Stop and Smell the Roses

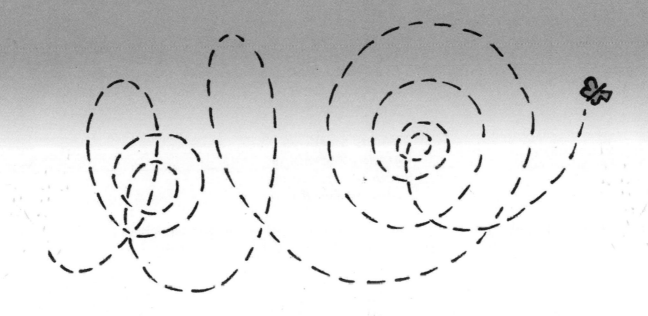

A 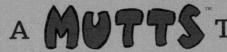 **MUTTS**™ TREASURY BY PATRICK M^cDONNELL

Andrews McMeel
Publishing, LLC
Kansas City

Other Books by Patrick McDonnell

THE BEST of MUTTS

The Best of Mutts

Mutts
Cats and Dogs: Mutts II
More Shtuff: Mutts III
Yesh!: Mutts IV
Our Mutts: Five
A Little Look-See: Mutts VI
What Now: Mutts VII
I Want to Be the Kitty: Mutts VIII
Dog-Eared: Mutts IX
Who Let the Cat Out: Mutts X
Everyday Mutts
Animal Friendly
Call of the Wild

Mutts Sundays
Sunday Mornings
Sunday Afternoons
Sunday Evenings

MUTTS
Shelter Stories
Love. Guaranteed.

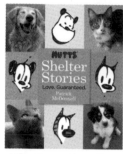

Shelter Stories

Mutts is distributed internationally by King Features Syndicate, Inc. For information write King Features Syndicate, Inc., 300 West Fifty-Seventh Street, New York, New York 10019.

 For information, write Andrews McMeel Publishing, LLC, an Andrews McMeel Universal company, 1130 Walnut Street, Kansas City, Missouri 64106.

09 10 11 12 13 BAM 10 9 8 7 6 5 4 3 2 1

ISBN-13: 978-0-7407-8146-9
ISBN-10: 0-7407-8146-4

Library of Congress Control Number: 2008936279

Stop and Smell the Roses is printed on recycled paper.

Mutts can be found on the Internet at
www.muttscomics.com

Cover design by Jeff Schulz, Command-Z Design.

Mutts lithograph on page 3 courtesy of Jack Gallery.

ATTENTION: SCHOOLS AND BUSINESSES

Andrews McMeel books are available at quantity discounts with bulk purchase for educational, business, or sales promotional use.
For information, please write to: Special Sales Department, Andrews McMeel Publishing, LLC, 1130 Walnut Street, Kansas City, Missouri 64106.

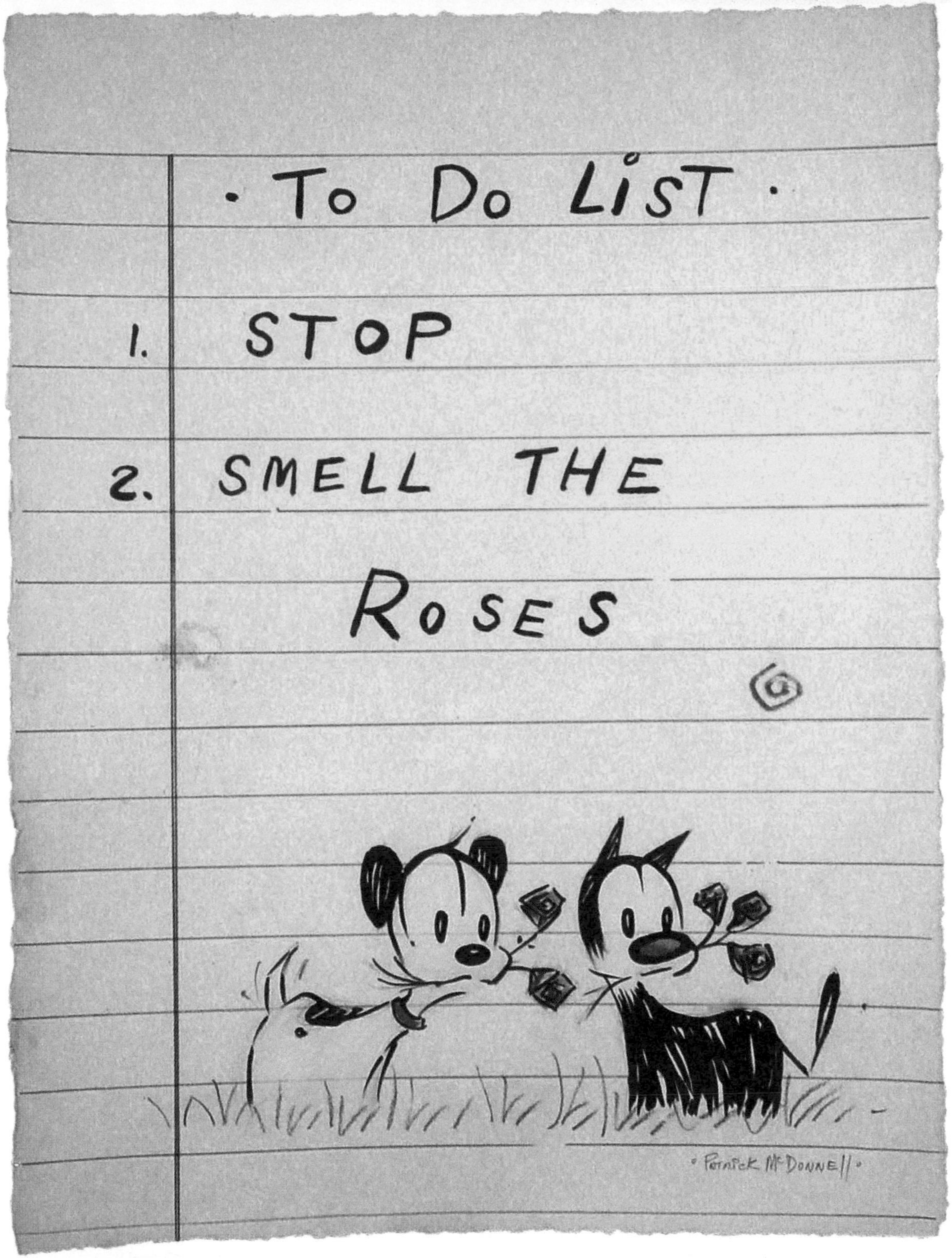
· TO DO LIST ·
1. STOP
2. SMELL THE
ROSES
PATRICK McDONNELL

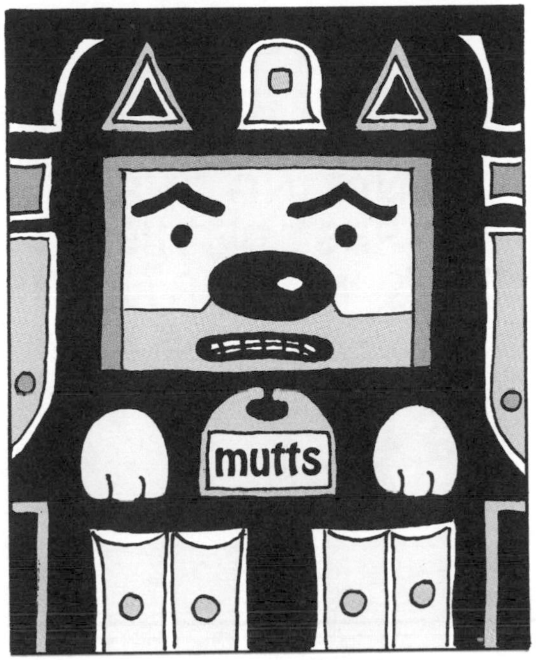
mutts

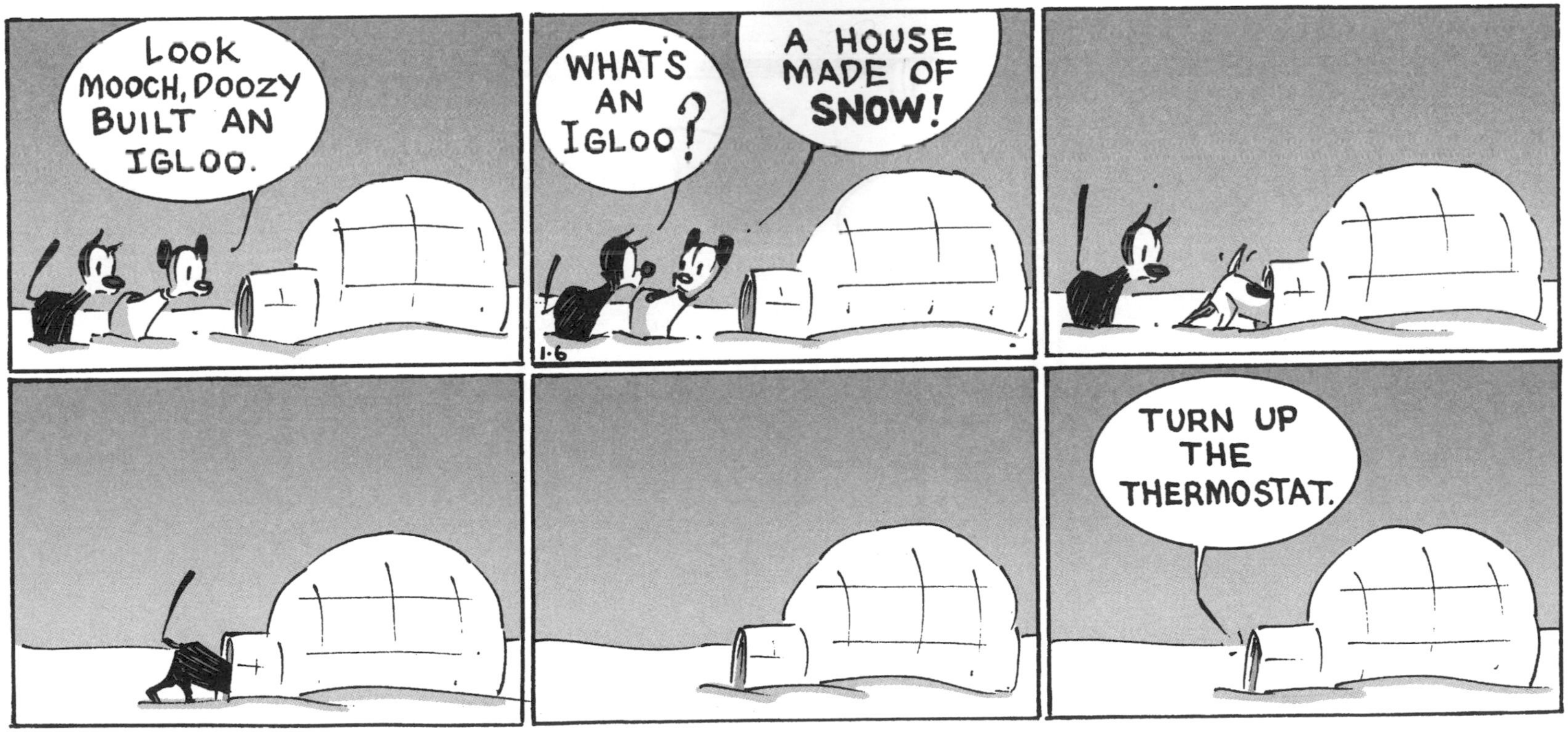
LOOK MOOCH, DOOZY BUILT AN IGLOO.
WHAT'S AN IGLOO?
A HOUSE MADE OF SNOW!
TURN UP THE THERMOSTAT.

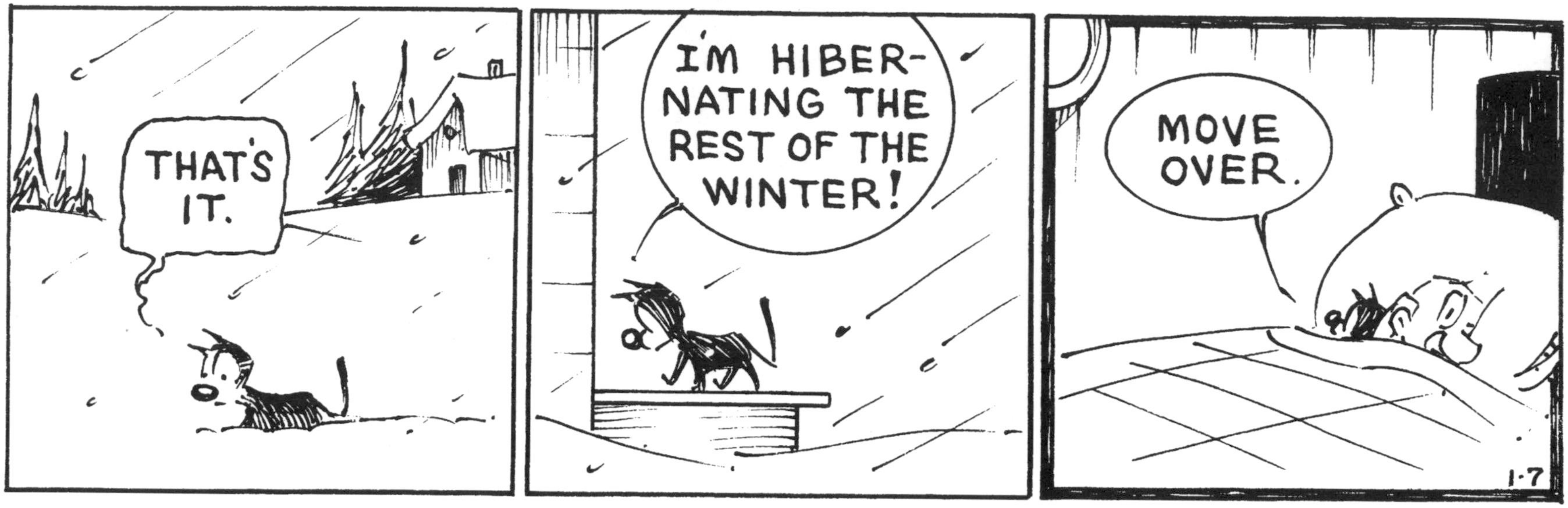
THAT'S IT.
I'M HIBERNATING THE REST OF THE WINTER!
MOVE OVER.
1·7

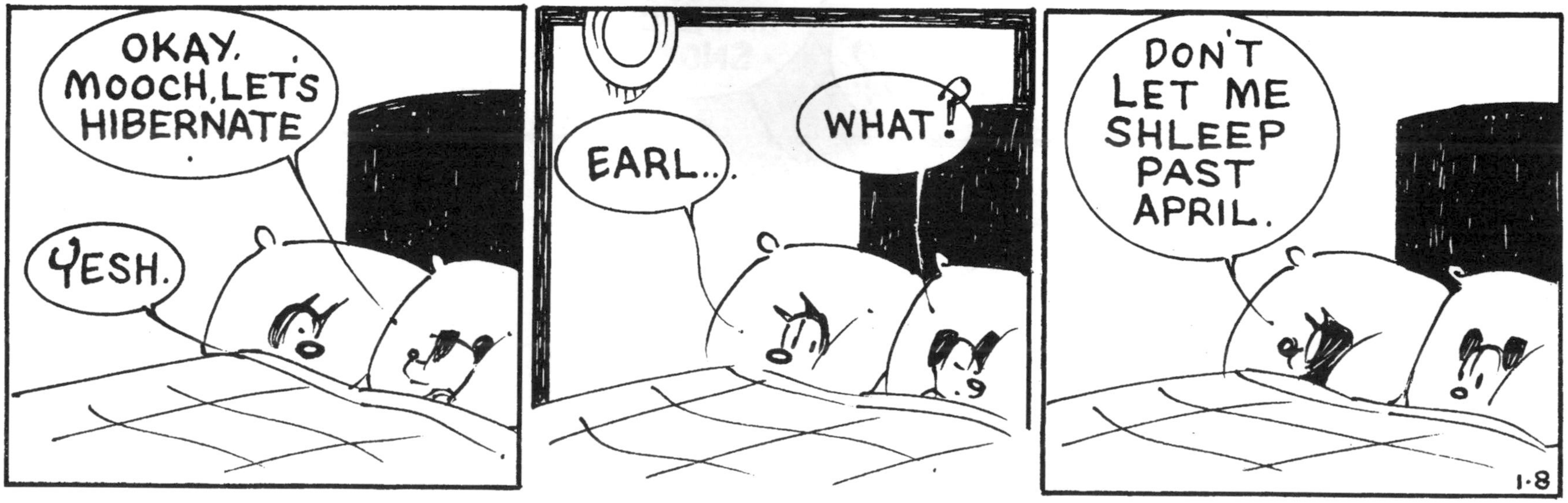
OKAY, MOOCH, LET'S HIBERNATE.
YESH.
EARL...
WHAT?
DON'T LET ME SHLEEP PAST APRIL.
1·8

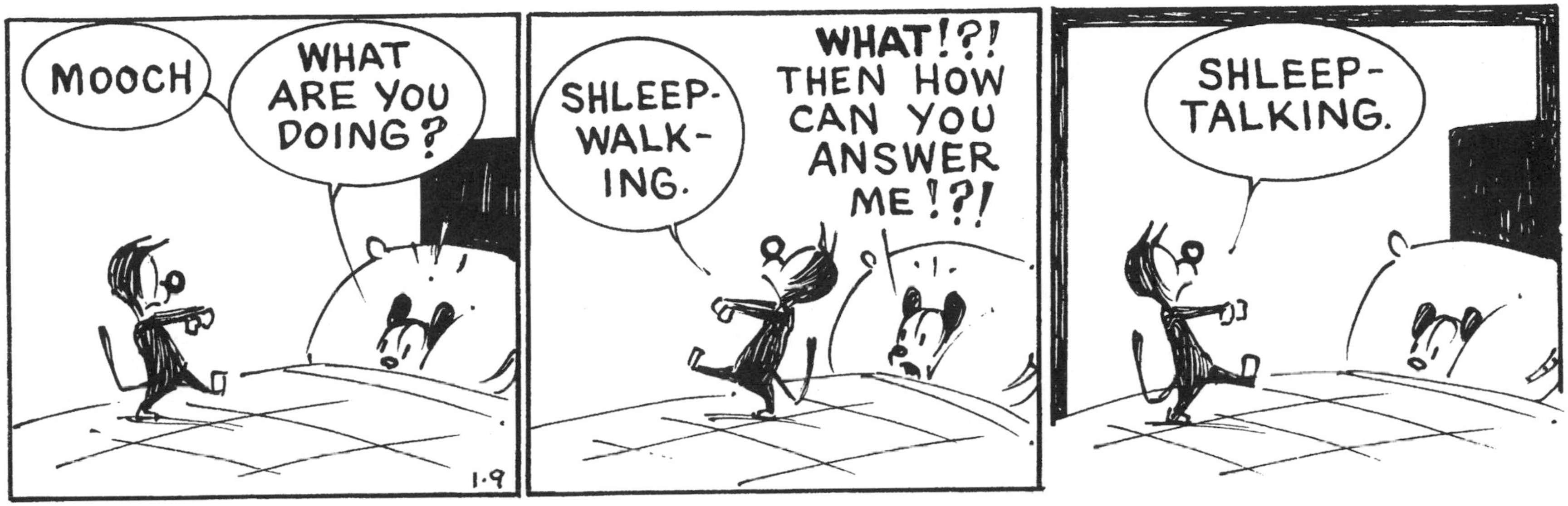
MOOCH
WHAT ARE YOU DOING?
SHLEEP-WALK-ING.
WHAT!?! THEN HOW CAN YOU ANSWER ME!?!
SHLEEP-TALKING.
1·9

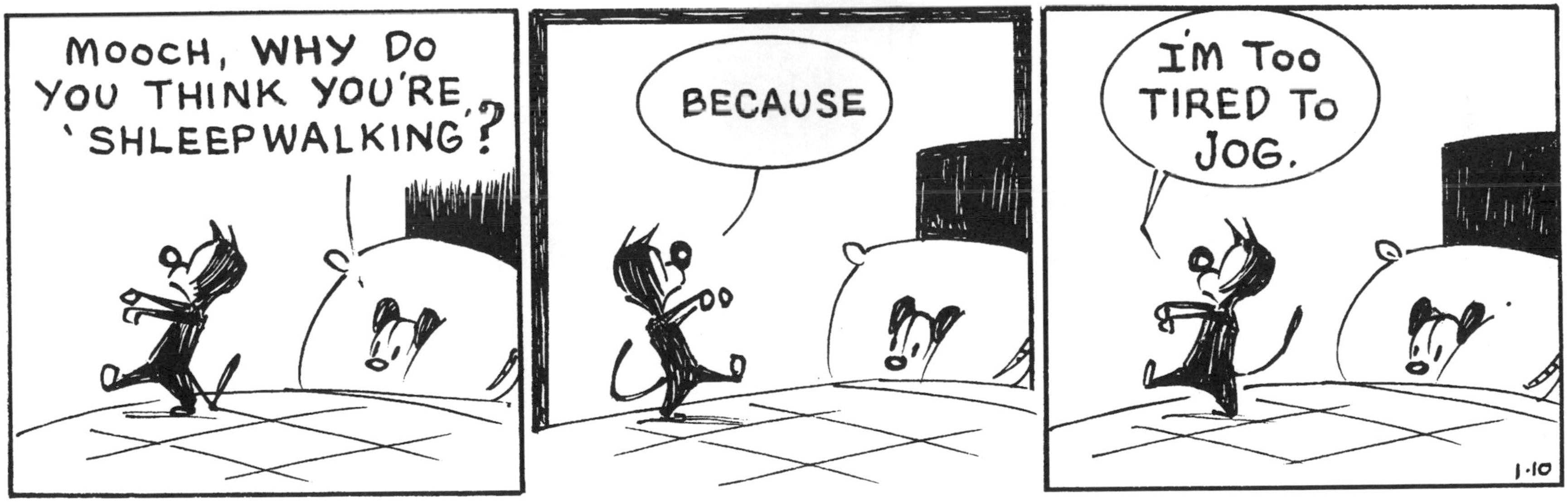
MOOCH, WHY DO YOU THINK YOU'RE 'SHLEEPWALKING'?
BECAUSE
I'M TOO TIRED TO JOG.
1·10

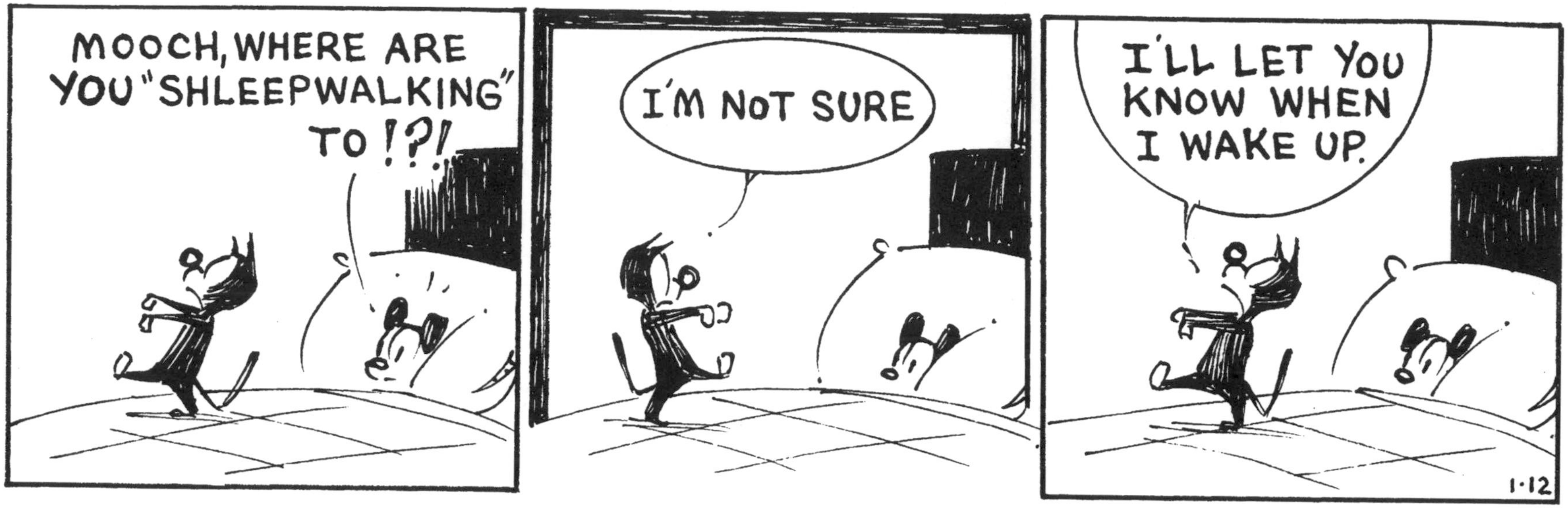
MOOCH, WHERE ARE YOU "SHLEEPWALKING" TO!?!
I'M NOT SURE
I'LL LET YOU KNOW WHEN I WAKE UP.
1·12

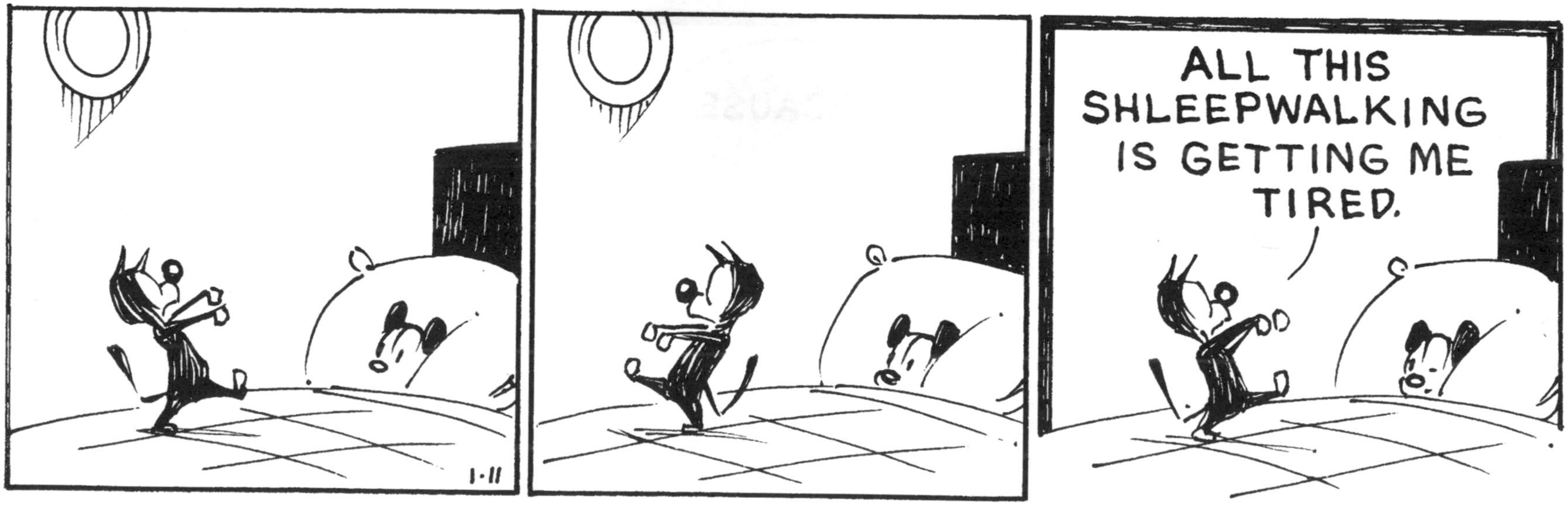
1·11
ALL THIS SHLEEPWALKING IS GETTING ME TIRED.

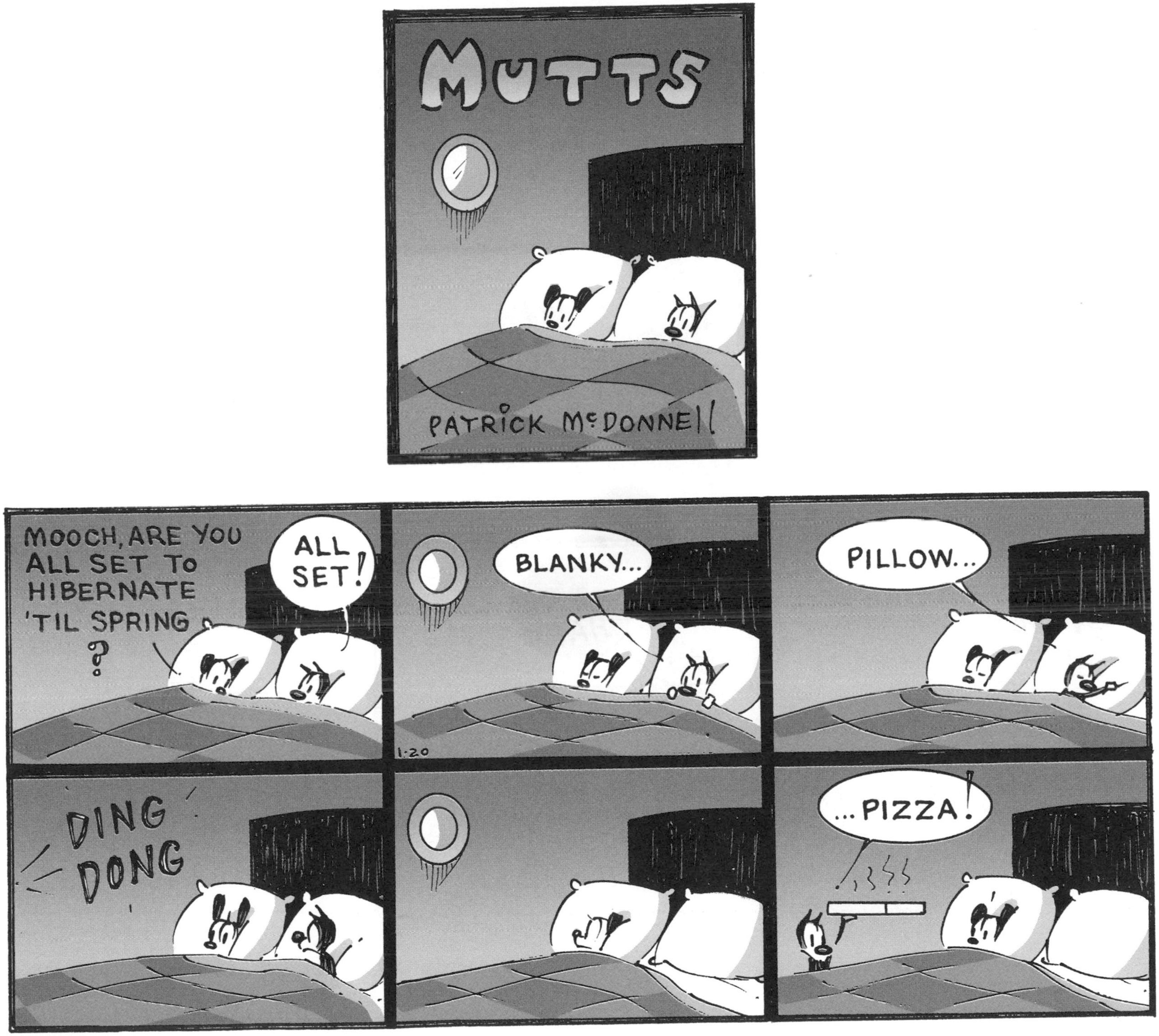
MUTTS
PATRICK McDONNELL
MOOCH, ARE YOU ALL SET TO HIBERNATE 'TIL SPRING?
ALL SET!
BLANKY...
1-20
PILLOW...
DING DONG
...PIZZA!

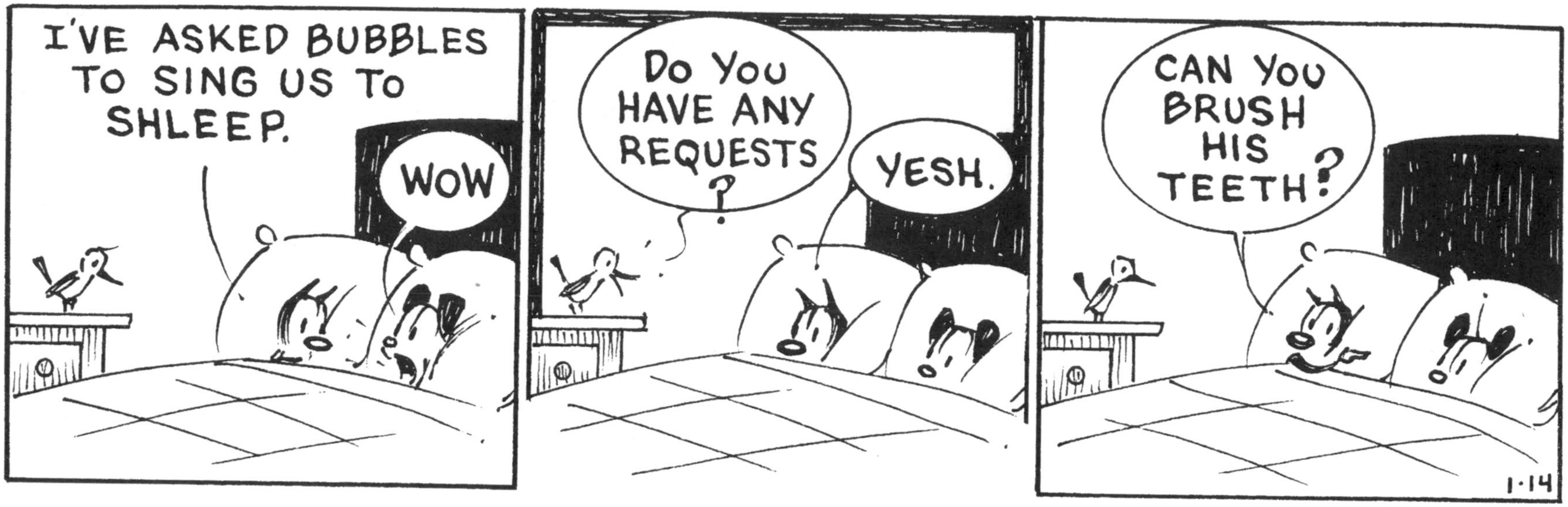
I'VE ASKED BUBBLES TO SING US TO SHLEEP.
WOW
DO YOU HAVE ANY REQUESTS?
YESH.
CAN YOU BRUSH HIS TEETH?
1·14

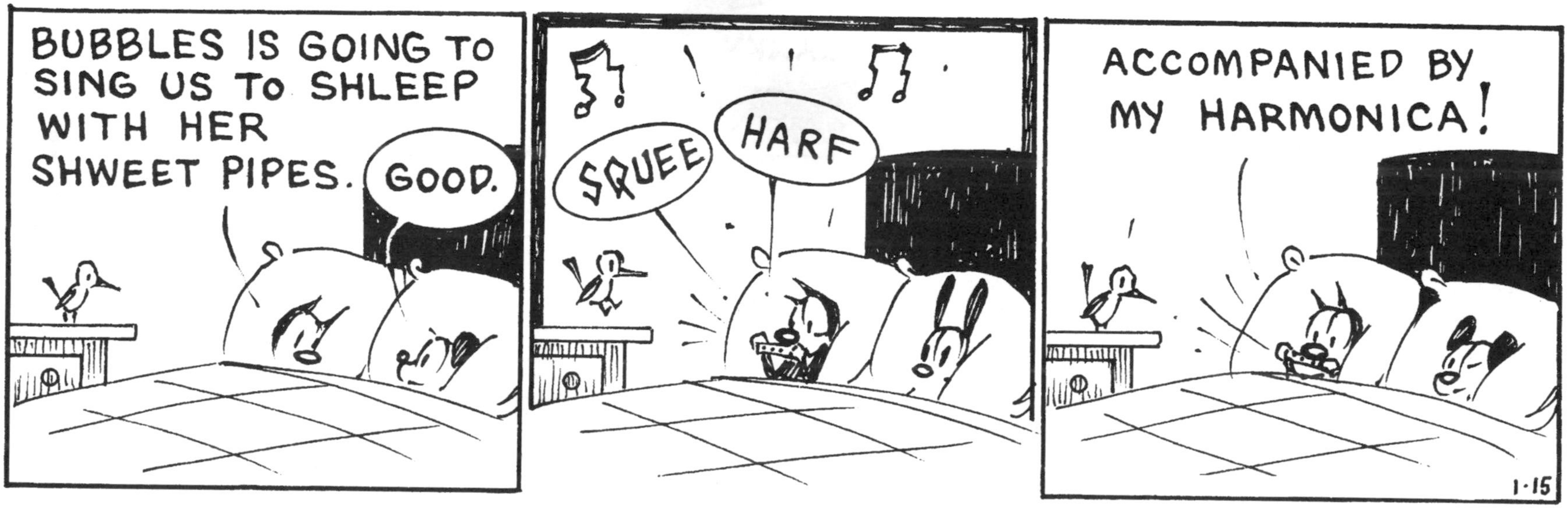
BUBBLES IS GOING TO SING US TO SHLEEP WITH HER SHWEET PIPES.
GOOD.
SQUEE
HARF
ACCOMPANIED BY MY HARMONICA!
1·15

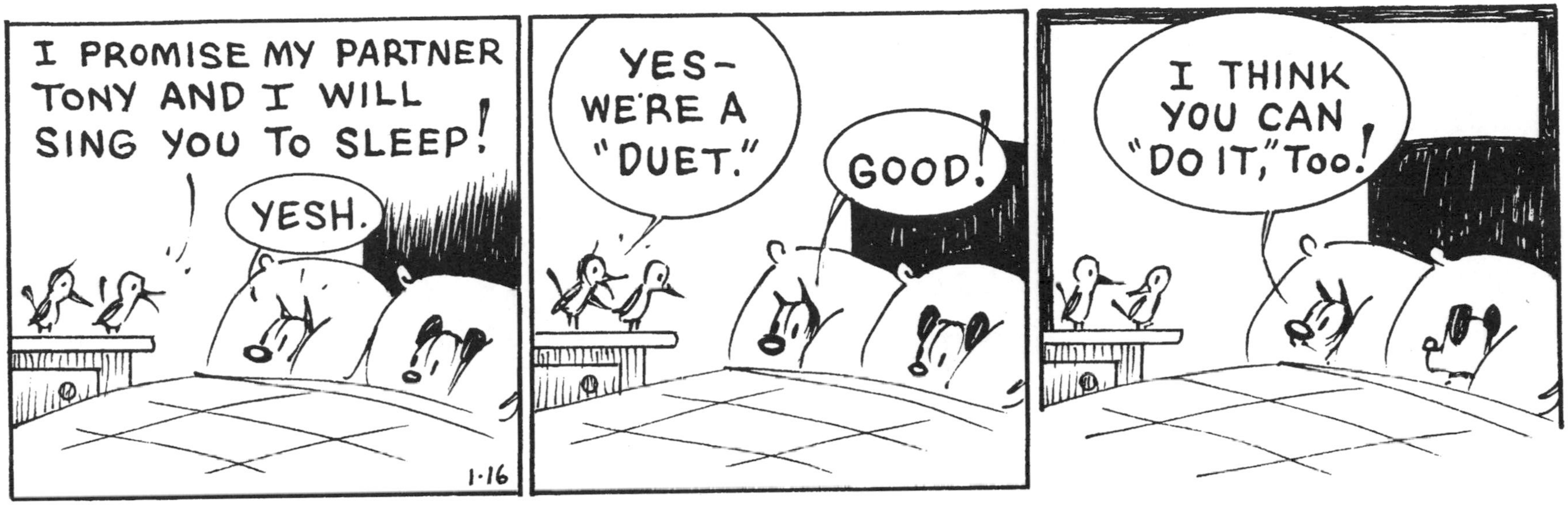
I PROMISE MY PARTNER TONY AND I WILL SING YOU TO SLEEP!
YESH.
YES– WE'RE A "DUET."
GOOD!
I THINK YOU CAN "DO IT," Too!
1·16

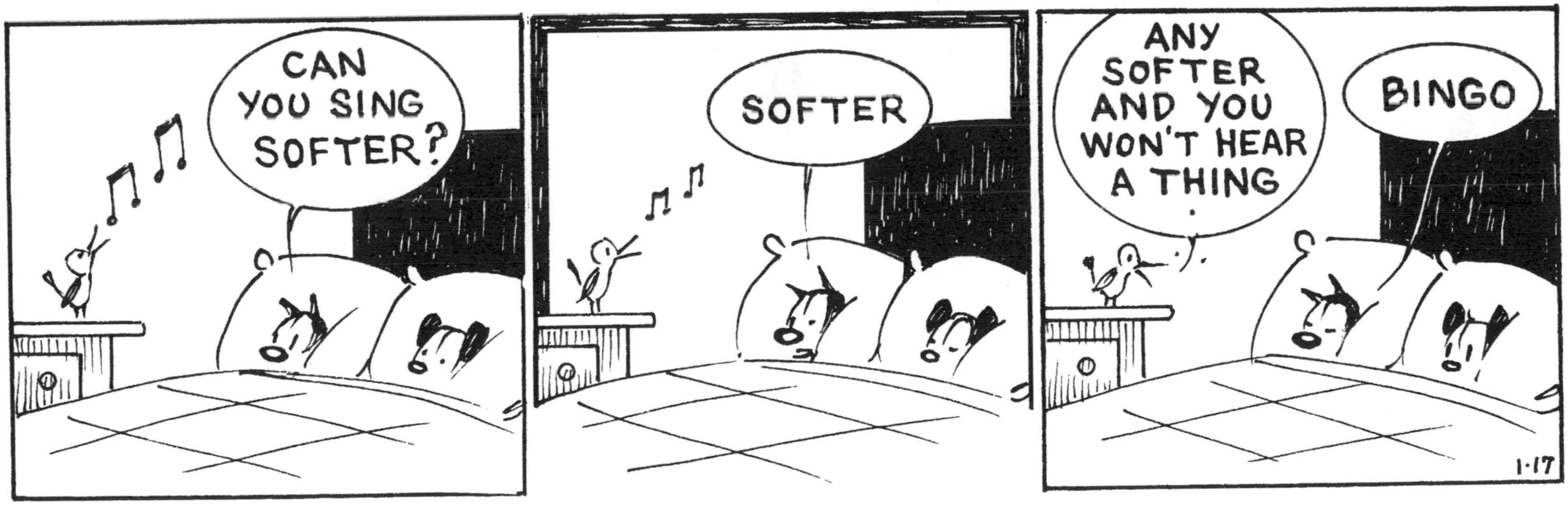
CAN YOU SING SOFTER?
SOFTER
ANY SOFTER AND YOU WON'T HEAR A THING
BINGO
1·17

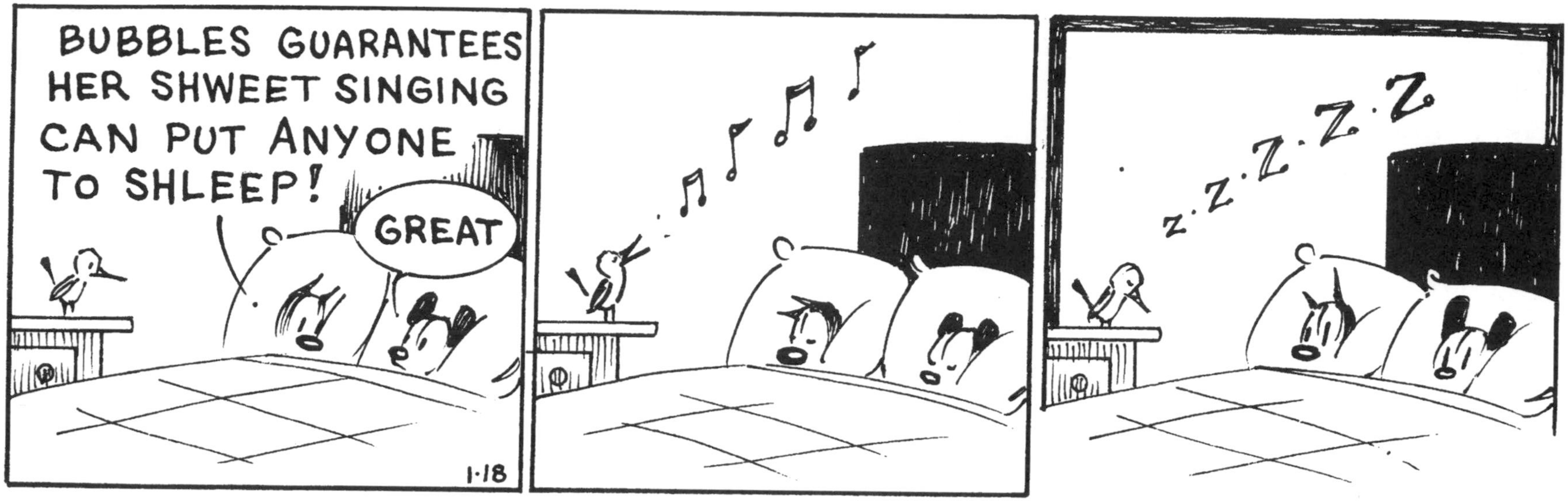
BUBBLES GUARANTEES HER SHWEET SINGING CAN PUT ANYONE TO SHLEEP!
GREAT
z·z·Z·Z·Z·Z
1·18

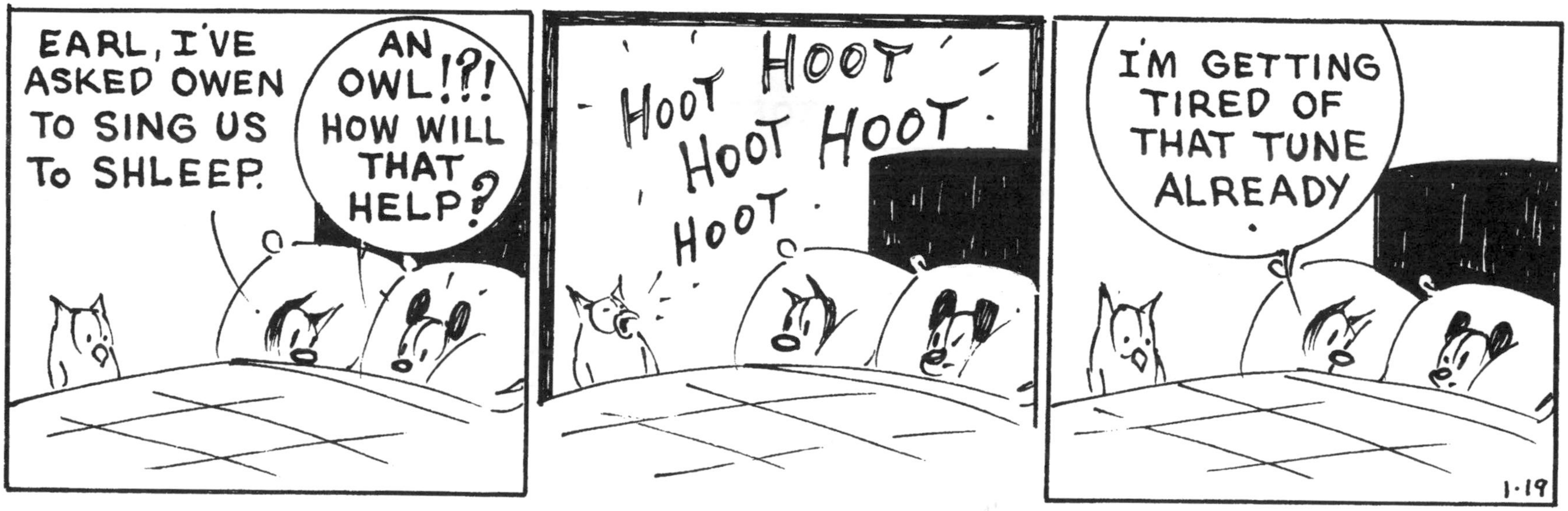
EARL, I'VE ASKED OWEN TO SING US TO SHLEEP.
AN OWL!?! HOW WILL THAT HELP?
HOOT HOOT HOOT HOOT HOOT
I'M GETTING TIRED OF THAT TUNE ALREADY.
1·19

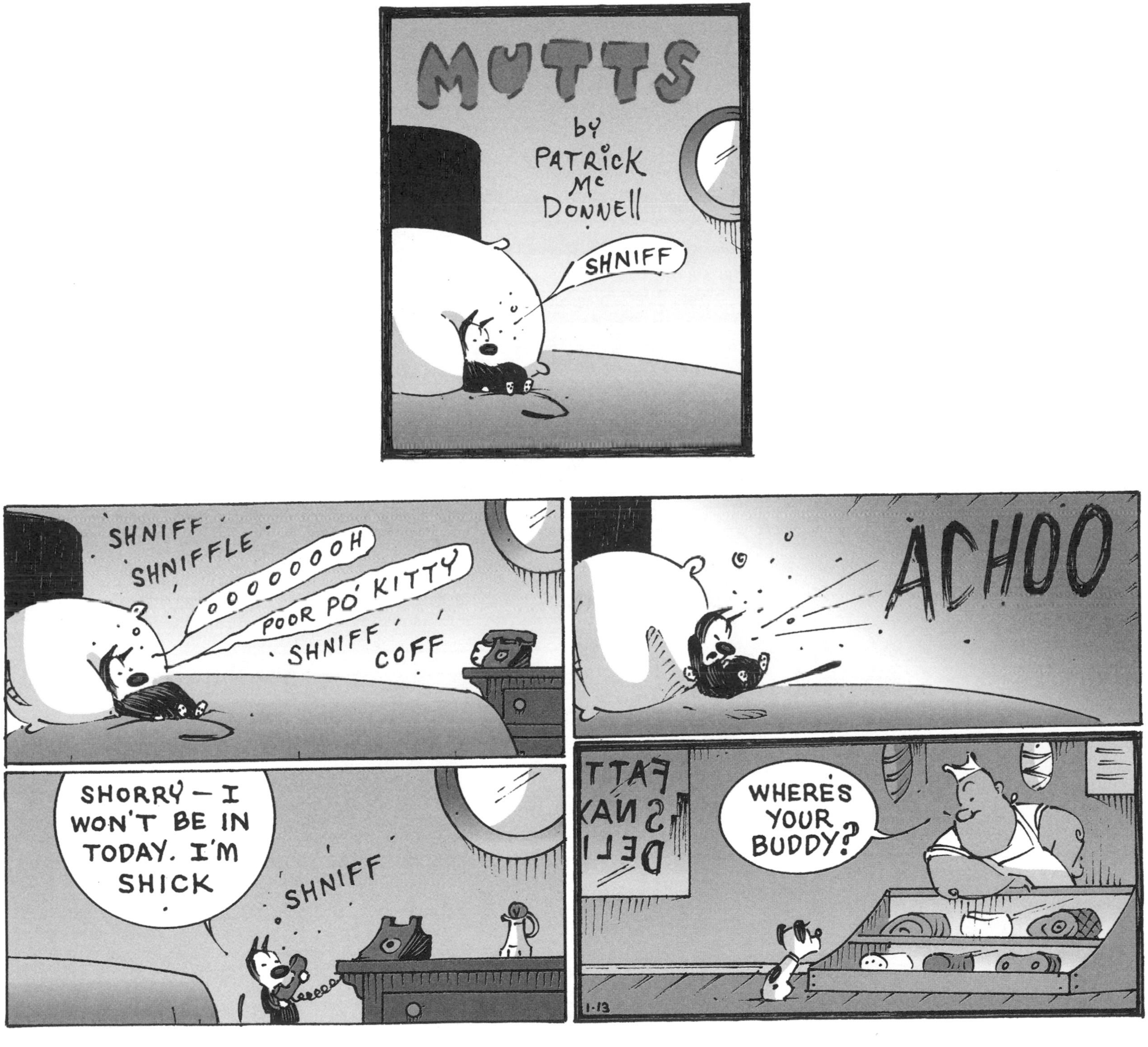
MUTTS
by PATRICK Mc DONNELL
SHNIFF
SHNIFF
SHNIFFLE
OOOOOOOOH
POOR PO' KITTY
SHNIFF
COFF
ACHOO
SHORRY — I WON'T BE IN TODAY. I'M SHICK
SHNIFF
WHERE'S YOUR BUDDY?
1-13

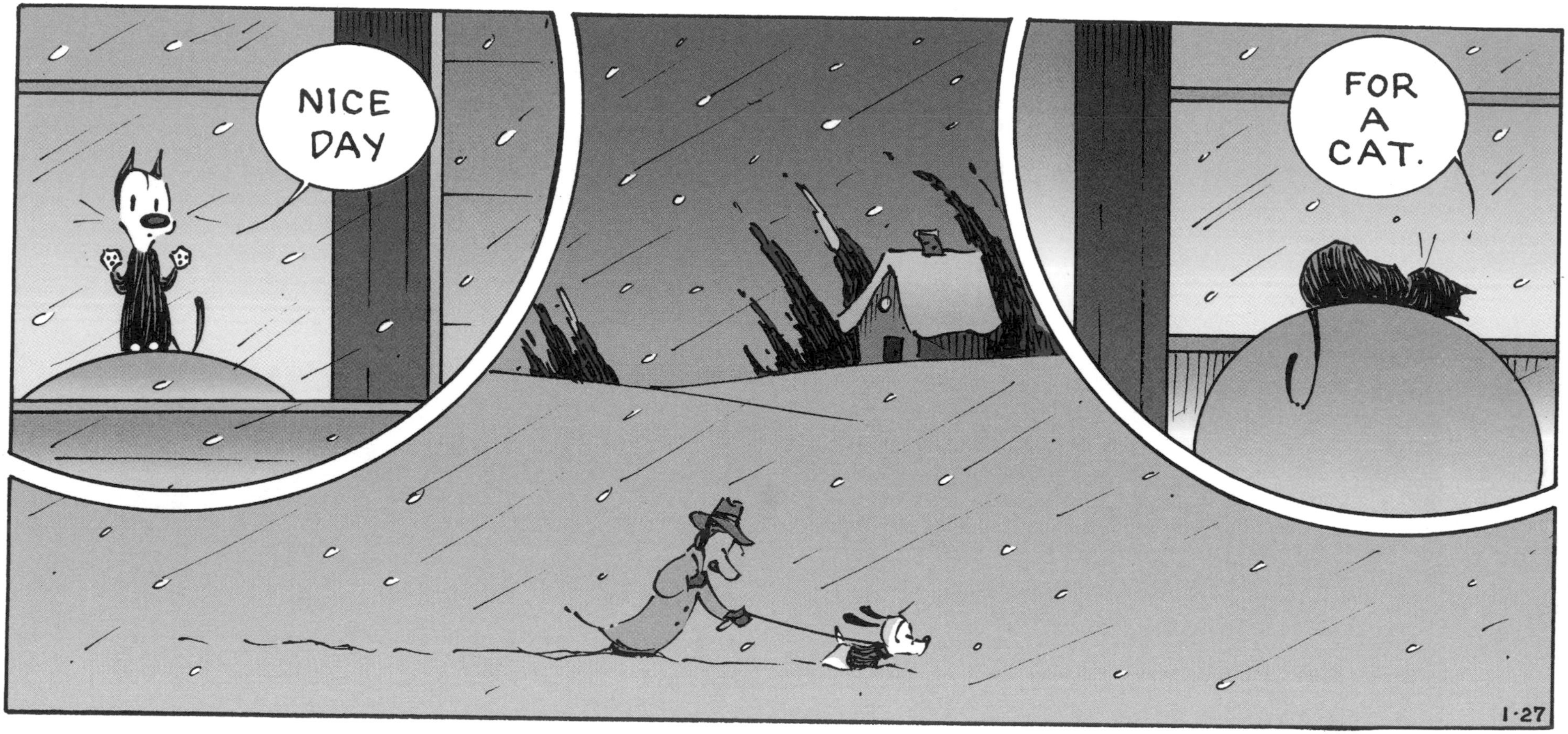
NICE DAY
FOR A CAT.
1·27

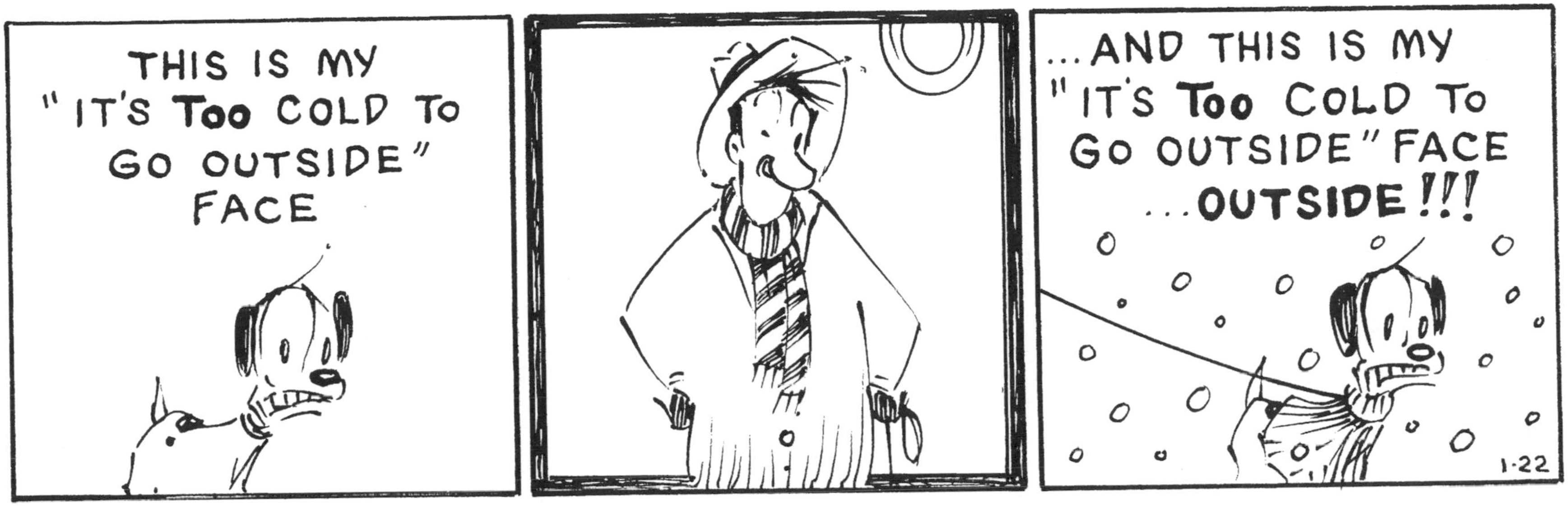
THIS IS MY "IT'S TOO COLD TO GO OUTSIDE" FACE
...AND THIS IS MY "IT'S TOO COLD TO GO OUTSIDE" FACE ...OUTSIDE!!!
1-22

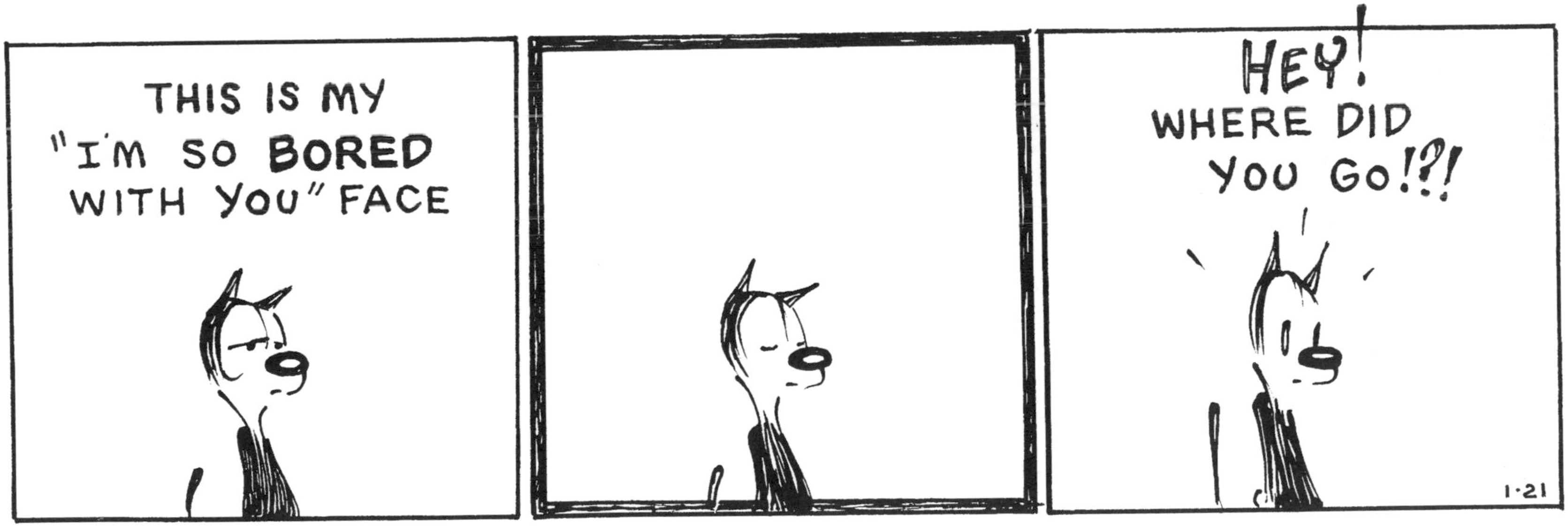
THIS IS MY "I'M SO BORED WITH YOU" FACE
HEY! WHERE DID YOU GO!?!
1-21

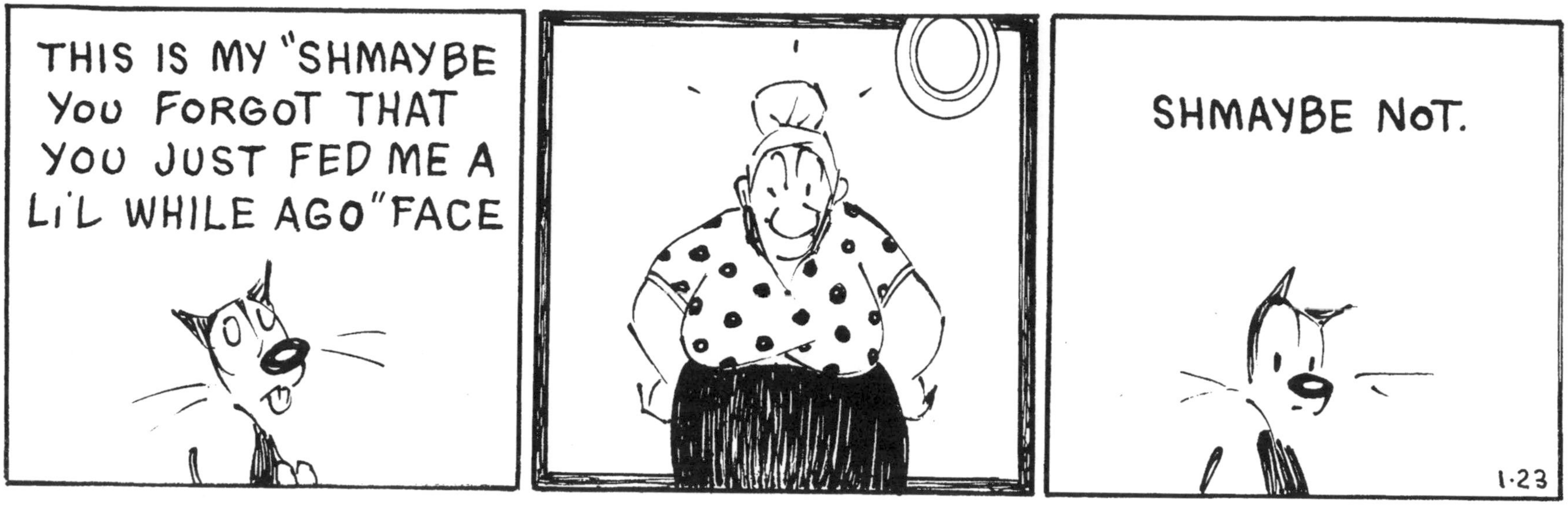
THIS IS MY "SHMAYBE YOU FORGOT THAT YOU JUST FED ME A LI'L WHILE AGO" FACE
SHMAYBE NOT.
1·23

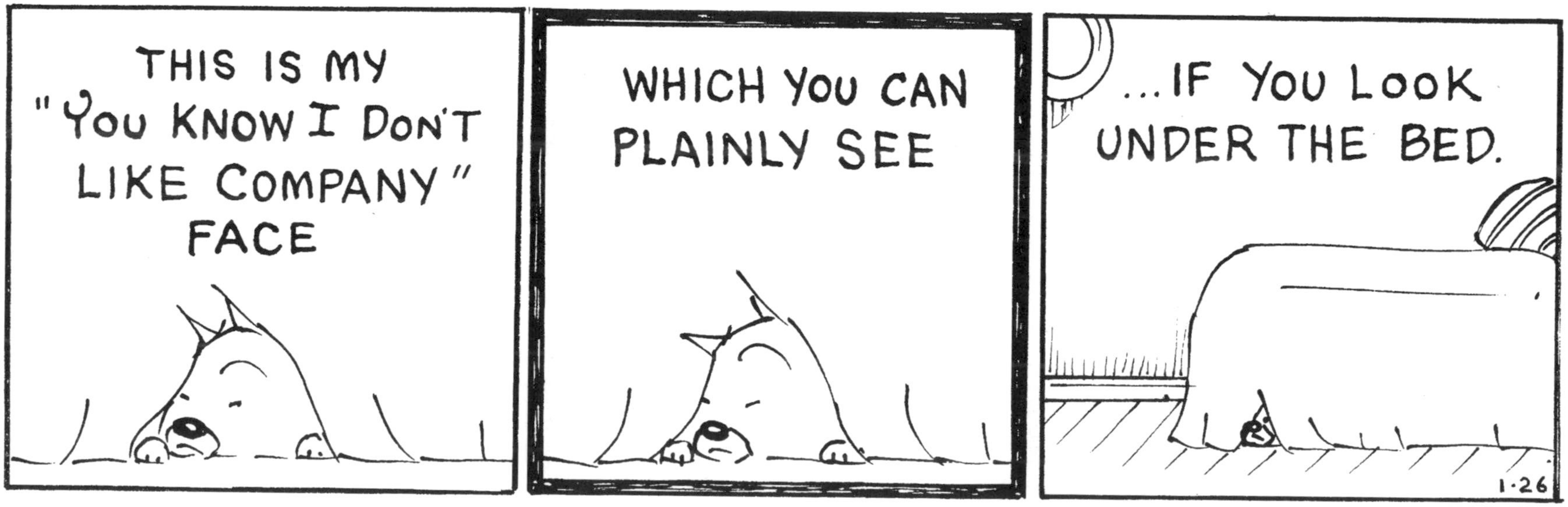
THIS IS MY "YOU KNOW I DON'T LIKE COMPANY" FACE
WHICH YOU CAN PLAINLY SEE
...IF YOU LOOK UNDER THE BED.
1·26

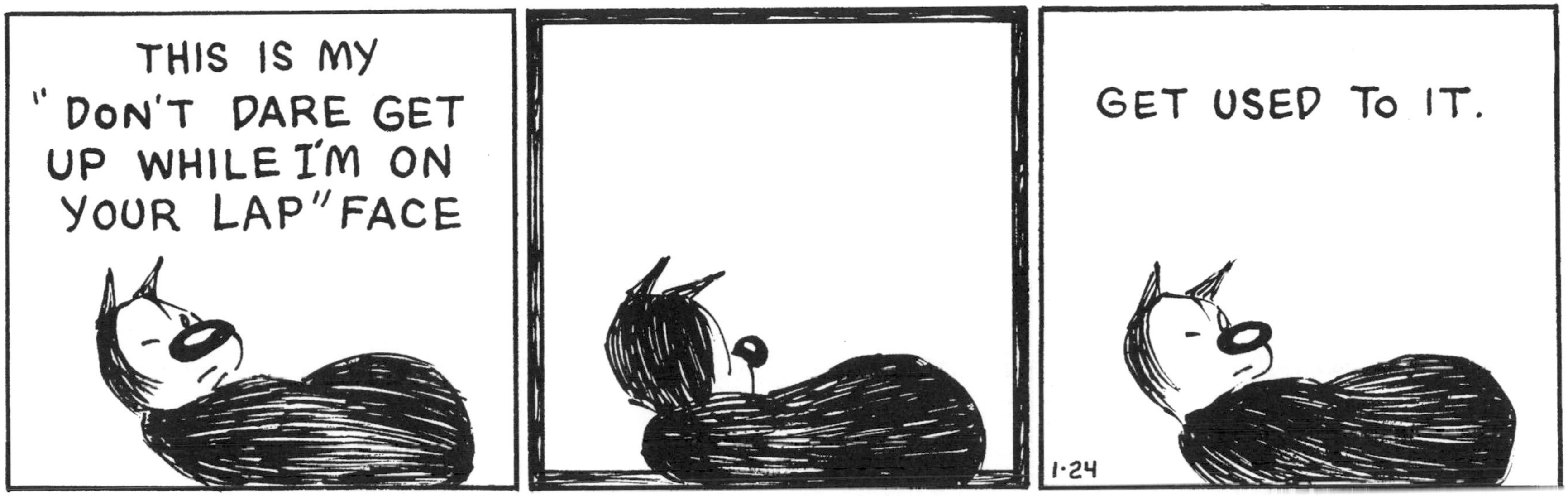
THIS IS MY "DON'T DARE GET UP WHILE I'M ON YOUR LAP" FACE
GET USED TO IT.
1·24

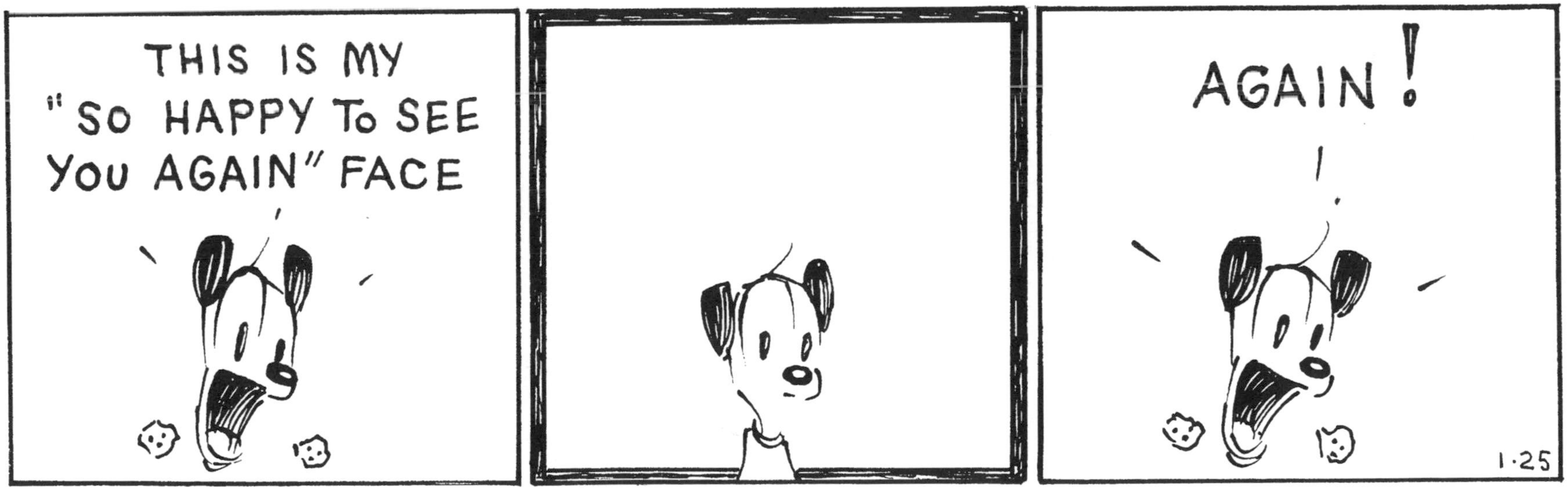
THIS IS MY "SO HAPPY TO SEE YOU AGAIN" FACE
AGAIN!
1·25

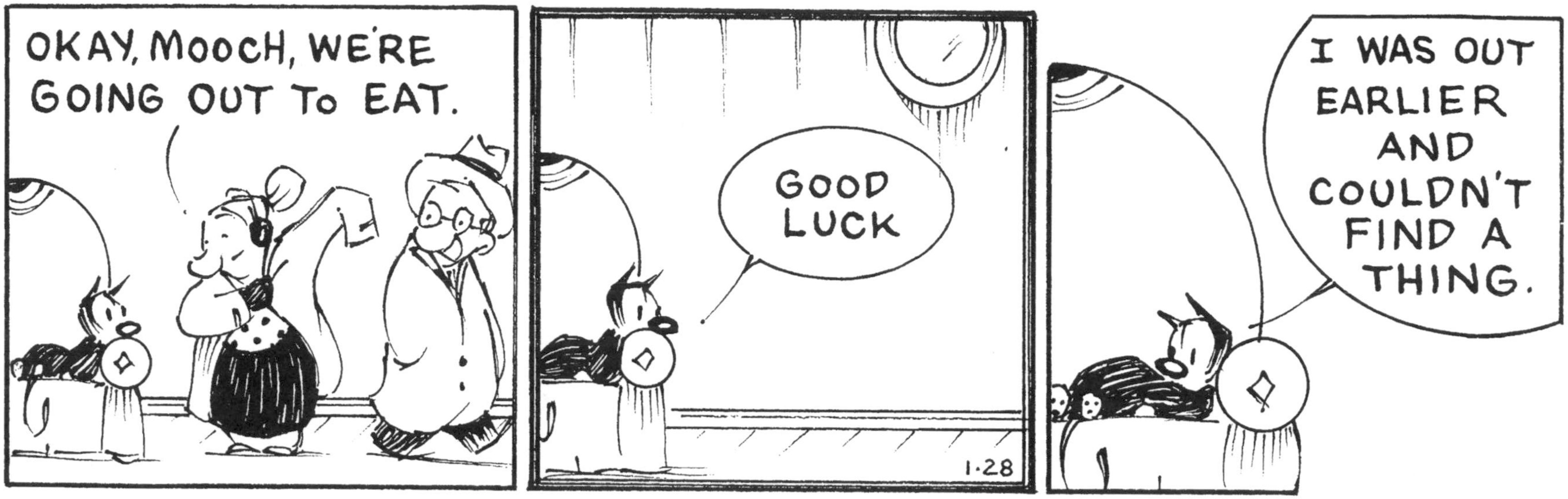
OKAY, MOOCH, WE'RE GOING OUT TO EAT.
GOOD LUCK
I WAS OUT EARLIER AND COULDN'T FIND A THING.

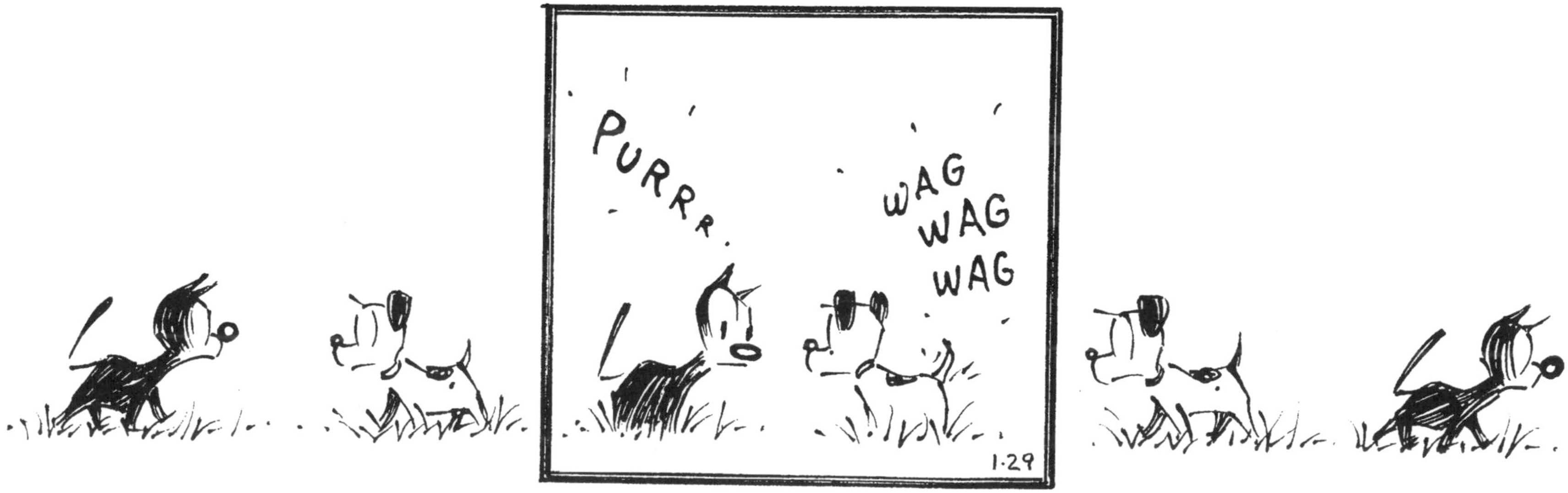
PURRRR.
WAG WAG WAG

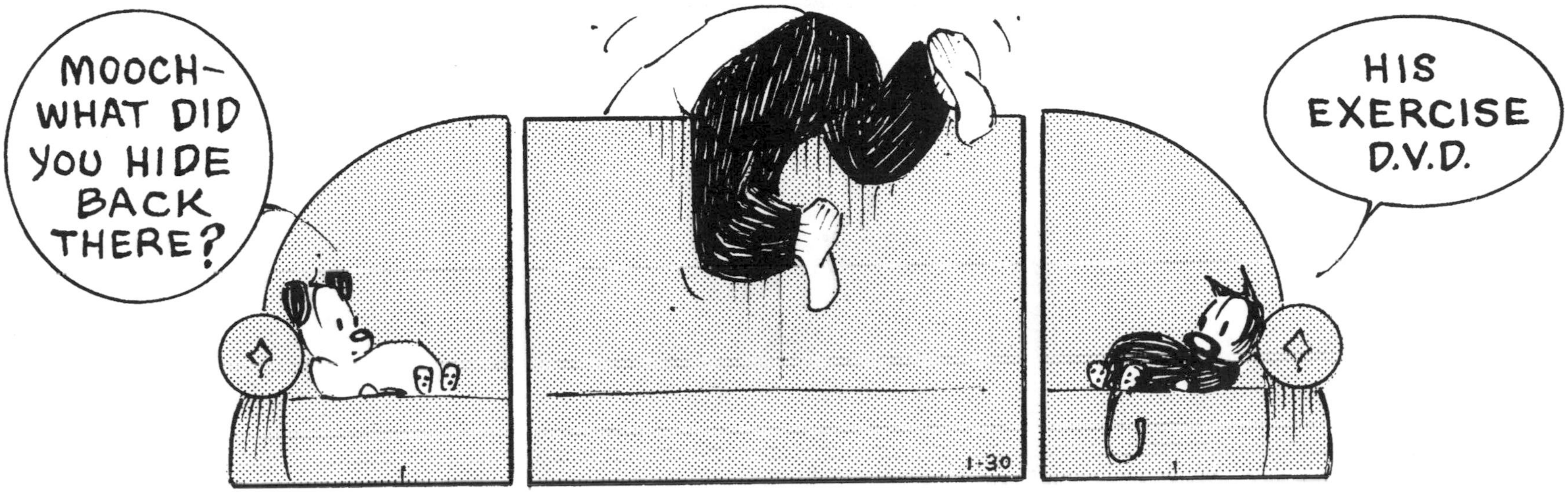
MOOCH-
WHAT DID
YOU HIDE
BACK
THERE?
HIS
EXERCISE
D.V.D.
1-30

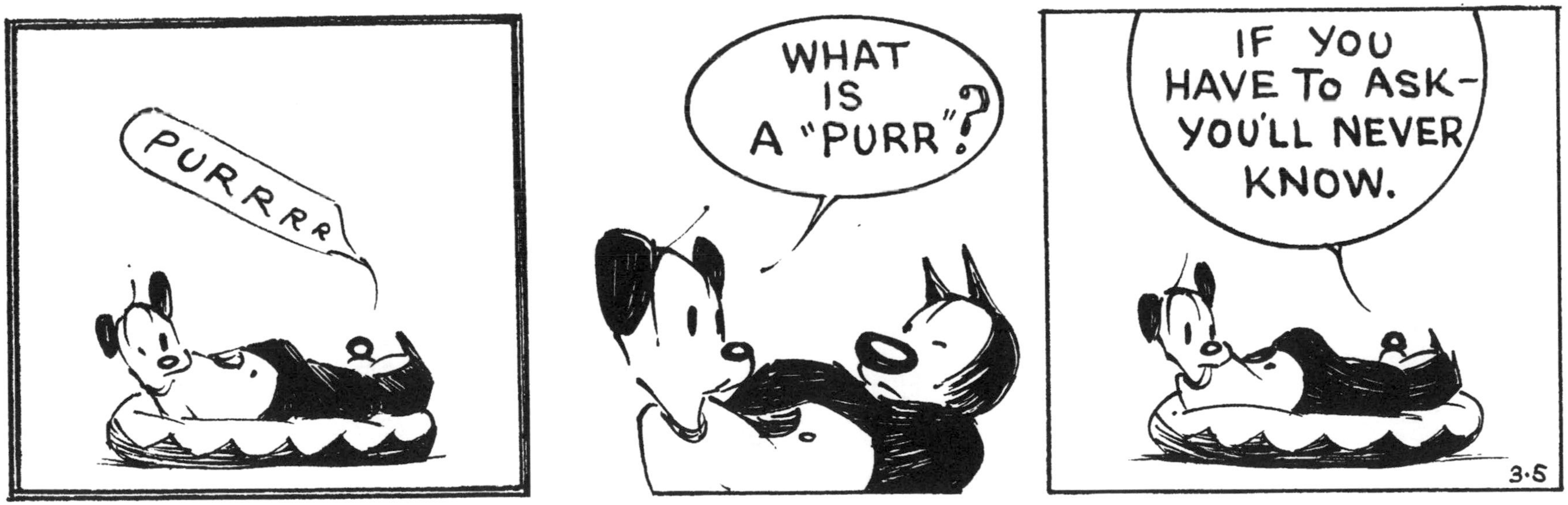
PURRRRR
WHAT
IS
A "PURR"?
IF YOU
HAVE To ASK-
YOU'LL NEVER
KNOW.
3-5

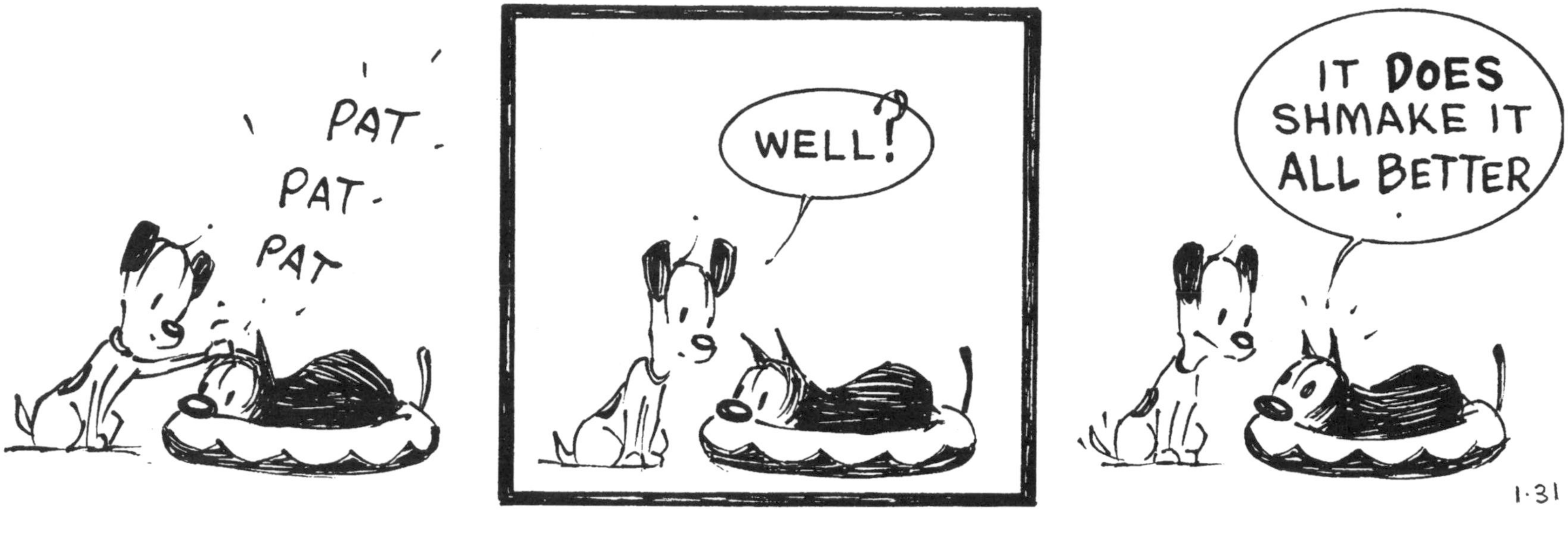
PAT
PAT
PAT
WELL?
IT **DOES** SHMAKE IT ALL BETTER
1·31

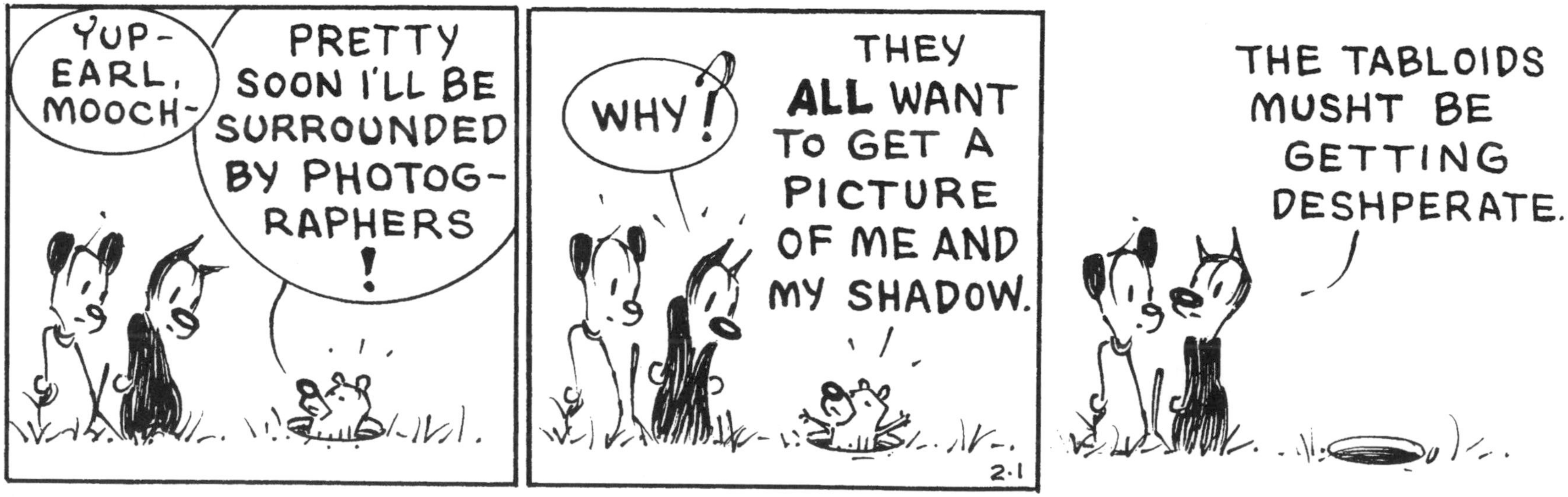
YUP- EARL, MOOCH-
PRETTY SOON I'LL BE SURROUNDED BY PHOTOGRAPHERS!
WHY?
THEY **ALL** WANT TO GET A PICTURE OF ME AND MY SHADOW.
2·1
THE TABLOIDS MUSHT BE GETTING DESHPERATE.

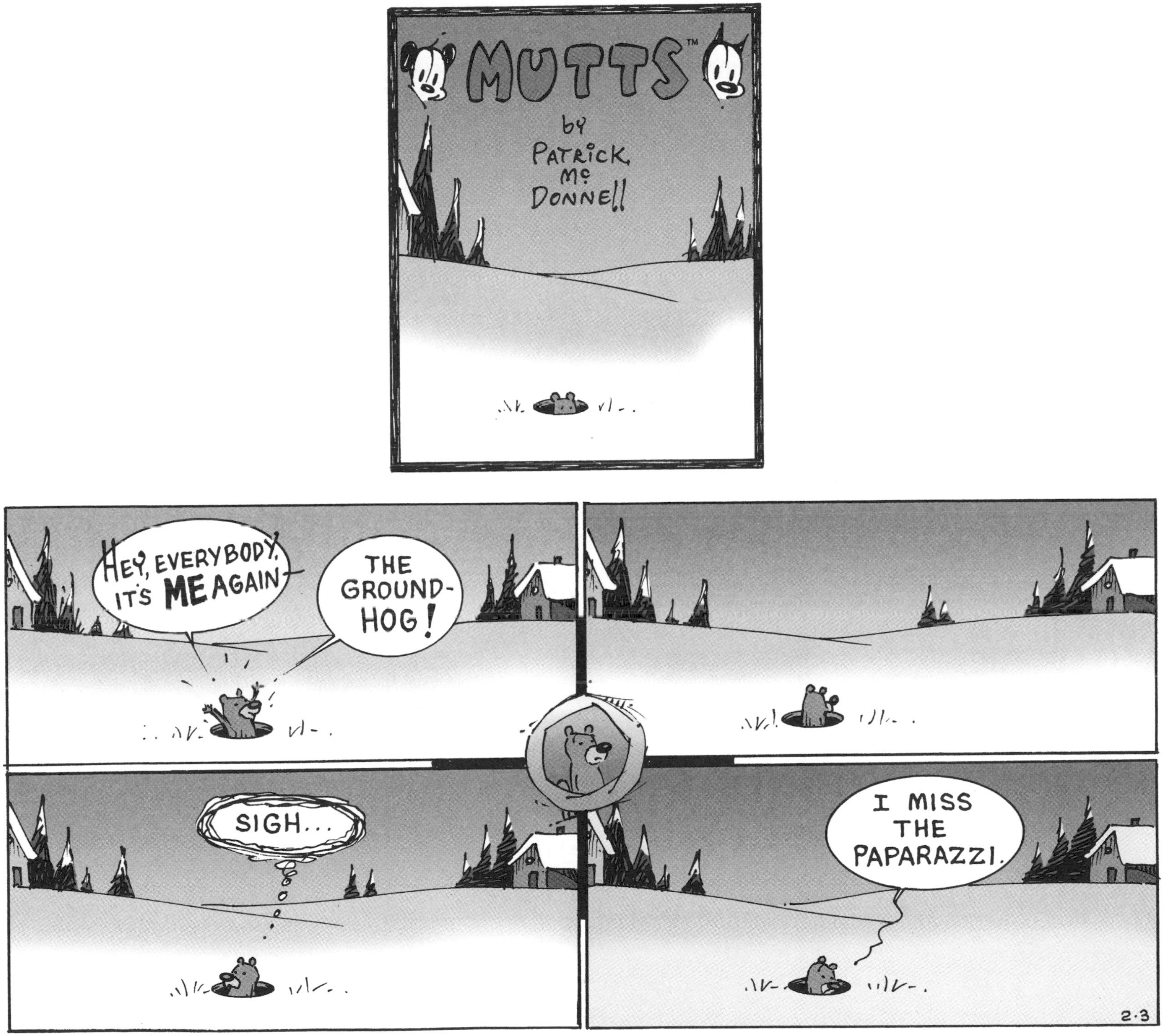
MUTTS™
by PATRICK MC DONNELL
HEY, EVERYBODY, IT'S ME AGAIN—
THE GROUND-HOG!
SIGH...
I MISS THE PAPARAZZI.
2·3

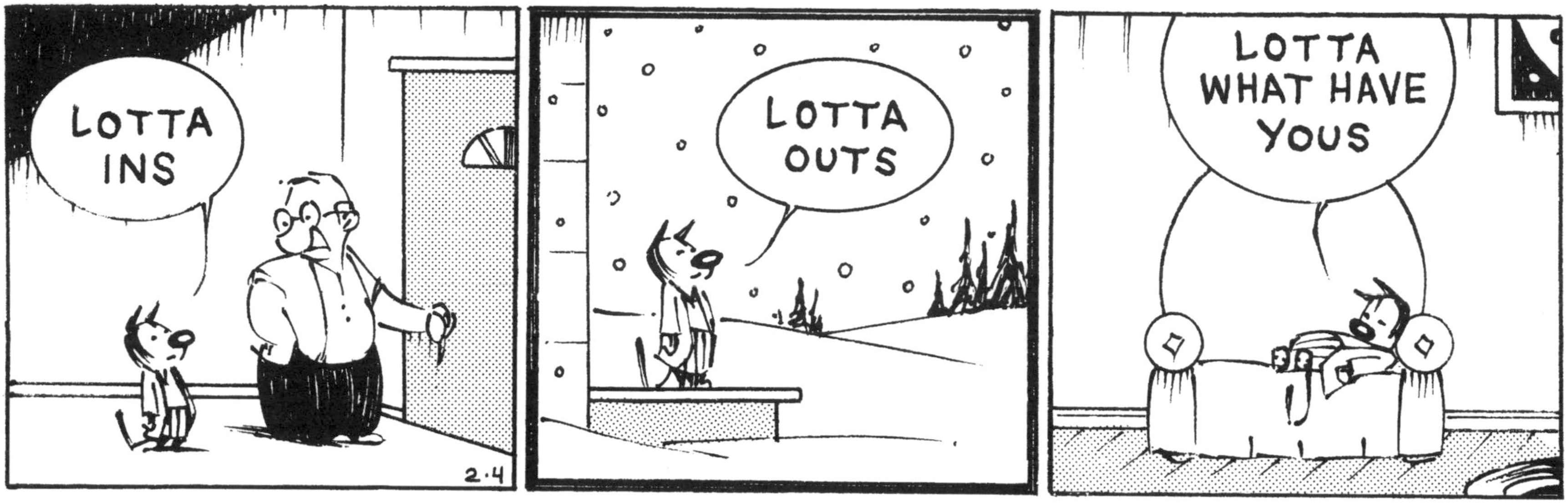
LOTTA INS
2·4
LOTTA OUTS
LOTTA WHAT HAVE YOUS

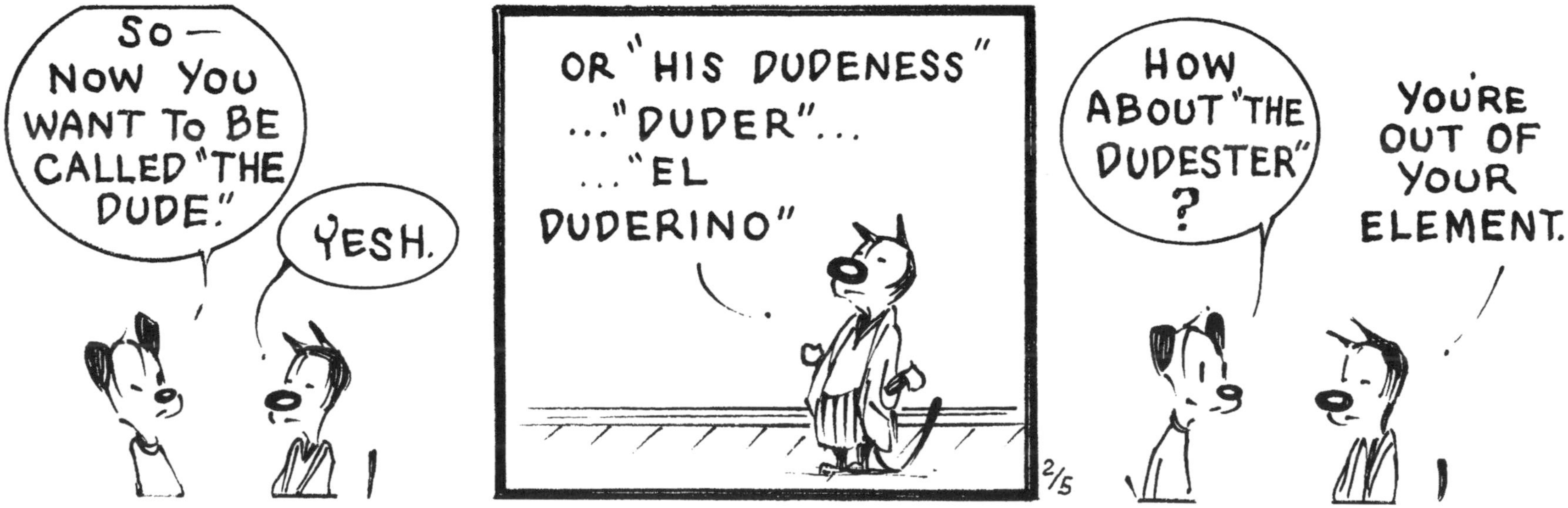
SO— NOW YOU WANT TO BE CALLED "THE DUDE."
YESH.
OR "HIS DUDENESS" ..."DUDER"... ..."EL DUDERINO"
2/5
HOW ABOUT "THE DUDESTER"?
YOU'RE OUT OF YOUR ELEMENT.

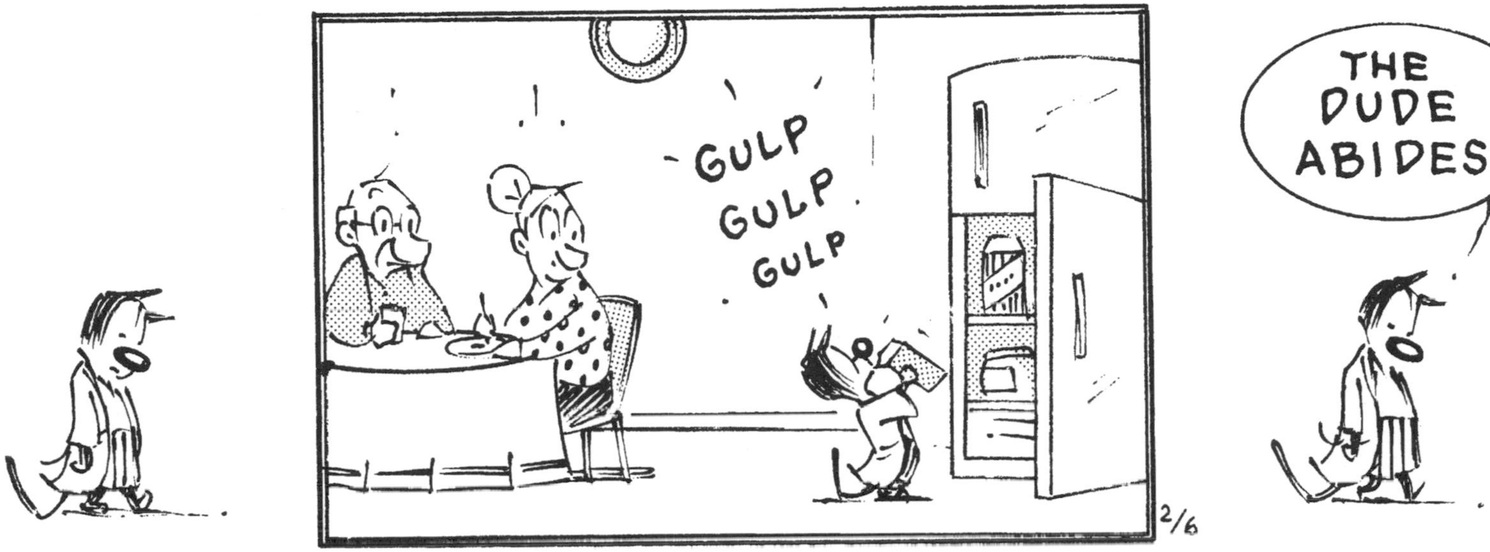
GULP
GULP
GULP
THE DUDE ABIDES.
2/6

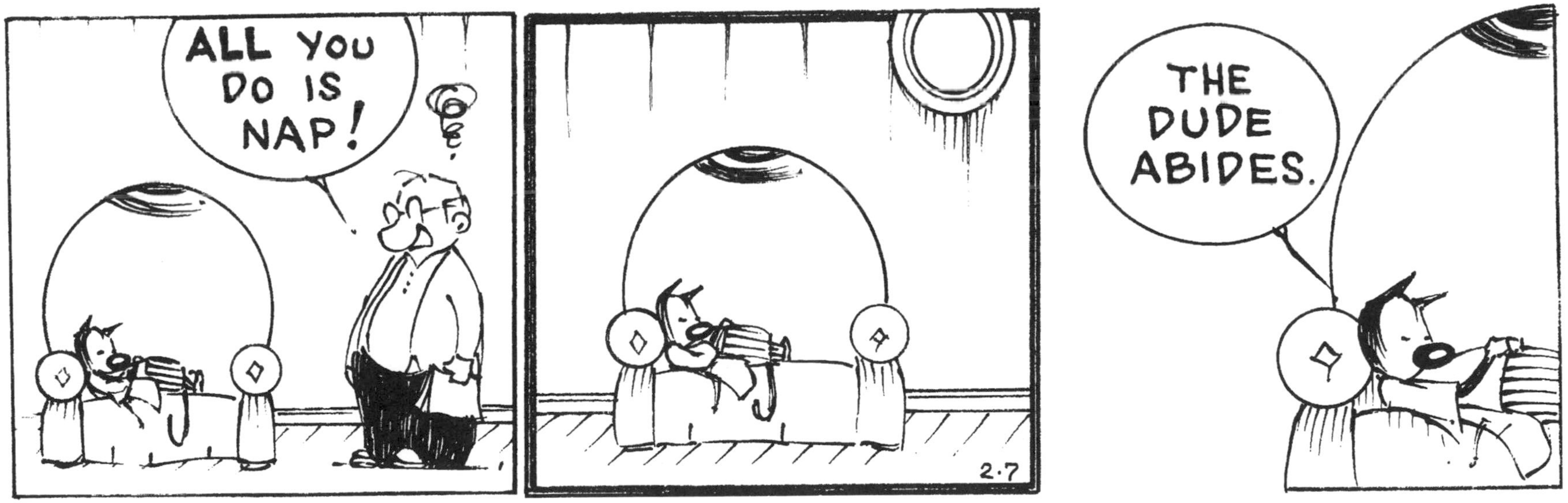
ALL YOU DO IS NAP!
2·7
THE DUDE ABIDES.

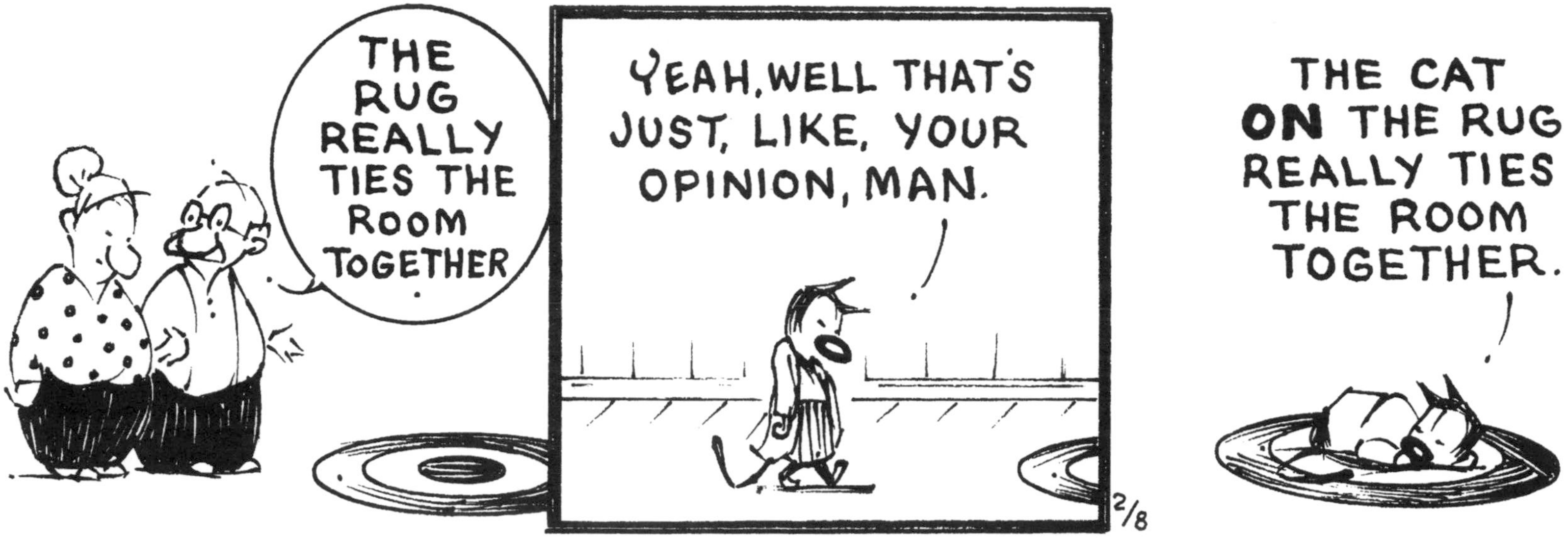
THE RUG REALLY TIES THE ROOM TOGETHER.
YEAH, WELL THAT'S JUST, LIKE, YOUR OPINION, MAN.
THE CAT **ON** THE RUG REALLY TIES THE ROOM TOGETHER.
2/8

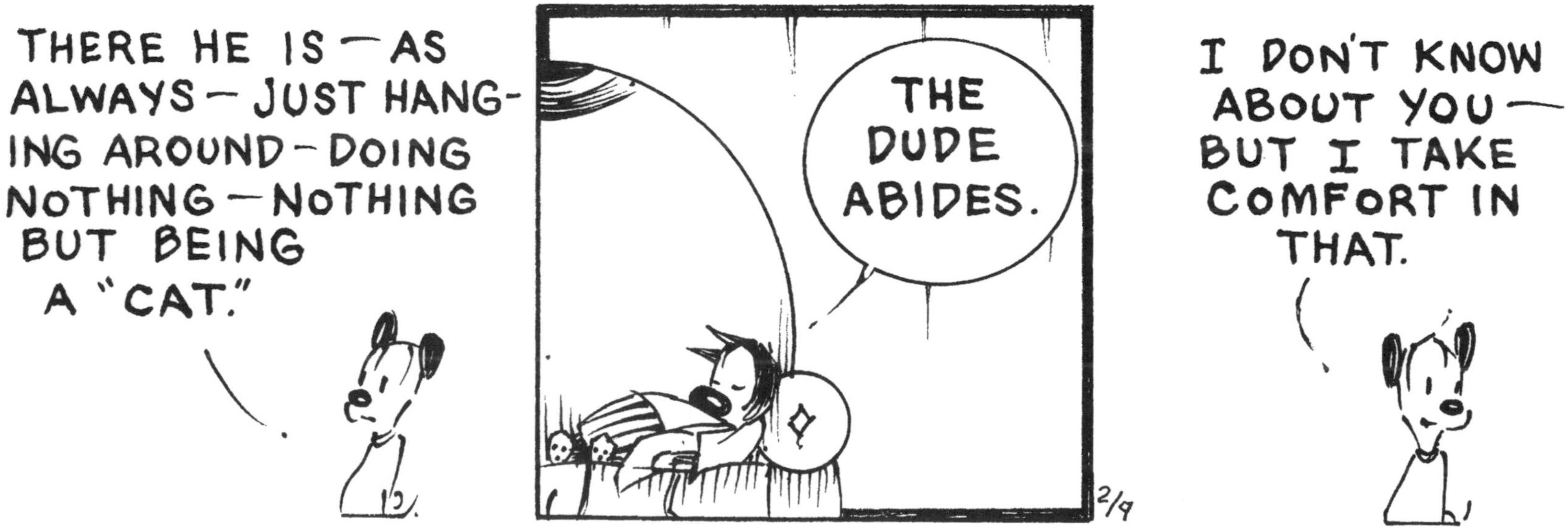
THERE HE IS—AS ALWAYS—JUST HANGING AROUND—DOING NOTHING—NOTHING BUT BEING A "CAT."
THE DUDE ABIDES.
I DON'T KNOW ABOUT YOU—BUT I TAKE COMFORT IN THAT.
2/9

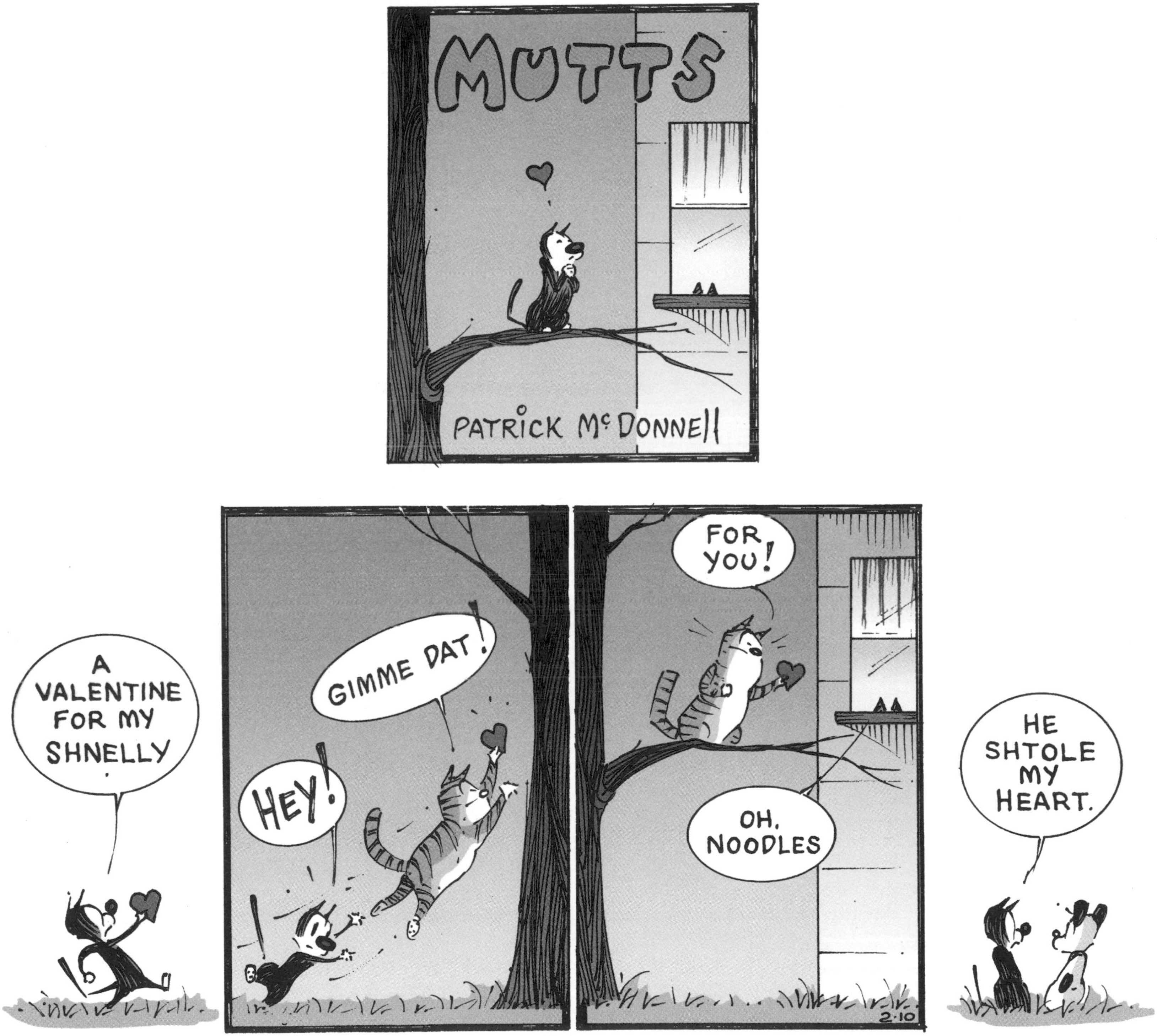
MUTTS
PATRICK McDONNELL
A VALENTINE FOR MY SHNELLY
HEY!
GIMME DAT!
FOR YOU!
OH, NOODLES
HE SHTOLE MY HEART.
2.10

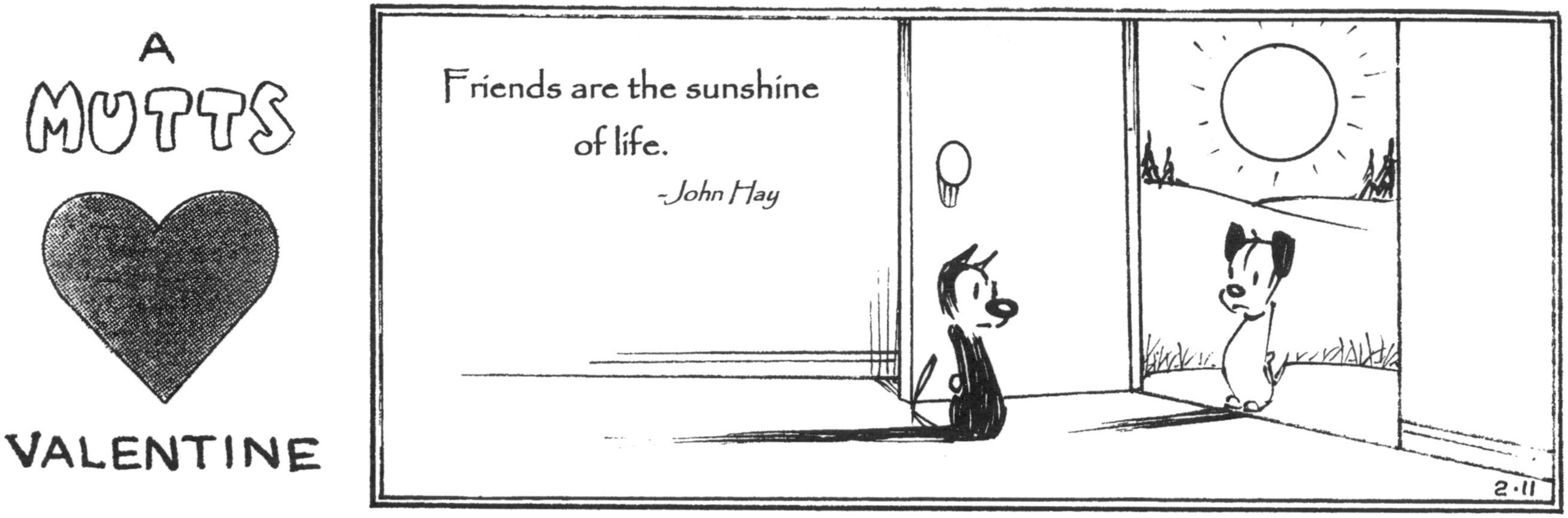
A MUTTS VALENTINE
Friends are the sunshine of life.
-John Hay
2.11

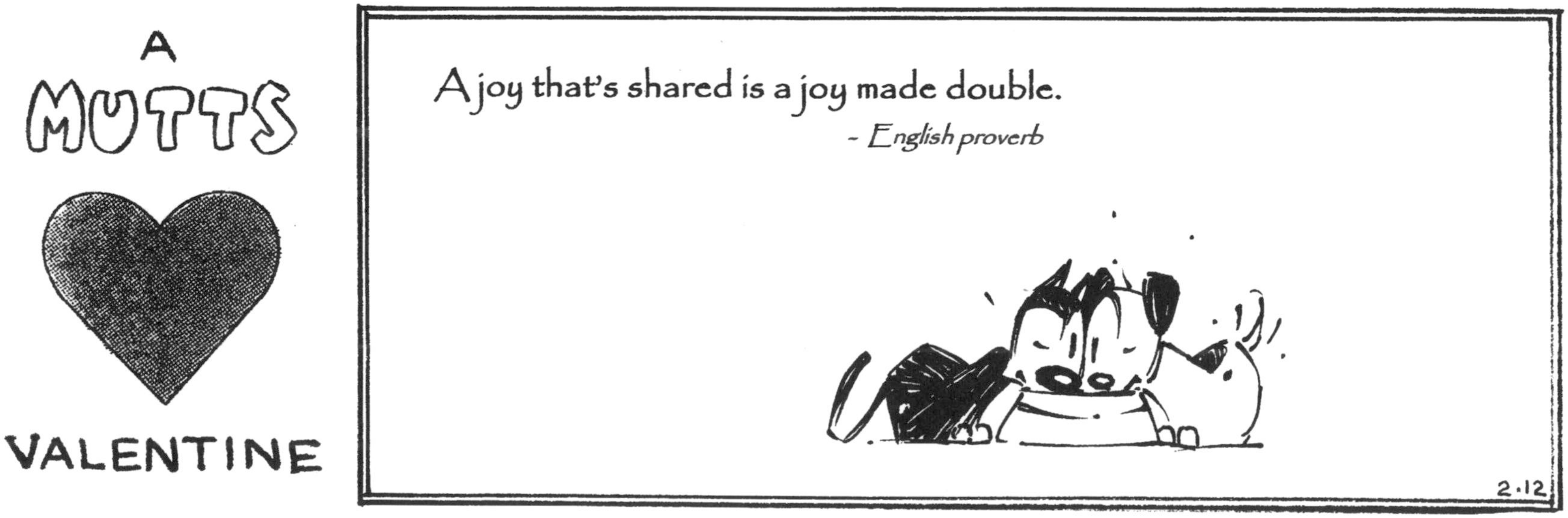
A MUTTS VALENTINE
A joy that's shared is a joy made double.
- English proverb
2.12

A MUTTS ♥ VALENTINE

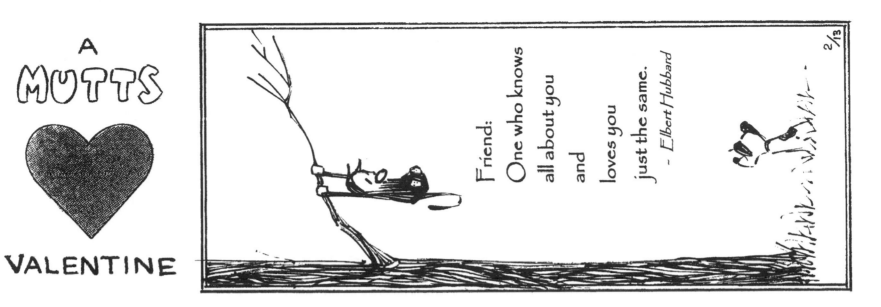

Friend:
One who knows
all about you
and
loves you
just the same.
— Elbert Hubbard

2/13

A MUTTS ♥ VALENTINE

Make yourself necessary to somebody.
— Ralph Waldo Emerson

2·14

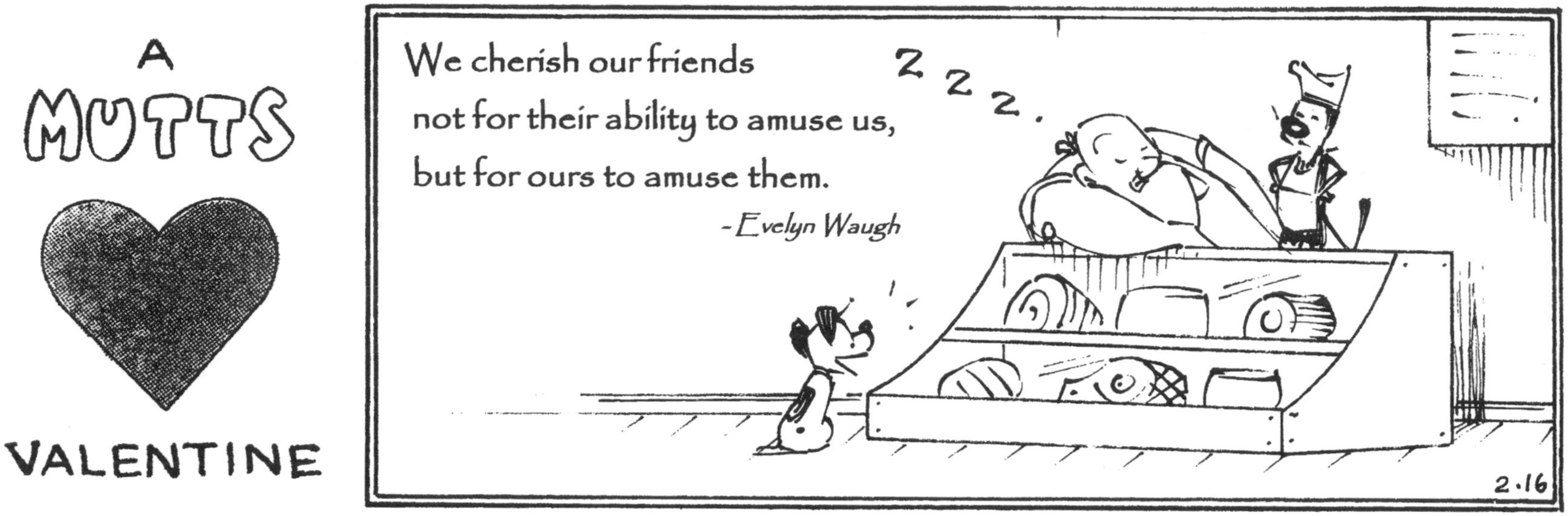
A MUTTS VALENTINE
We cherish our friends
not for their ability to amuse us,
but for ours to amuse them.
- Evelyn Waugh
Z Z Z .
2.16

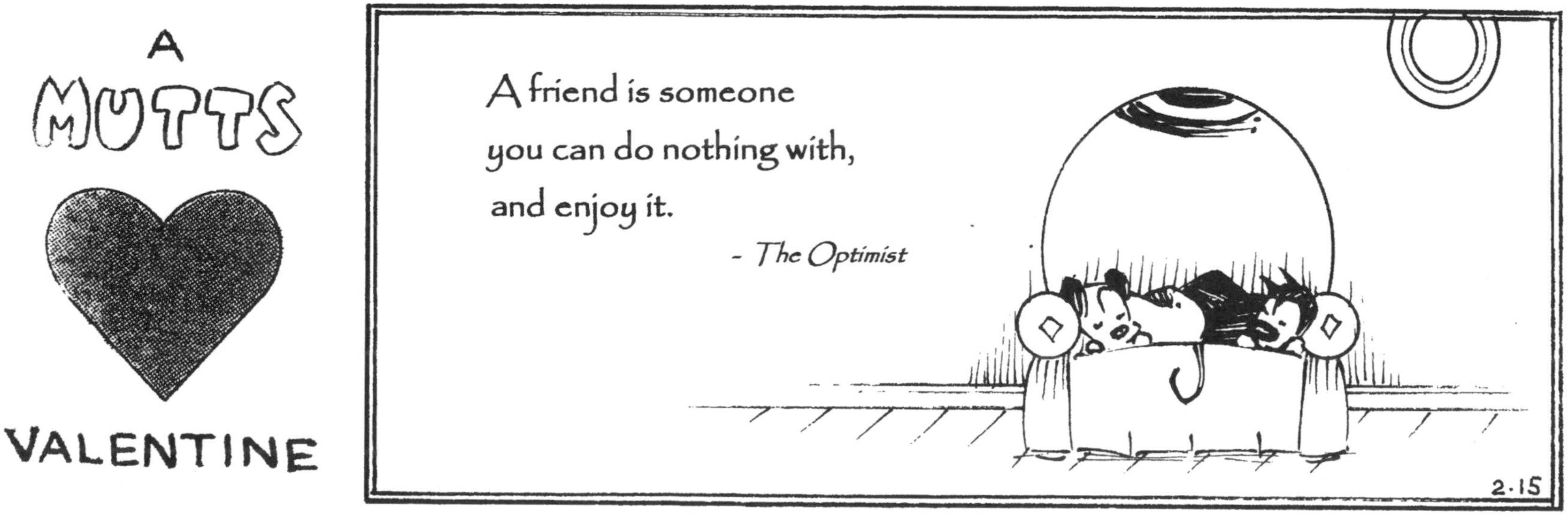
A MUTTS VALENTINE
A friend is someone
you can do nothing with,
and enjoy it.
- The Optimist
2.15

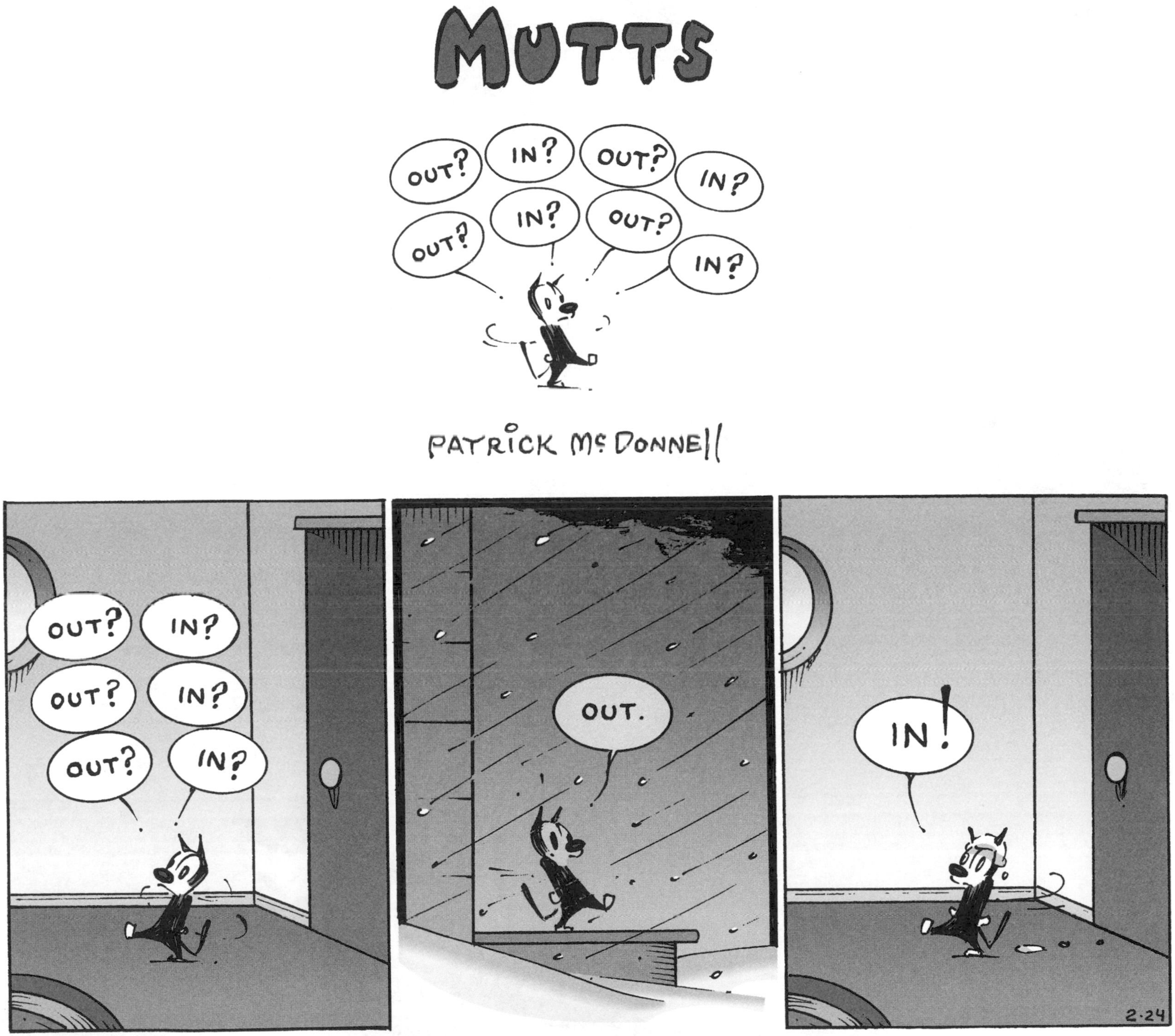
MUTTS
OUT?
IN?
OUT?
IN?
OUT?
IN?
OUT?
IN?
PATRICK McDONNELL
OUT?
IN?
OUT?
IN?
OUT?
IN?
OUT.
IN!
2·24

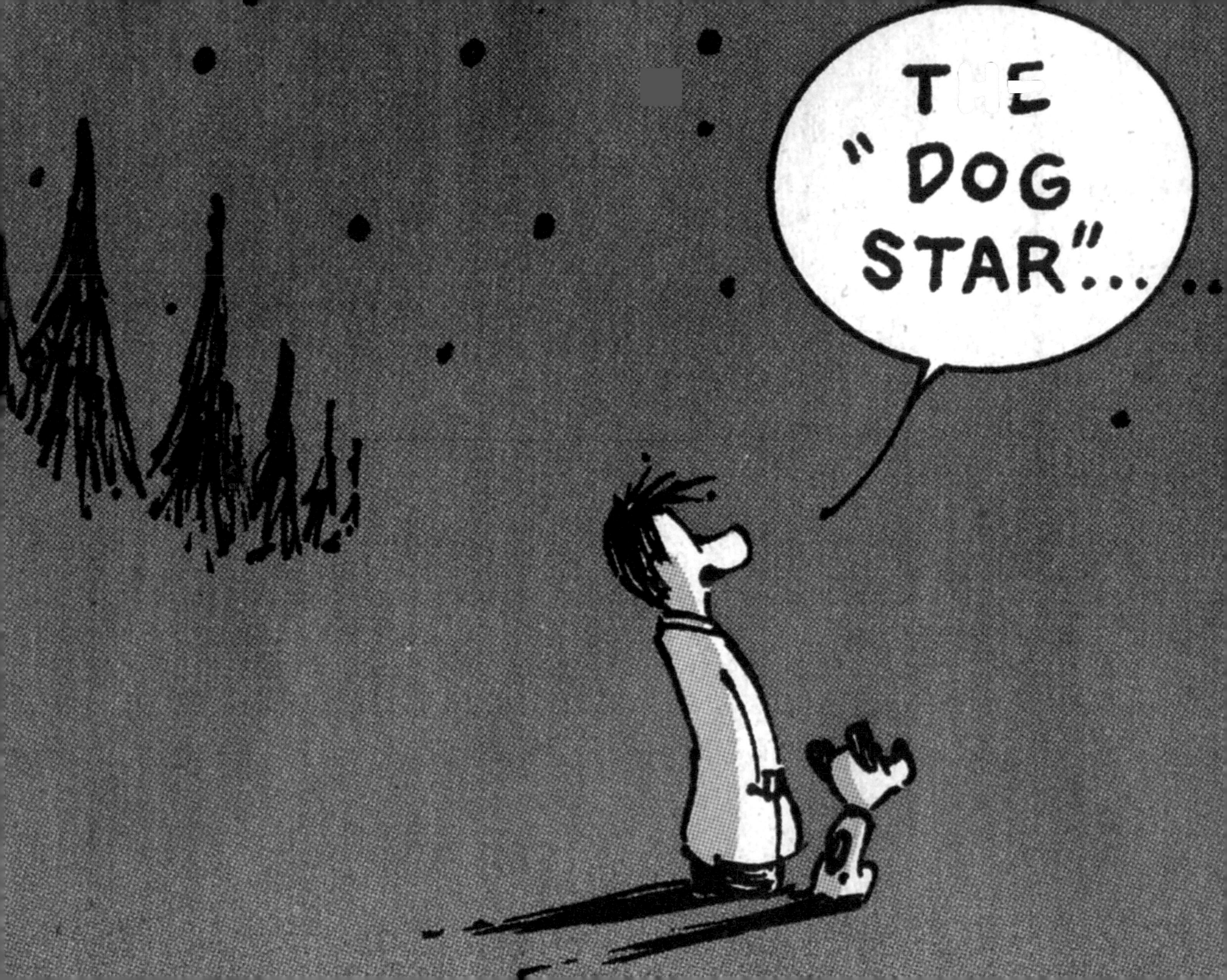
THE "DOG STAR"...

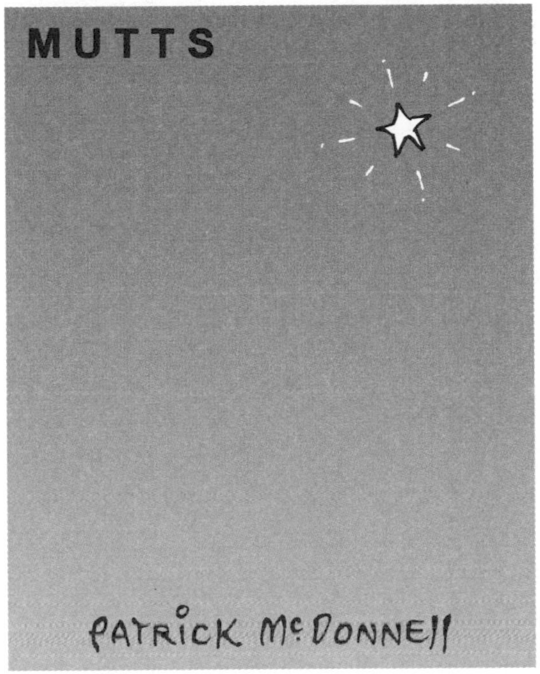
MUTTS
PATRICK McDONNELL

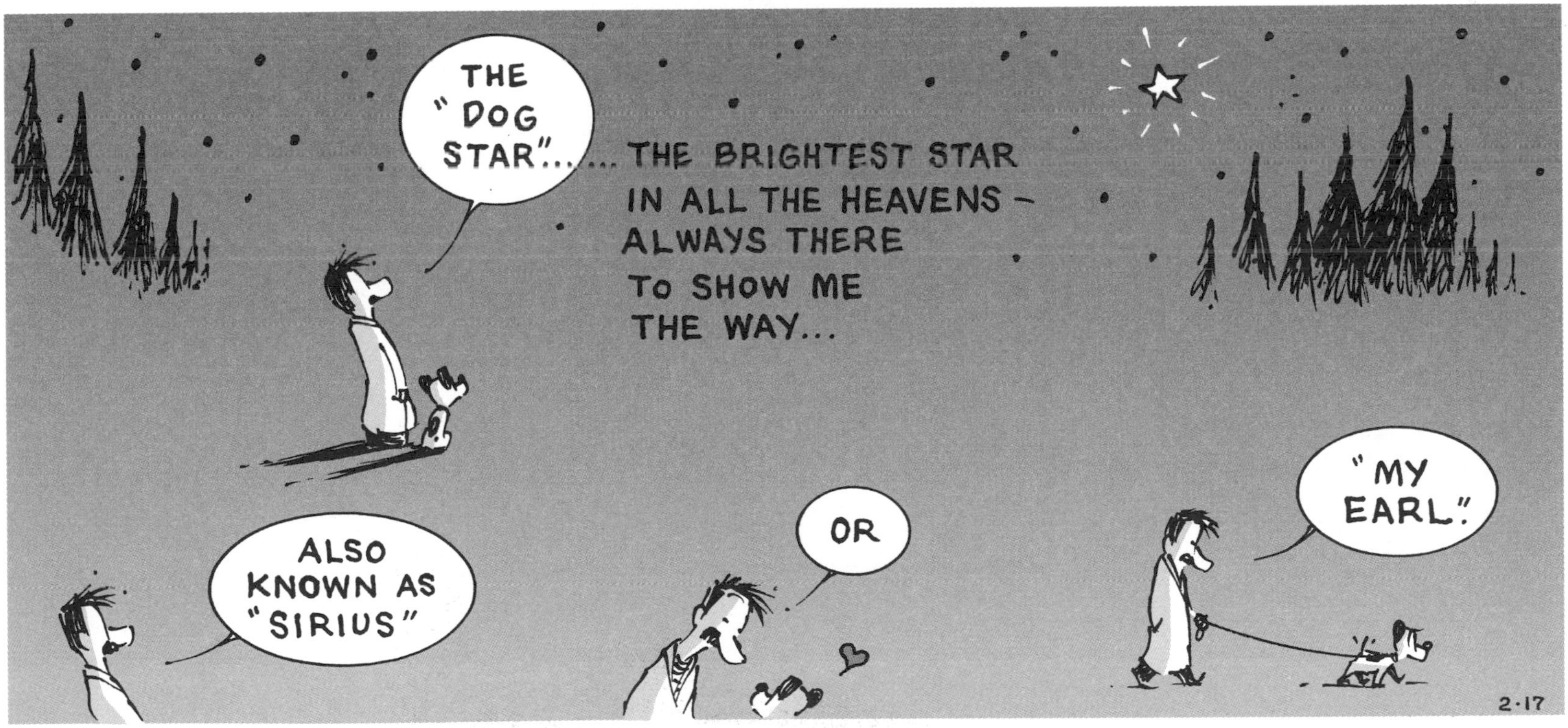
THE "DOG STAR"......
THE BRIGHTEST STAR IN ALL THE HEAVENS – ALWAYS THERE TO SHOW ME THE WAY...
ALSO KNOWN AS "SIRIUS"
OR
"MY EARL."
2·17

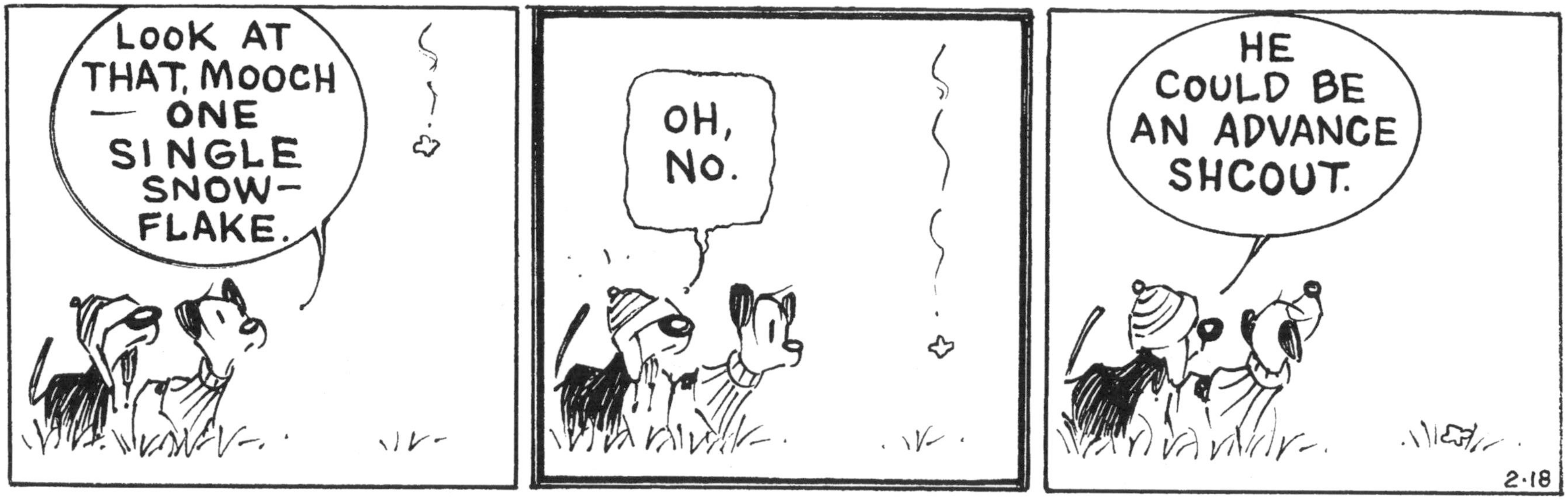
LOOK AT THAT, MOOCH — ONE SINGLE SNOW-FLAKE.
OH, NO.
HE COULD BE AN ADVANCE SHCOUT.
2·18

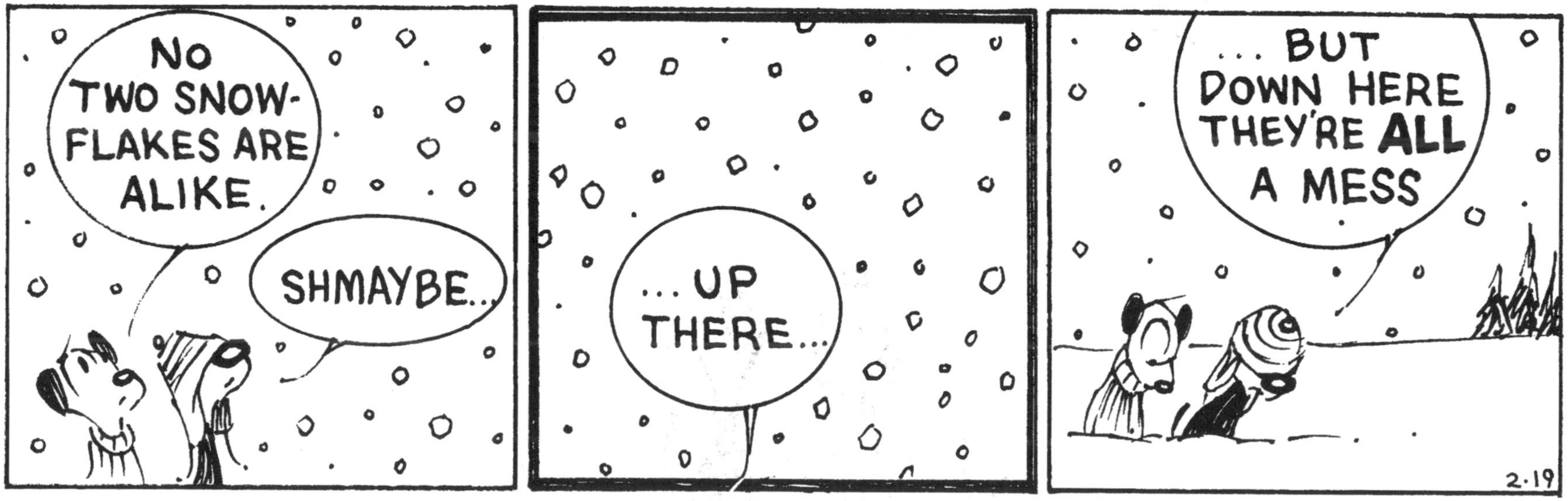
NO TWO SNOW-FLAKES ARE ALIKE.
SHMAYBE...
...UP THERE...
...BUT DOWN HERE THEY'RE **ALL** A MESS
2·19

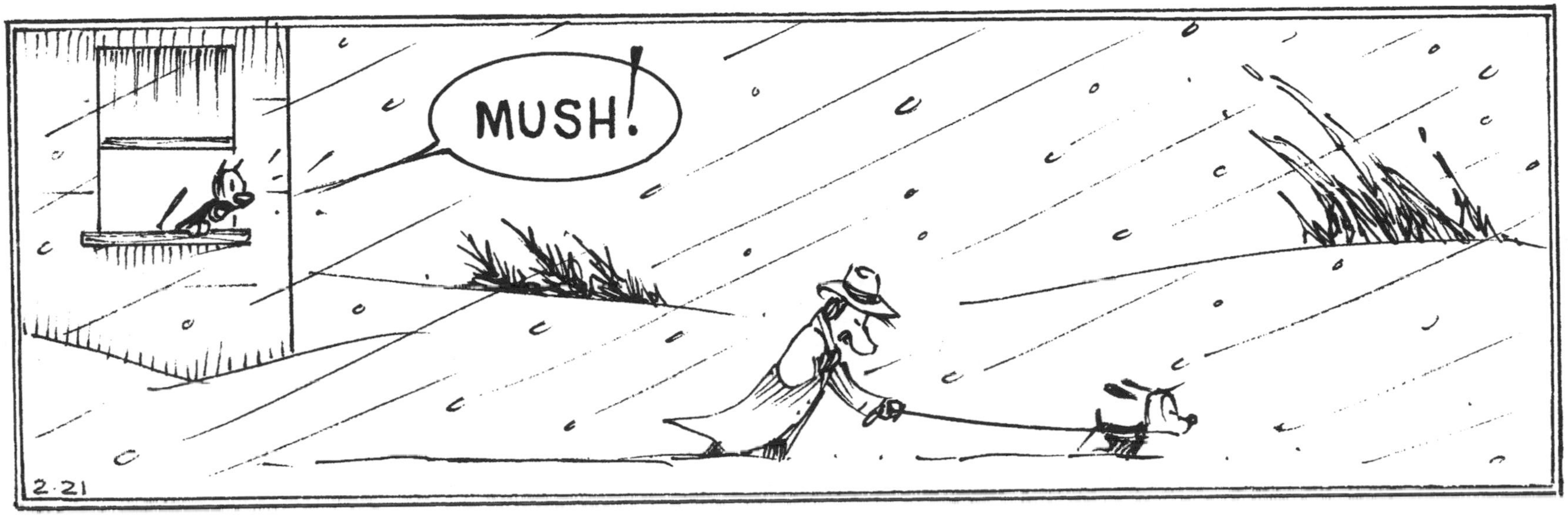
MUSH!
2·21

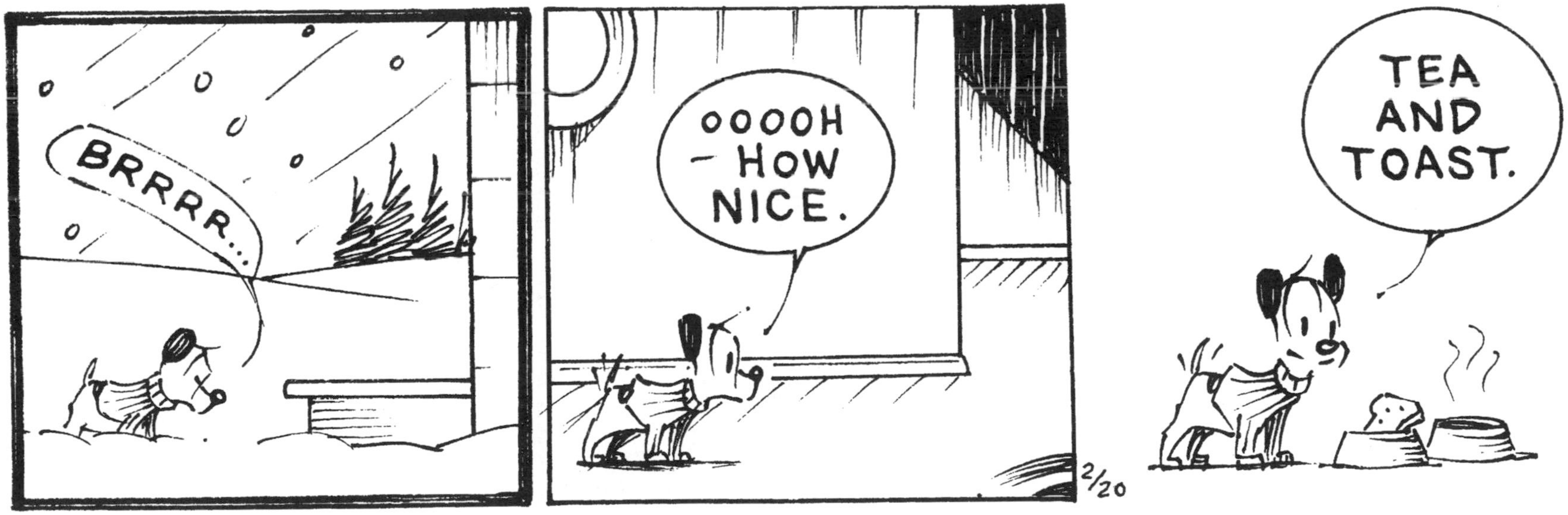
BRRRRR...
OOOOH – HOW NICE.
TEA AND TOAST.
2/20

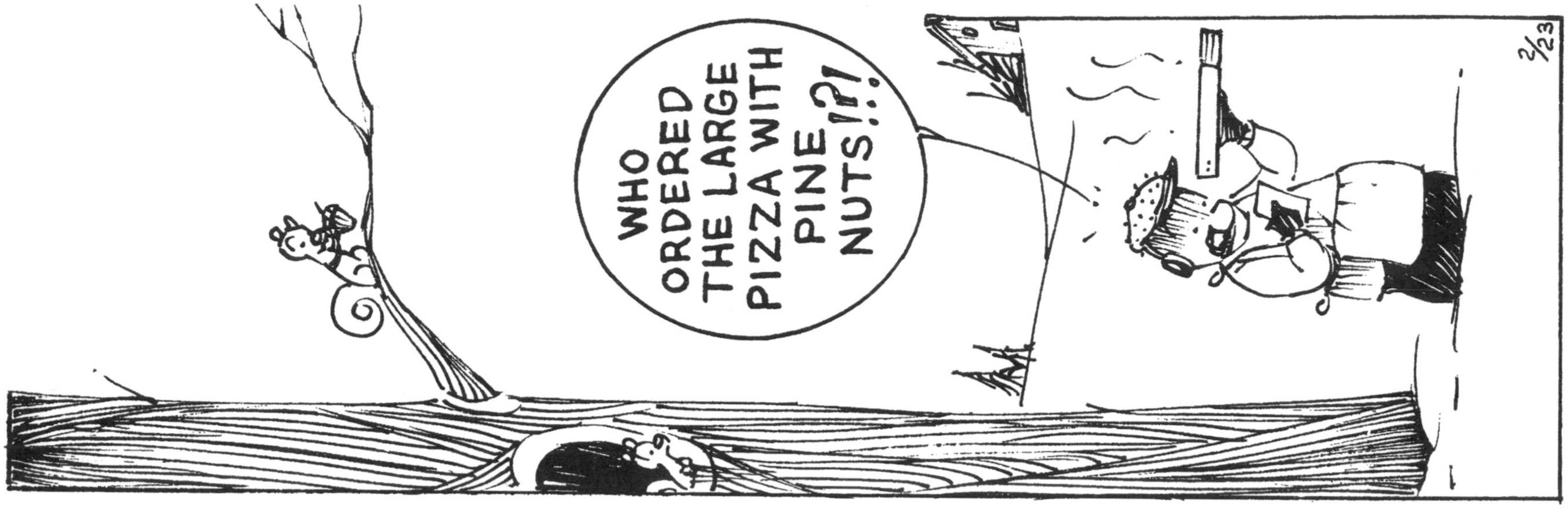
WHO ORDERED THE LARGE PIZZA WITH PINE NUTS!!?!
2/23

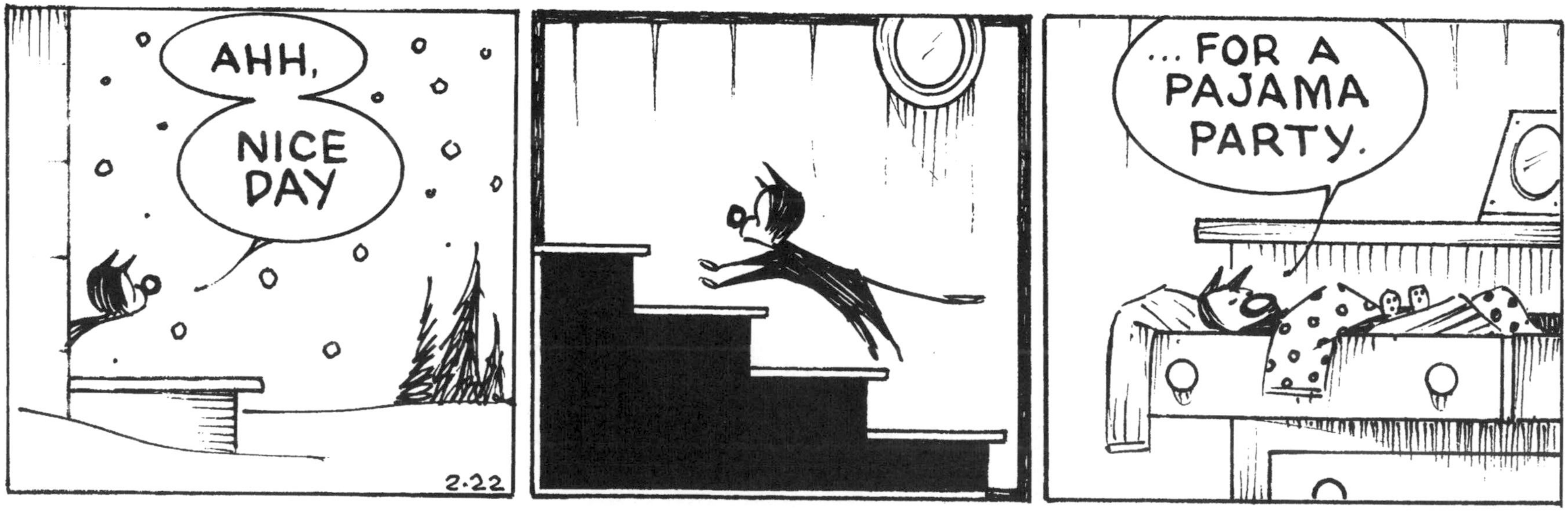
AHH,
NICE DAY
2.22
...FOR A PAJAMA PARTY.

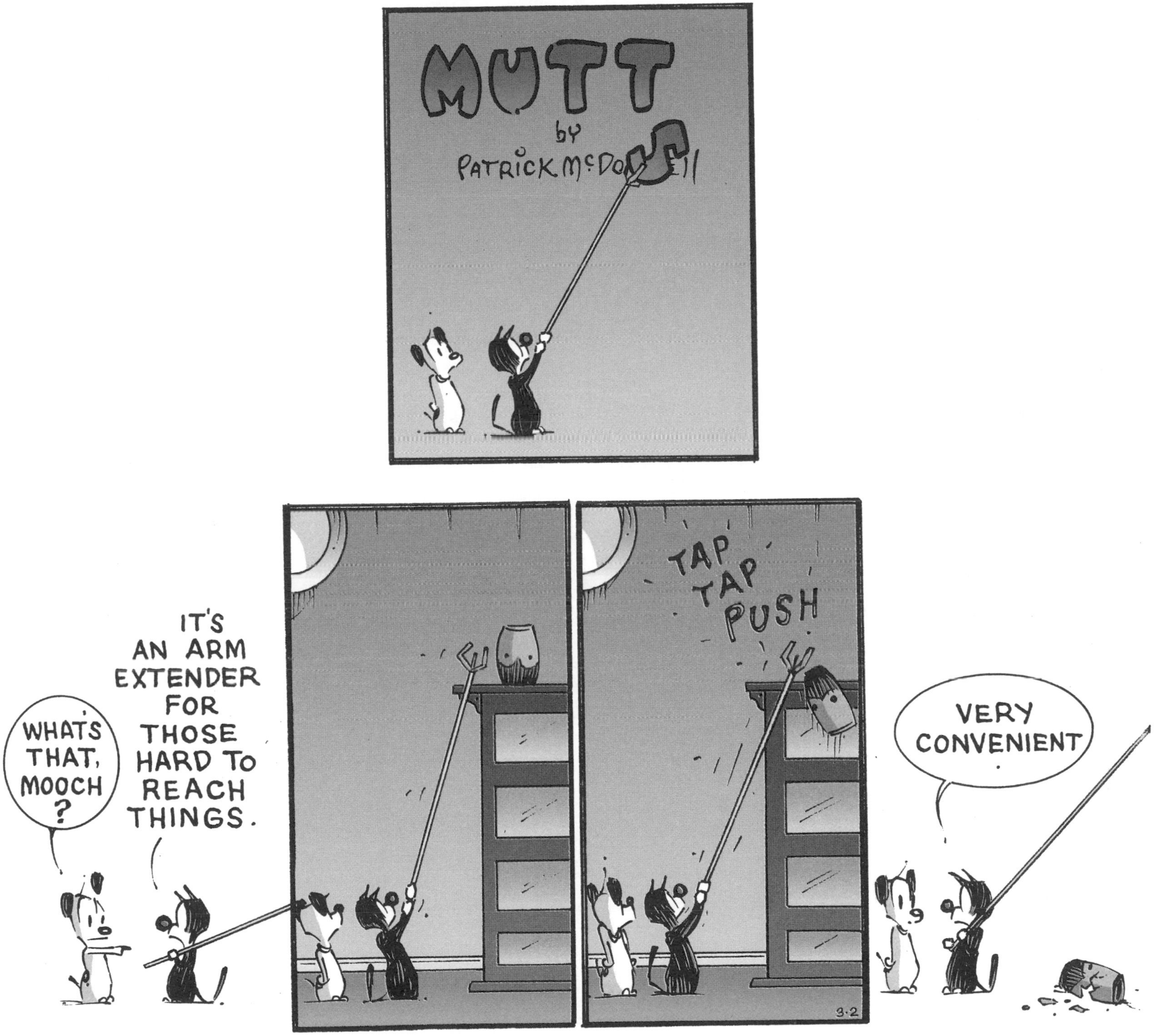
MUTT
by
PATRICK McDONNELL
WHATS THAT, MOOCH?
IT'S AN ARM EXTENDER FOR THOSE HARD TO REACH THINGS.
TAP TAP PUSH
VERY CONVENIENT
3·2

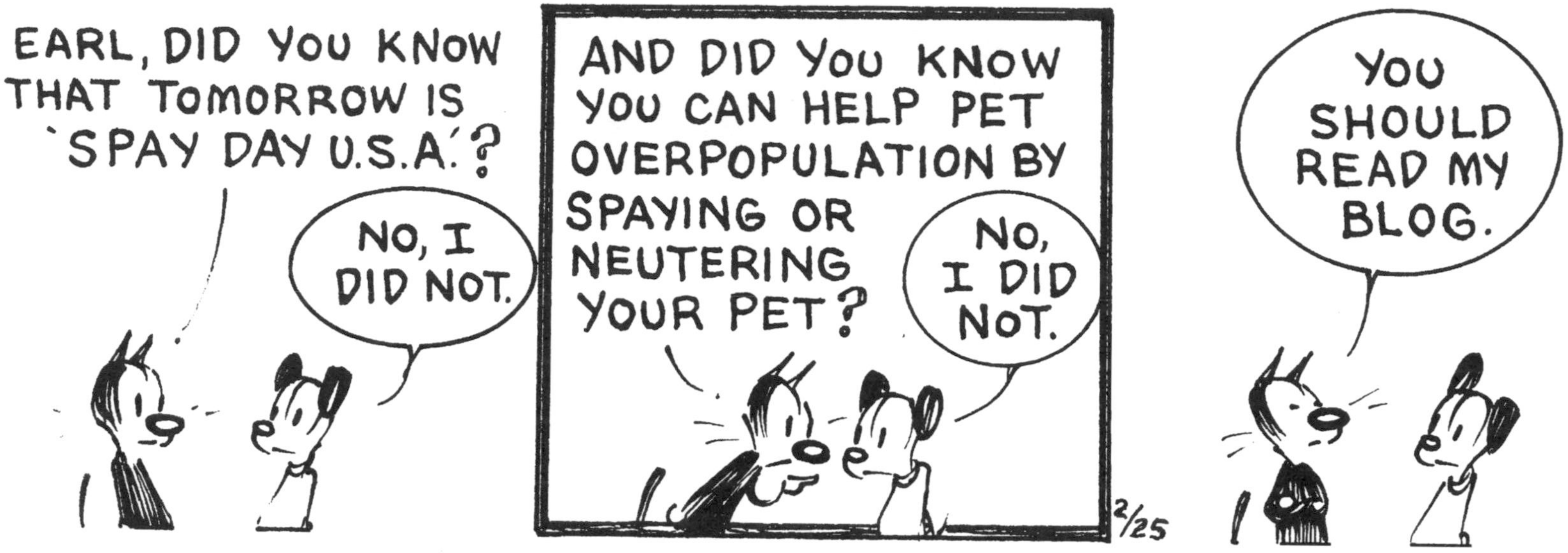
EARL, DID YOU KNOW THAT TOMORROW IS 'SPAY DAY U.S.A.'?
NO, I DID NOT.
AND DID YOU KNOW YOU CAN HELP PET OVERPOPULATION BY SPAYING OR NEUTERING YOUR PET?
NO, I DID NOT.
YOU SHOULD READ MY BLOG.
2/25

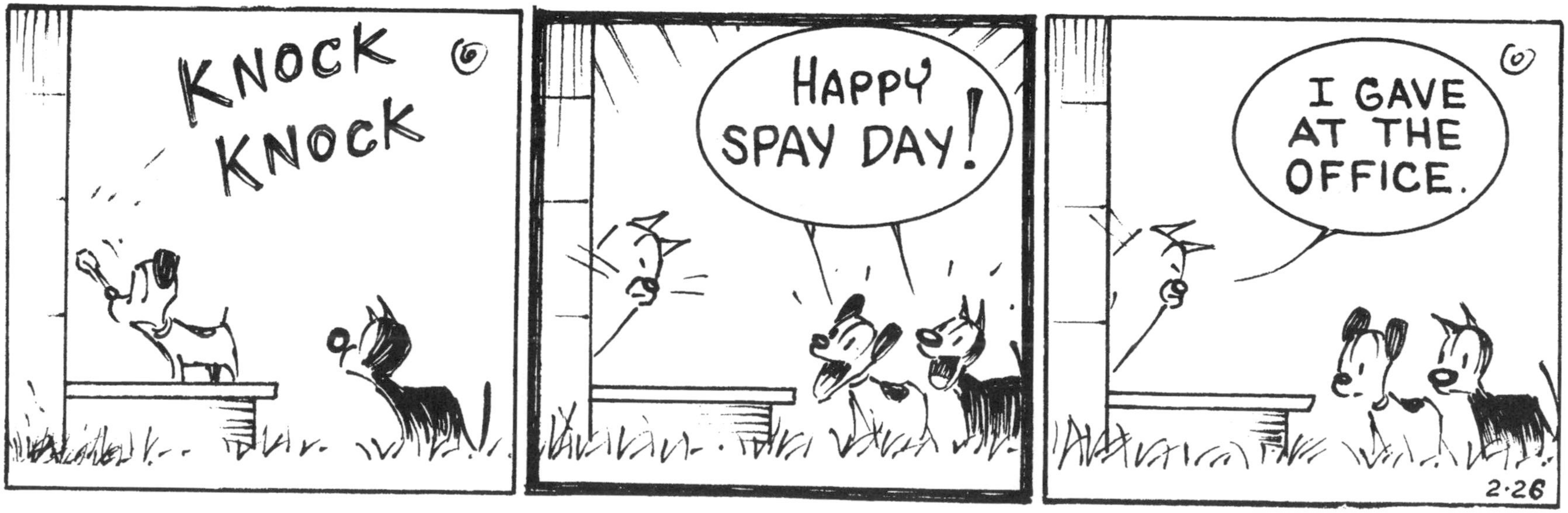
KNOCK KNOCK
HAPPY SPAY DAY!
I GAVE AT THE OFFICE.
2·26

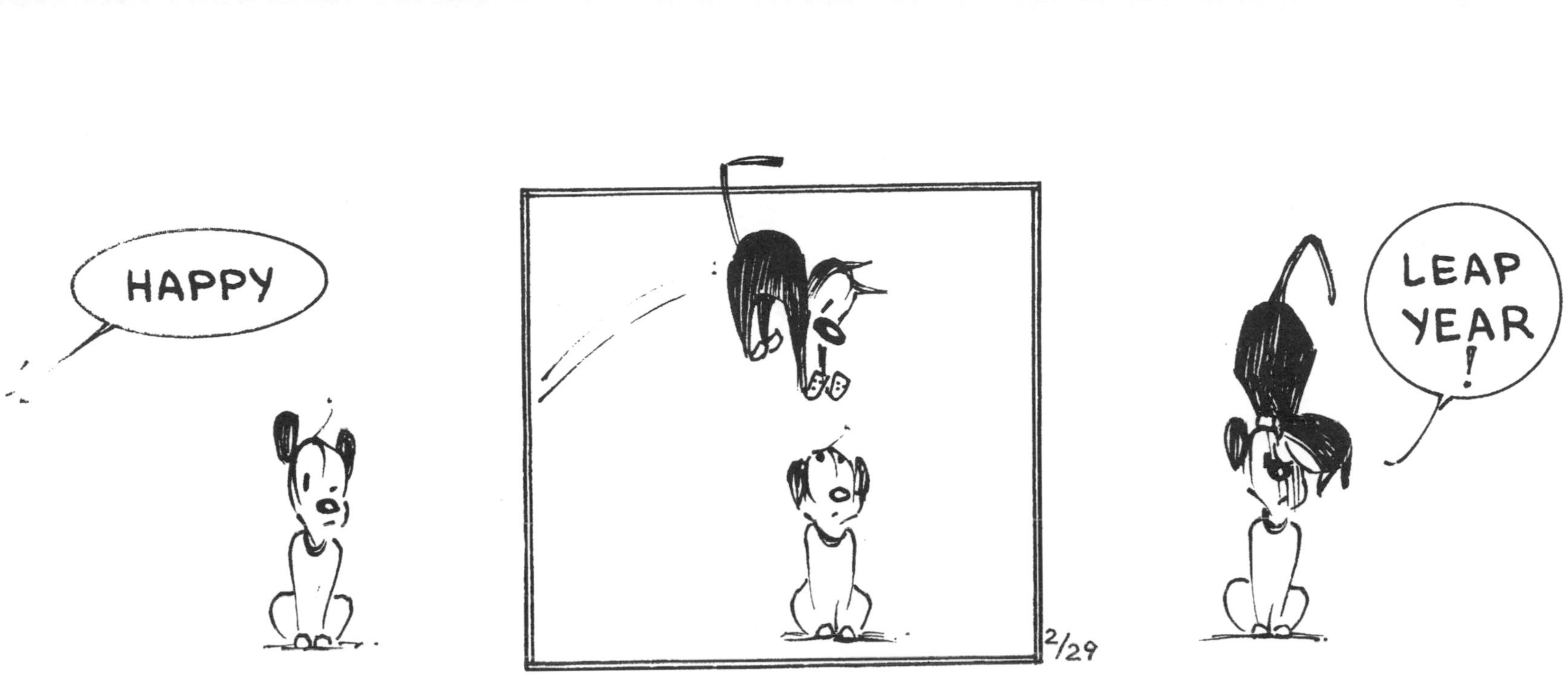
HAPPY
LEAP YEAR!
2/29

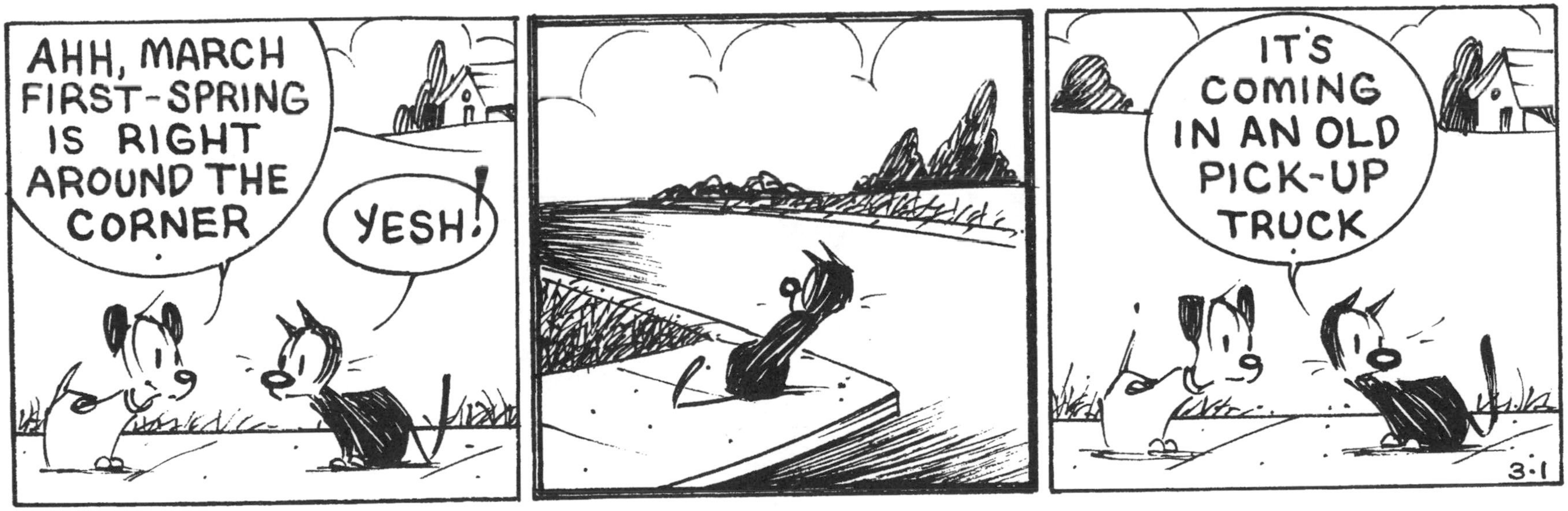
AHH, MARCH FIRST-SPRING IS RIGHT AROUND THE CORNER
YESH!
IT'S COMING IN AN OLD PICK-UP TRUCK
3-1

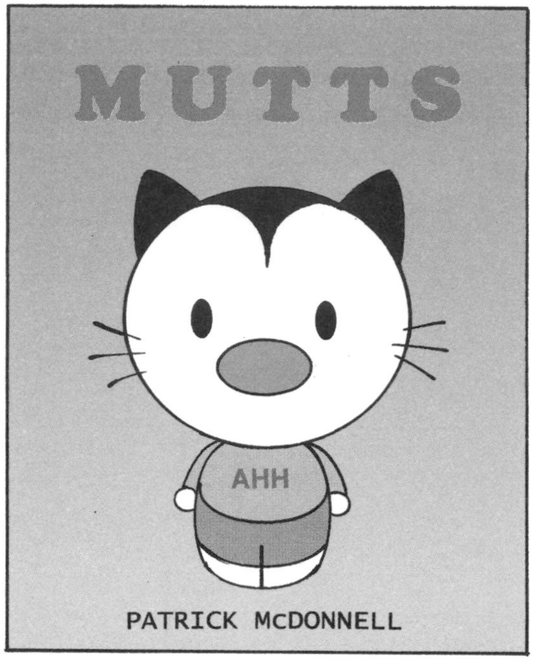
MUTTS
AHH
PATRICK McDONNELL

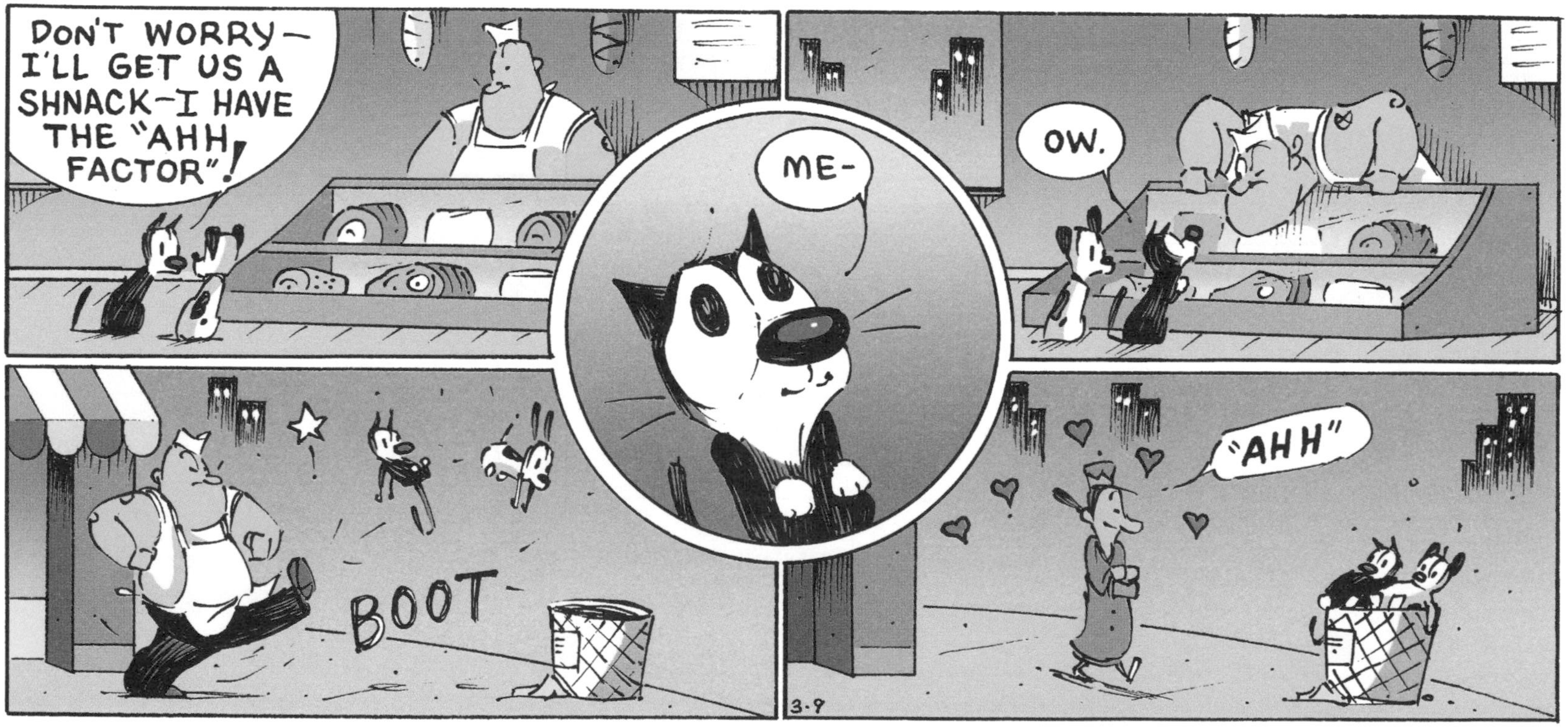
DON'T WORRY— I'LL GET US A SHNACK—I HAVE THE "AHH FACTOR"!
ME-
OW.
BOOT
"AHH"
3-9

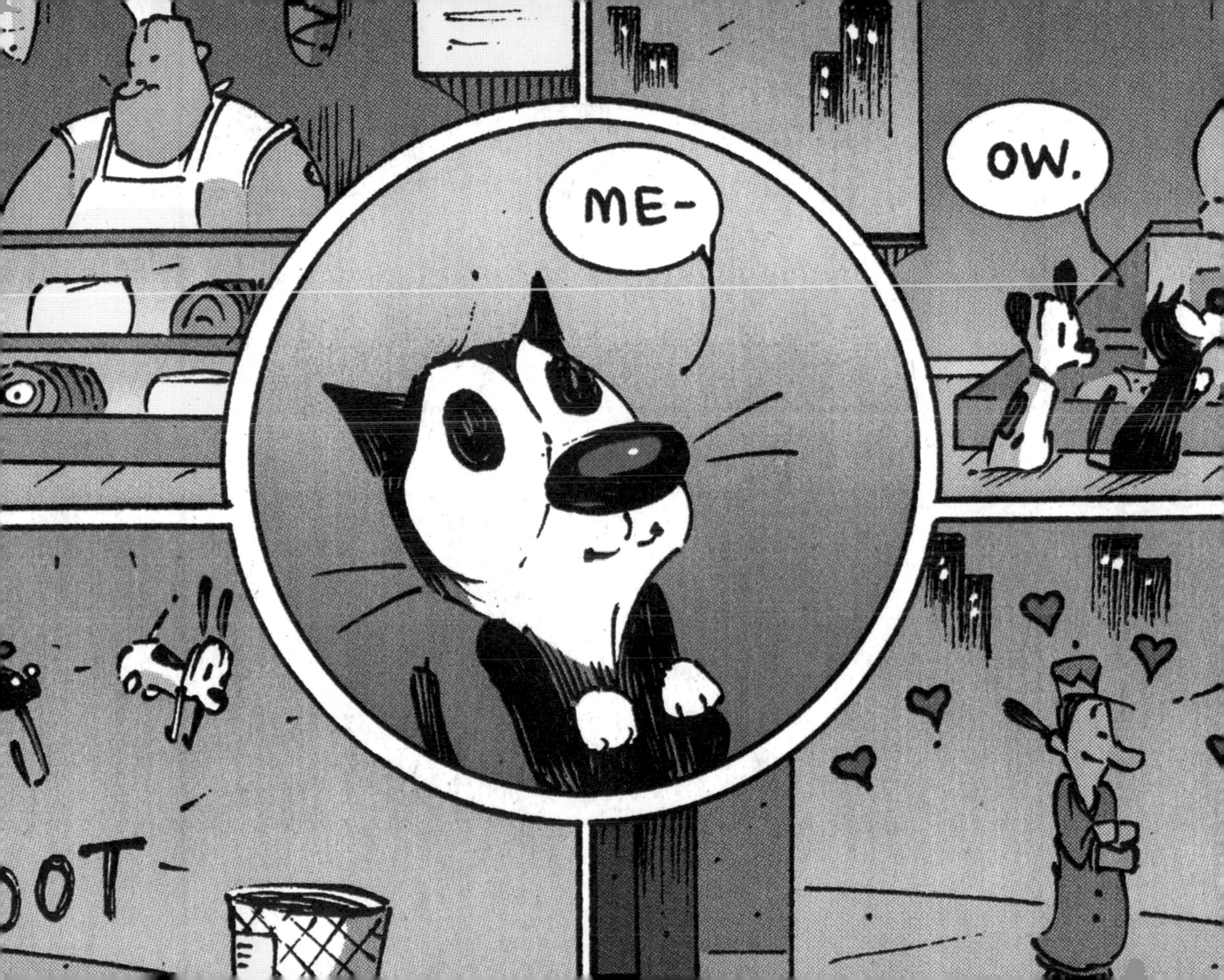
ME-
OW.
OOT-

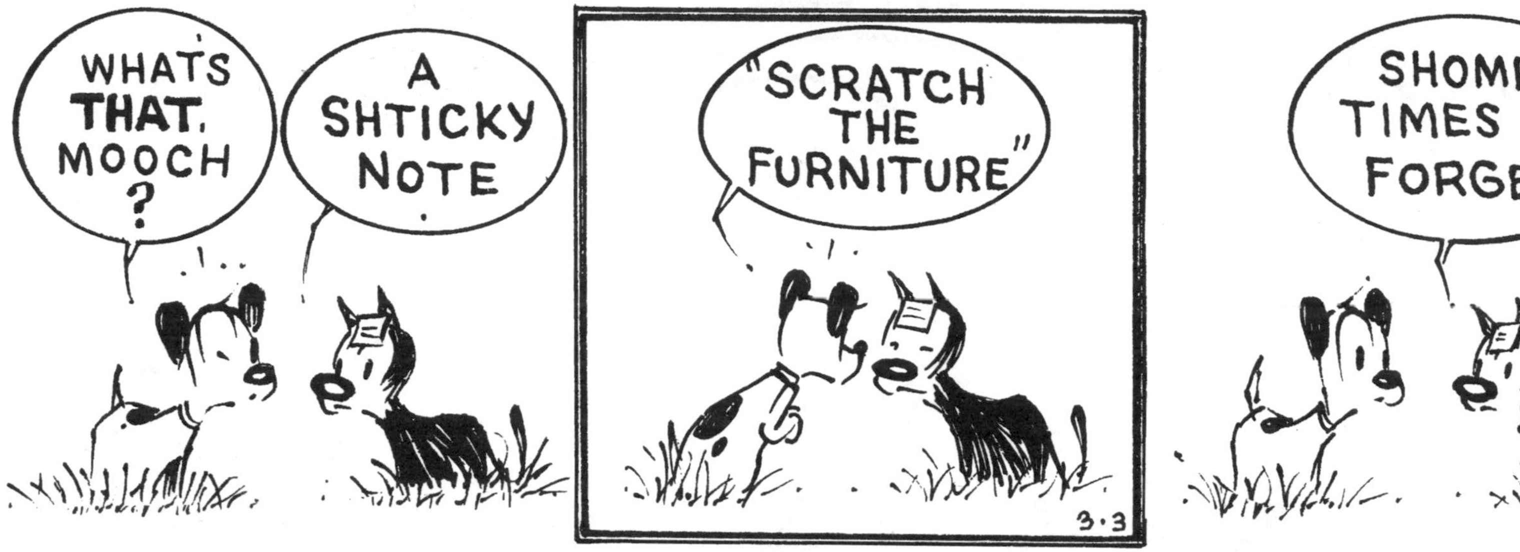
WHAT'S THAT, MOOCH ?
A SHTICKY NOTE
"SCRATCH THE FURNITURE"
SHOME-TIMES I FORGET.
3·3

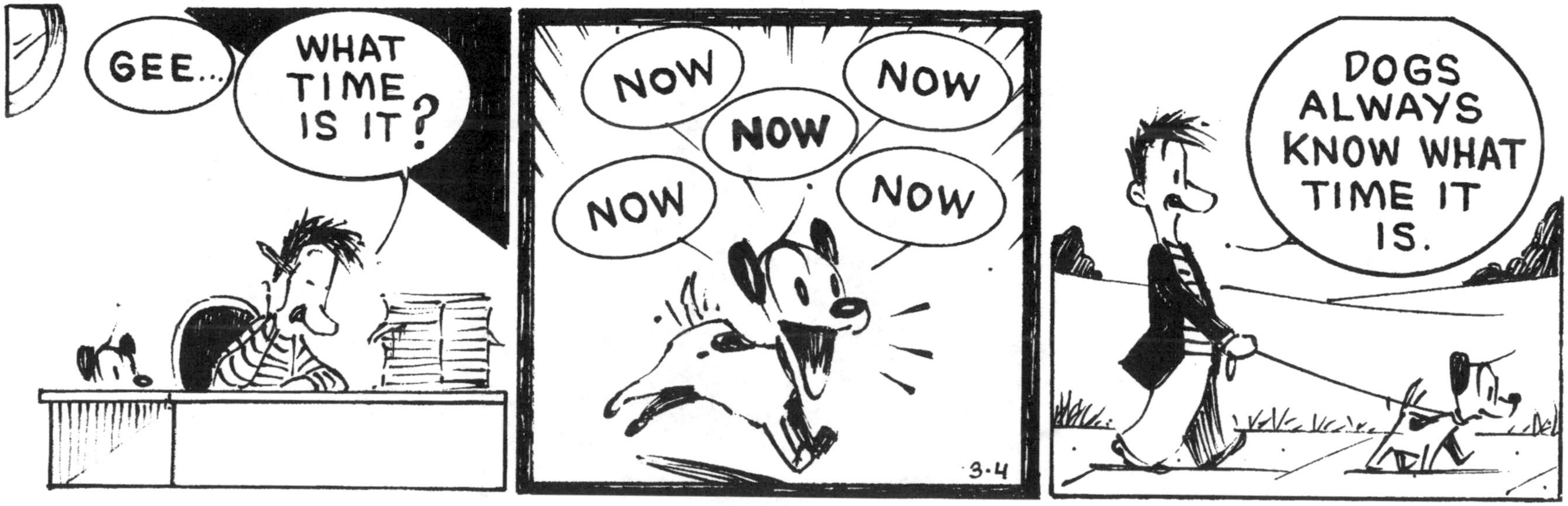
GEE...
WHAT TIME IS IT ?
NOW
NOW
NOW
NOW
NOW
3·4
DOGS ALWAYS KNOW WHAT TIME IT IS.

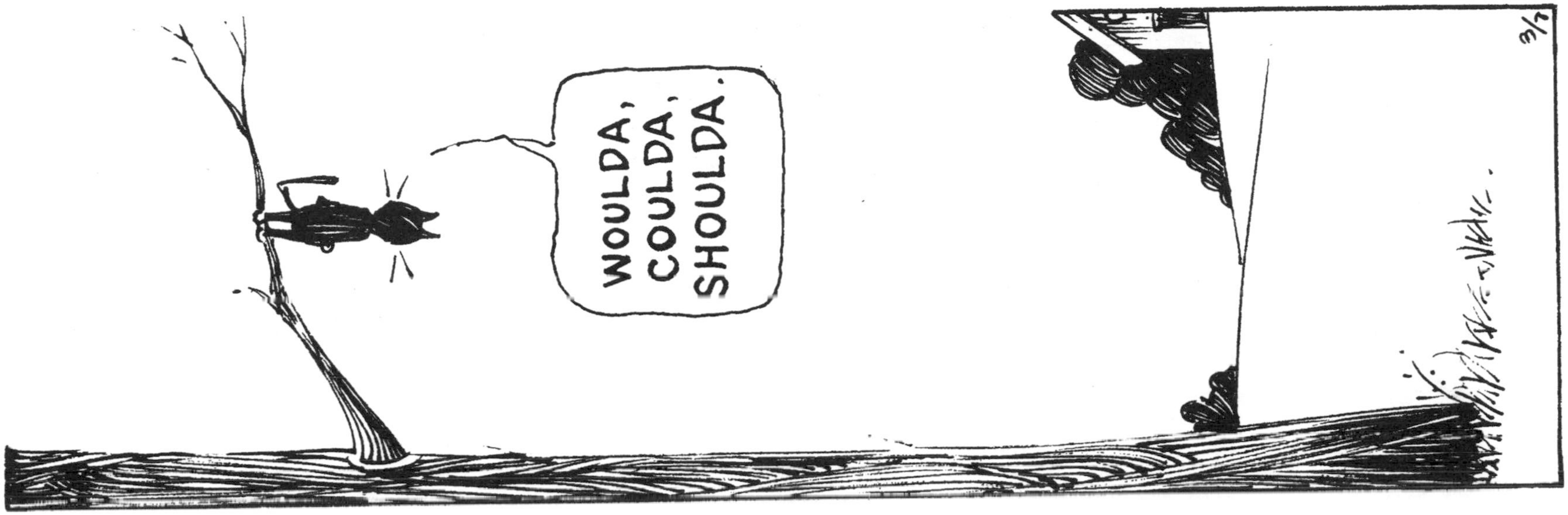
WOULDA, COULDA, SHOULDA.
3/7

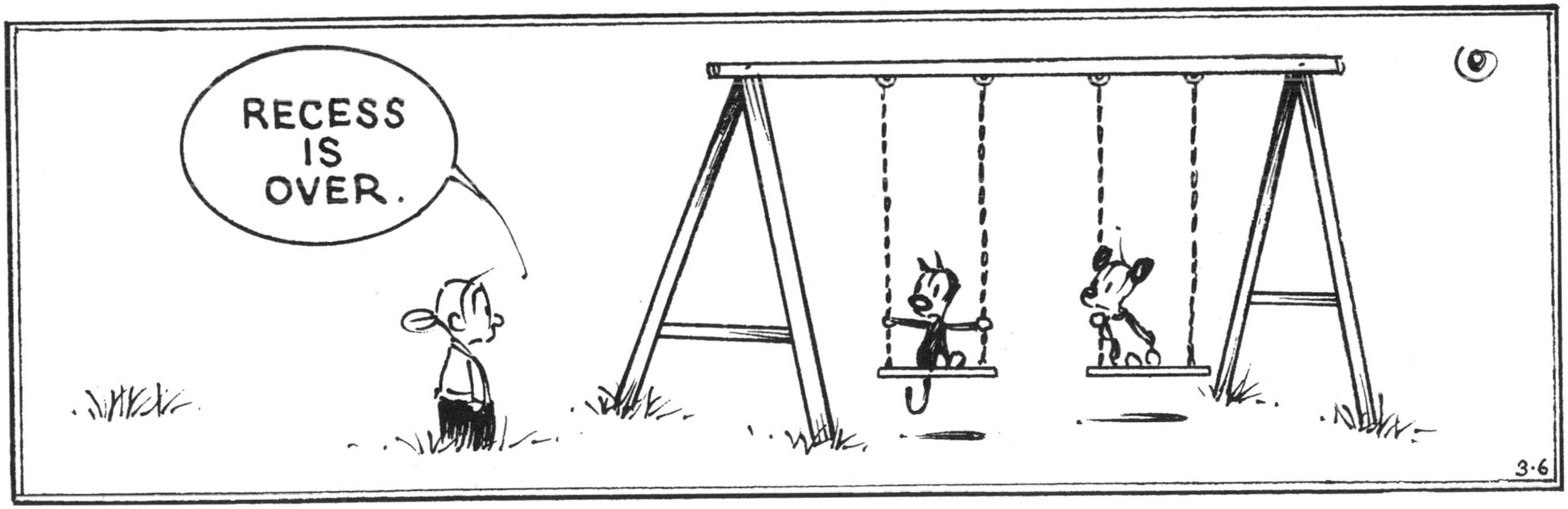
RECESS IS OVER.
3·6

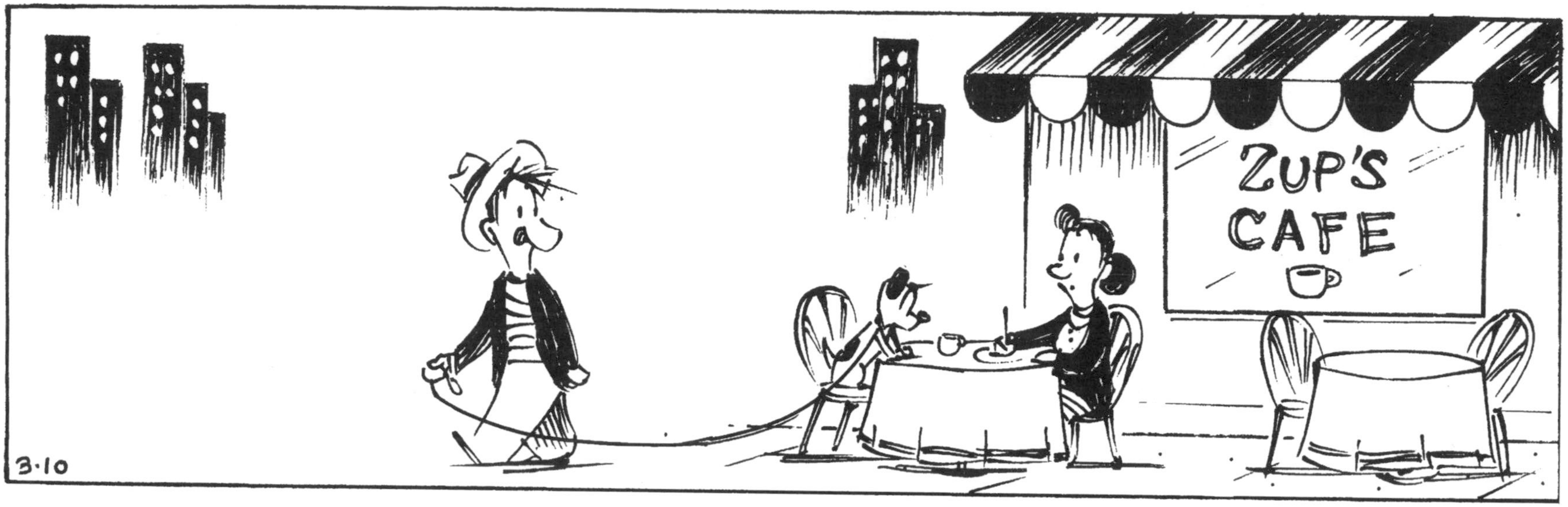
ZUP'S CAFE
3·10

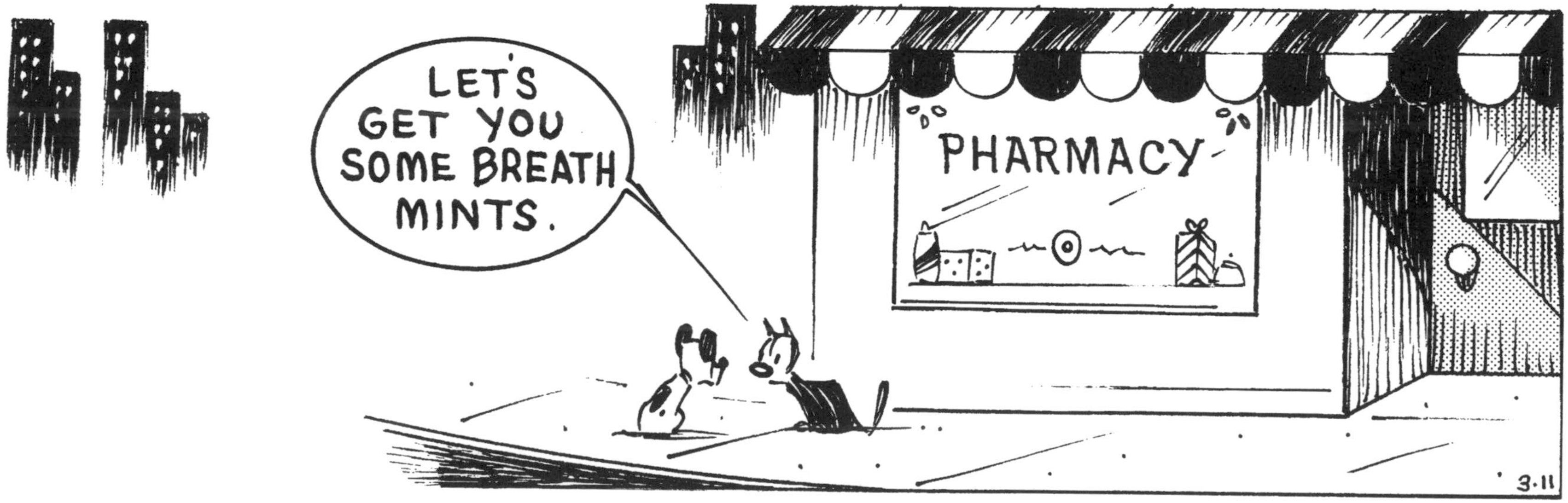
LET'S GET YOU SOME BREATH MINTS.
PHARMACY
3·11

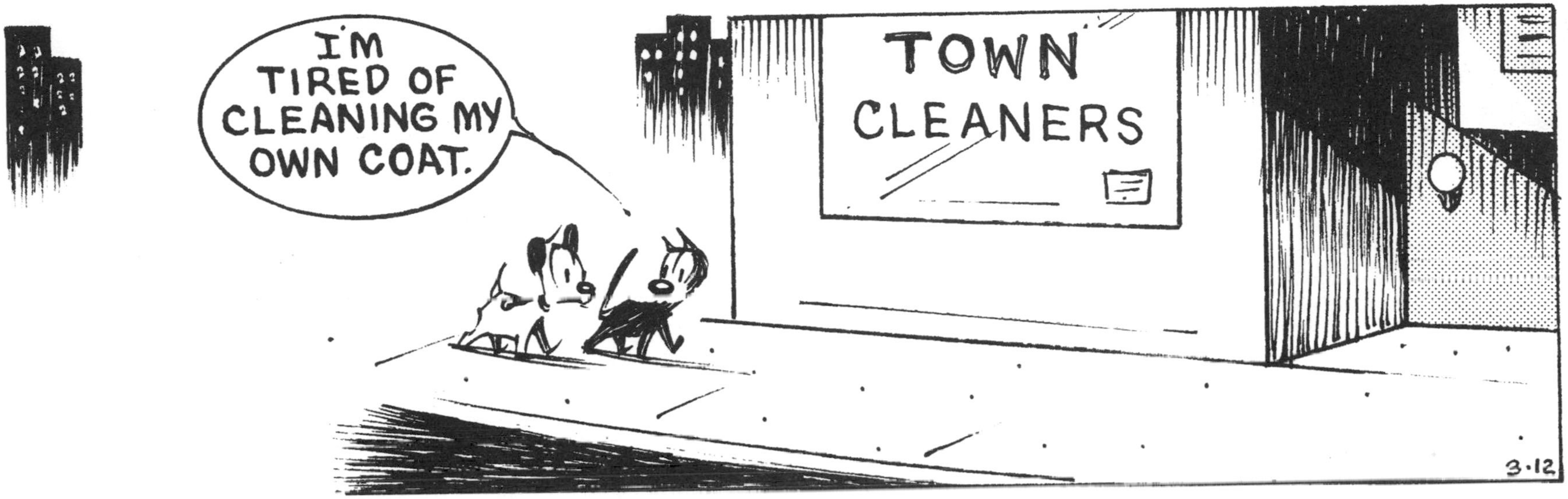
I'M TIRED OF CLEANING MY OWN COAT.
TOWN CLEANERS
3·12

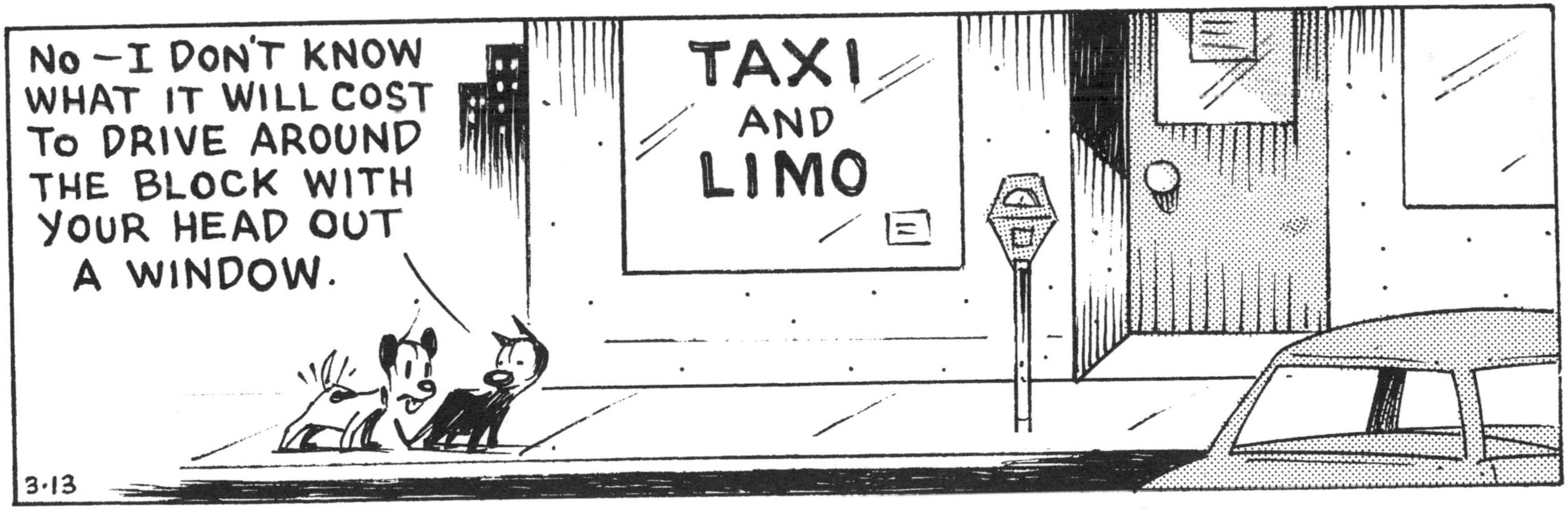
No — I DON'T KNOW WHAT IT WILL COST TO DRIVE AROUND THE BLOCK WITH YOUR HEAD OUT A WINDOW.
TAXI AND LIMO
3·13

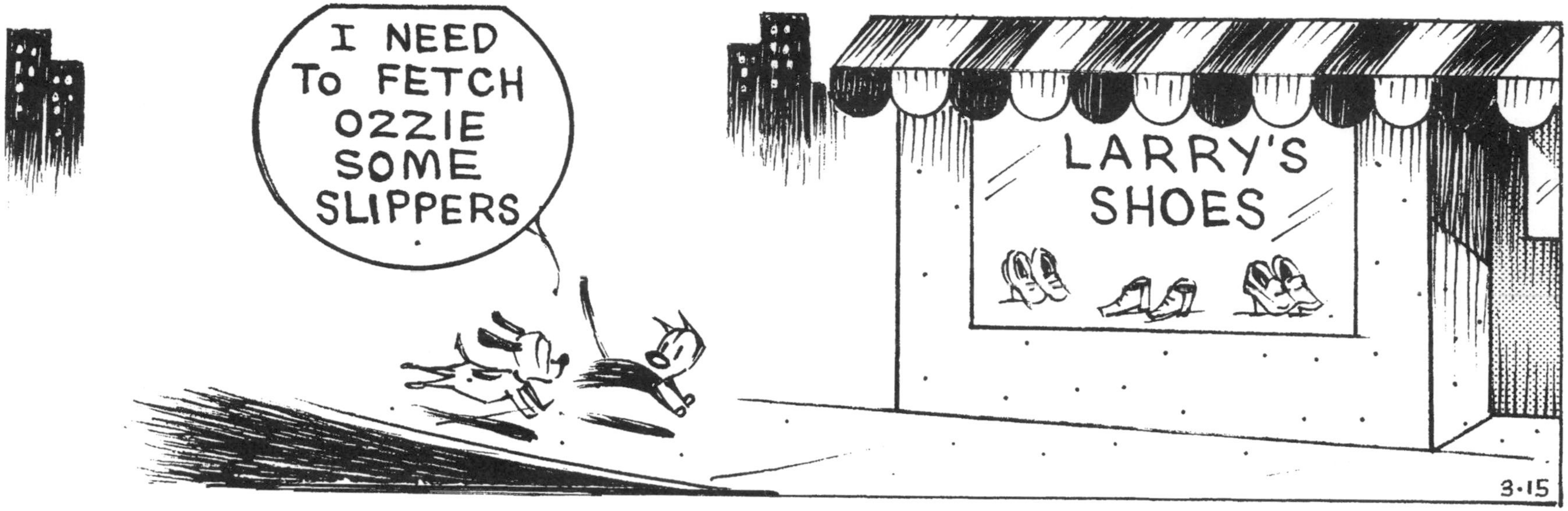
I NEED To FETCH OZZIE SOME SLIPPERS
LARRY'S SHOES
3·15

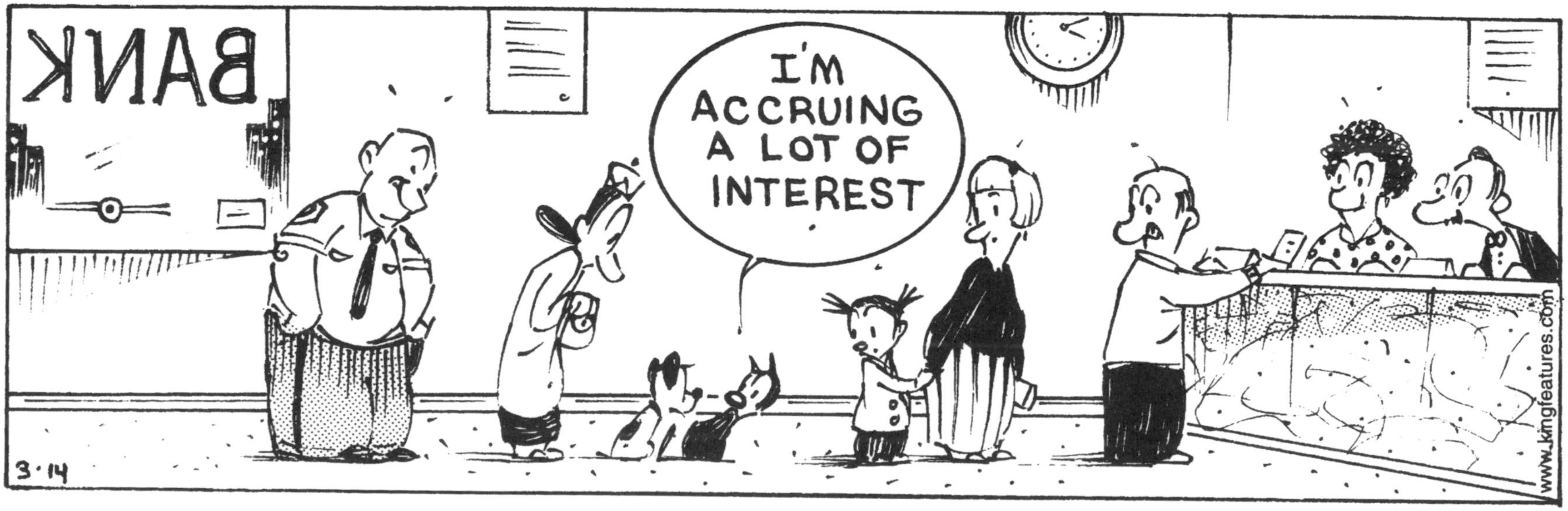
BANK
I'M ACCRUING A LOT OF INTEREST
3·14
www.kingfeatures.com

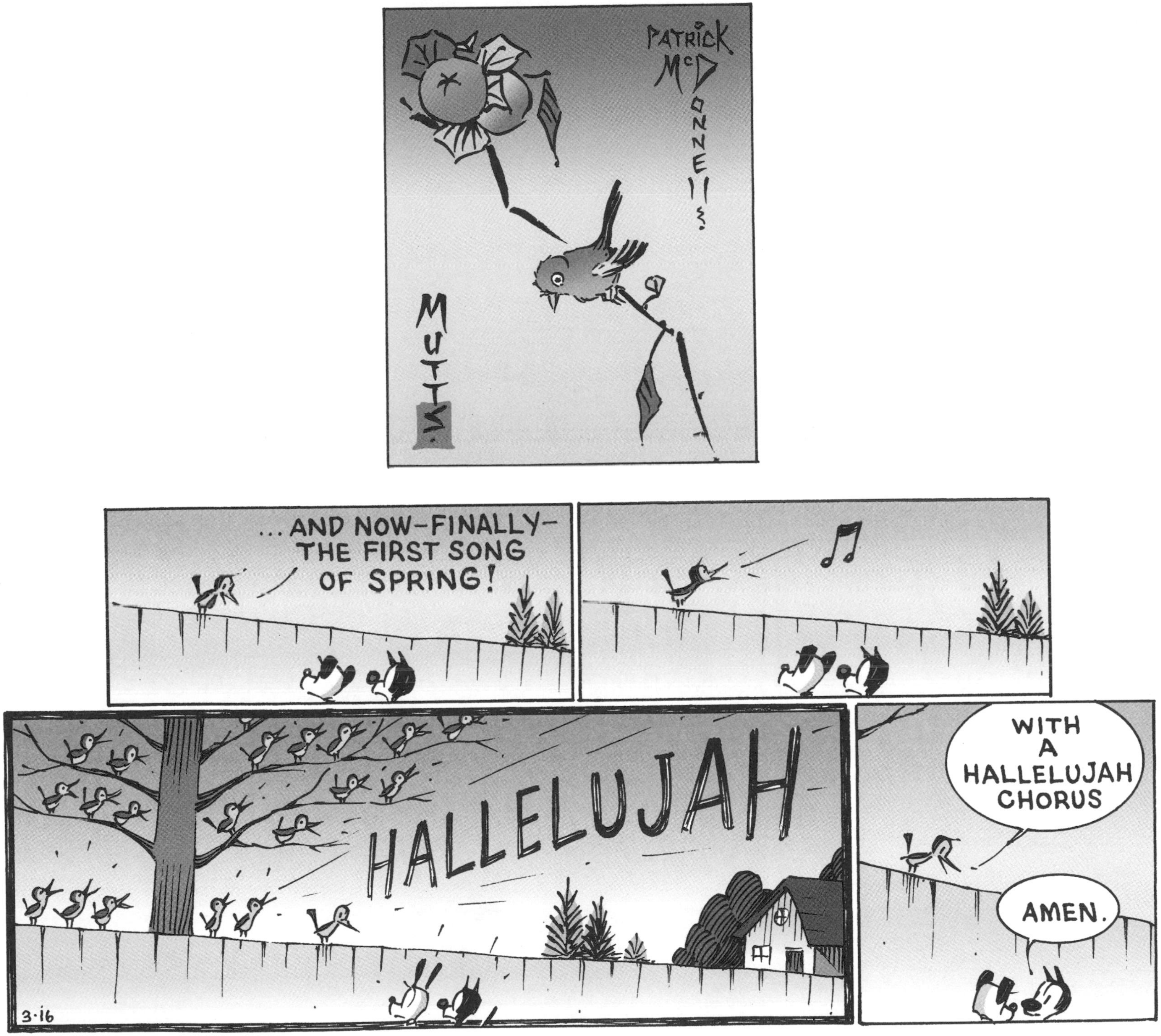
PATRICK McDONNELL
MUTTS
... AND NOW—FINALLY—THE FIRST SONG OF SPRING!
HALLELUJAH
WITH A HALLELUJAH CHORUS
AMEN.
3·16

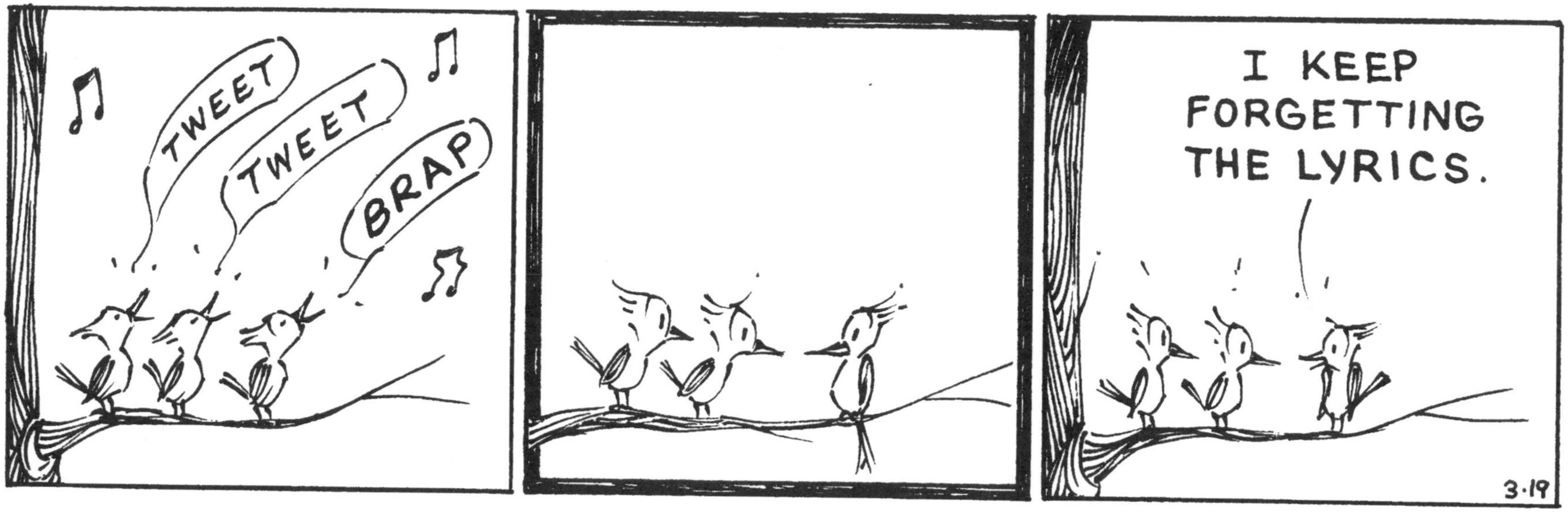
TWEET
TWEET
BRAP
I KEEP FORGETTING THE LYRICS.
3·19

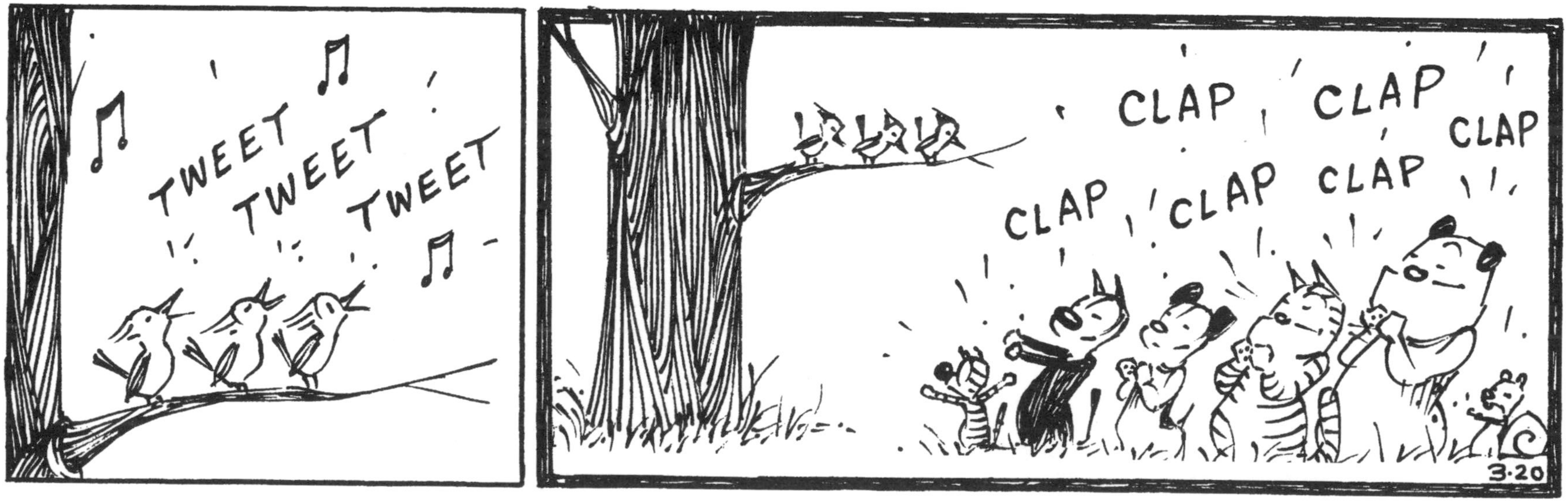
TWEET
TWEET
TWEET
CLAP CLAP CLAP CLAP CLAP CLAP CLAP
3·20

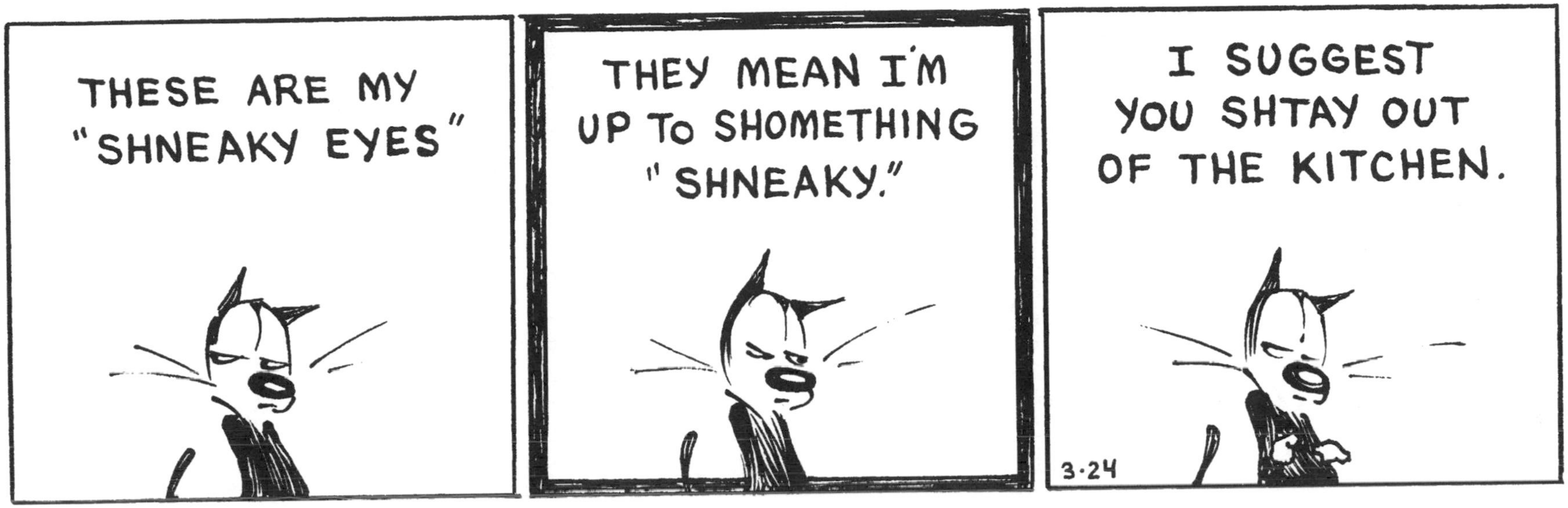
THESE ARE MY "SHNEAKY EYES"
THEY MEAN I'M UP TO SHOMETHING "SHNEAKY."
I SUGGEST YOU SHTAY OUT OF THE KITCHEN.
3·24

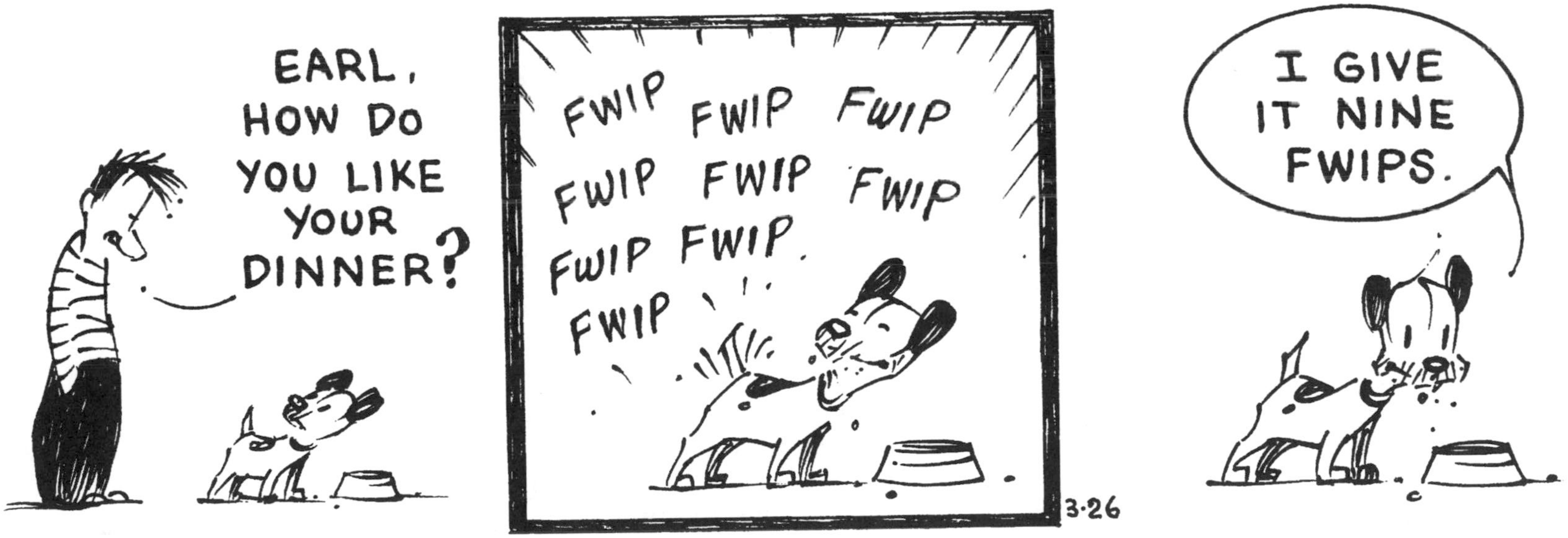
EARL, HOW DO YOU LIKE YOUR DINNER?
FWIP FWIP FWIP FWIP FWIP FWIP FWIP FWIP. FWIP
3·26
I GIVE IT NINE FWIPS.

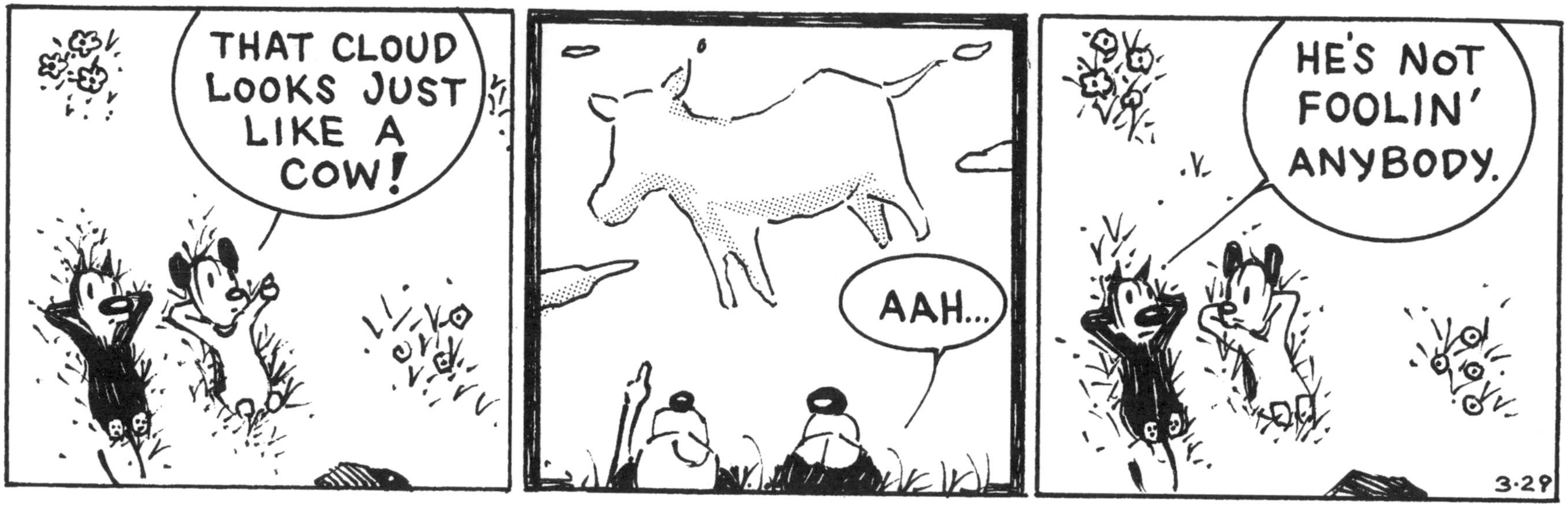
THAT CLOUD LOOKS JUST LIKE A COW!
AAH...
HE'S NOT FOOLIN' ANYBODY.
3·29

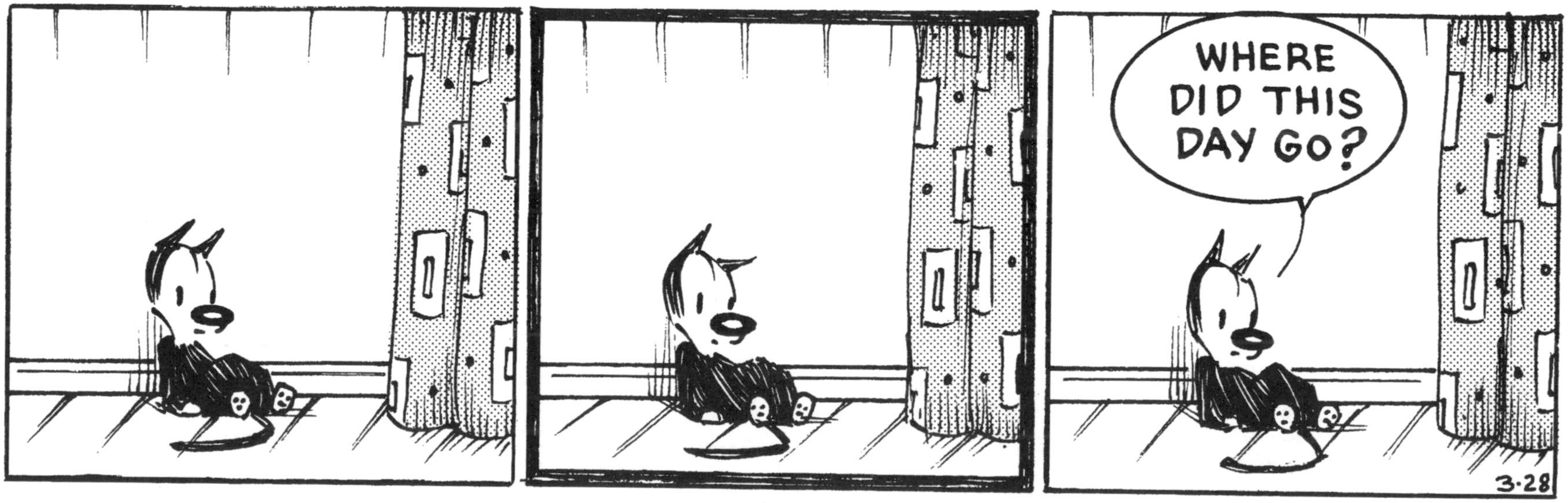
WHERE DID THIS DAY GO?
3·28

MUTTS
McDONNELL

OWERS
SALE
WOW.
WHAT HOLE DID HE CRAWL OUT OF?
3·23
...AND HOW DID HE GET SO BIG!?!
I'LL TAKE A LITTLE LOOK-SEE.
WELL...?
CHOCOLATE
AND
JELLY BEANS
THAT'LL DO IT.

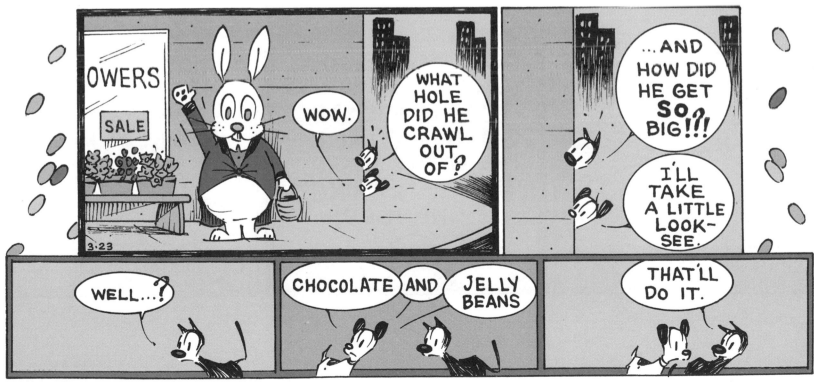

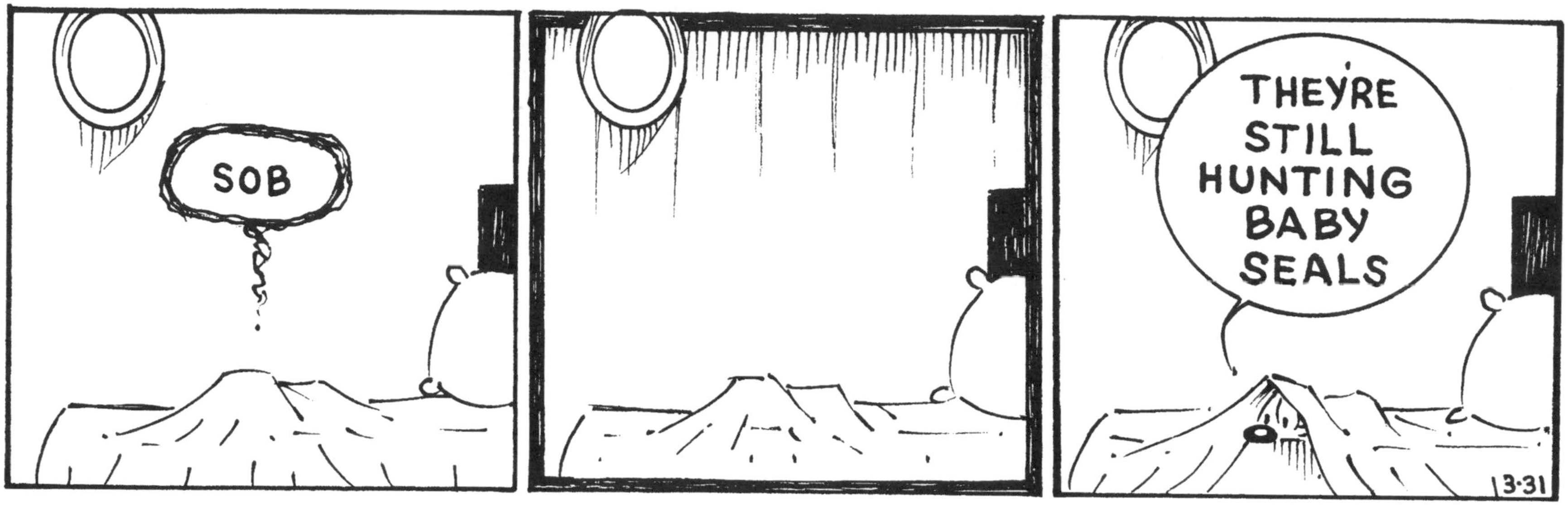
SOB
THEY'RE STILL HUNTING BABY SEALS
3·31

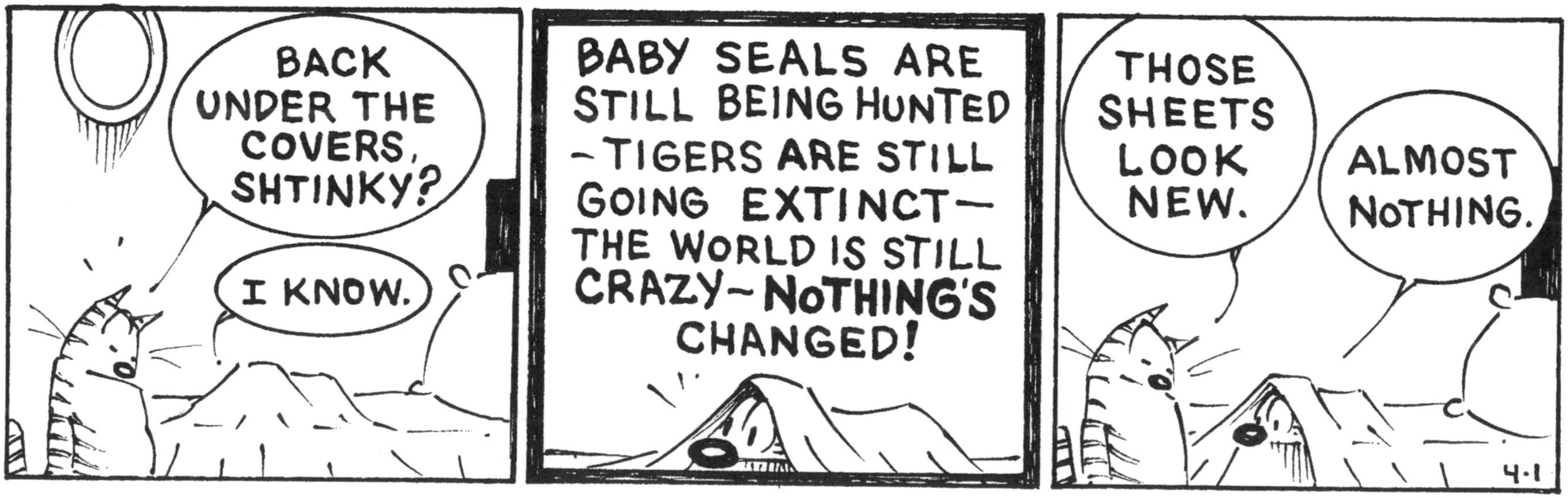
BACK UNDER THE COVERS, SHTINKY?
I KNOW.
BABY SEALS ARE STILL BEING HUNTED — TIGERS ARE STILL GOING EXTINCT — THE WORLD IS STILL CRAZY — NOTHING'S CHANGED!
THOSE SHEETS LOOK NEW.
ALMOST NOTHING.
4·1

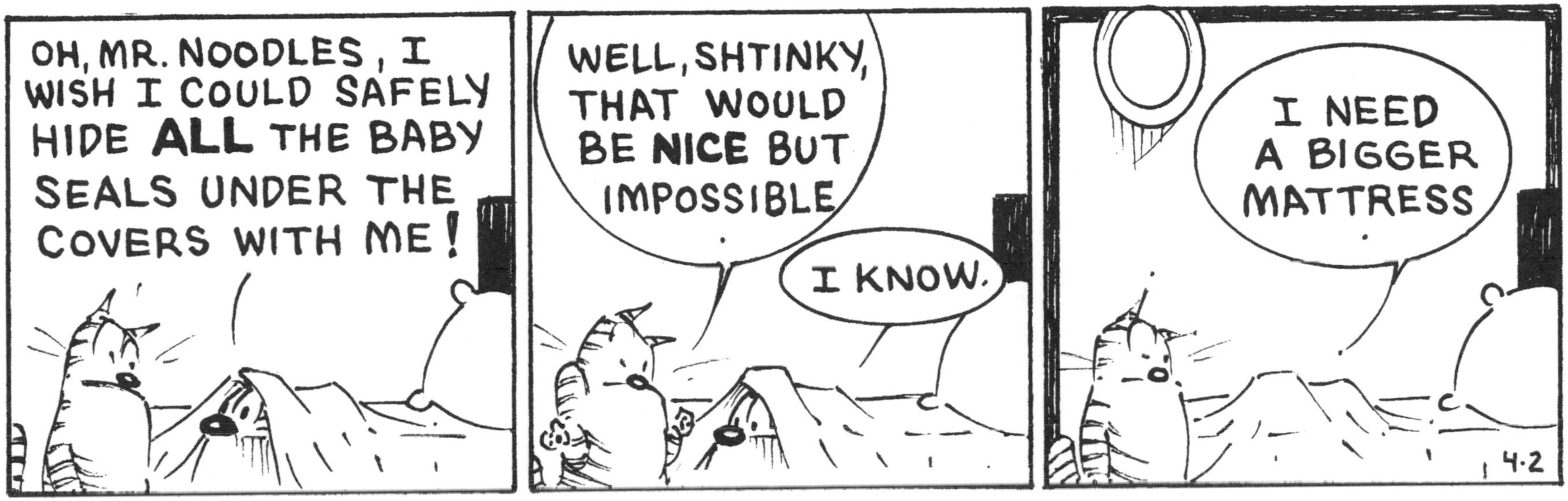
OH, MR. NOODLES, I WISH I COULD SAFELY HIDE **ALL** THE BABY SEALS UNDER THE COVERS WITH ME!
WELL, SHTINKY, THAT WOULD BE **NICE** BUT IMPOSSIBLE.
I KNOW.
I NEED A BIGGER MATTRESS.
4·2

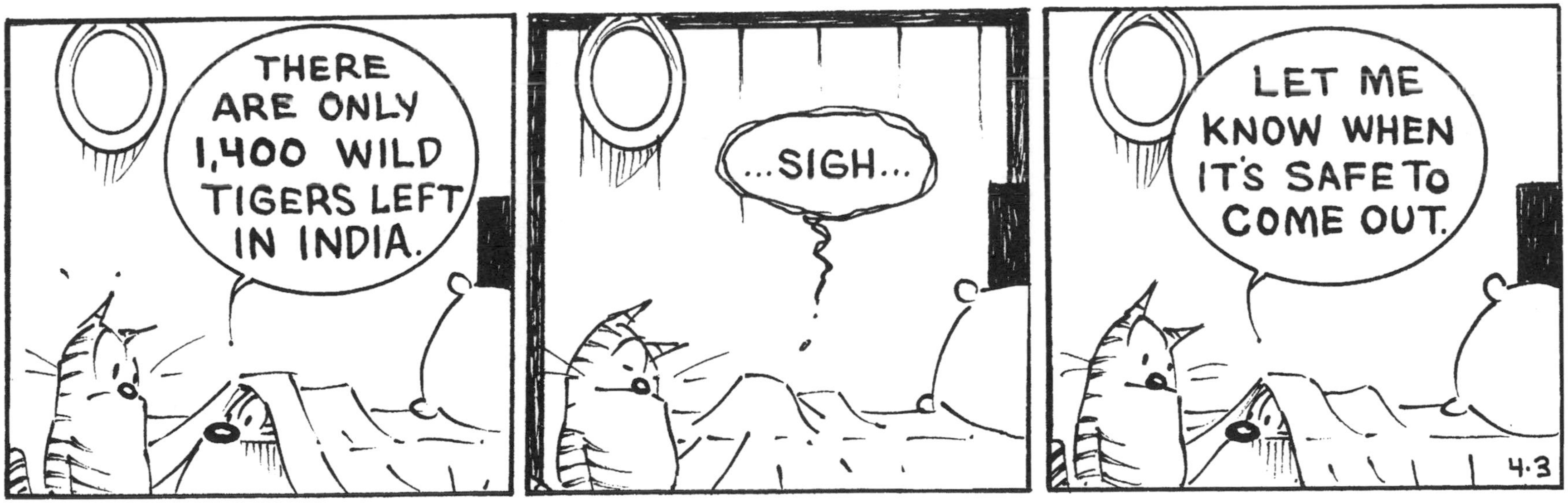
THERE ARE ONLY 1,400 WILD TIGERS LEFT IN INDIA.
...SIGH...
LET ME KNOW WHEN IT'S SAFE TO COME OUT.
4·3

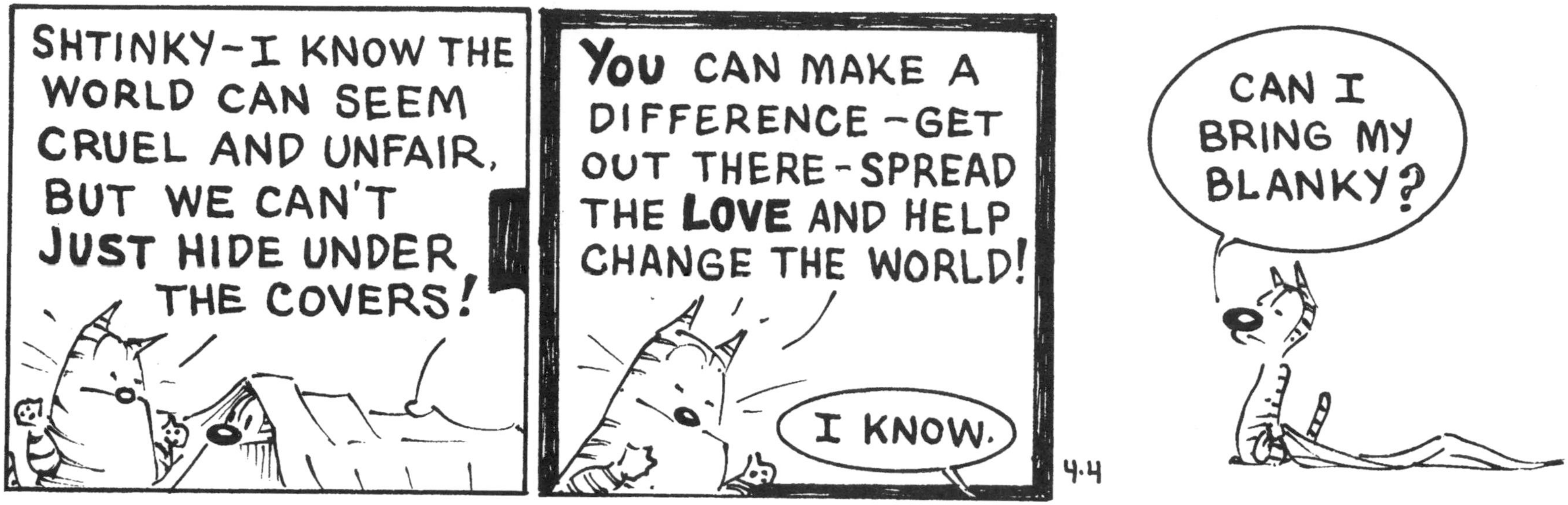
SHTINKY–I KNOW THE WORLD CAN SEEM CRUEL AND UNFAIR, BUT WE CAN'T **JUST** HIDE UNDER THE COVERS!
YOU CAN MAKE A DIFFERENCE–GET OUT THERE–SPREAD THE **LOVE** AND HELP CHANGE THE WORLD!
I KNOW.
4·4
CAN I BRING MY BLANKY?

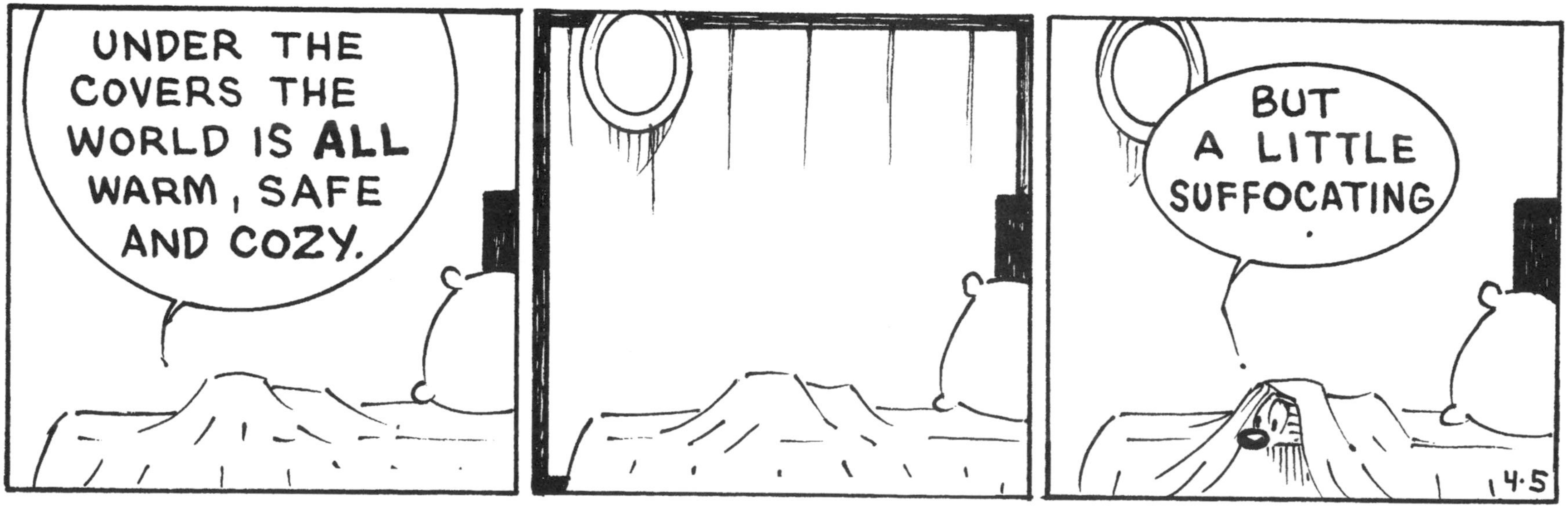
UNDER THE COVERS THE WORLD IS **ALL** WARM, SAFE AND COZY.
BUT A LITTLE SUFFOCATING.
4·5

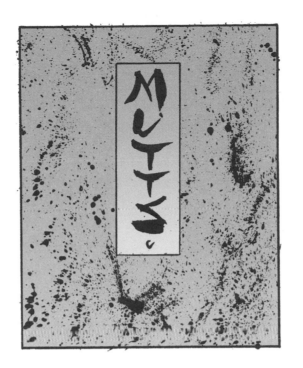

SITTING QUIETLY,   DOING NOTHING,

SPRING COMES,

AND THE GRASS GROWS BY ITSELF.

3·30

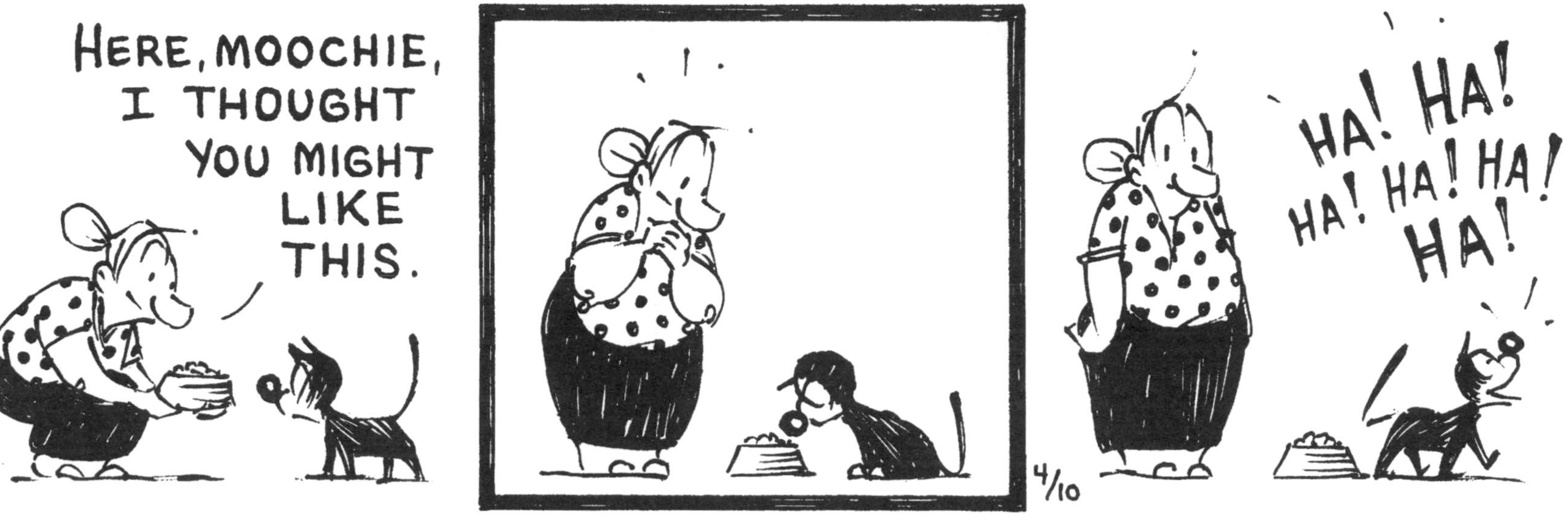
HERE, MOOCHIE, I THOUGHT YOU MIGHT LIKE THIS.
4/10
HA! HA! HA! HA! HA! HA!

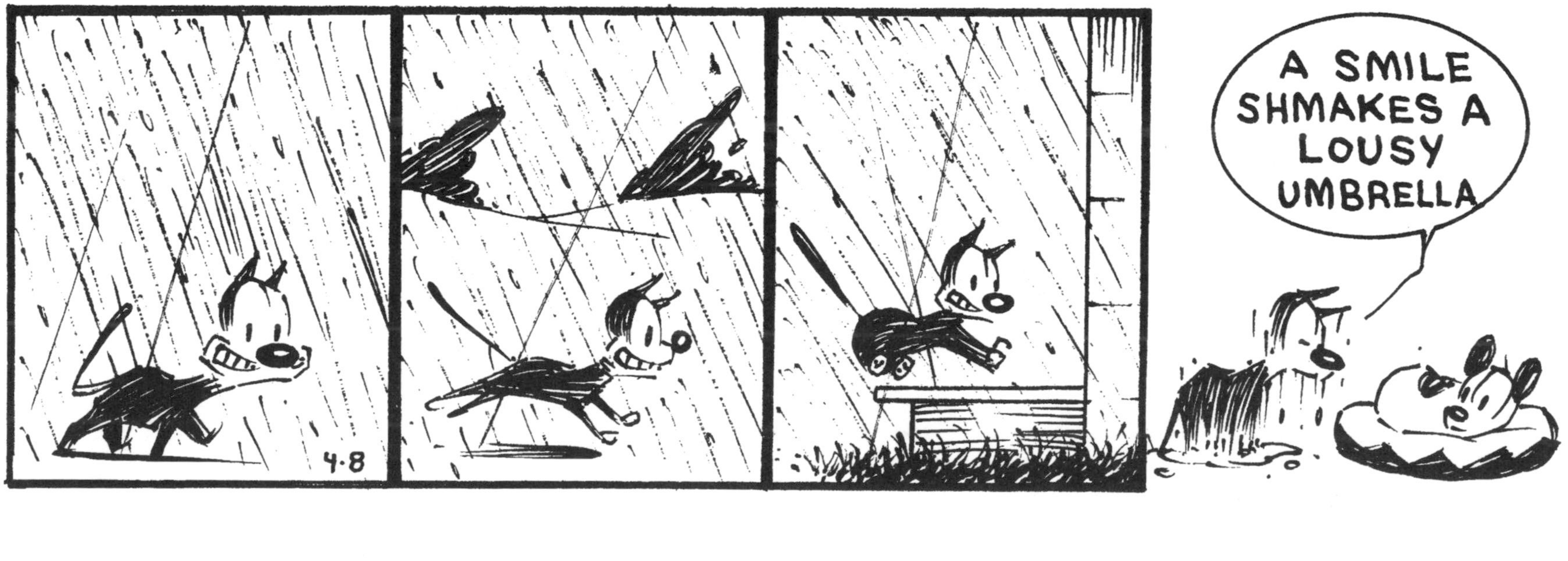
4·8
A SMILE SHMAKES A LOUSY UMBRELLA

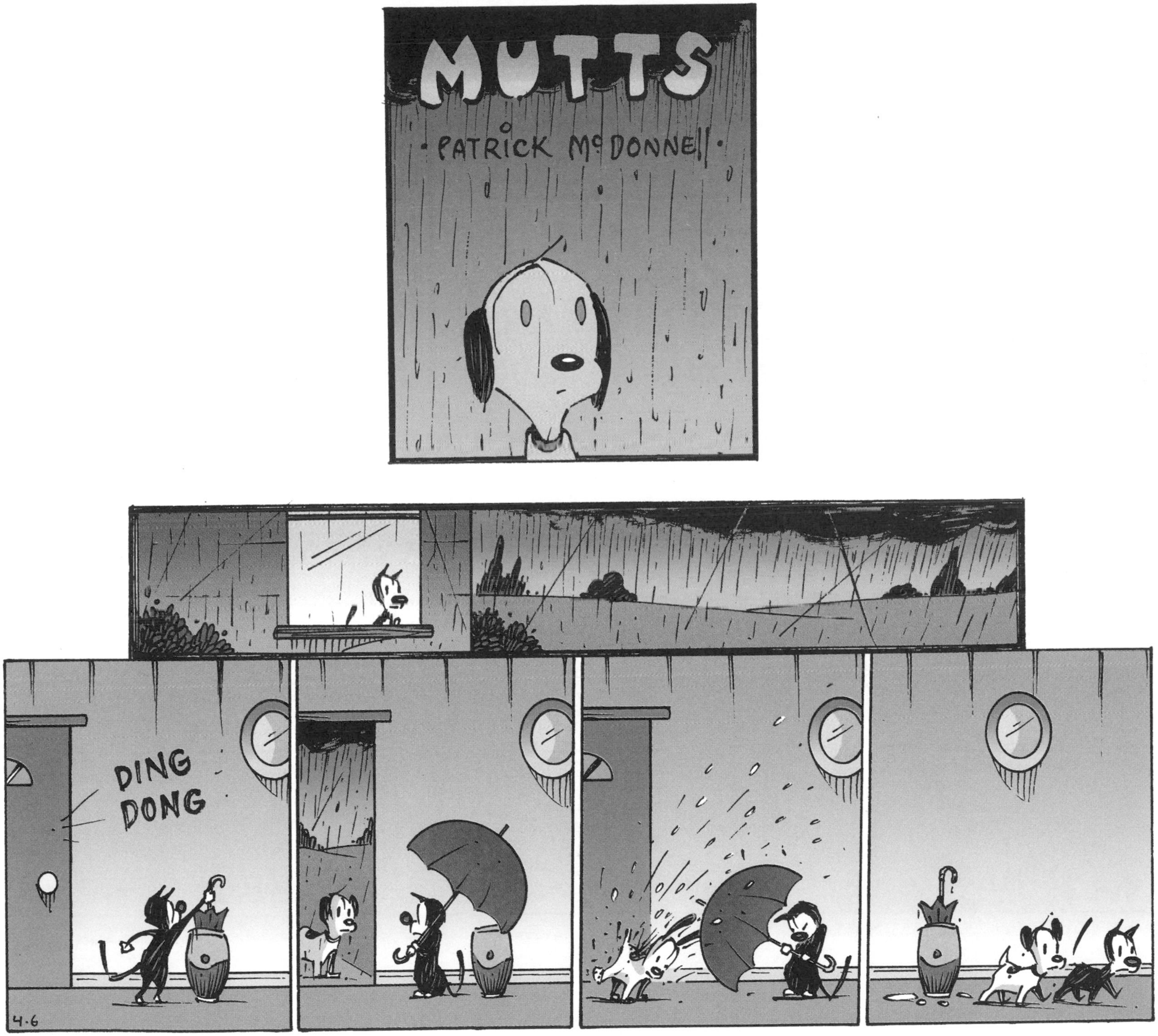
MUTTS
PATRICK McDONNELL
DING DONG
4.6

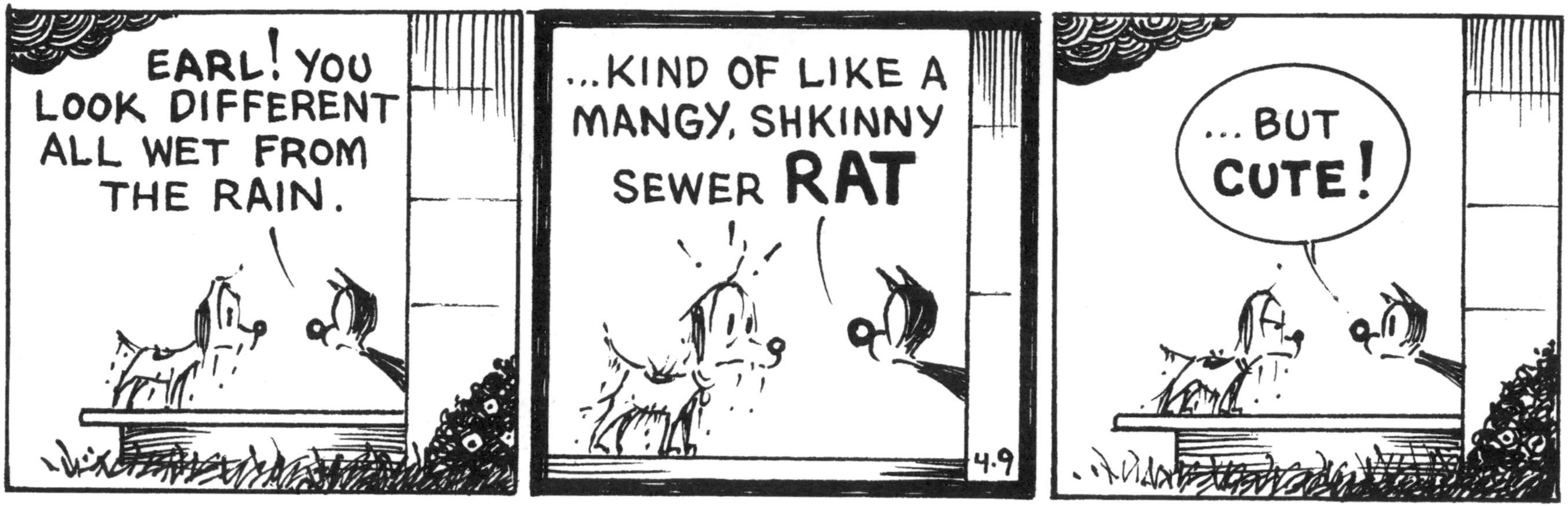
EARL! YOU LOOK DIFFERENT ALL WET FROM THE RAIN.
...KIND OF LIKE A MANGY, SHKINNY SEWER RAT
4.9
...BUT CUTE!

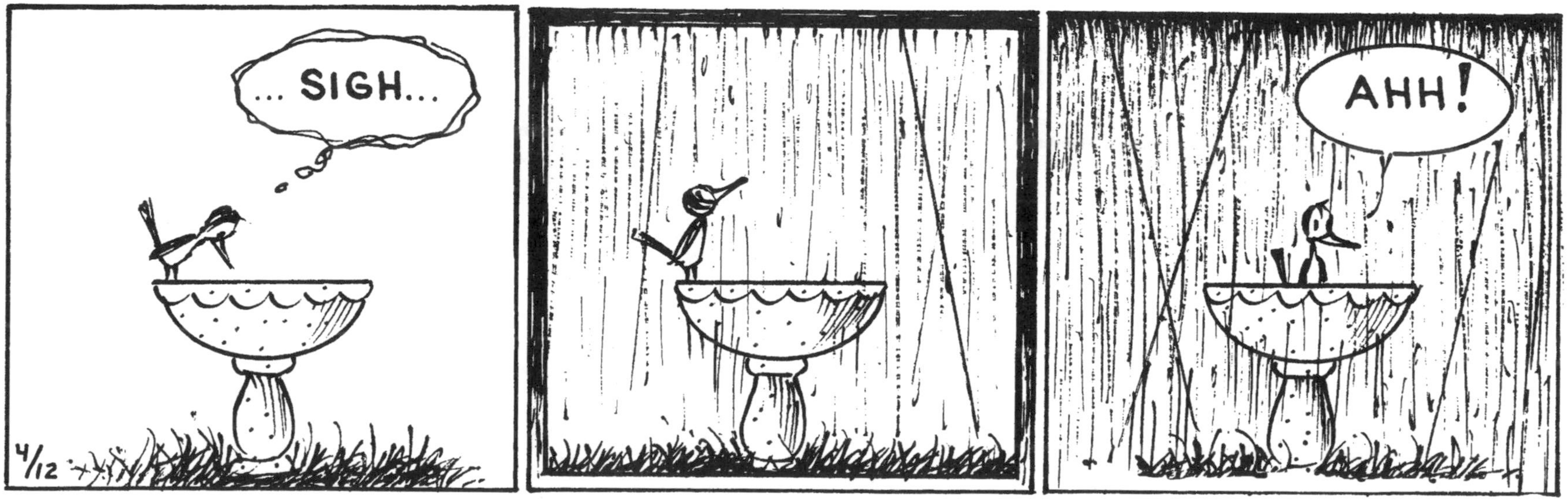
...SIGH...
4/12
AHH!

MUTTS
by
PATRICK
Mc DONNELL
SHTUPID
CLOUD.
4-27

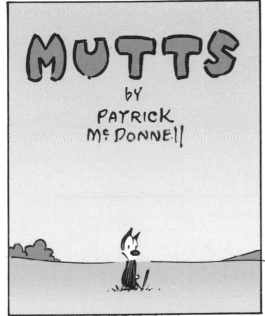

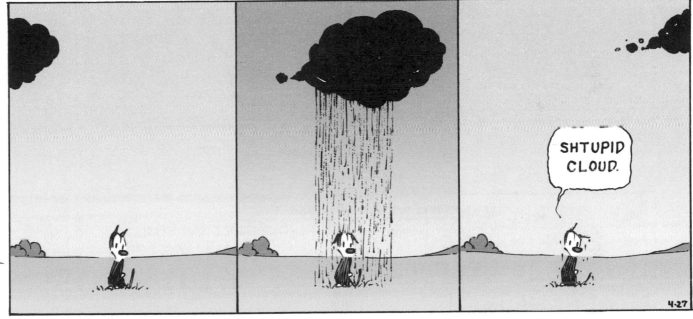

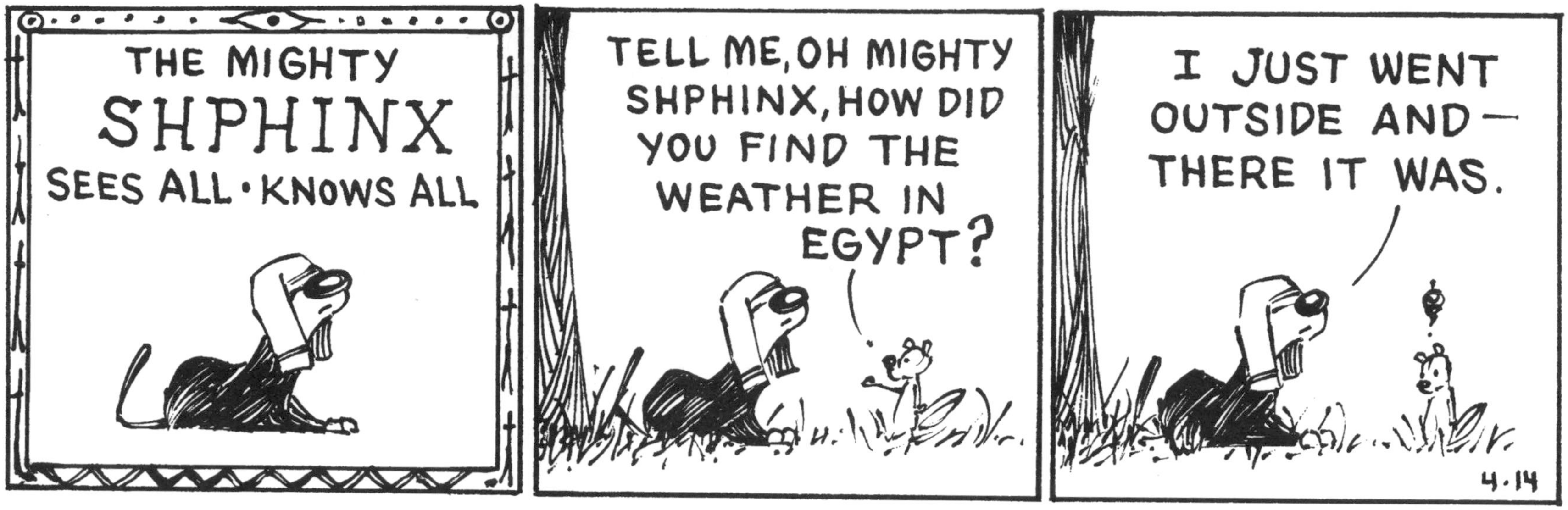
THE MIGHTY SHPHINX SEES ALL • KNOWS ALL
TELL ME, OH MIGHTY SHPHINX, HOW DID YOU FIND THE WEATHER IN EGYPT?
I JUST WENT OUTSIDE AND— THERE IT WAS.
4·14

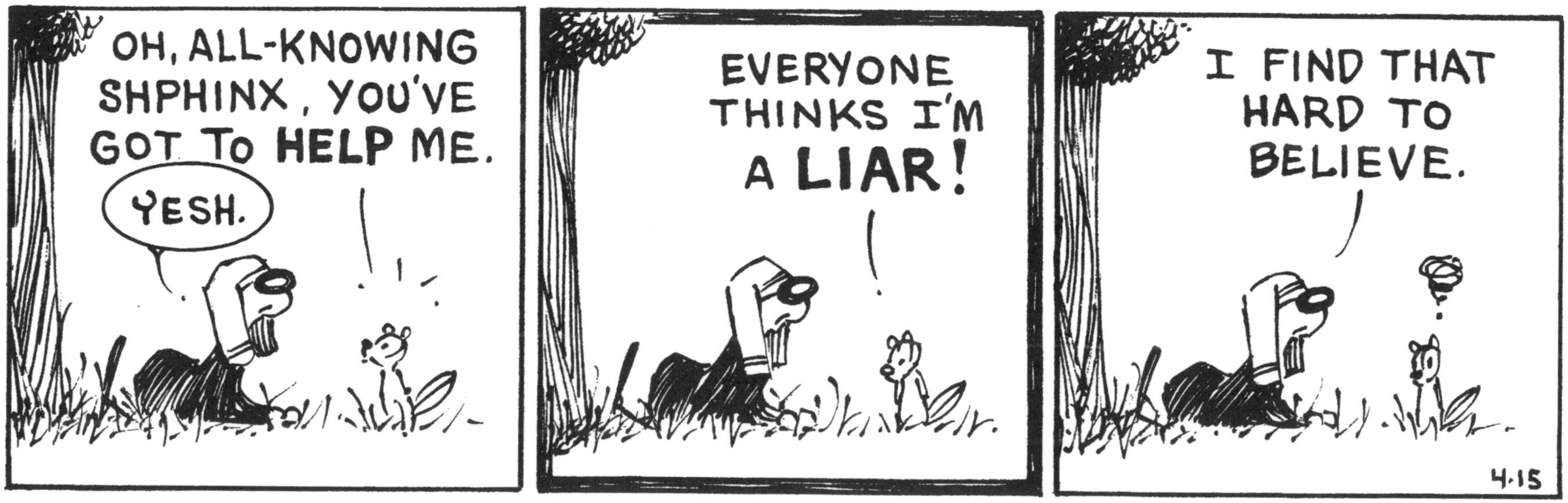
OH, ALL-KNOWING SHPHINX, YOU'VE GOT TO HELP ME.
YESH.
EVERYONE THINKS I'M A LIAR!
I FIND THAT HARD TO BELIEVE.
4·15

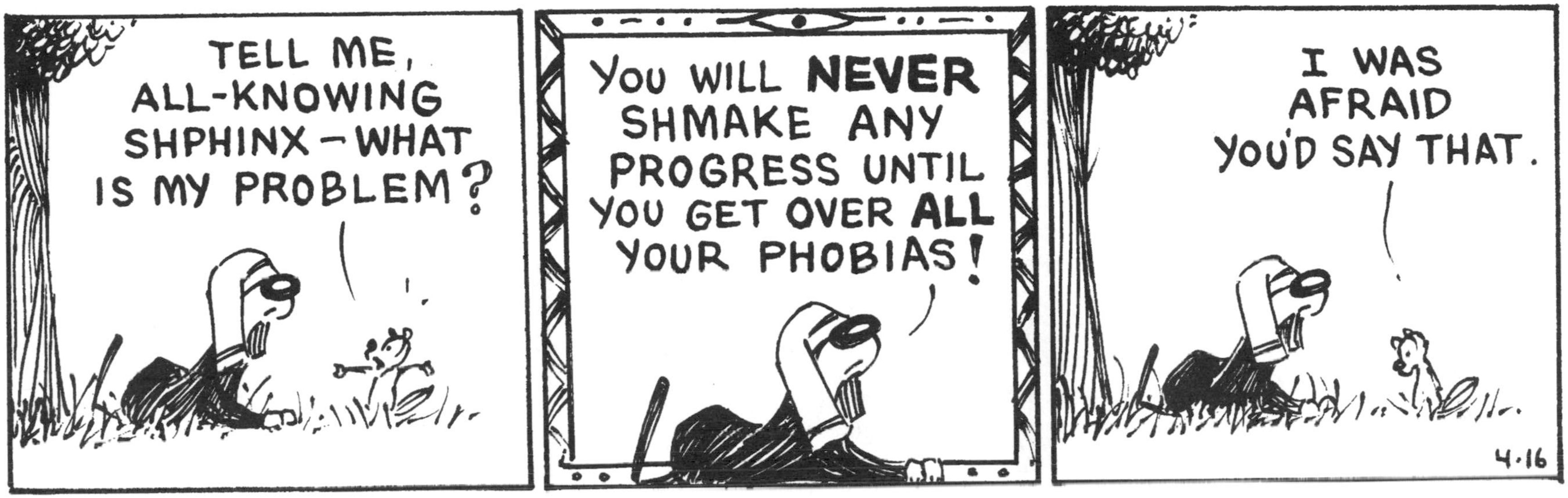
TELL ME, ALL-KNOWING SHPHINX – WHAT IS MY PROBLEM?
YOU WILL **NEVER** SHMAKE ANY PROGRESS UNTIL YOU GET OVER **ALL** YOUR PHOBIAS!
I WAS AFRAID YOU'D SAY THAT.
4·16

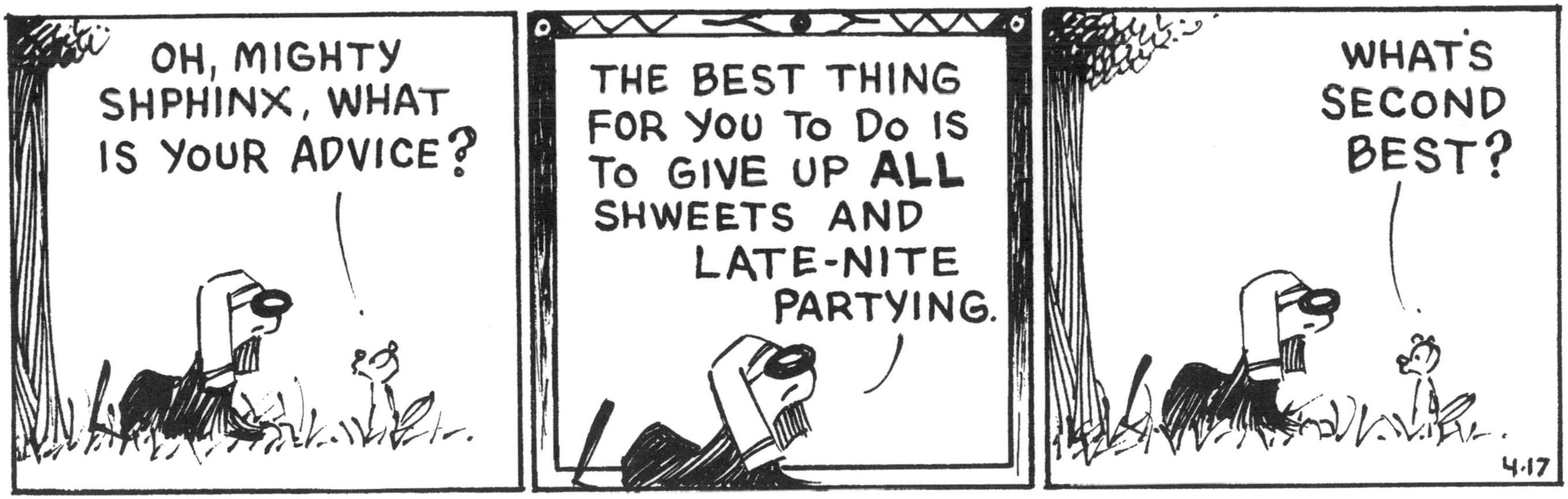
OH, MIGHTY SHPHINX, WHAT IS YOUR ADVICE?
THE BEST THING FOR YOU TO DO IS TO GIVE UP **ALL** SHWEETS AND LATE-NITE PARTYING.
WHAT'S SECOND BEST?
4·17

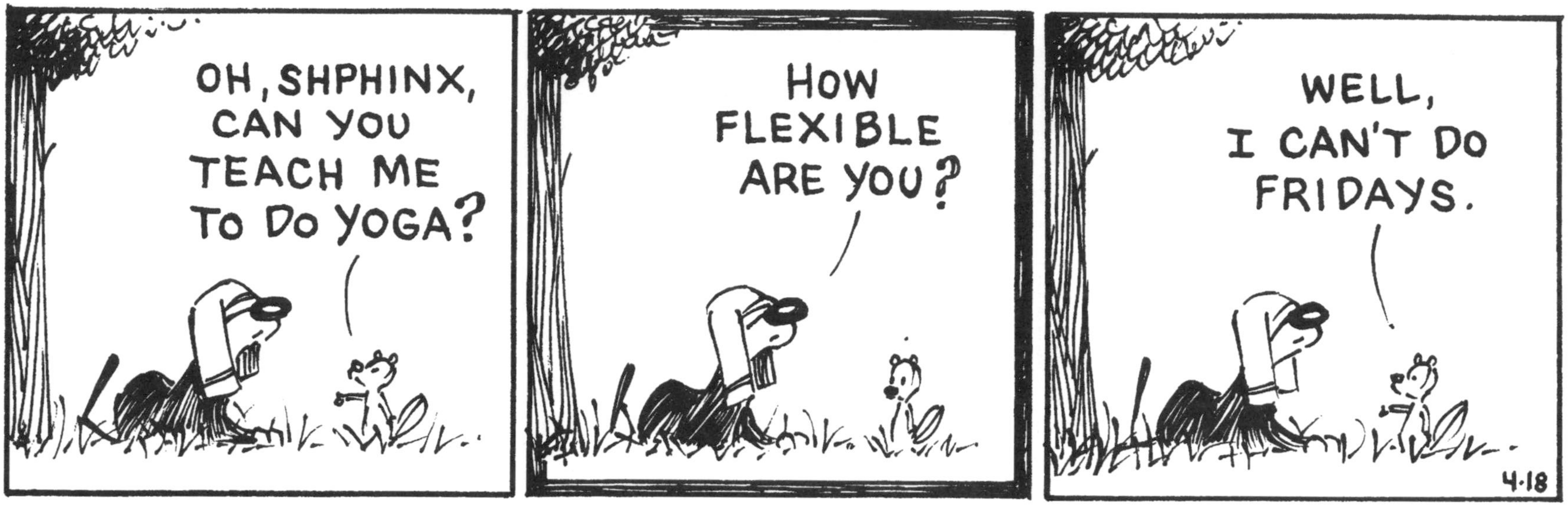
OH, SHPHINX, CAN YOU TEACH ME TO DO YOGA?
HOW FLEXIBLE ARE YOU?
WELL, I CAN'T DO FRIDAYS.
4·18

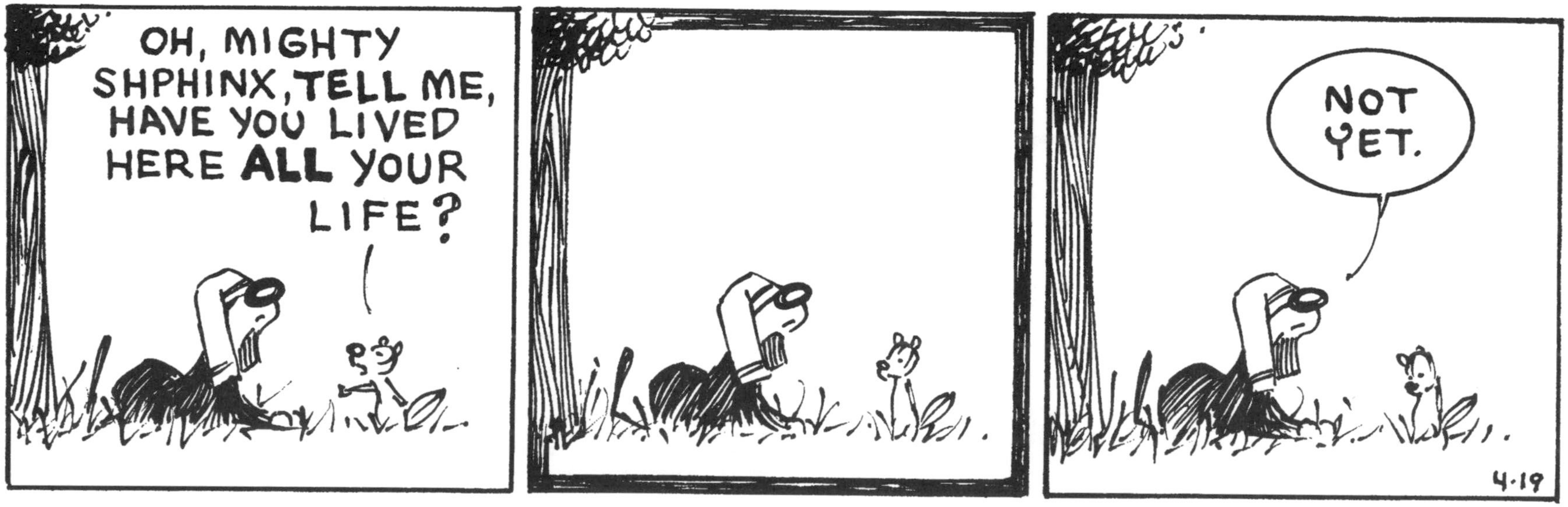
OH, MIGHTY SHPHINX, TELL ME, HAVE YOU LIVED HERE ALL YOUR LIFE?
NOT YET.
4·19

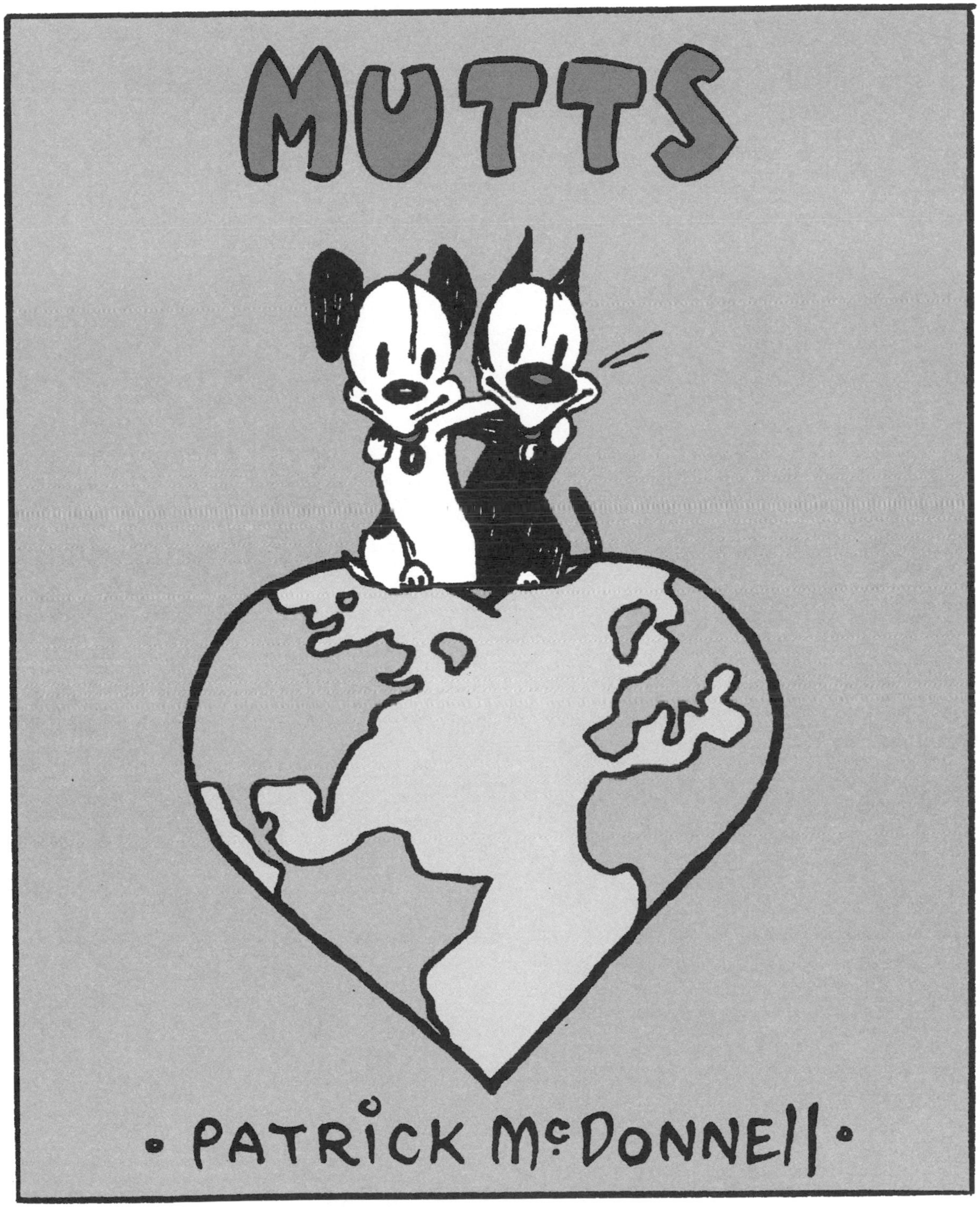
MUTTS
PATRICK McDONNELL

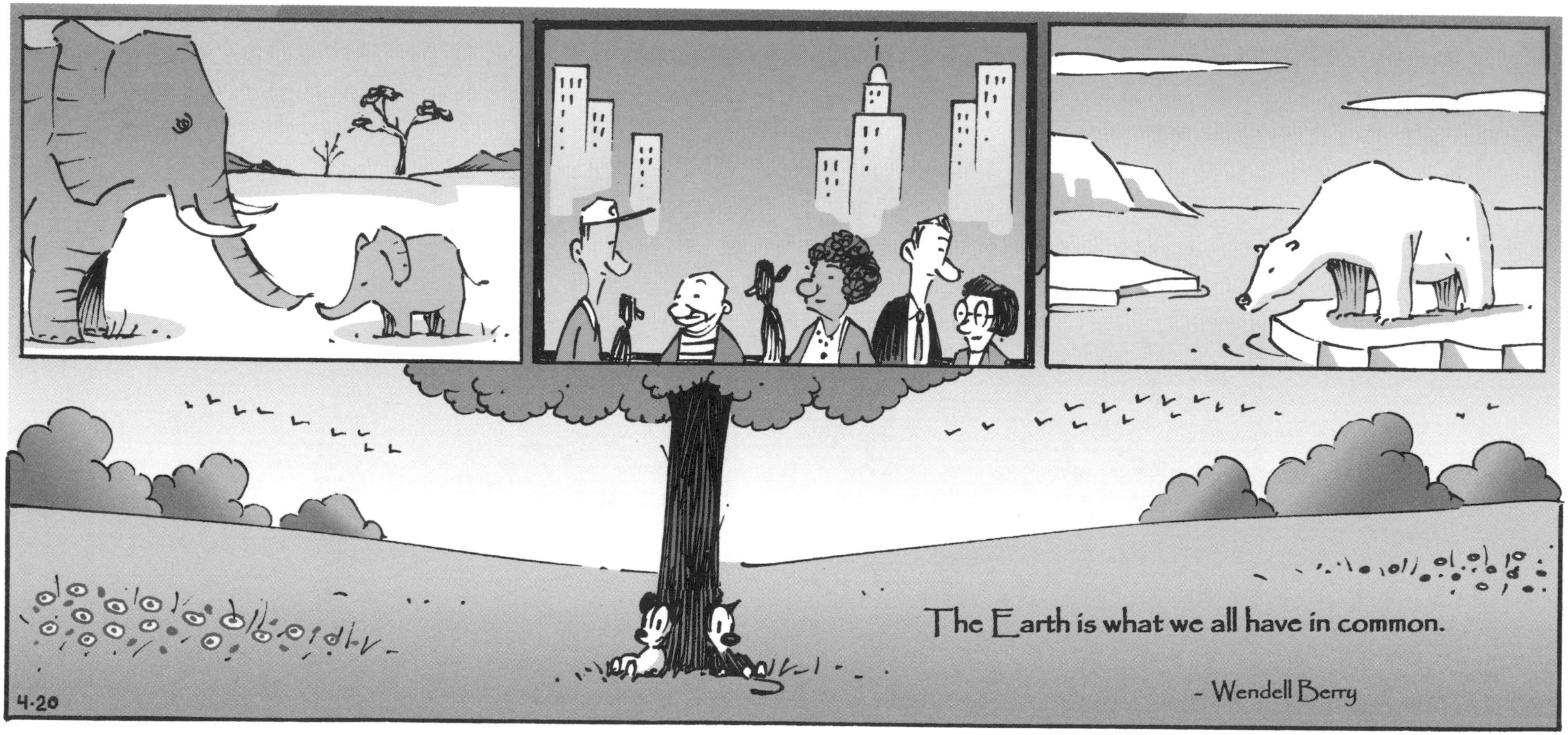

The Earth is what we all have in common.
- Wendell Berry
4·20

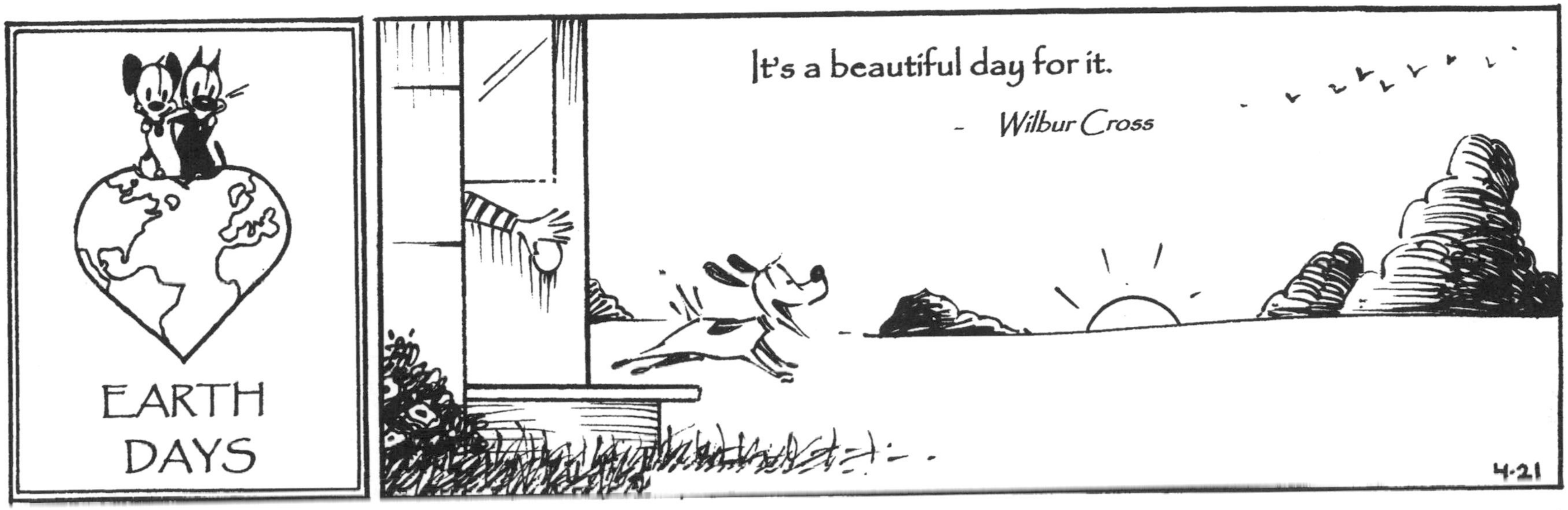
EARTH DAYS
It's a beautiful day for it.
- Wilbur Cross
4-21

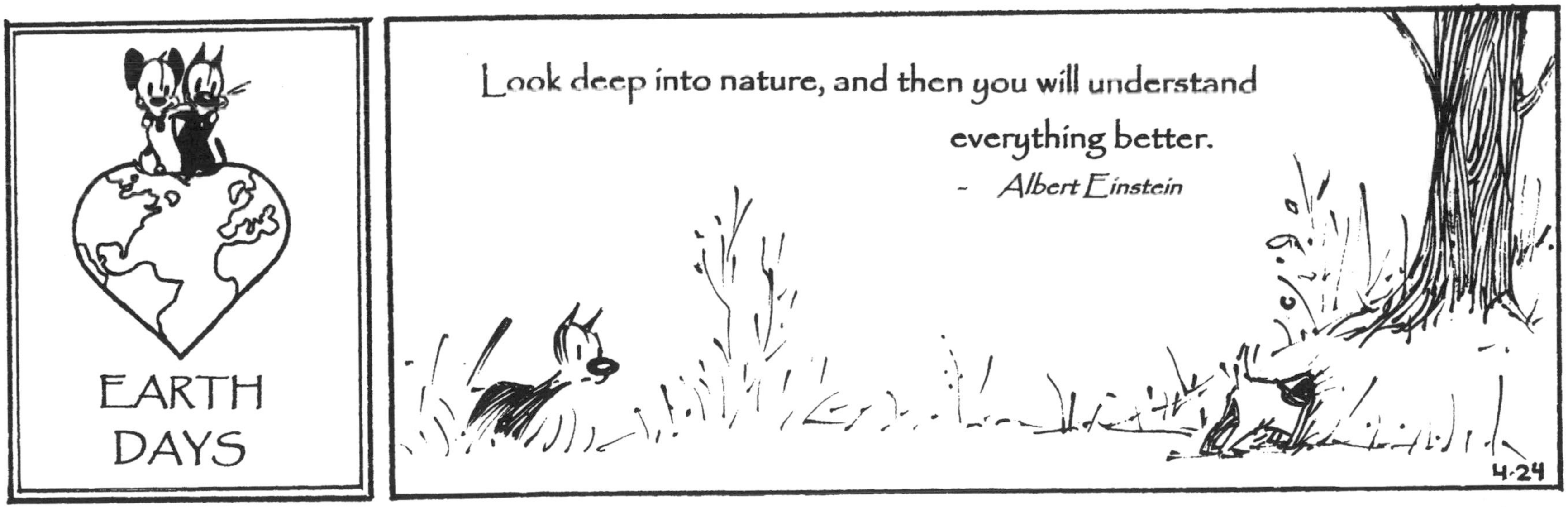
EARTH DAYS
Look deep into nature, and then you will understand everything better.
- Albert Einstein
4-24

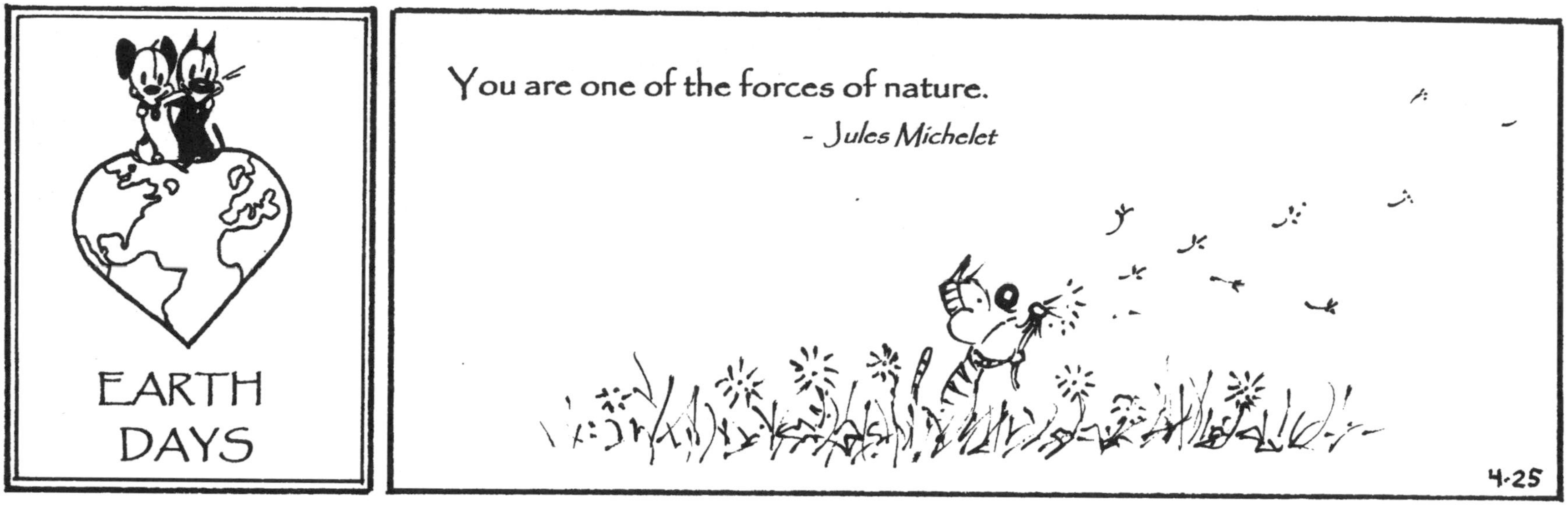
EARTH DAYS
You are one of the forces of nature.
- Jules Michelet
4-25

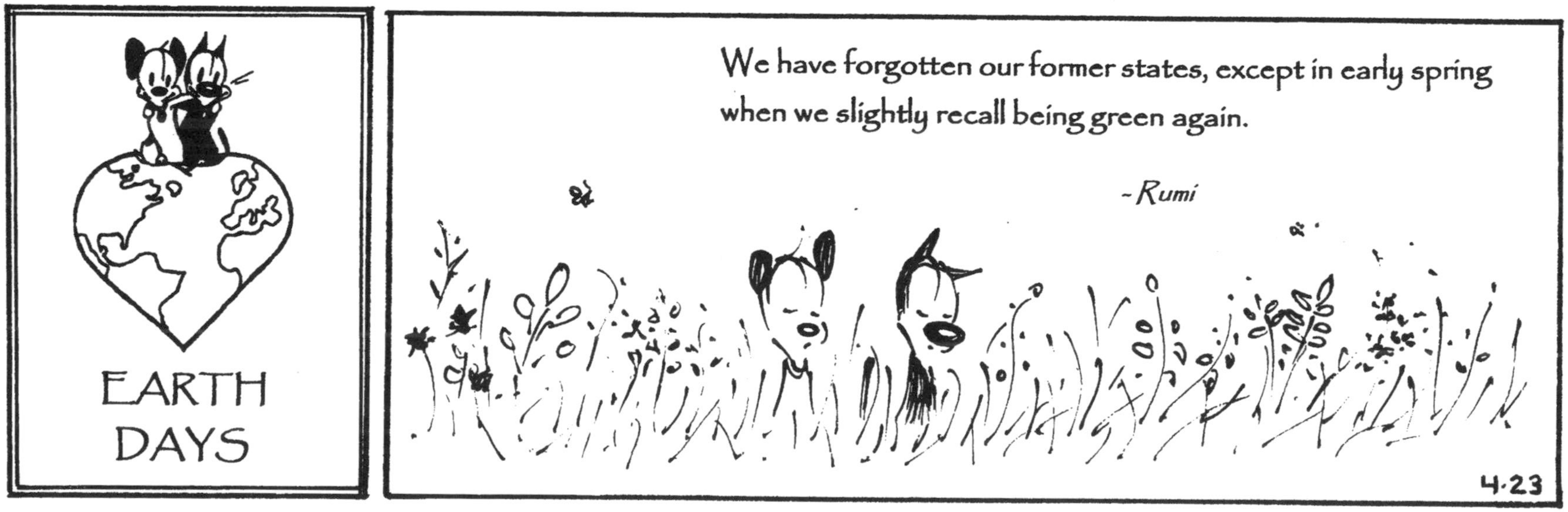
EARTH DAYS
We have forgotten our former states, except in early spring when we slightly recall being green again.
-Rumi
4-23

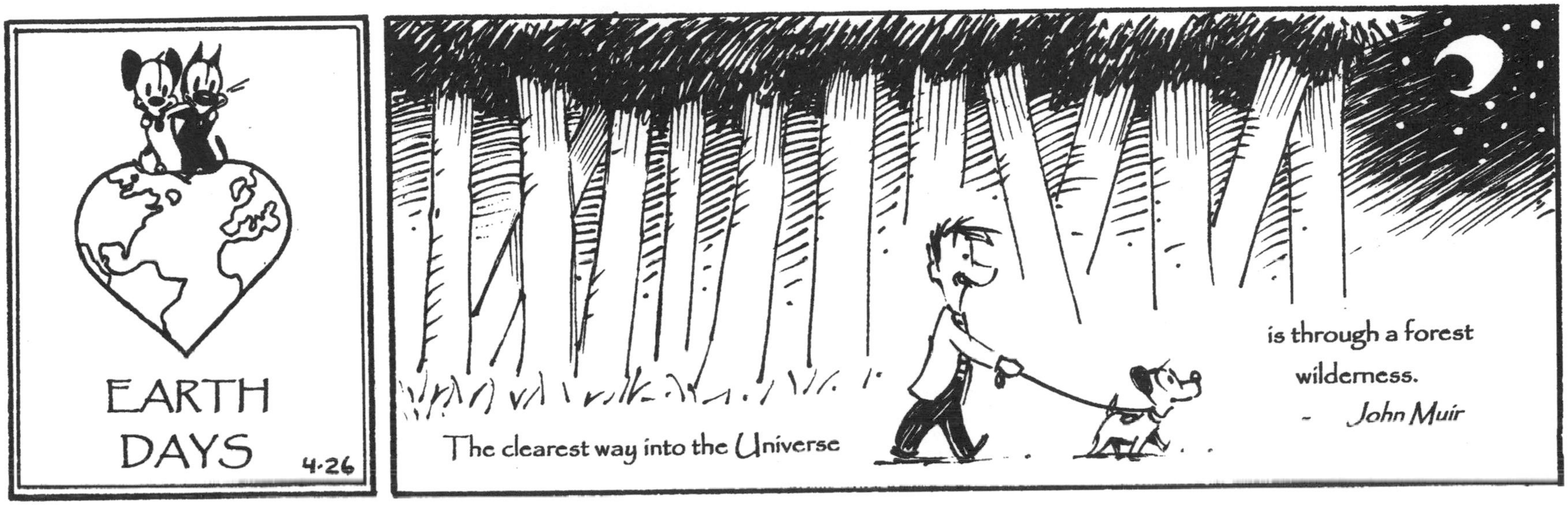
EARTH DAYS
4·26
The clearest way into the Universe
is through a forest wilderness.
- John Muir

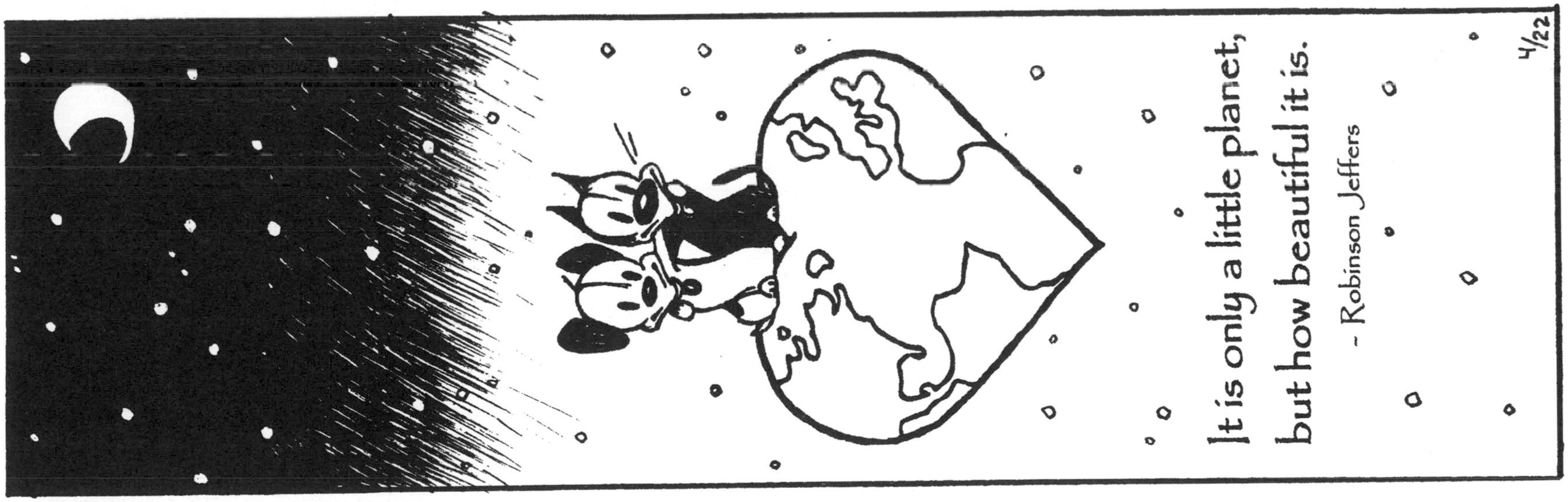
It is only a little planet,
but how beautiful it is.
- Robinson Jeffers
4/22

MUTTS
Shelter
Stories
PATRICK McDONNELL

5.4
ANIMAL
SHELTE
Love. Guaranteed.

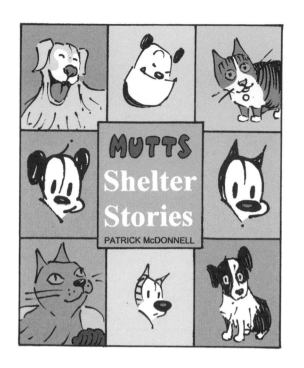

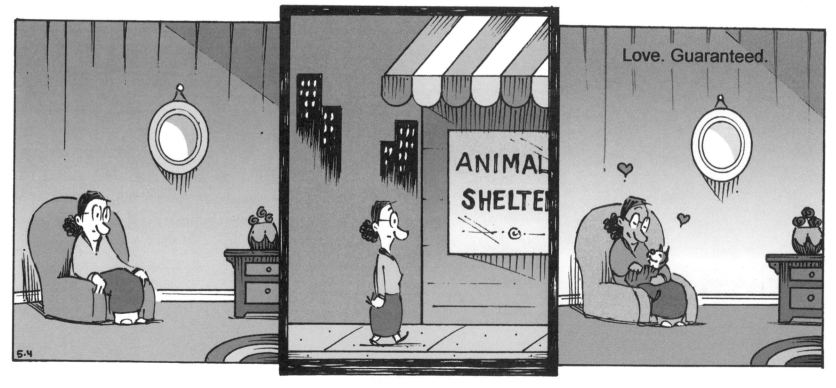

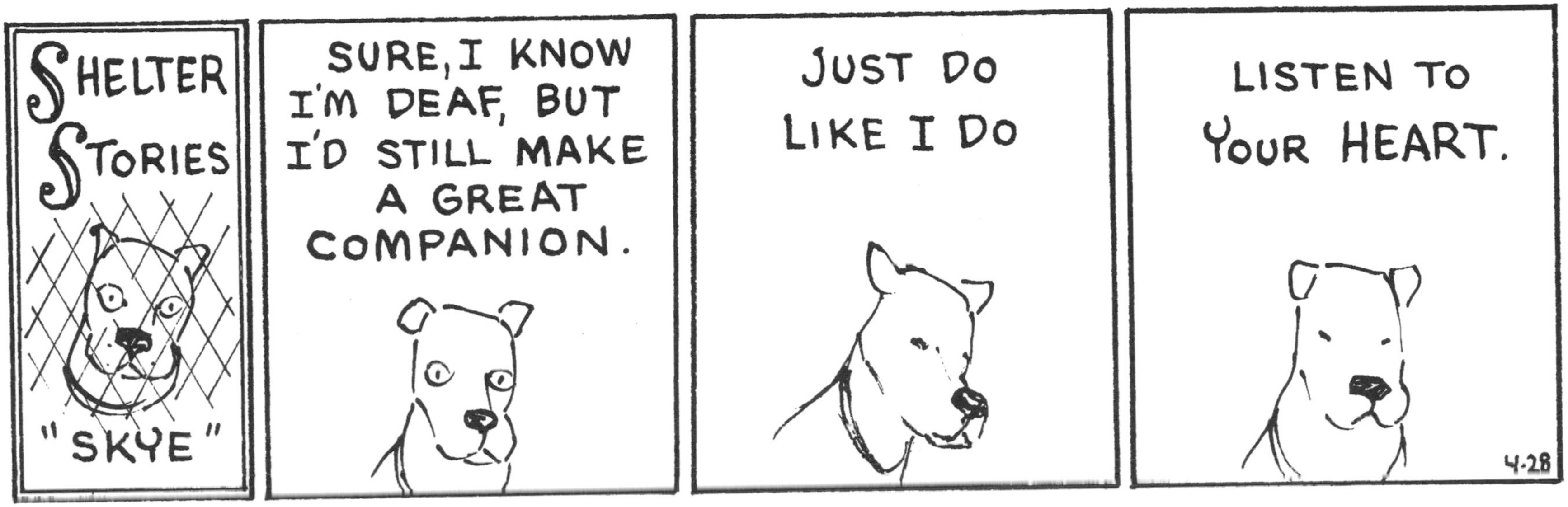
SHELTER STORIES
"SKYE"
SURE, I KNOW I'M DEAF, BUT I'D STILL MAKE A GREAT COMPANION.
JUST DO LIKE I DO
LISTEN TO YOUR HEART.
4·28

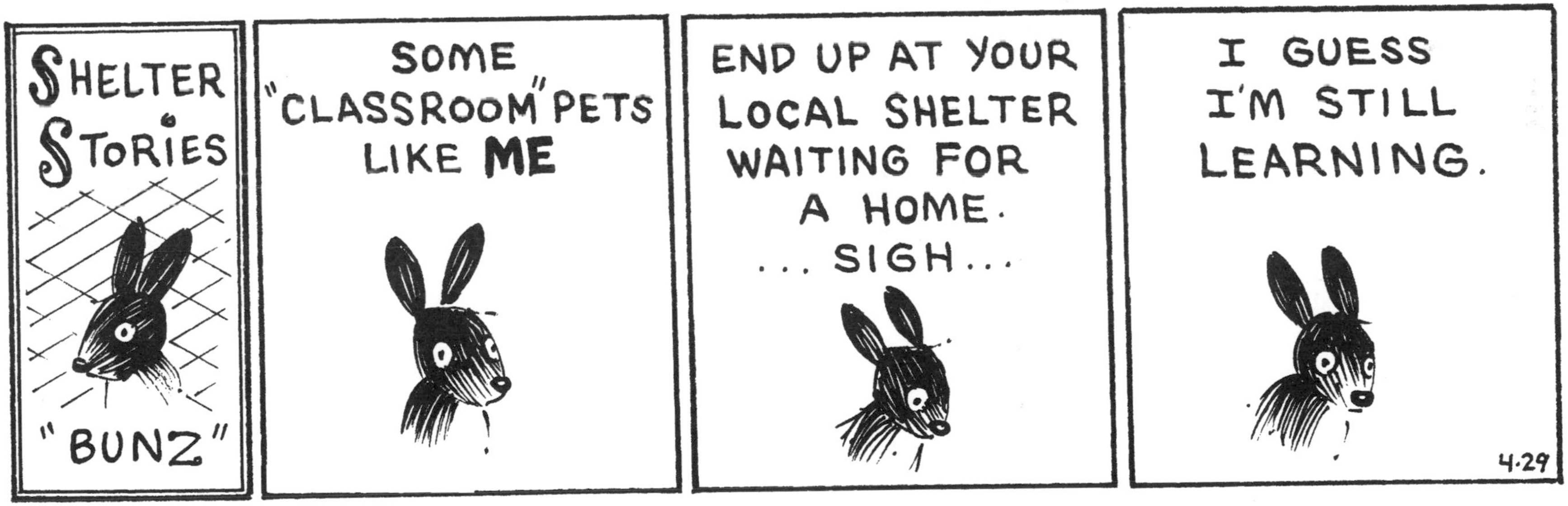
SHELTER STORIES
"BUNZ"
SOME "CLASSROOM" PETS LIKE ME
END UP AT YOUR LOCAL SHELTER WAITING FOR A HOME.
... SIGH ...
I GUESS I'M STILL LEARNING.
4·29

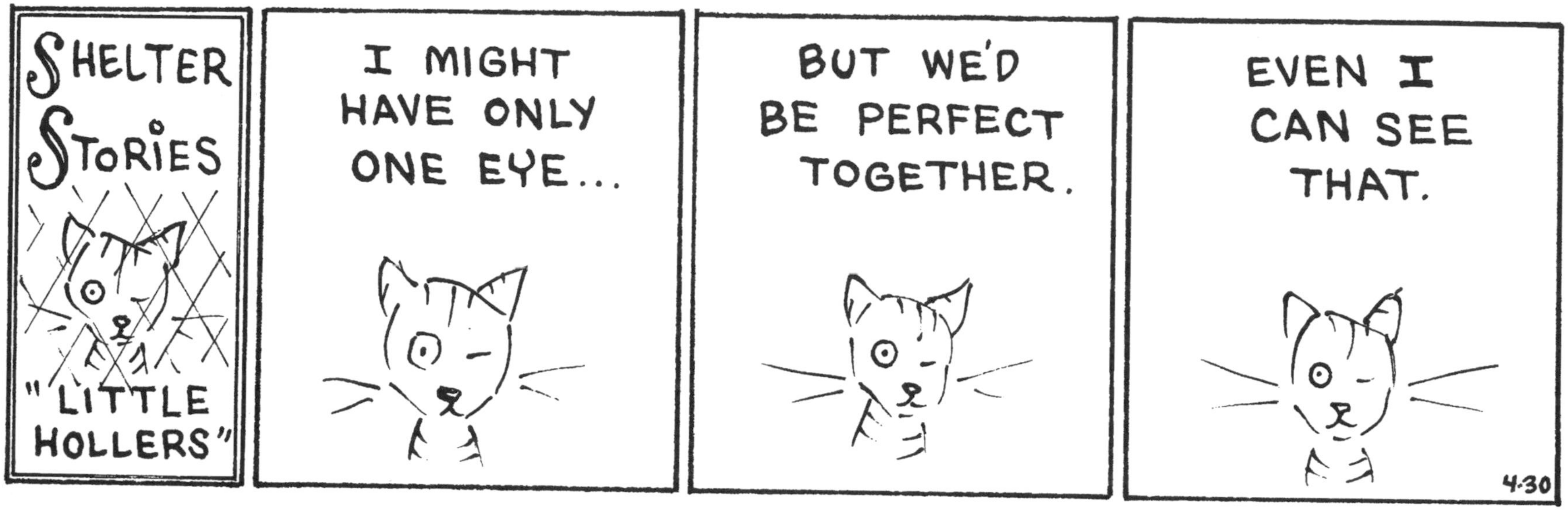
SHELTER STORIES
"LITTLE HOLLERS"
I MIGHT HAVE ONLY ONE EYE...
BUT WE'D BE PERFECT TOGETHER.
EVEN I CAN SEE THAT.
4·30

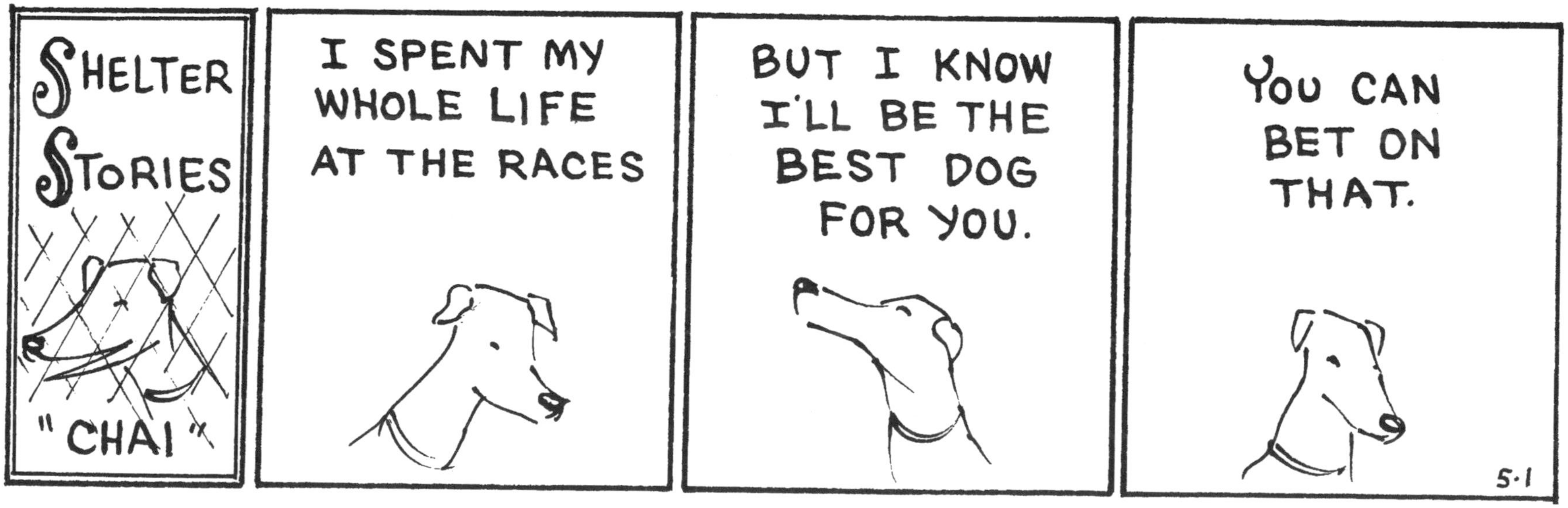
SHELTER STORIES
"CHAI"
I SPENT MY WHOLE LIFE AT THE RACES
BUT I KNOW I'LL BE THE BEST DOG FOR YOU.
YOU CAN BET ON THAT.
5·1

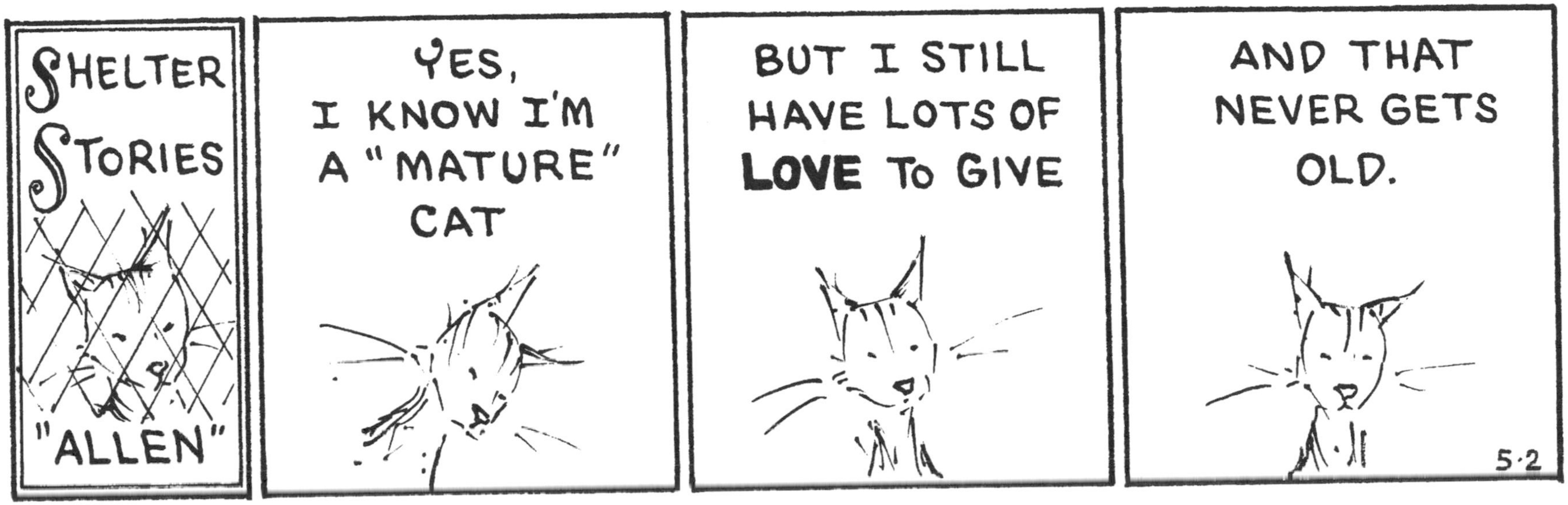
SHELTER STORIES
"ALLEN"
YES, I KNOW I'M A "MATURE" CAT
BUT I STILL HAVE LOTS OF **LOVE** TO GIVE
AND THAT NEVER GETS OLD.
5·2

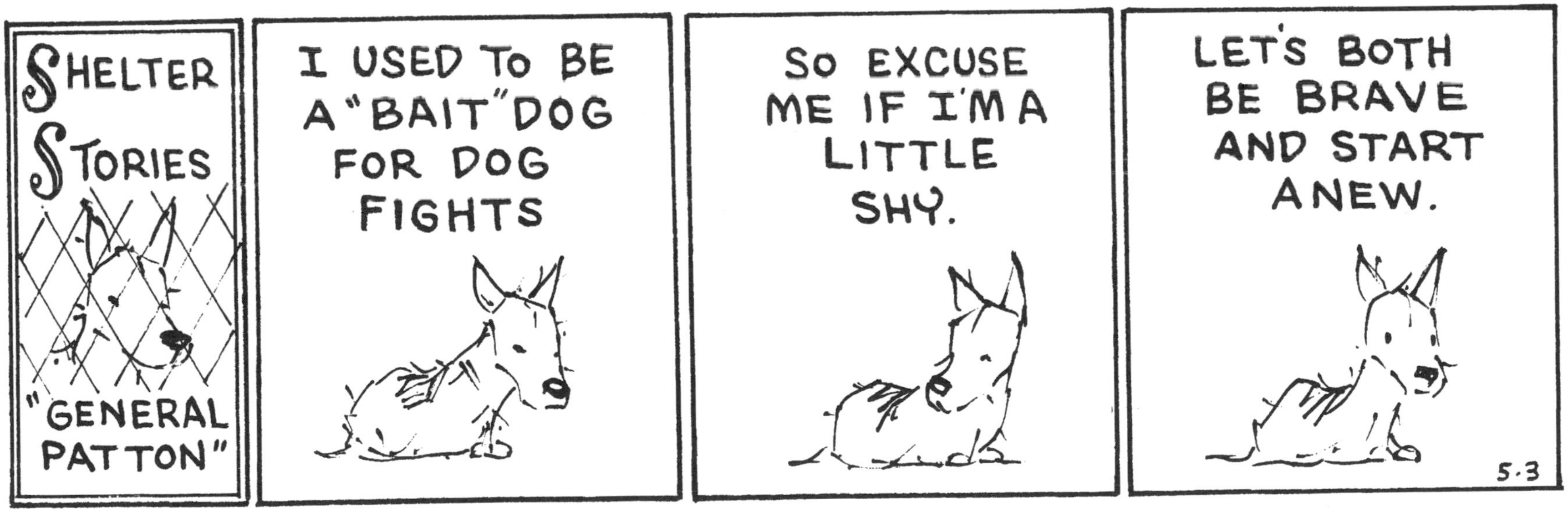
SHELTER STORIES
"GENERAL PATTON"
I USED TO BE A "BAIT" DOG FOR DOG FIGHTS
SO EXCUSE ME IF I'M A LITTLE SHY.
LET'S BOTH BE BRAVE AND START ANEW.
5·3

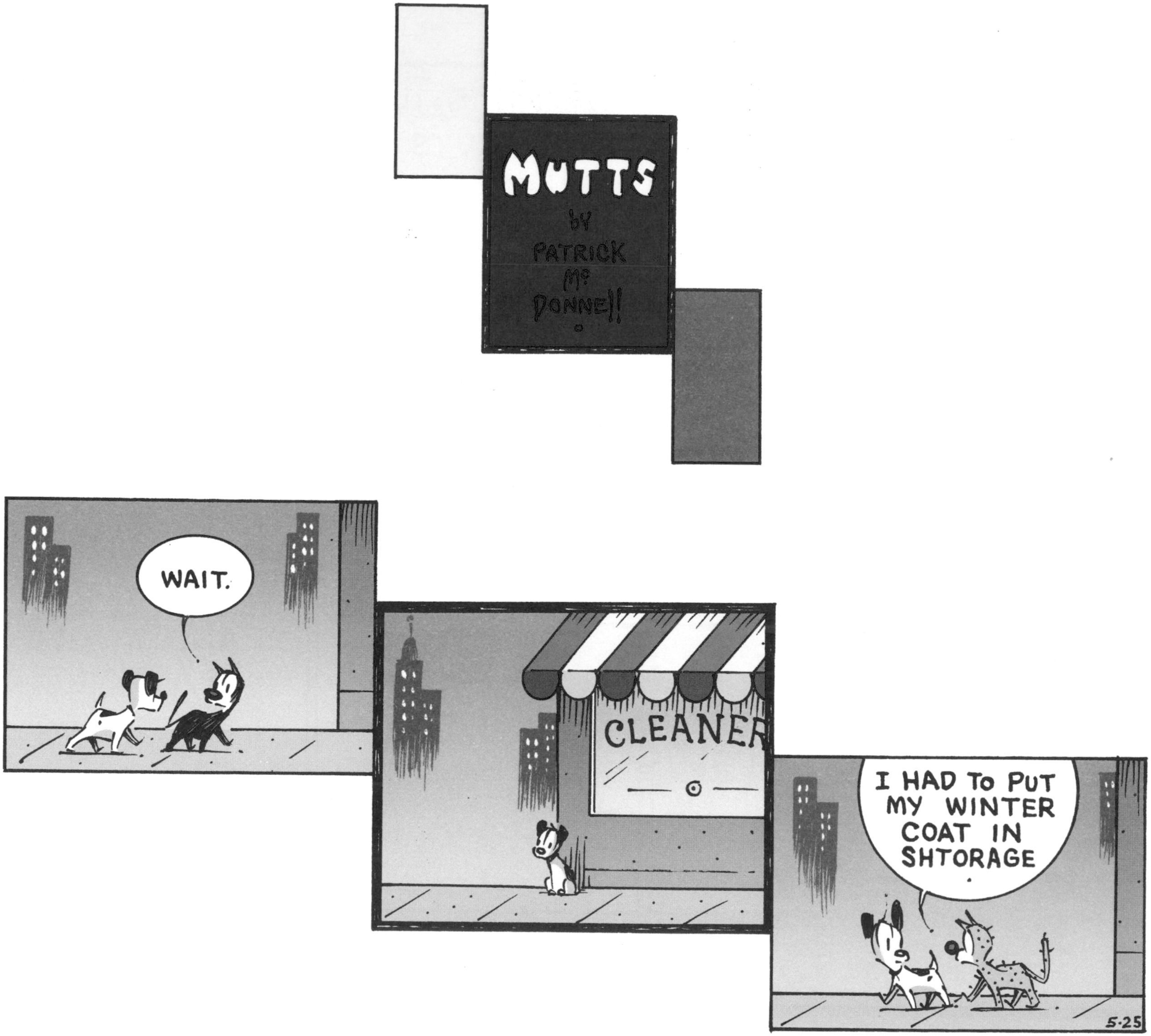
MUTTS
by
PATRICK
McDONNELL
WAIT.
CLEANER
I HAD TO PUT MY WINTER COAT IN SHTORAGE
5·25

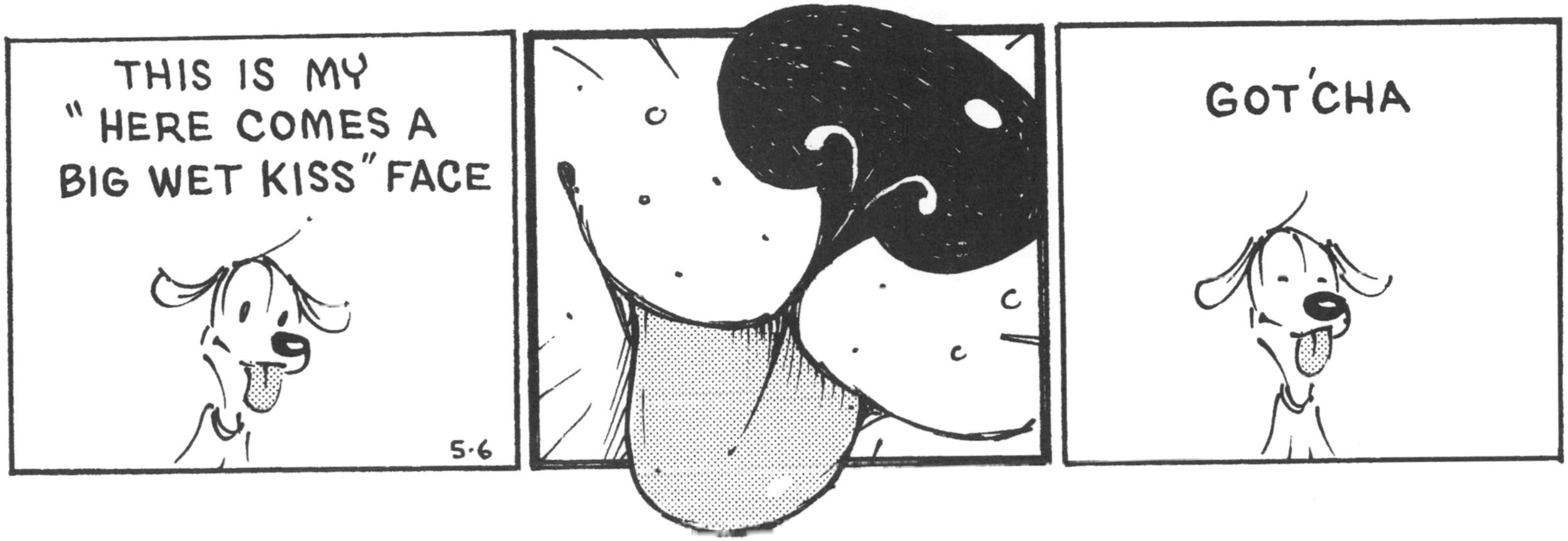
THIS IS MY "HERE COMES A BIG WET KISS" FACE
5·6
GOT'CHA

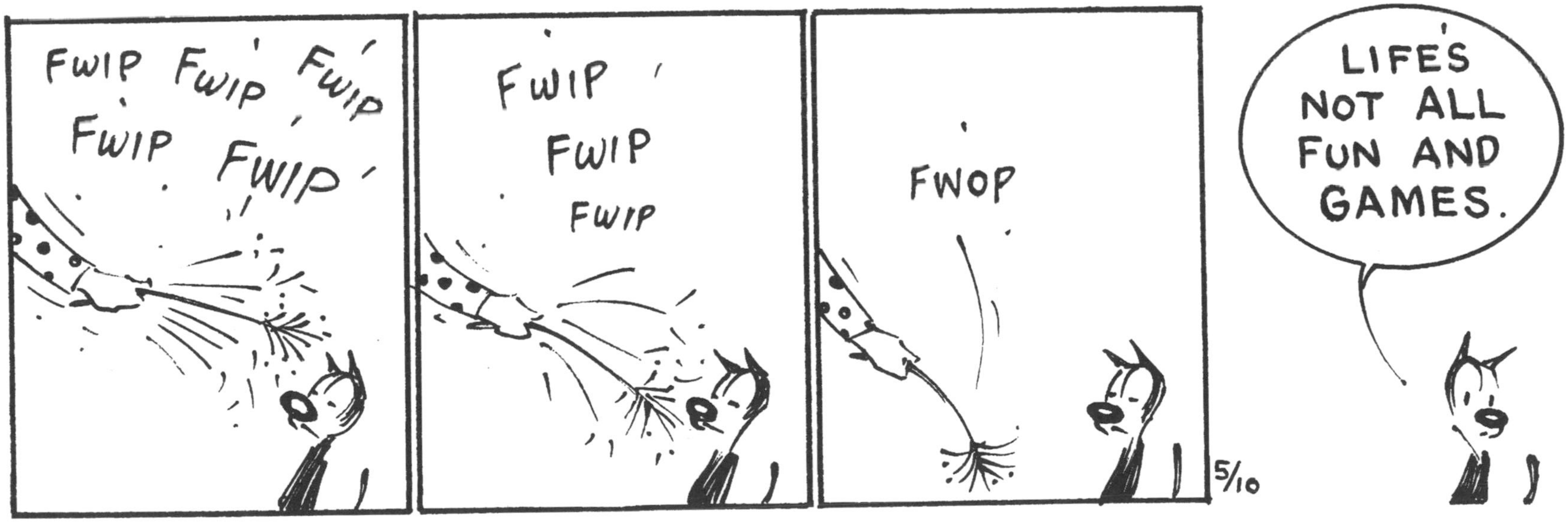
FWIP FWIP FWIP
FWIP FWIP
FWIP
FWIP
FWIP
FWOP
5/10
LIFE'S NOT ALL FUN AND GAMES.

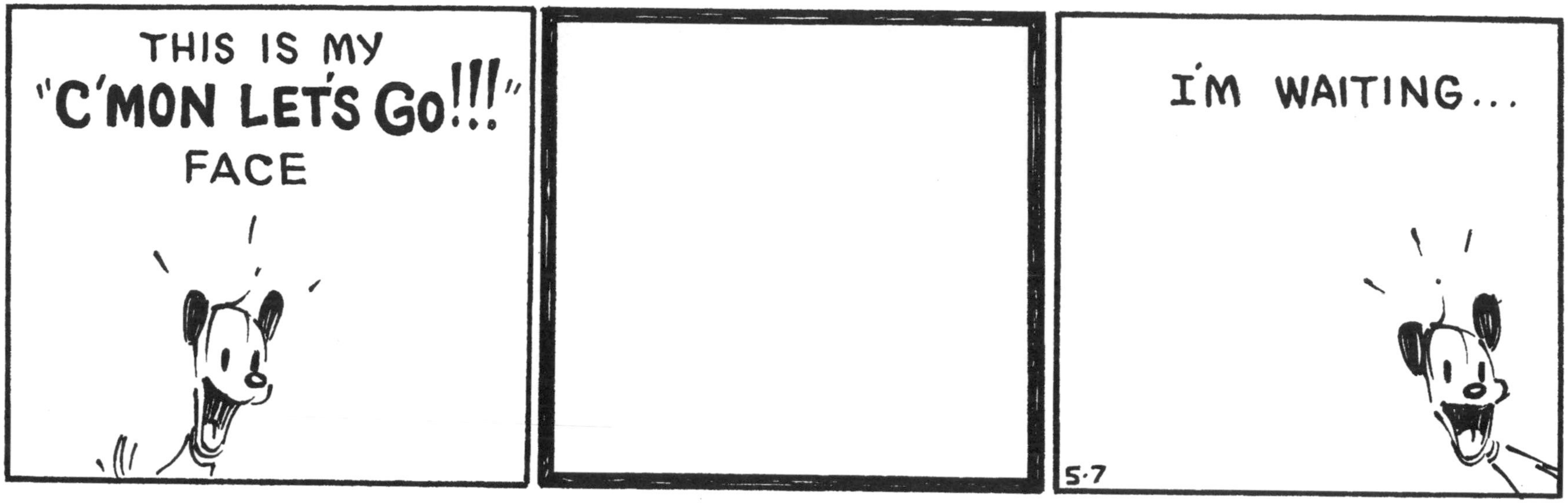
THIS IS MY "C'MON LET'S GO!!!" FACE
I'M WAITING...
5·7

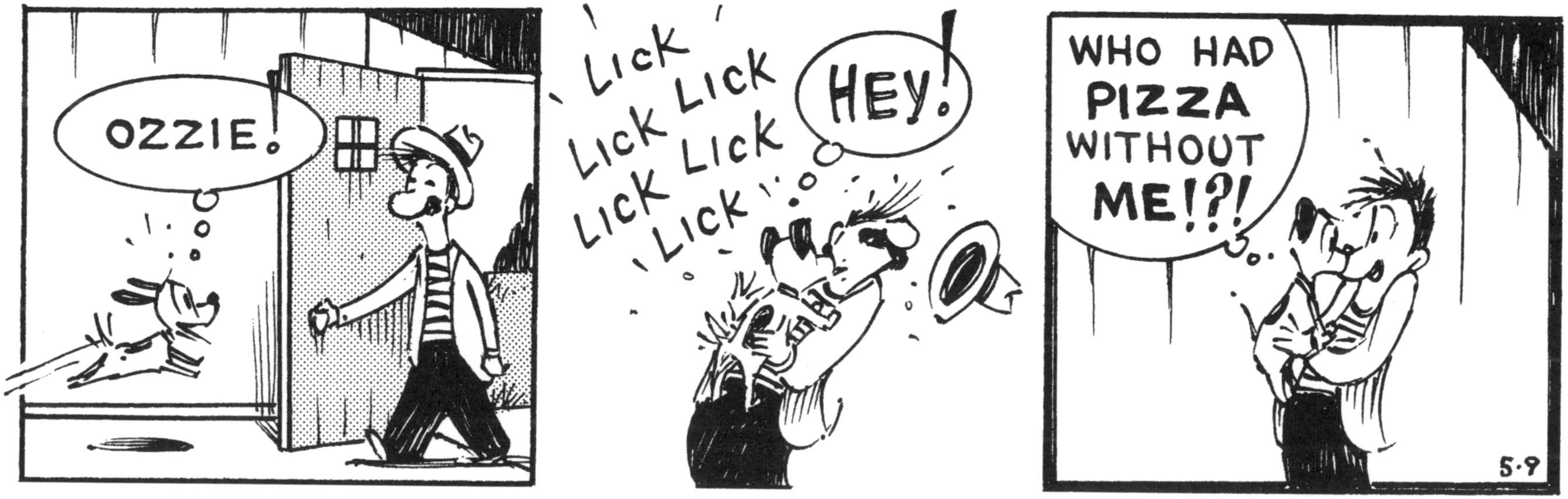
OZZIE!
LICK LICK LICK LICK LICK LICK
HEY!
WHO HAD PIZZA WITHOUT ME!?!
5·9

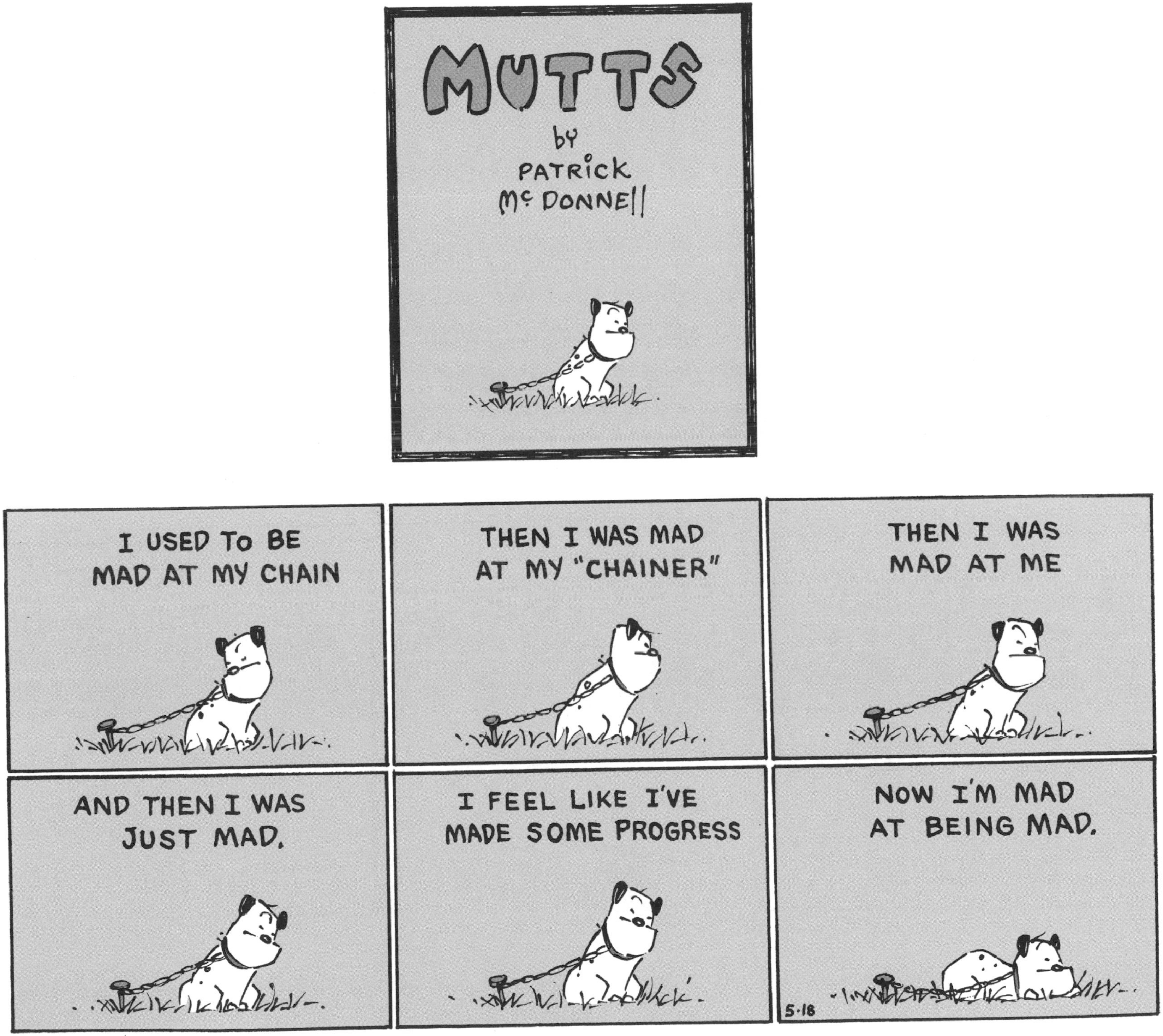
MUTTS
by PATRICK McDONNELL
I USED To BE MAD AT MY CHAIN
THEN I WAS MAD AT MY "CHAINER"
THEN I WAS MAD AT ME
AND THEN I WAS JUST MAD.
I FEEL LIKE I'VE MADE SOME PROGRESS
NOW I'M MAD AT BEING MAD.
5·18

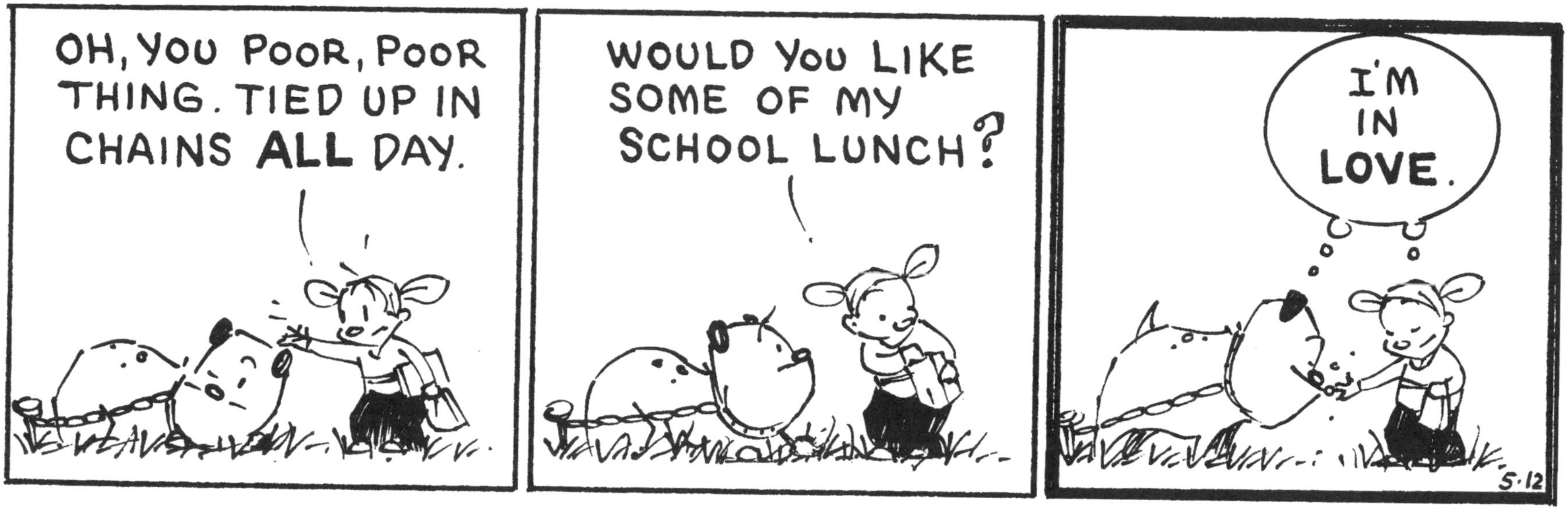
OH, YOU POOR, POOR THING. TIED UP IN CHAINS ALL DAY.
WOULD YOU LIKE SOME OF MY SCHOOL LUNCH?
I'M IN LOVE.
5·12

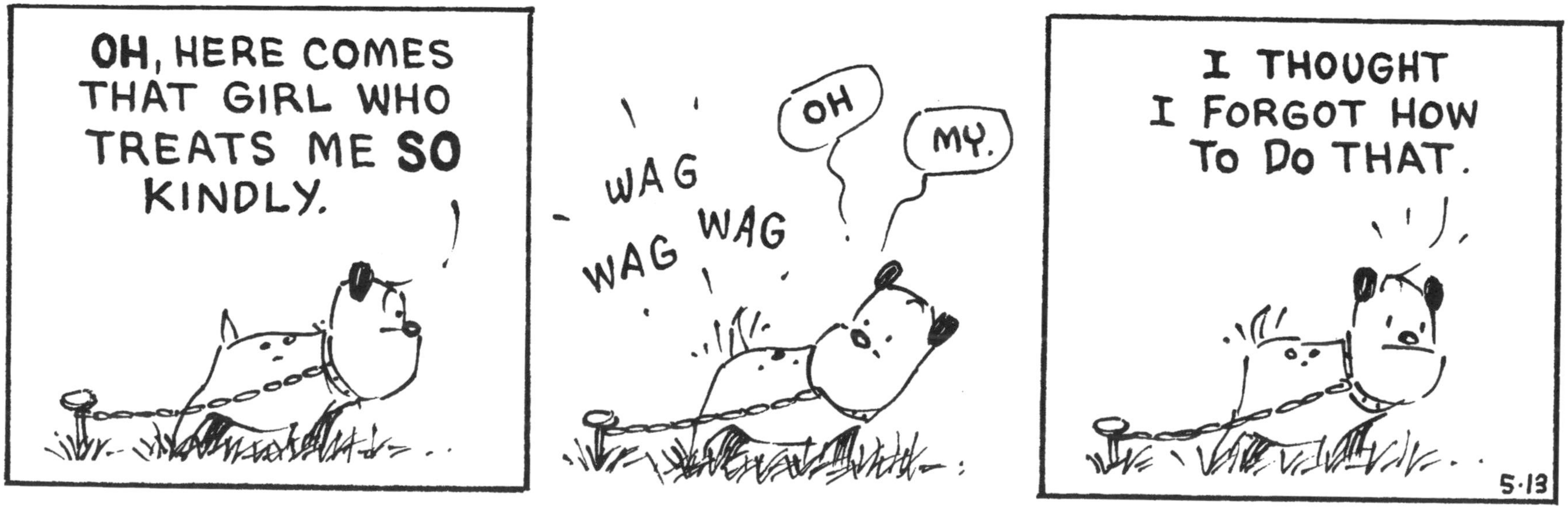
OH, HERE COMES THAT GIRL WHO TREATS ME SO KINDLY.
WAG WAG WAG
OH
MY.
I THOUGHT I FORGOT HOW TO DO THAT.
5·13

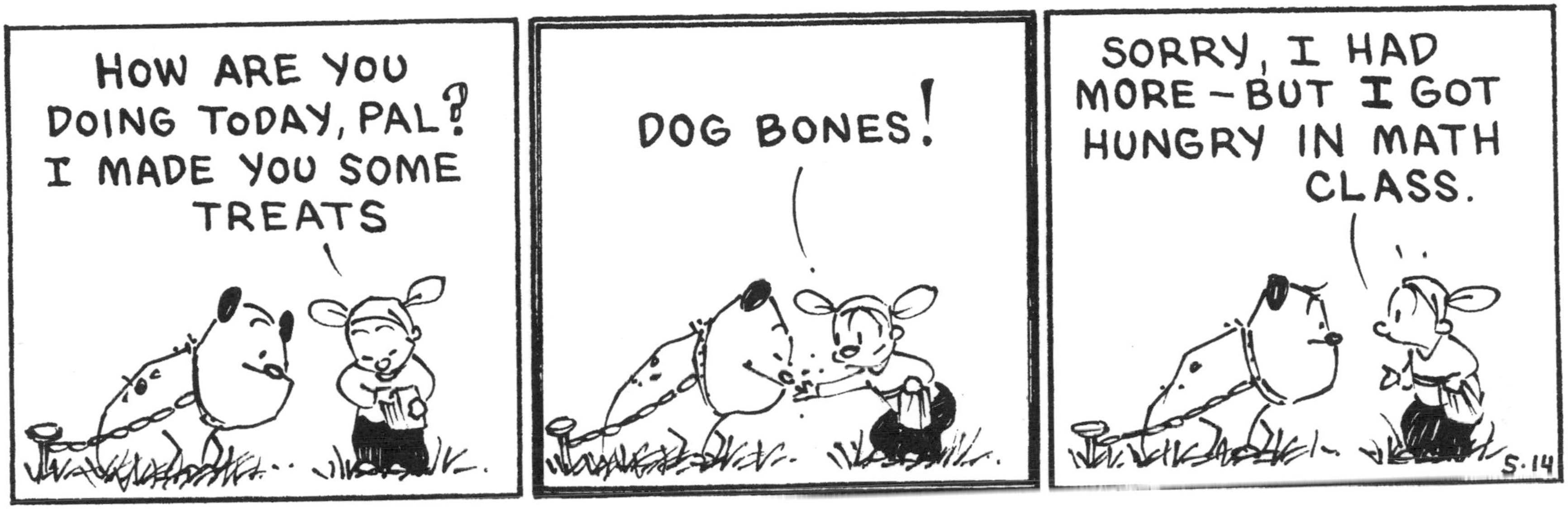
HOW ARE YOU DOING TODAY, PAL? I MADE YOU SOME TREATS
DOG BONES!
SORRY, I HAD MORE—BUT I GOT HUNGRY IN MATH CLASS.
5·14

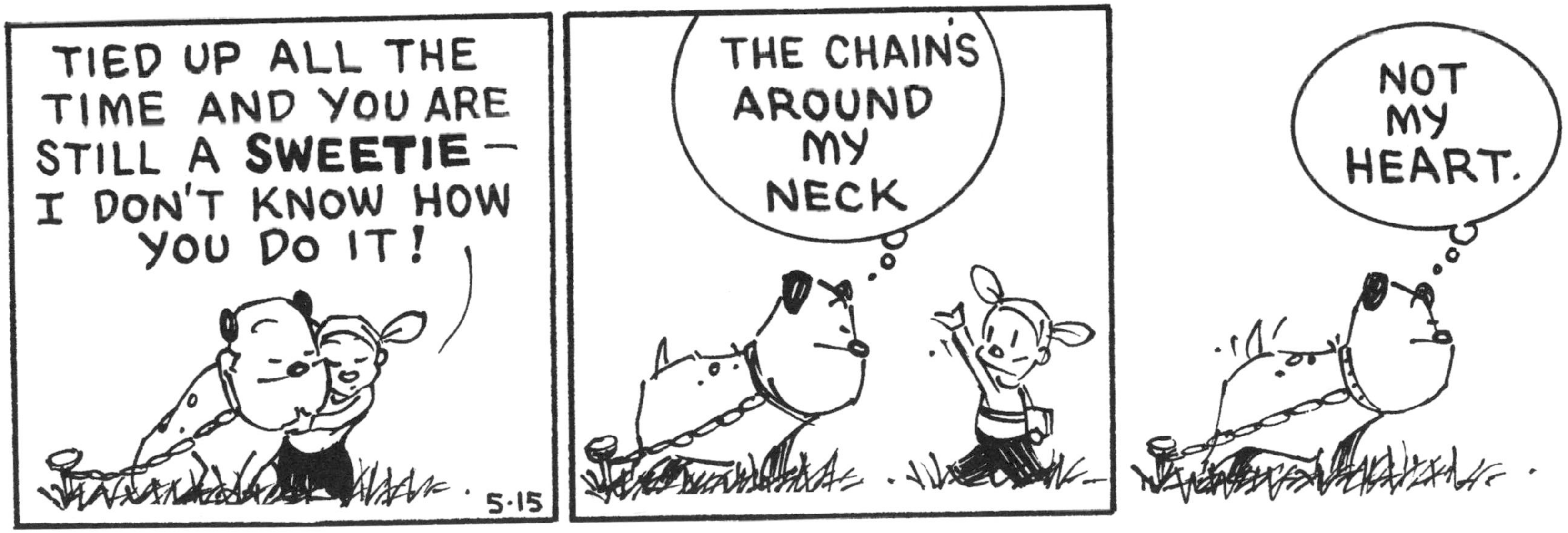
TIED UP ALL THE TIME AND YOU ARE STILL A **SWEETIE**—I DON'T KNOW HOW YOU DO IT!
5·15
THE CHAINS AROUND MY NECK
NOT MY HEART.

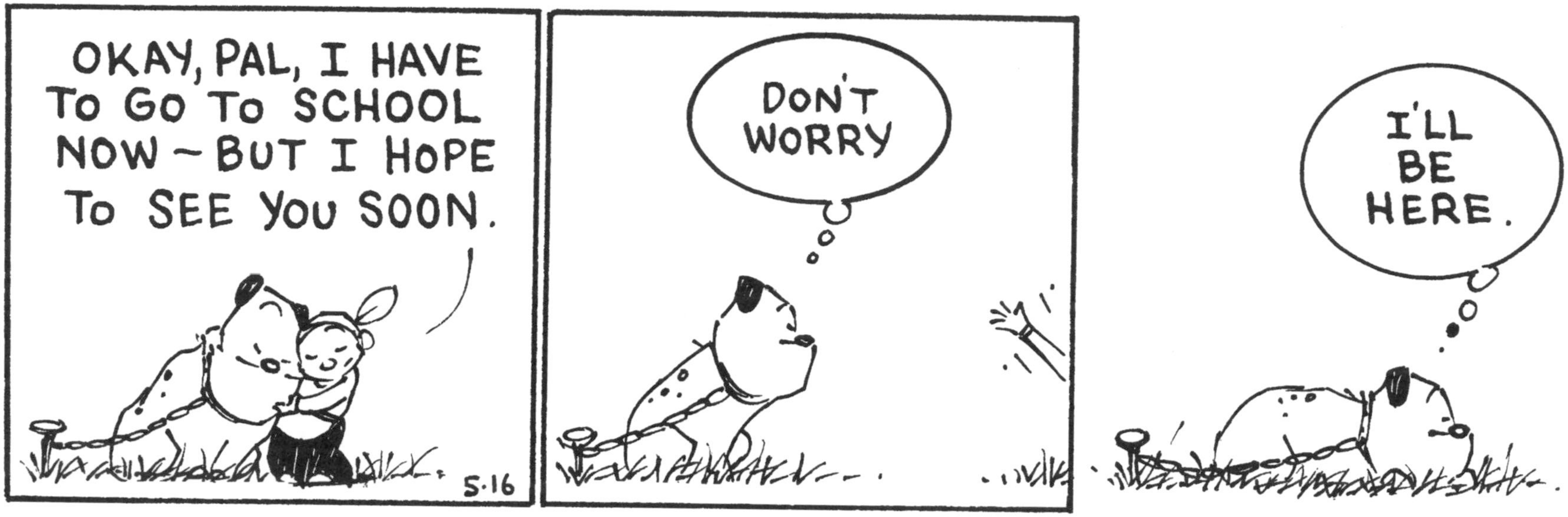
OKAY, PAL, I HAVE TO GO TO SCHOOL NOW ~ BUT I HOPE TO SEE YOU SOON.
5·16
DON'T WORRY
I'LL BE HERE.

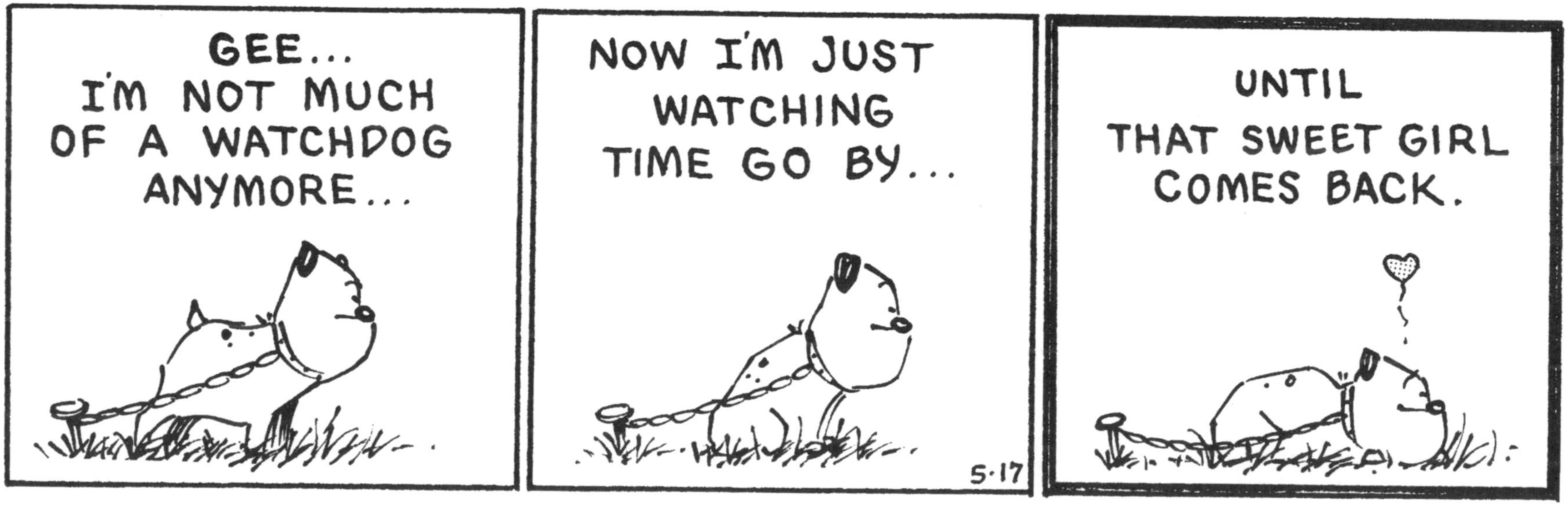
GEE... I'M NOT MUCH OF A WATCHDOG ANYMORE...
NOW I'M JUST WATCHING TIME GO BY...
5·17
UNTIL THAT SWEET GIRL COMES BACK.

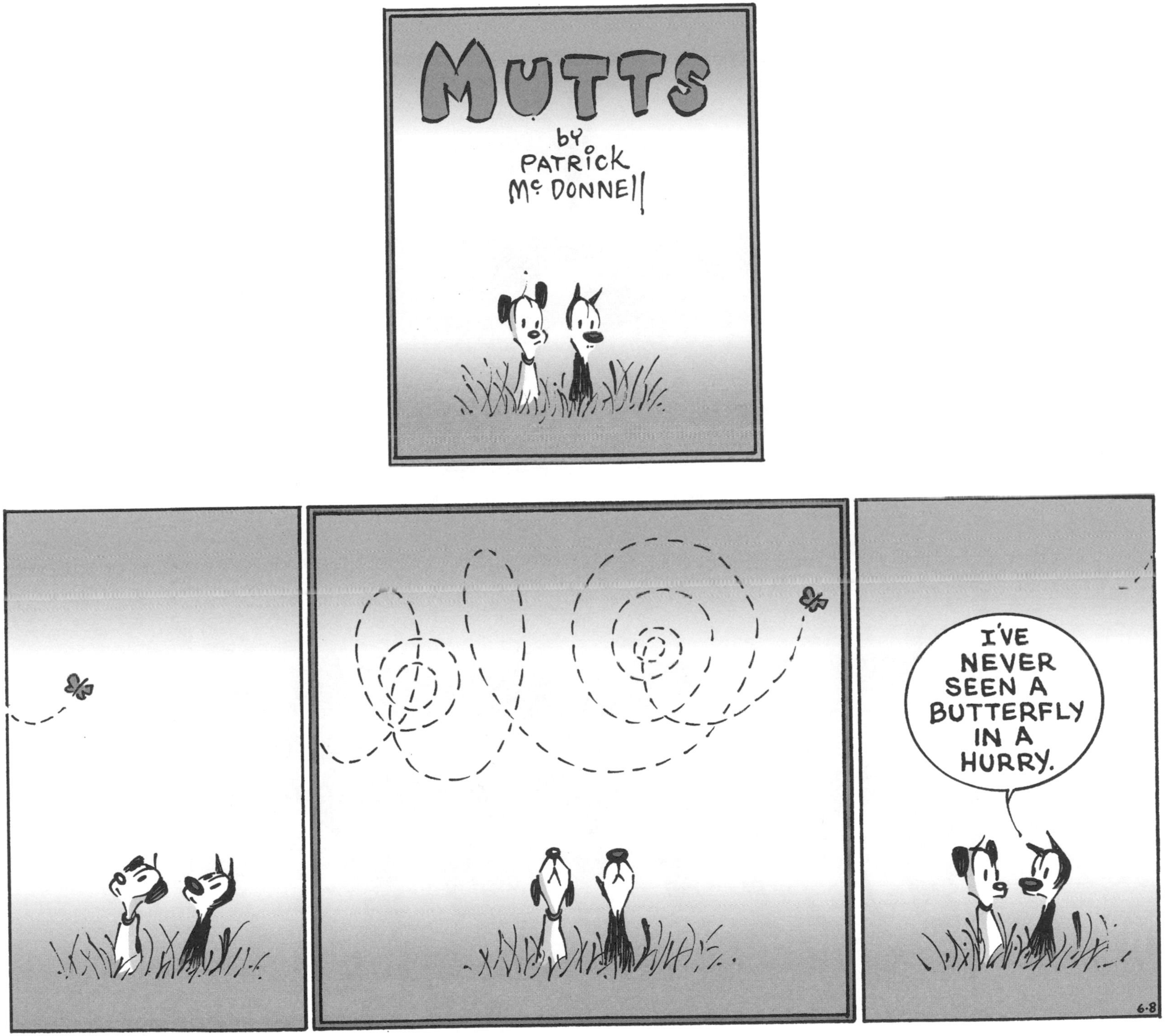
MUTTS
by PATRICK McDONNELL
I'VE NEVER SEEN A BUTTERFLY IN A HURRY.
6-8

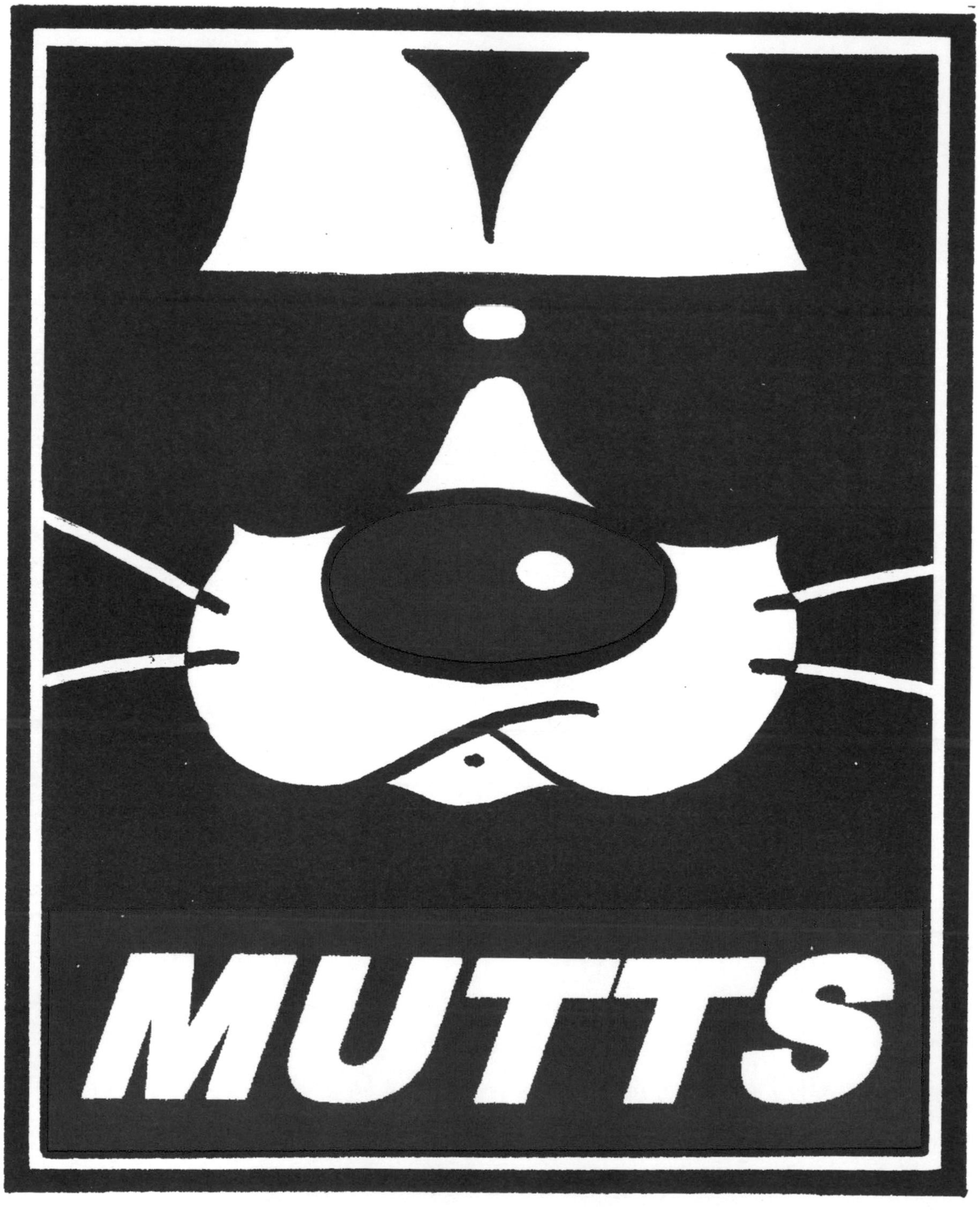
MUTTS

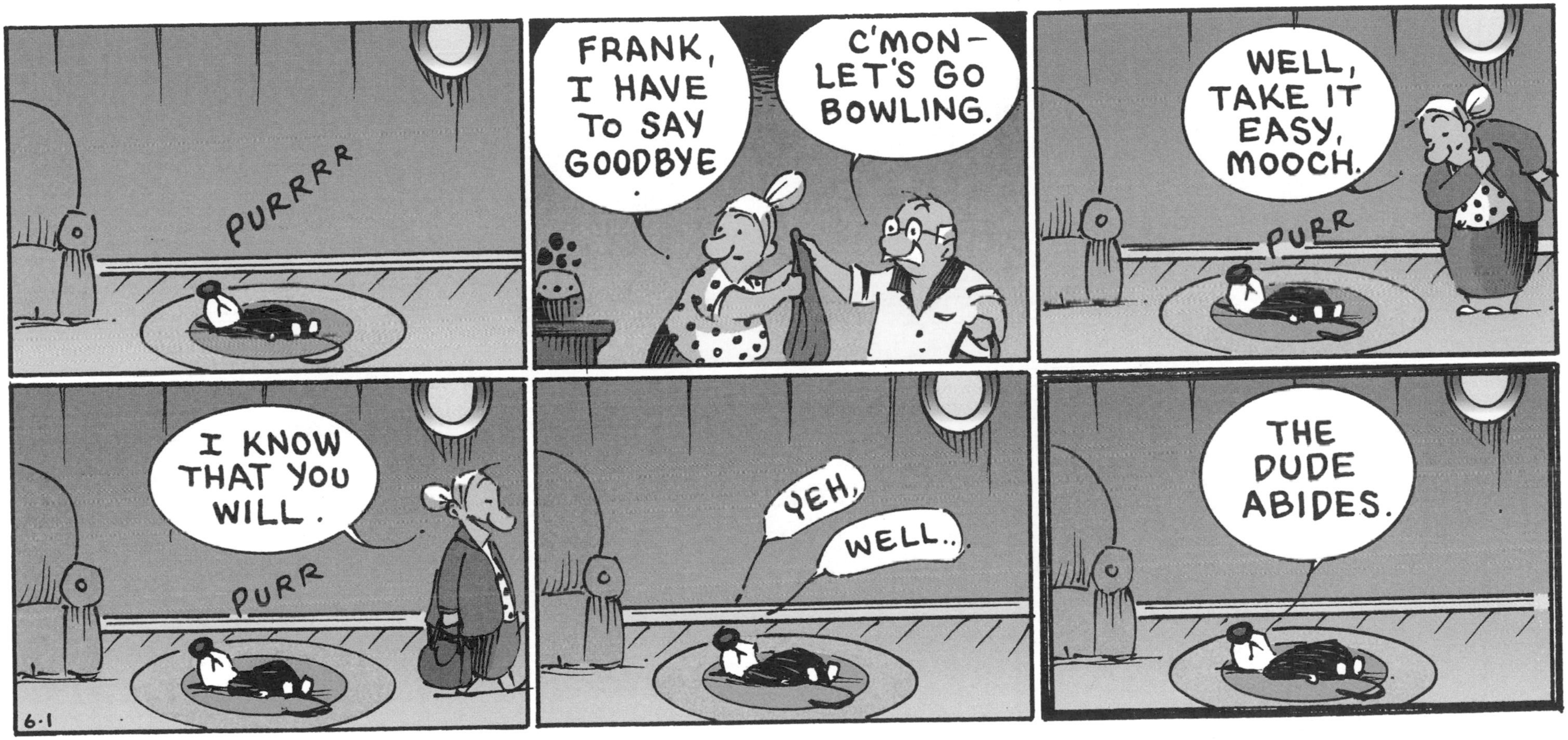
PURRRR
FRANK, I HAVE TO SAY GOODBYE.
C'MON– LET'S GO BOWLING.
WELL, TAKE IT EASY, MOOCH.
PURR
I KNOW THAT YOU WILL.
PURR
6·1
YEH,
WELL..
THE DUDE ABIDES.

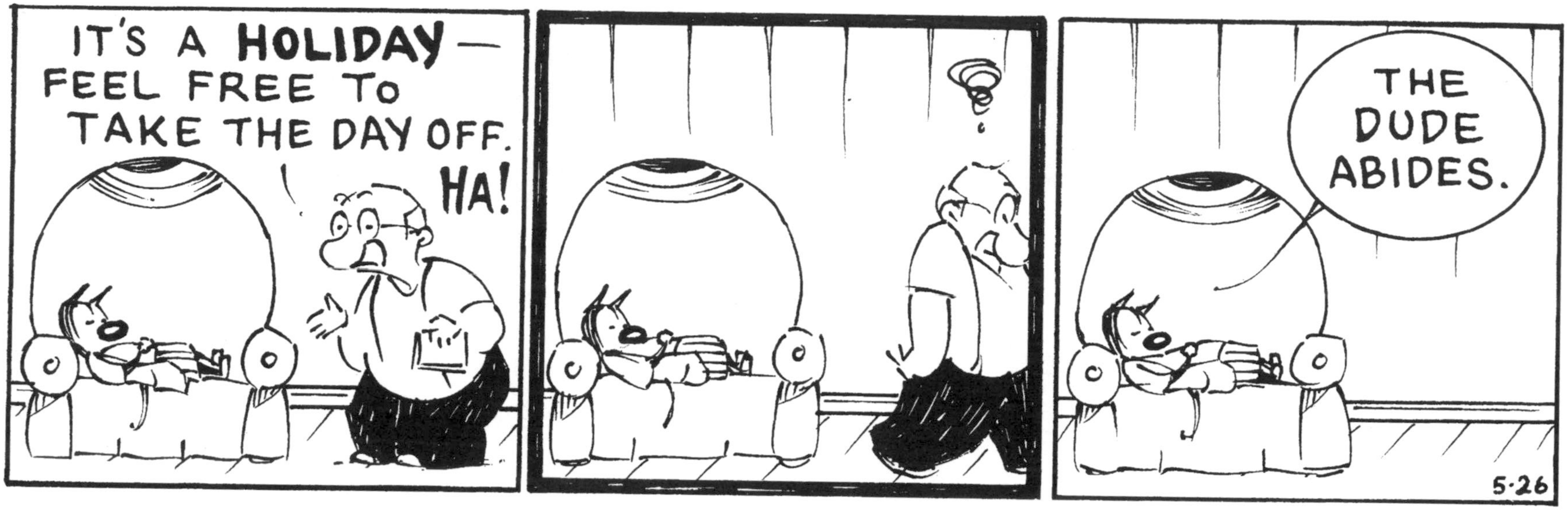
IT'S A **HOLIDAY**— FEEL FREE TO TAKE THE DAY OFF.
HA!
THE DUDE ABIDES.
5·26

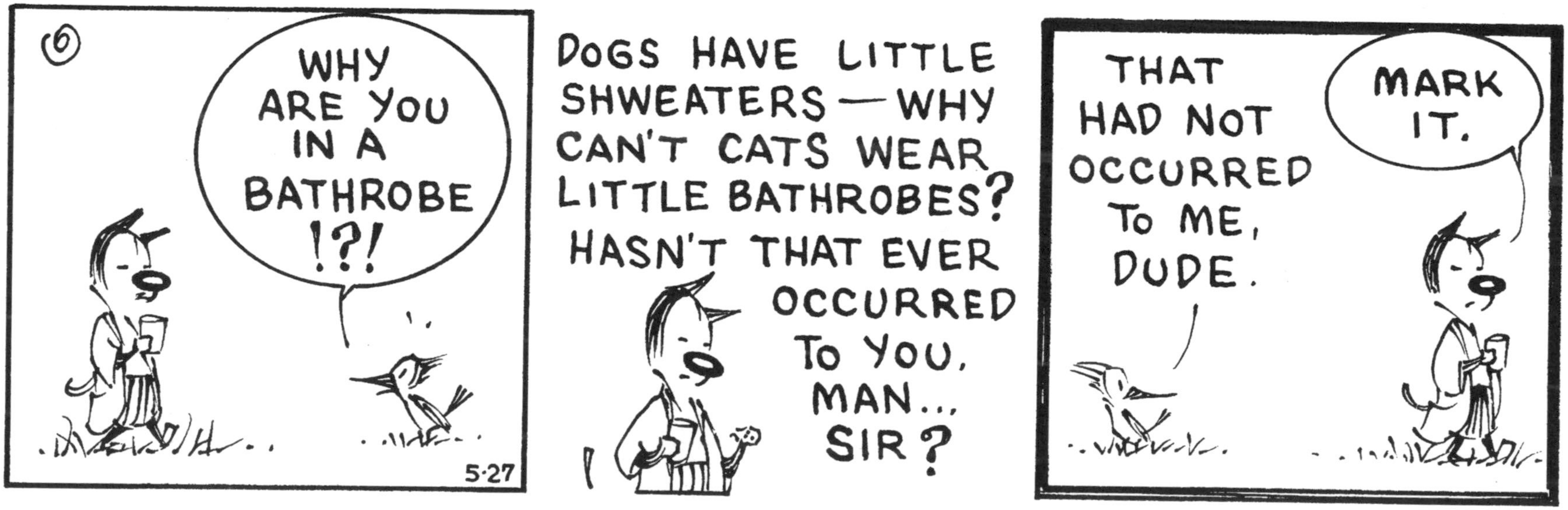
WHY ARE YOU IN A BATHROBE !?!
5·27
DOGS HAVE LITTLE SHWEATERS—WHY CAN'T CATS WEAR LITTLE BATHROBES? HASN'T THAT EVER OCCURRED TO YOU, MAN... SIR?
THAT HAD NOT OCCURRED TO ME, DUDE.
MARK IT.

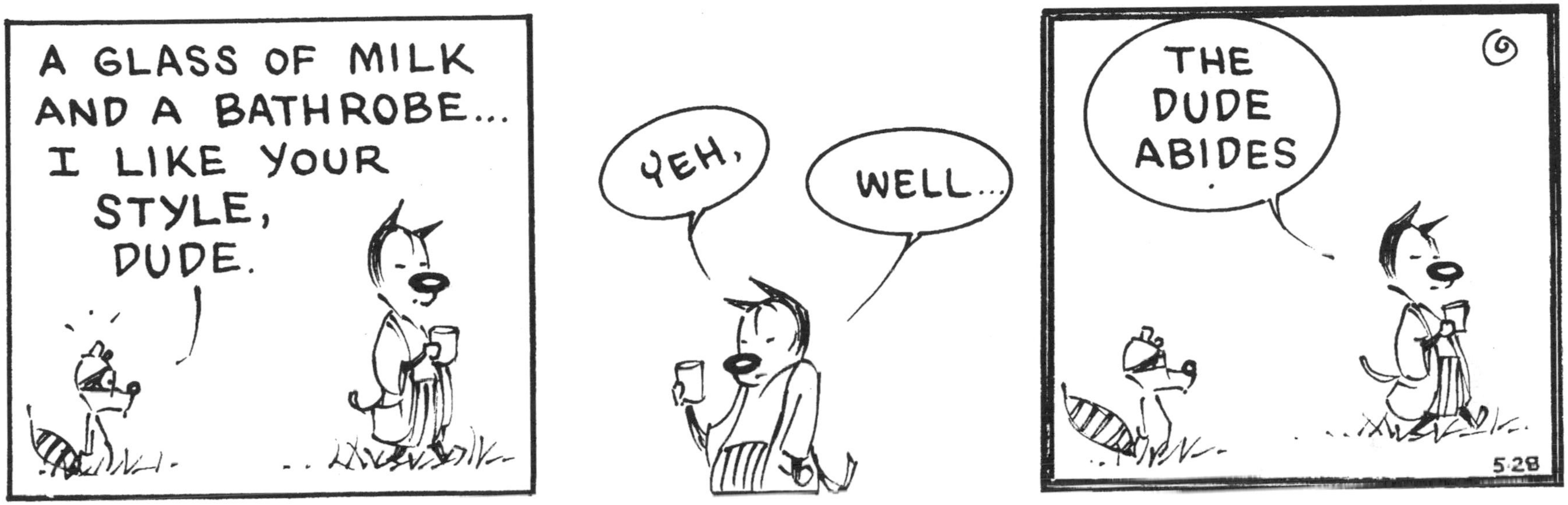
A GLASS OF MILK AND A BATHROBE... I LIKE YOUR STYLE, DUDE.
YEH,
WELL...
THE DUDE ABIDES
5·28

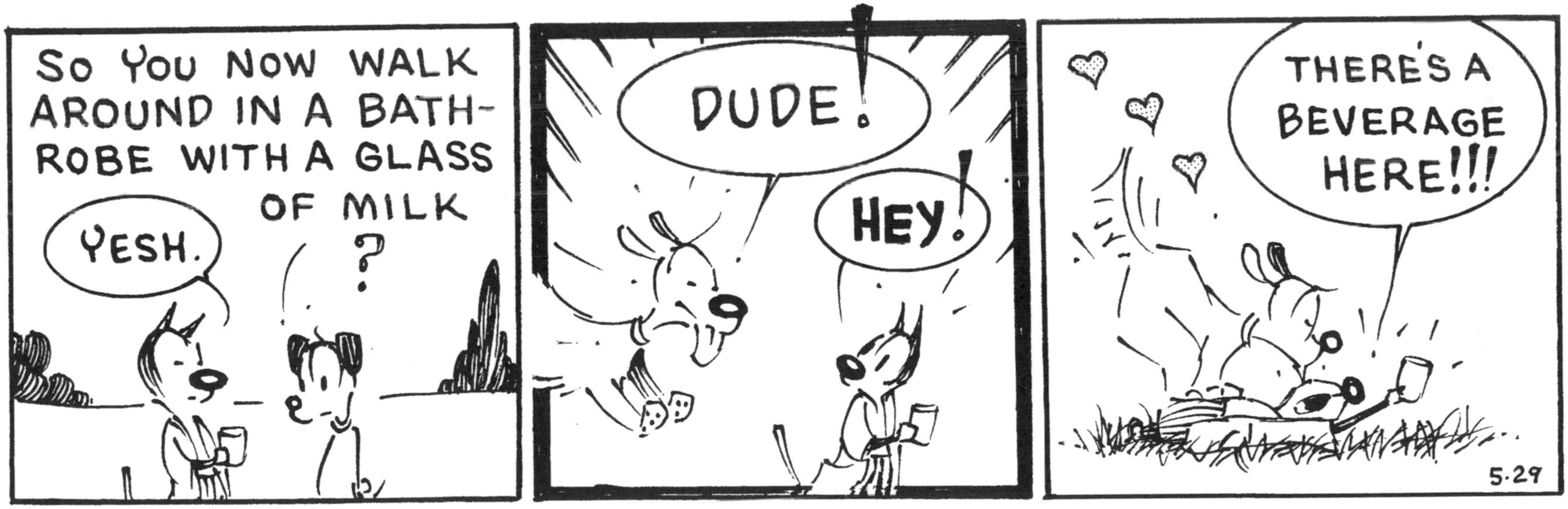
SO YOU NOW WALK AROUND IN A BATH-ROBE WITH A GLASS OF MILK
YESH.
?
DUDE!
HEY!
THERE'S A BEVERAGE HERE!!!
5·29

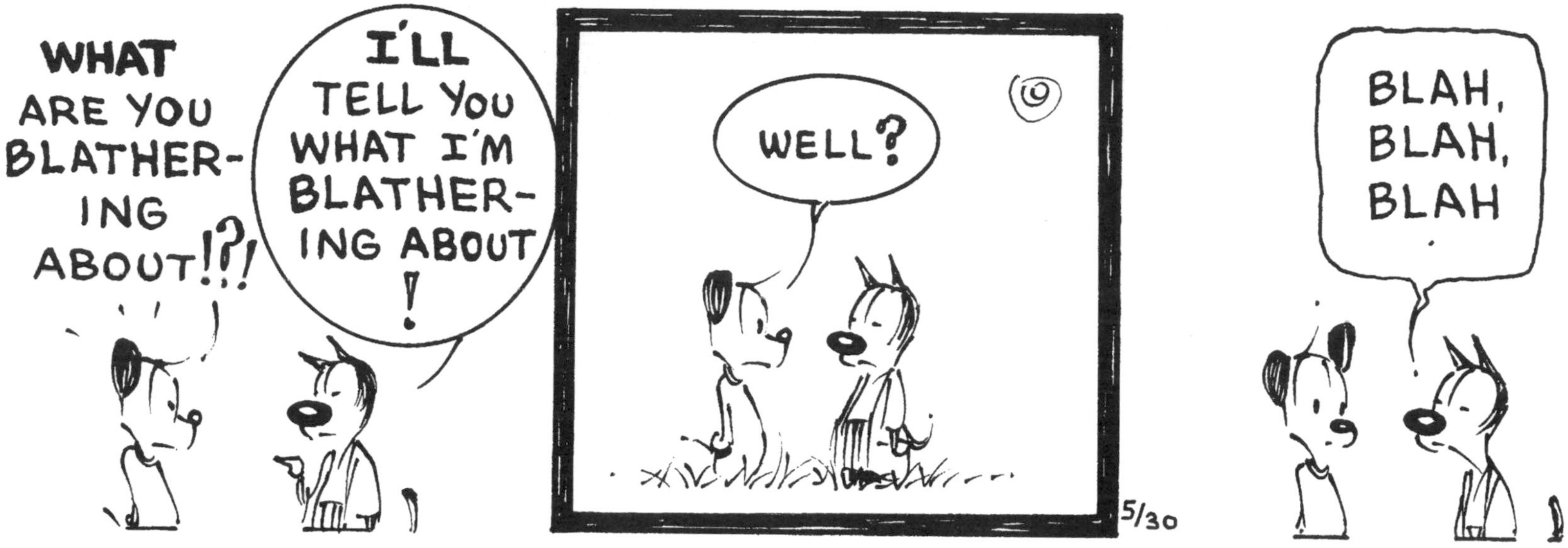
WHAT ARE YOU BLATHER-ING ABOUT!?!
I'LL TELL YOU WHAT I'M BLATHER-ING ABOUT!
WELL?
BLAH, BLAH, BLAH
5/30

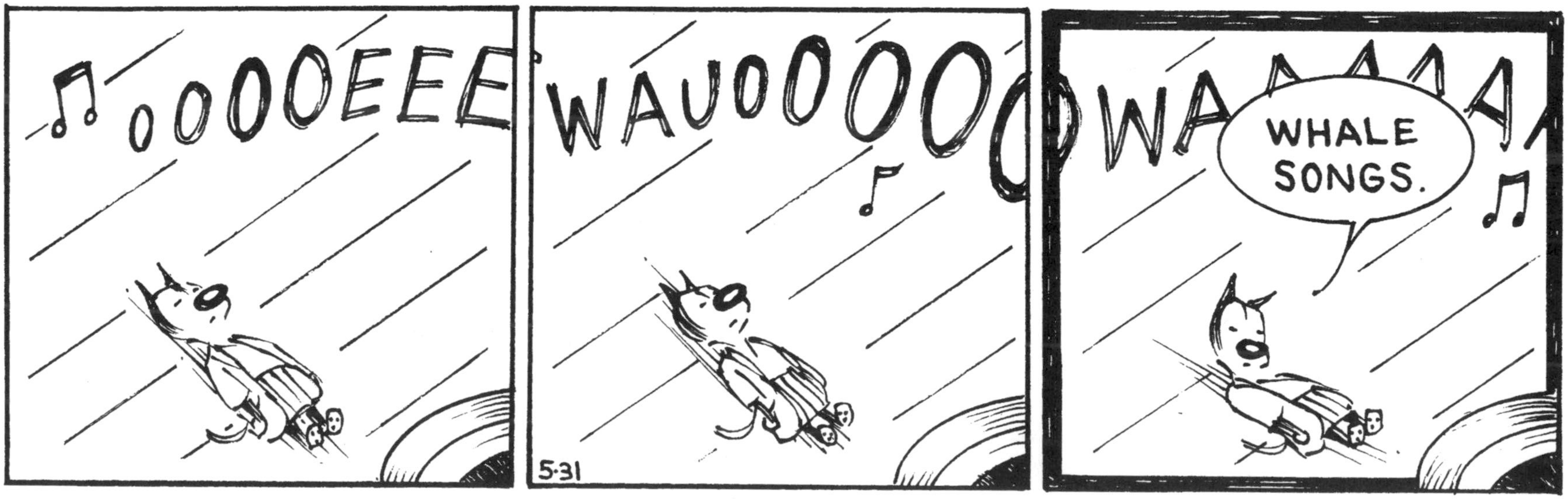
OOOOEEE
WAUOOOOO
WAAAAA
WHALE SONGS.
5·31

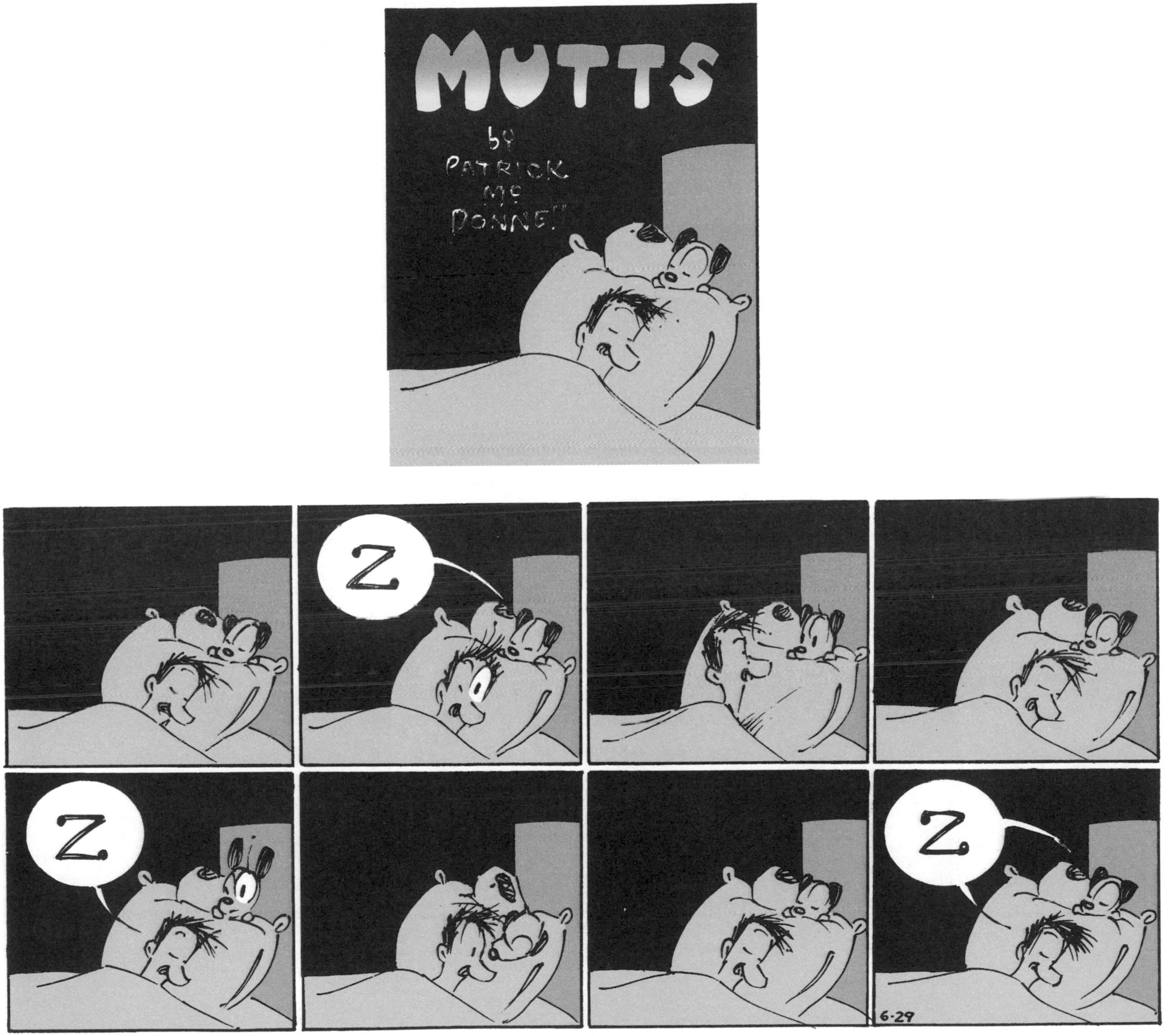
MUTTS
by PATRICK McDONNELL
Z
Z
Z
6-29

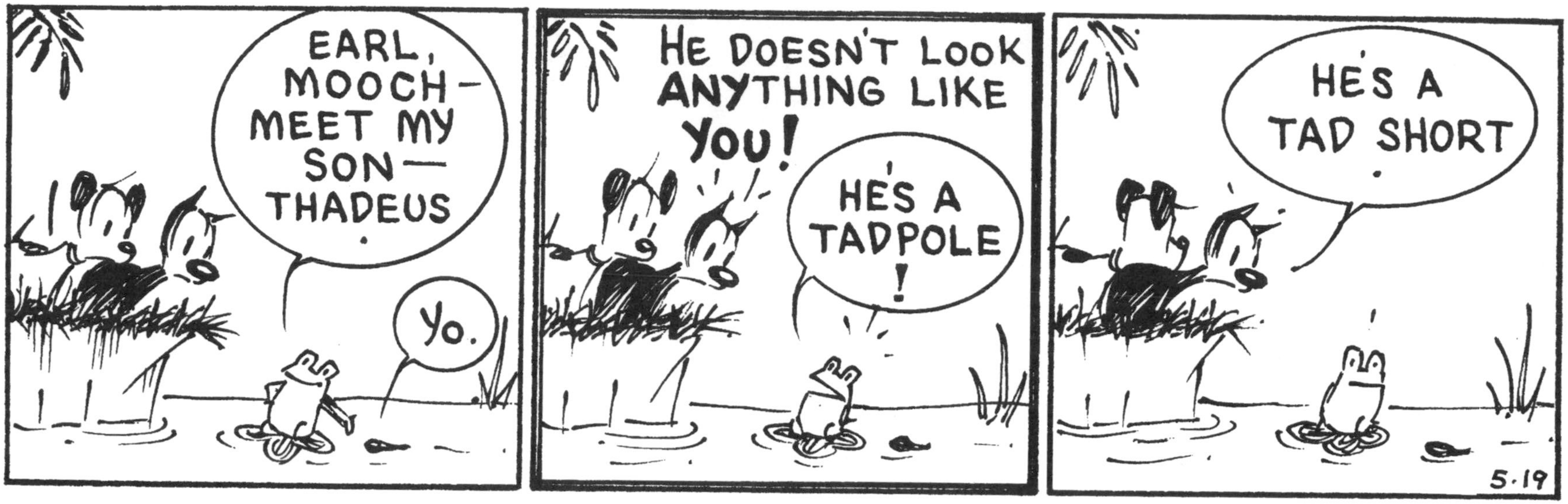
EARL, MOOCH– MEET MY SON– THADEUS.
YO.
HE DOESN'T LOOK ANYTHING LIKE YOU!
HE'S A TADPOLE!
HE'S A TAD SHORT.
5·19

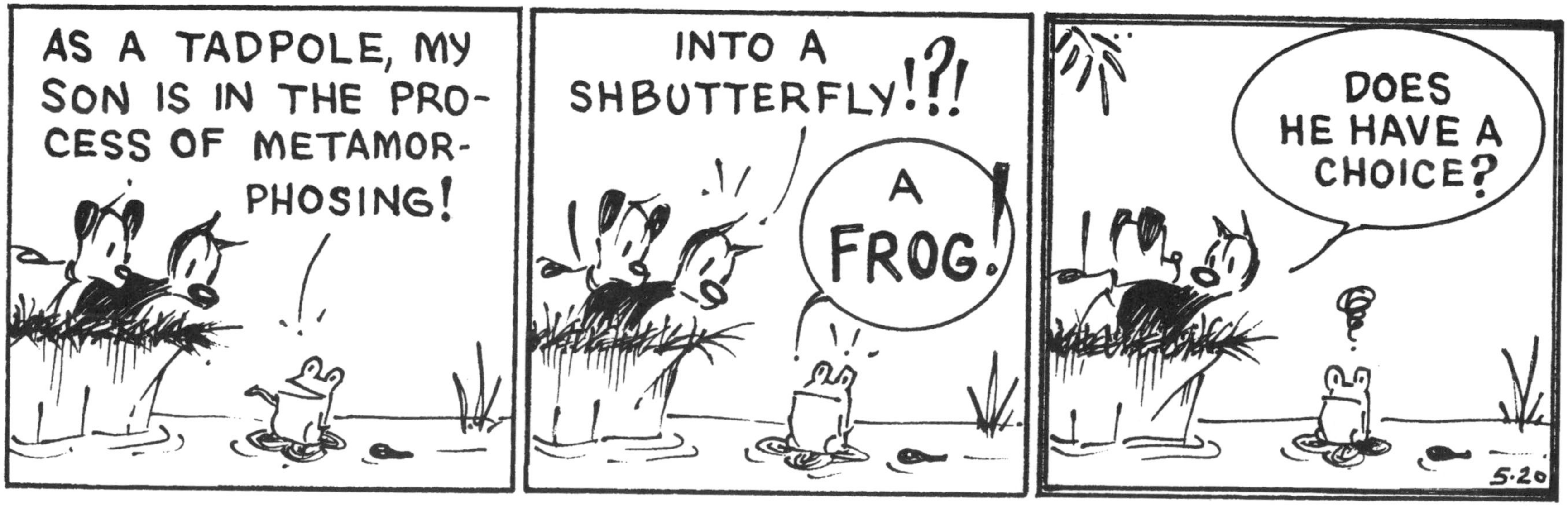
AS A TADPOLE, MY SON IS IN THE PRO-CESS OF METAMOR-PHOSING!
INTO A SHBUTTERFLY!?!
A FROG!
DOES HE HAVE A CHOICE?
5·20

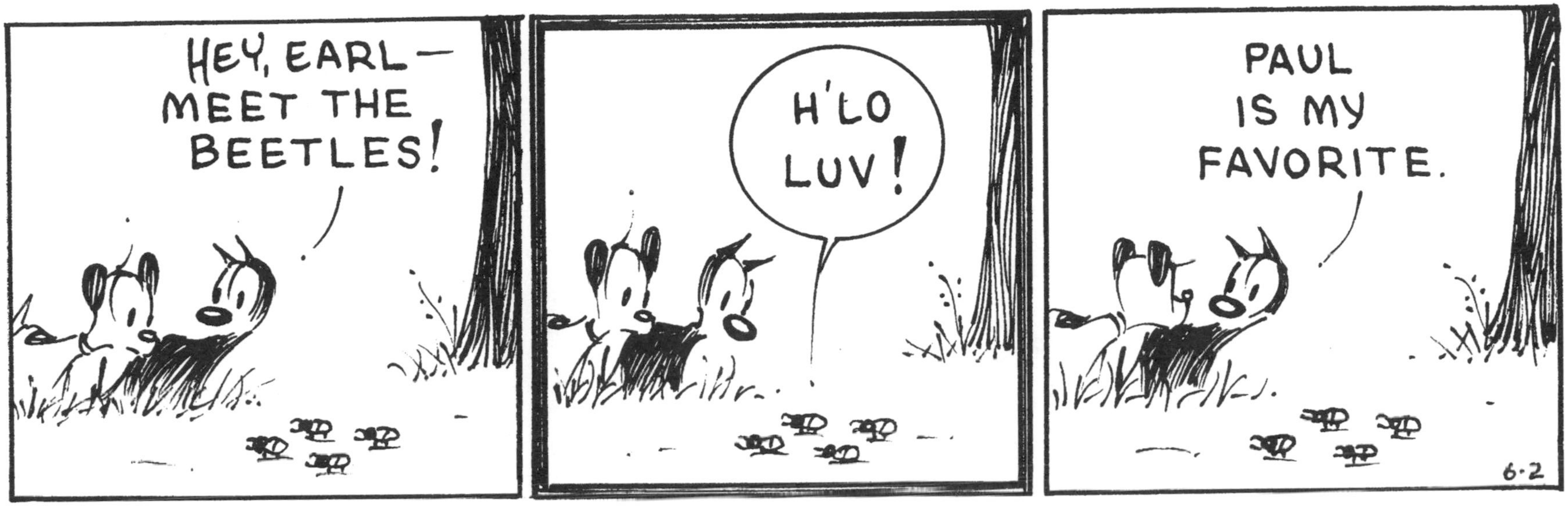
HEY, EARL—
MEET THE
BEETLES!
H'LO
LUV!
PAUL
IS MY
FAVORITE.
6·2

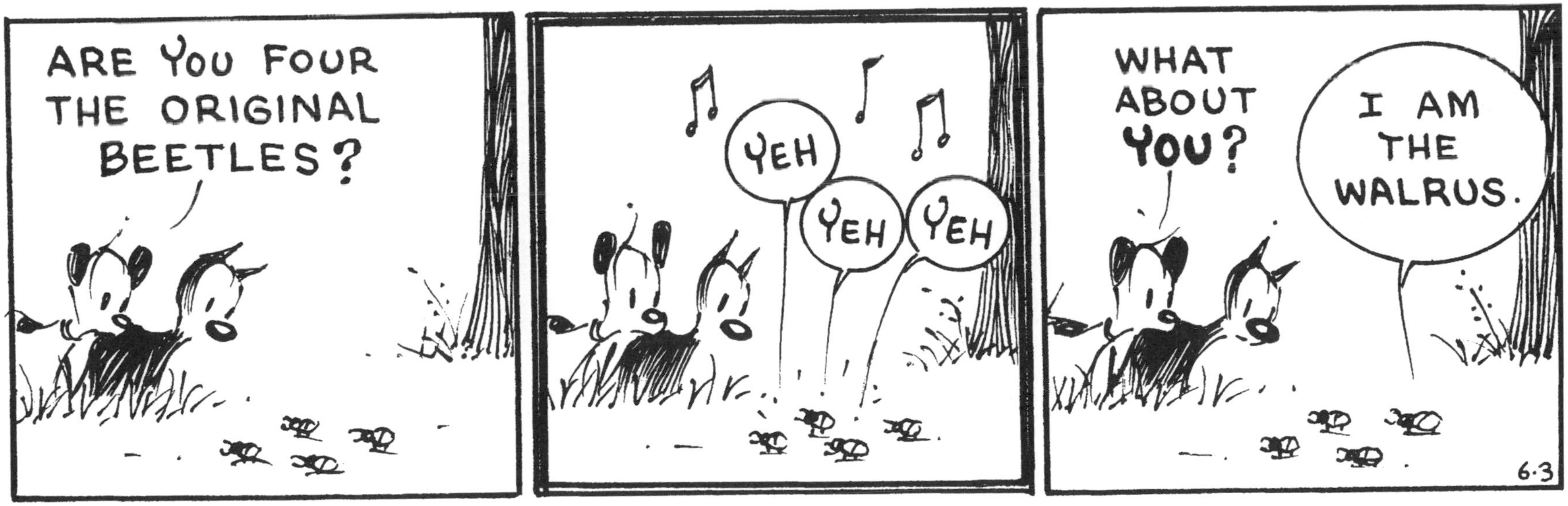
ARE YOU FOUR
THE ORIGINAL
BEETLES?
YEH
YEH
YEH
WHAT
ABOUT
YOU?
I AM
THE
WALRUS.
6·3

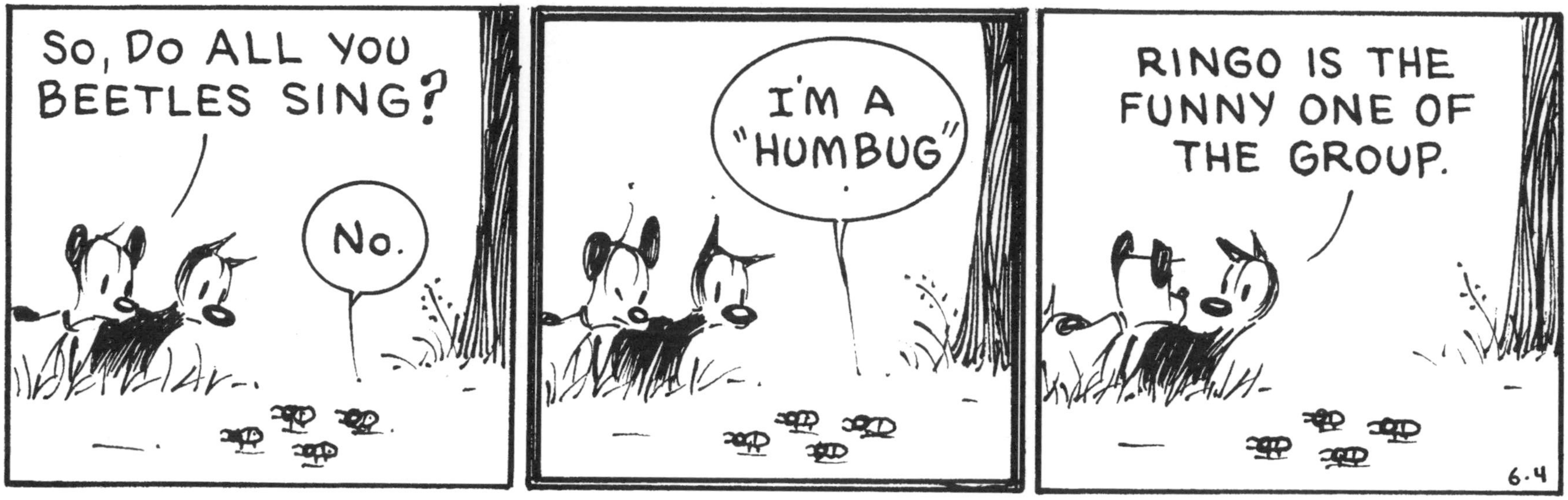
So, DO ALL YOU BEETLES SING?
No.
I'M A "HUMBUG"
RINGO IS THE FUNNY ONE OF THE GROUP.
6·4

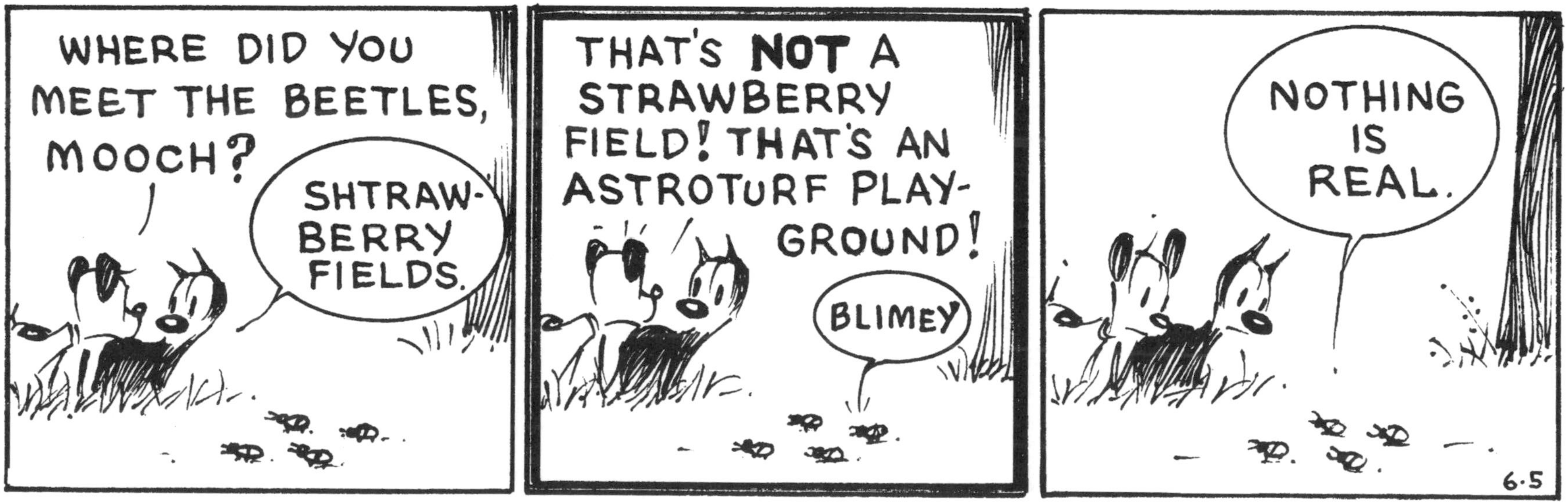
WHERE DID YOU MEET THE BEETLES, MOOCH?
SHTRAW-BERRY FIELDS.
THAT'S **NOT** A STRAWBERRY FIELD! THAT'S AN ASTROTURF PLAY-GROUND!
BLIMEY
NOTHING IS REAL.
6·5

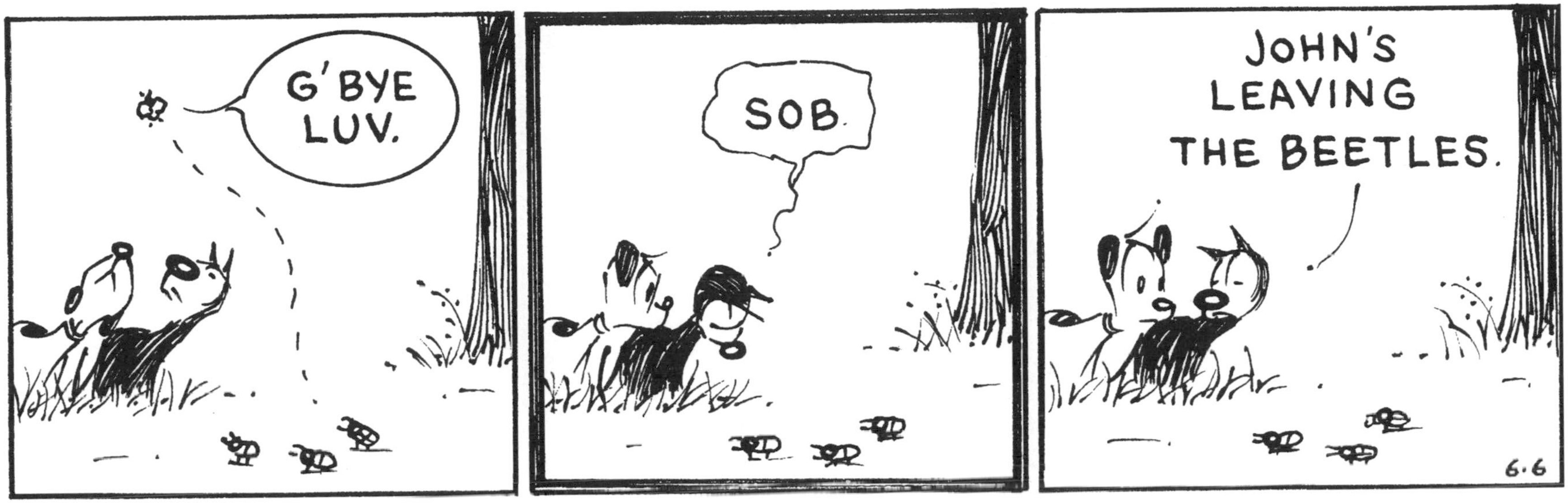
G'BYE LUV.
SOB.
JOHN'S LEAVING THE BEETLES.
6.6

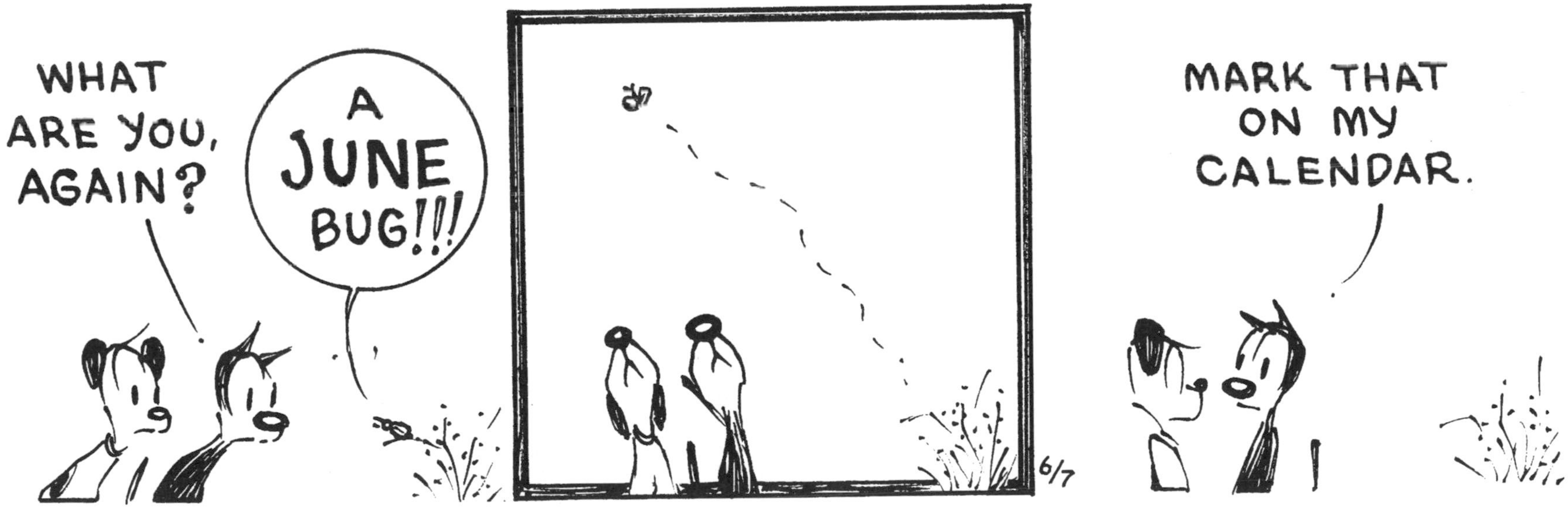
WHAT ARE YOU, AGAIN?
A JUNE BUG!!!
6/7
MARK THAT ON MY CALENDAR.

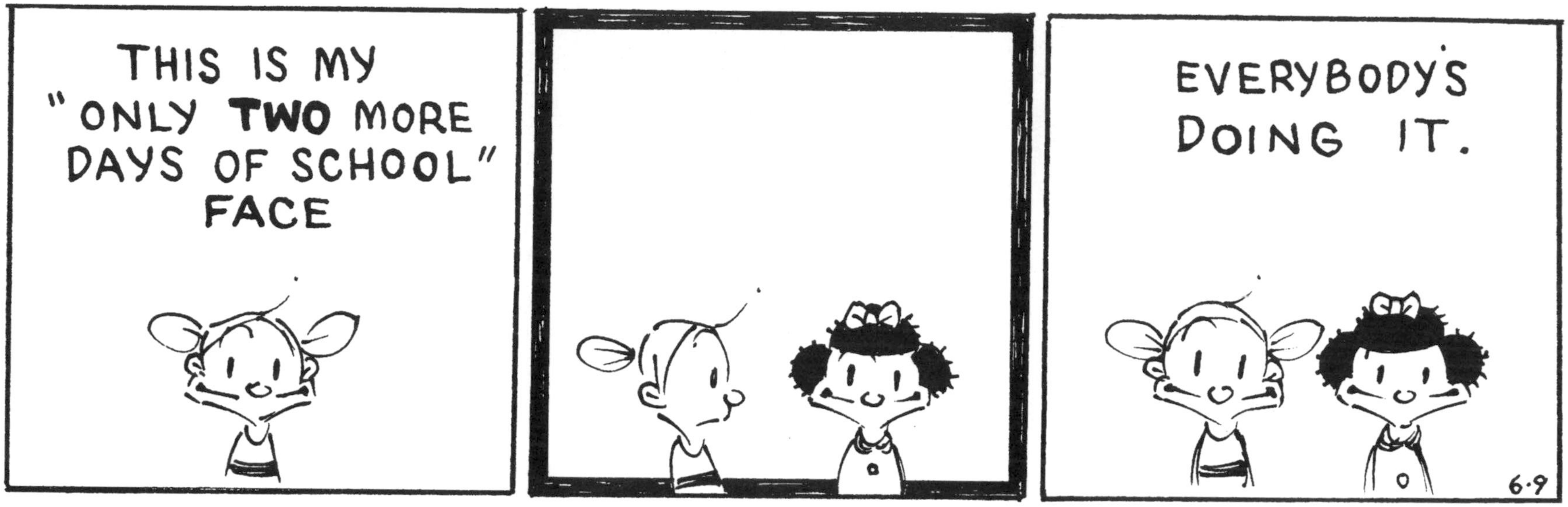
THIS IS MY "ONLY **TWO** MORE DAYS OF SCHOOL" FACE
EVERYBODY'S DOING IT.
6·9

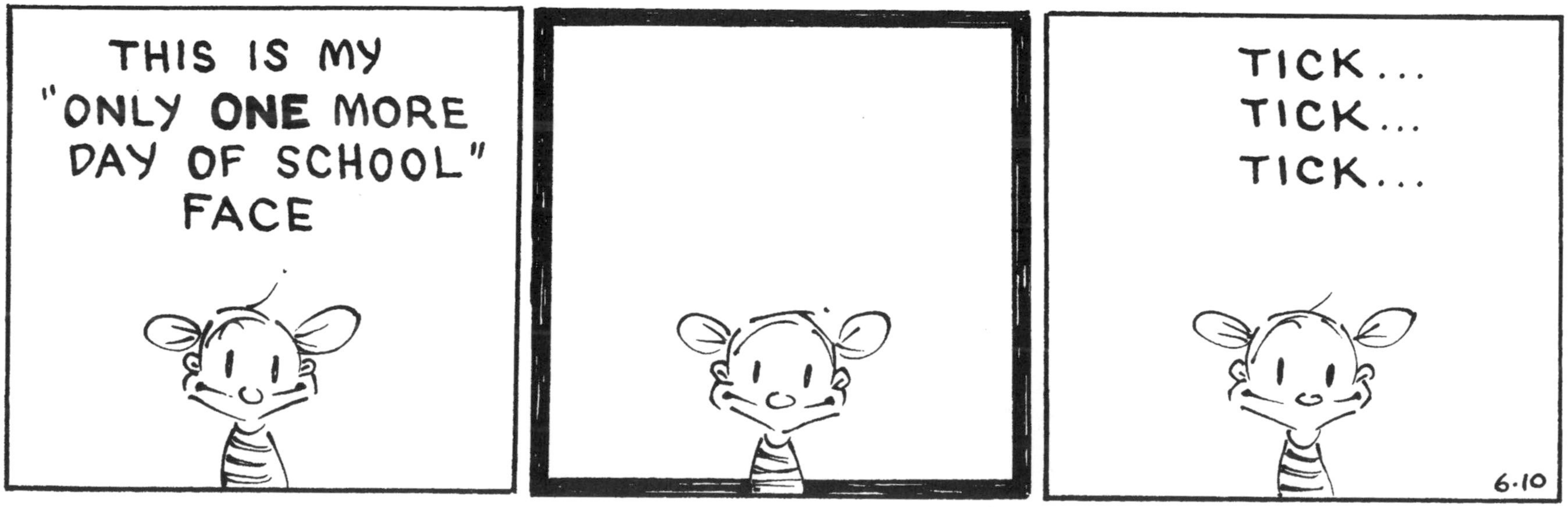
THIS IS MY "ONLY **ONE** MORE DAY OF SCHOOL" FACE
TICK...
TICK...
TICK...
6·10

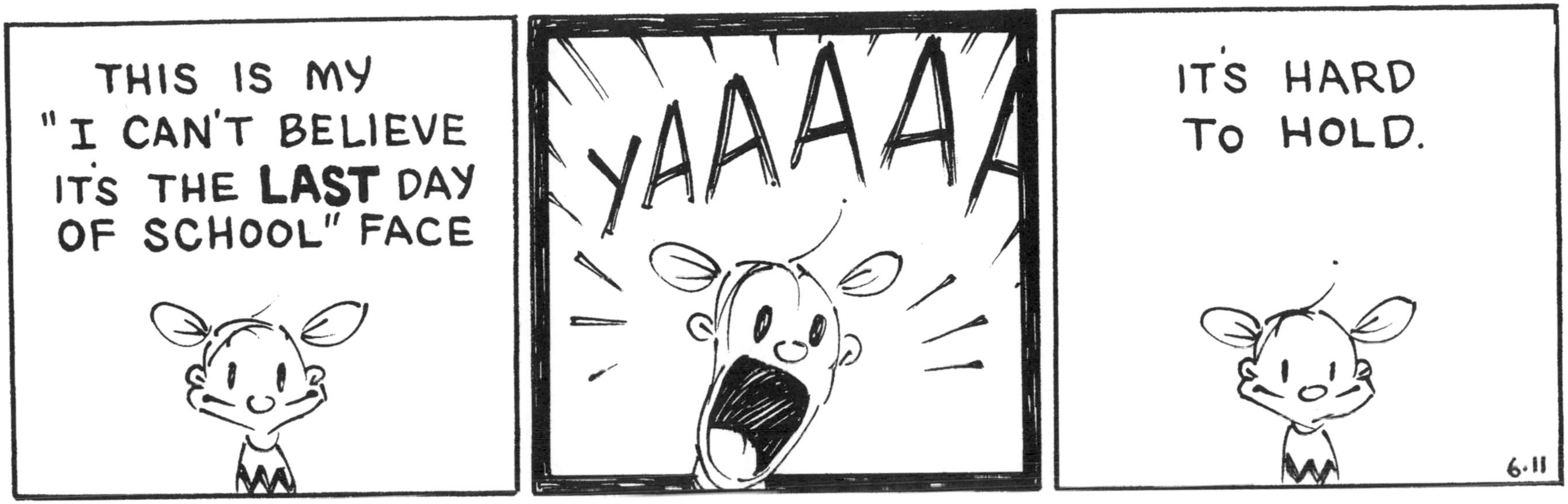
THIS IS MY "I CAN'T BELIEVE IT'S THE LAST DAY OF SCHOOL" FACE
YAAAAA
IT'S HARD TO HOLD.
6-11

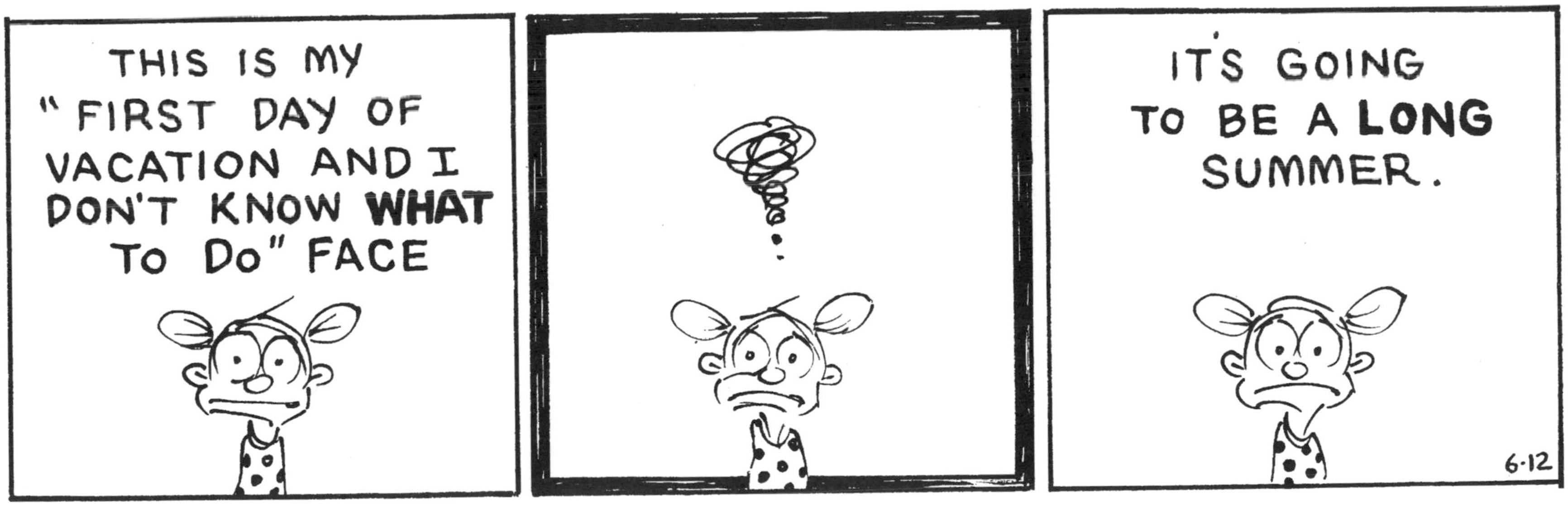
THIS IS MY "FIRST DAY OF VACATION AND I DON'T KNOW WHAT TO DO" FACE
IT'S GOING TO BE A LONG SUMMER.
6-12

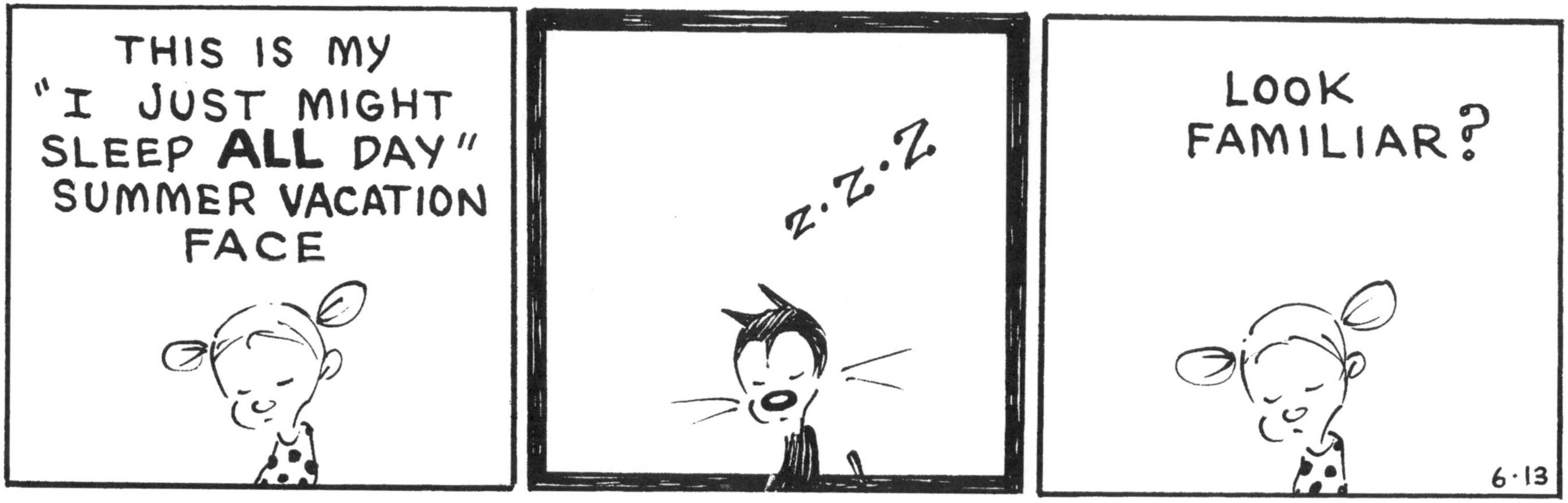
THIS IS MY "I JUST MIGHT SLEEP ALL DAY" SUMMER VACATION FACE
Z.Z.Z
LOOK FAMILIAR?
6·13

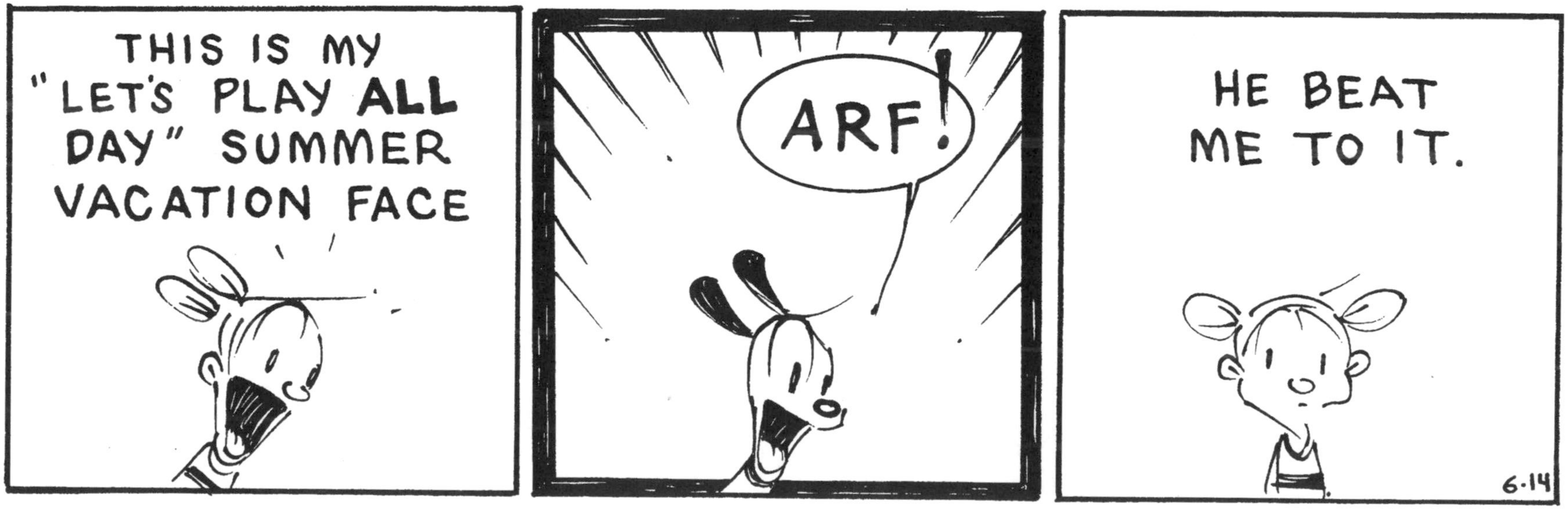
THIS IS MY "LET'S PLAY ALL DAY" SUMMER VACATION FACE
ARF!
HE BEAT ME TO IT.
6·14

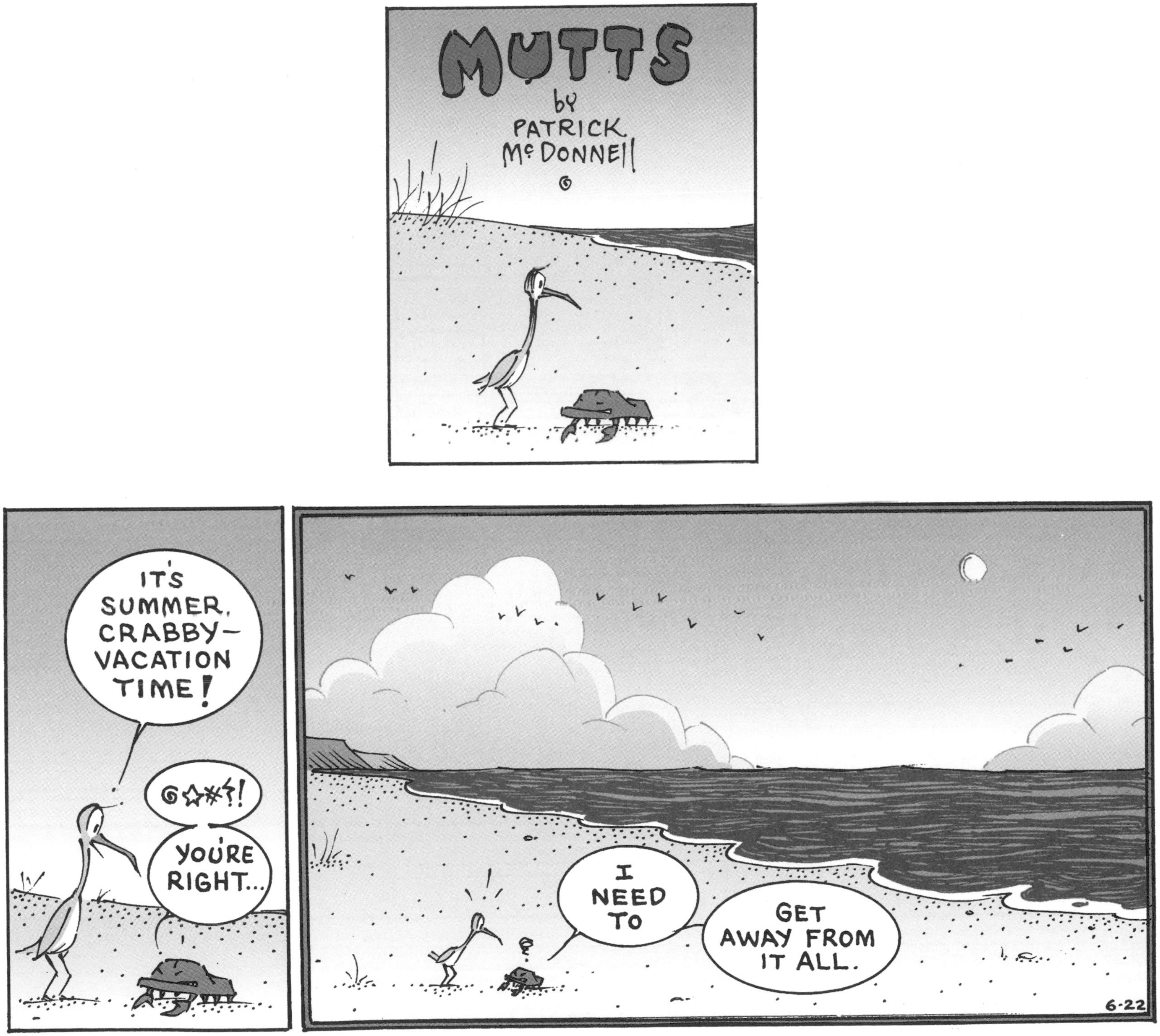
MUTTS
by
PATRICK McDONNELL
©
IT'S SUMMER, CRABBY— VACATION TIME!
YOU'RE RIGHT...
I NEED TO
GET AWAY FROM IT ALL.
6-22

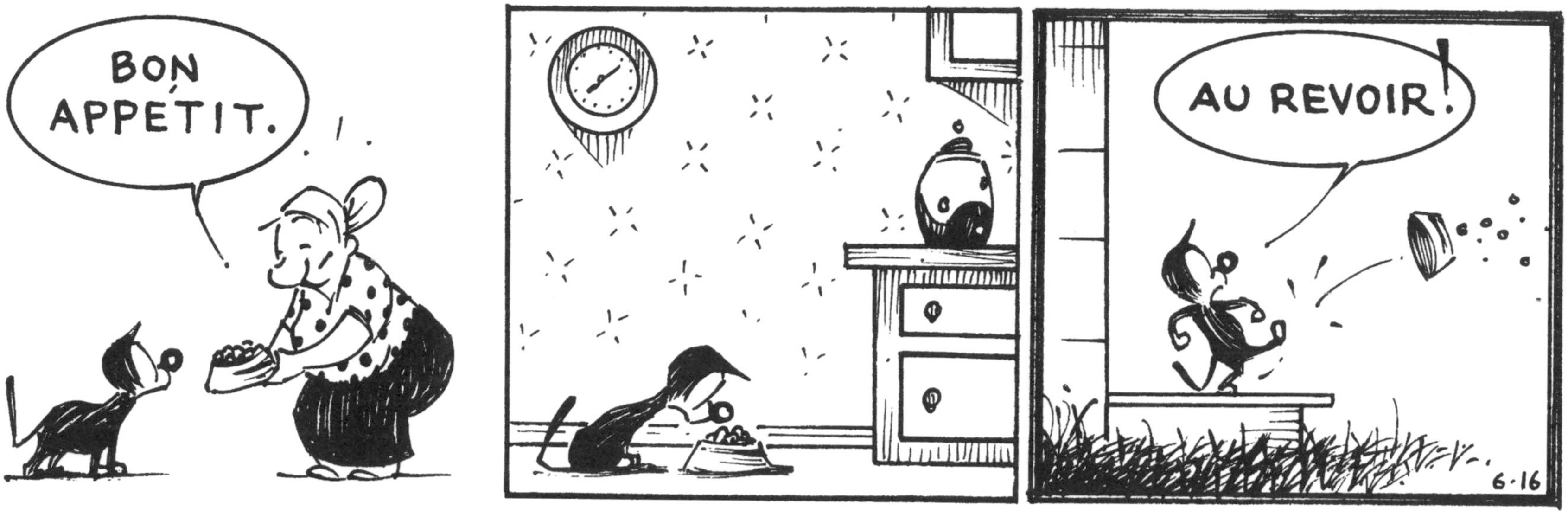
BON APPÉTIT.
AU REVOIR!
6·16

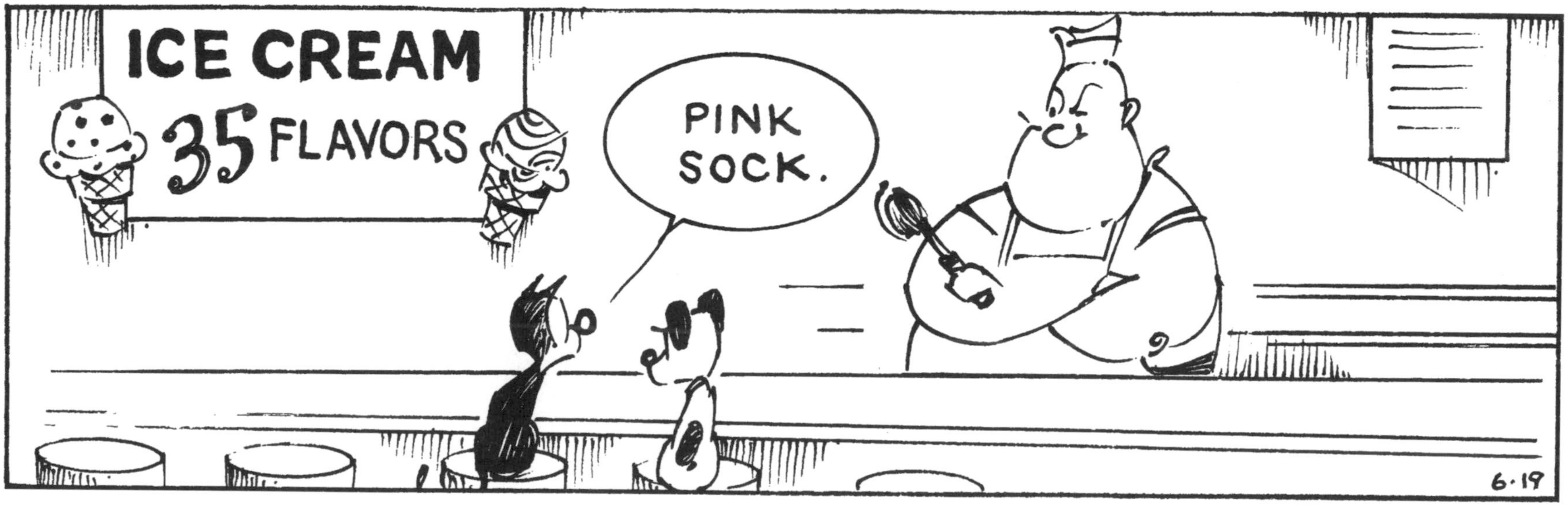
ICE CREAM
35 FLAVORS
PINK SOCK.
6·19

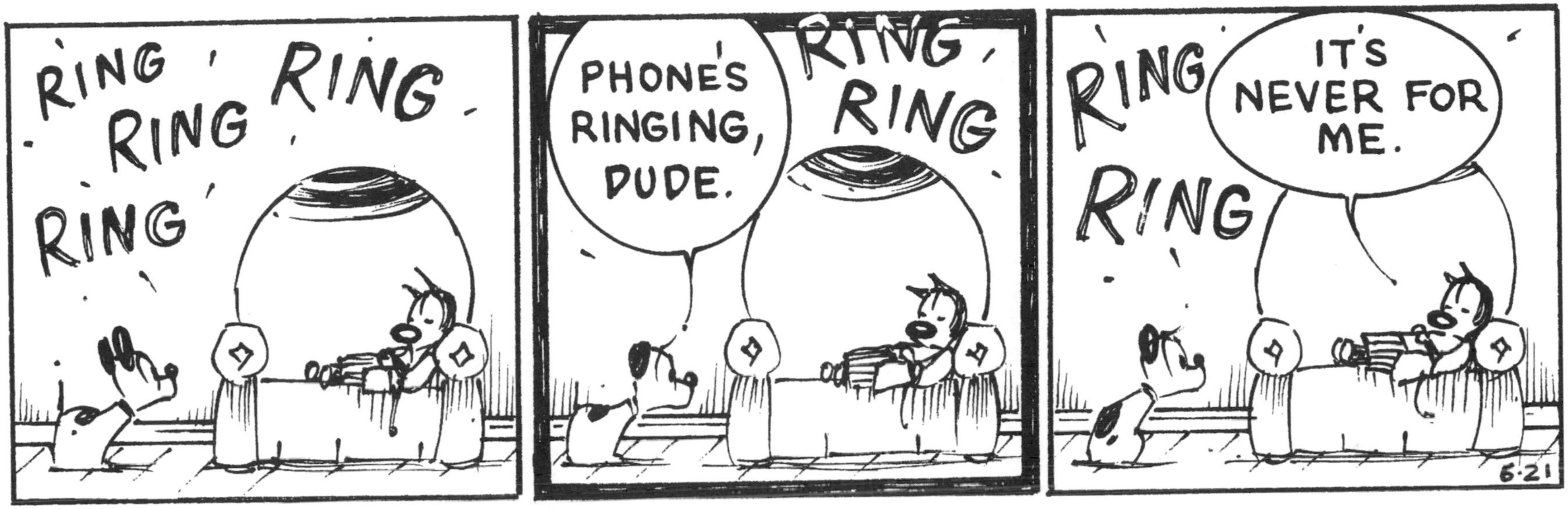
RING RING RING RING
PHONE'S RINGING, DUDE.
RING RING
RING RING
IT'S NEVER FOR ME.
6·21

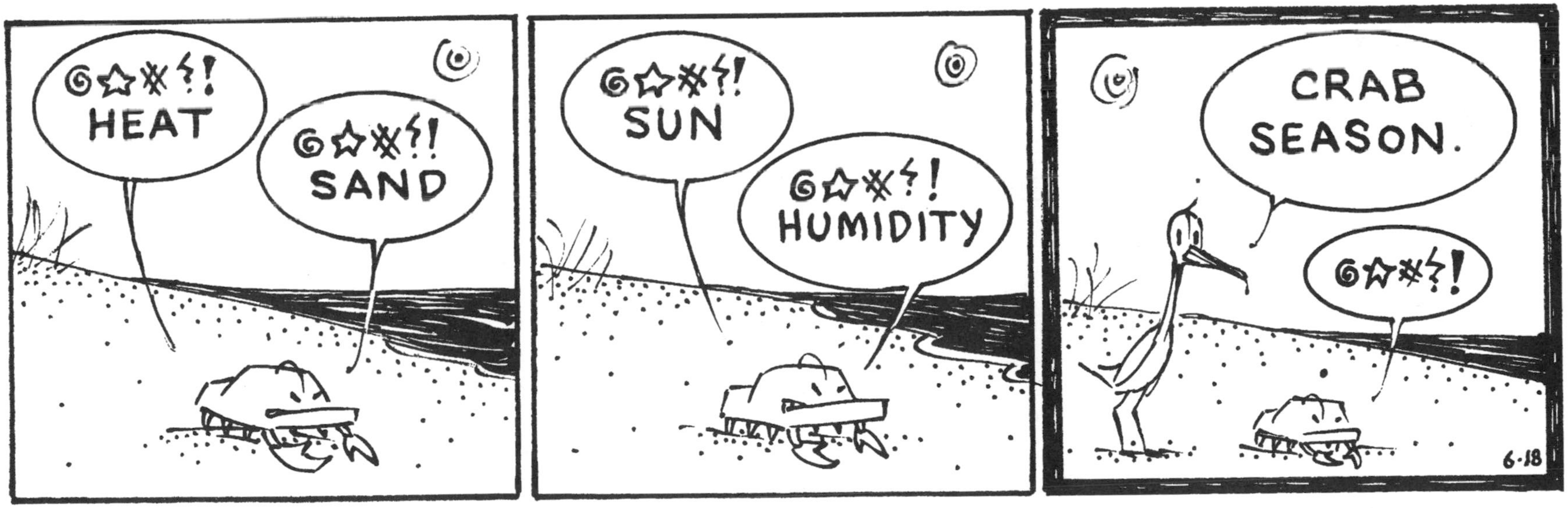
HEAT
SAND
SUN
HUMIDITY
CRAB SEASON.
6·18

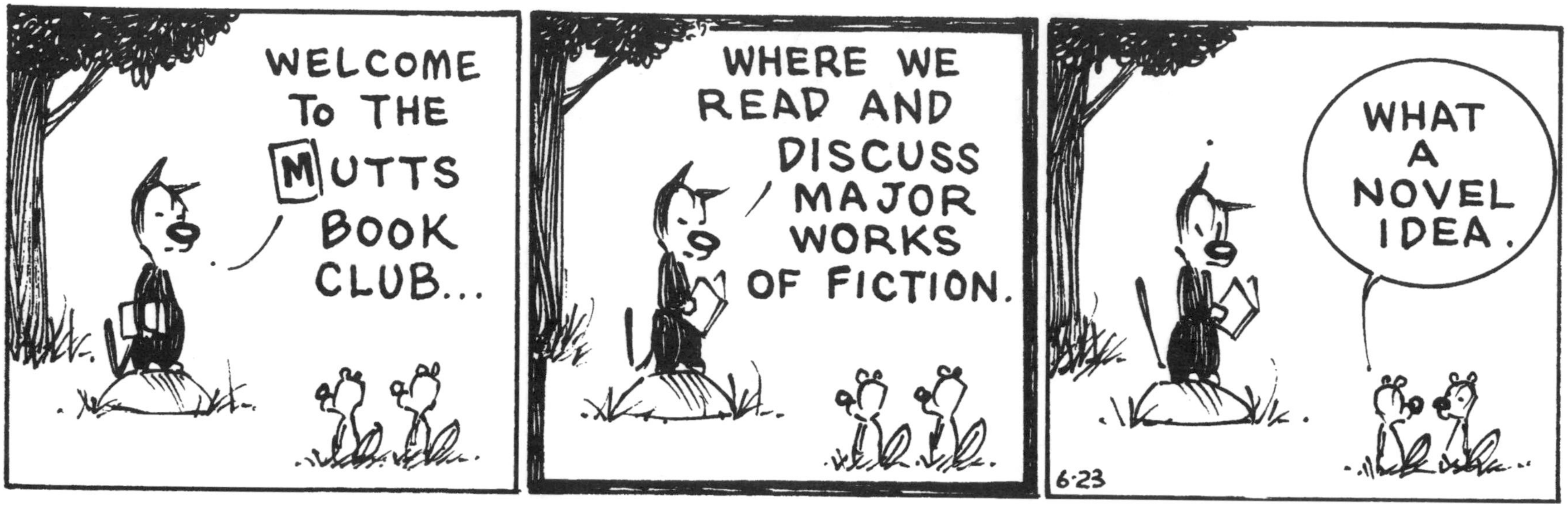
WELCOME TO THE MUTTS BOOK CLUB...
WHERE WE READ AND DISCUSS MAJOR WORKS OF FICTION.
WHAT A NOVEL IDEA.
6·23

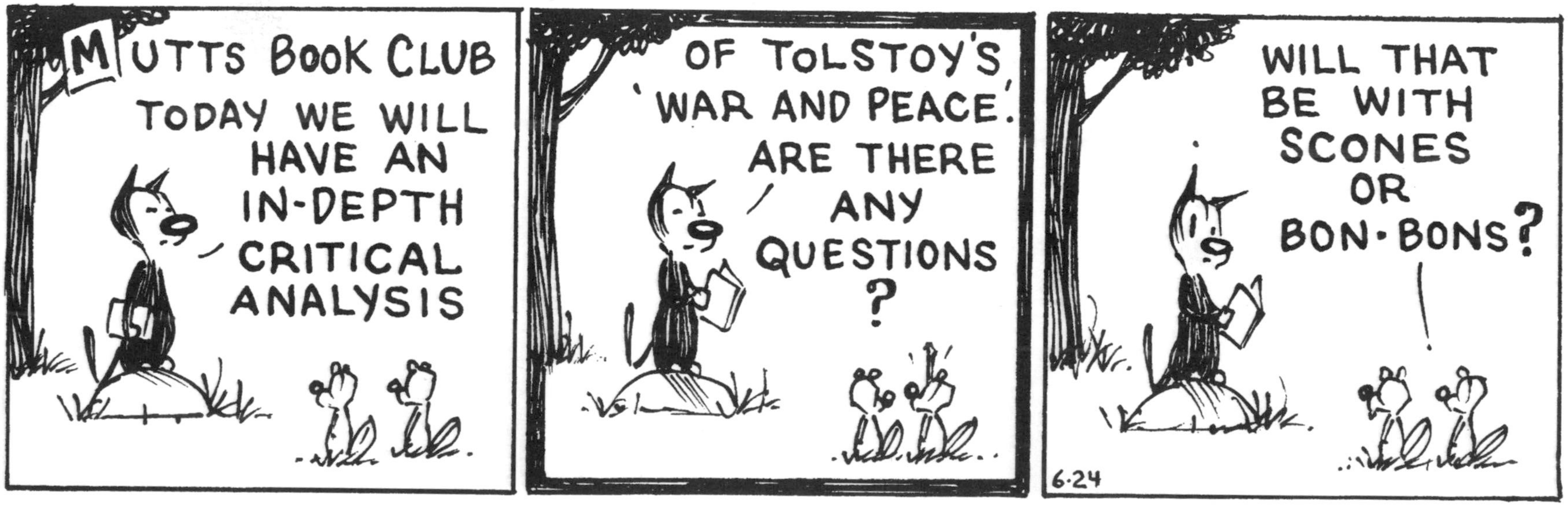
MUTTS BOOK CLUB
TODAY WE WILL HAVE AN IN-DEPTH CRITICAL ANALYSIS
OF TOLSTOY'S 'WAR AND PEACE'. ARE THERE ANY QUESTIONS?
WILL THAT BE WITH SCONES OR BON·BONS?
6·24

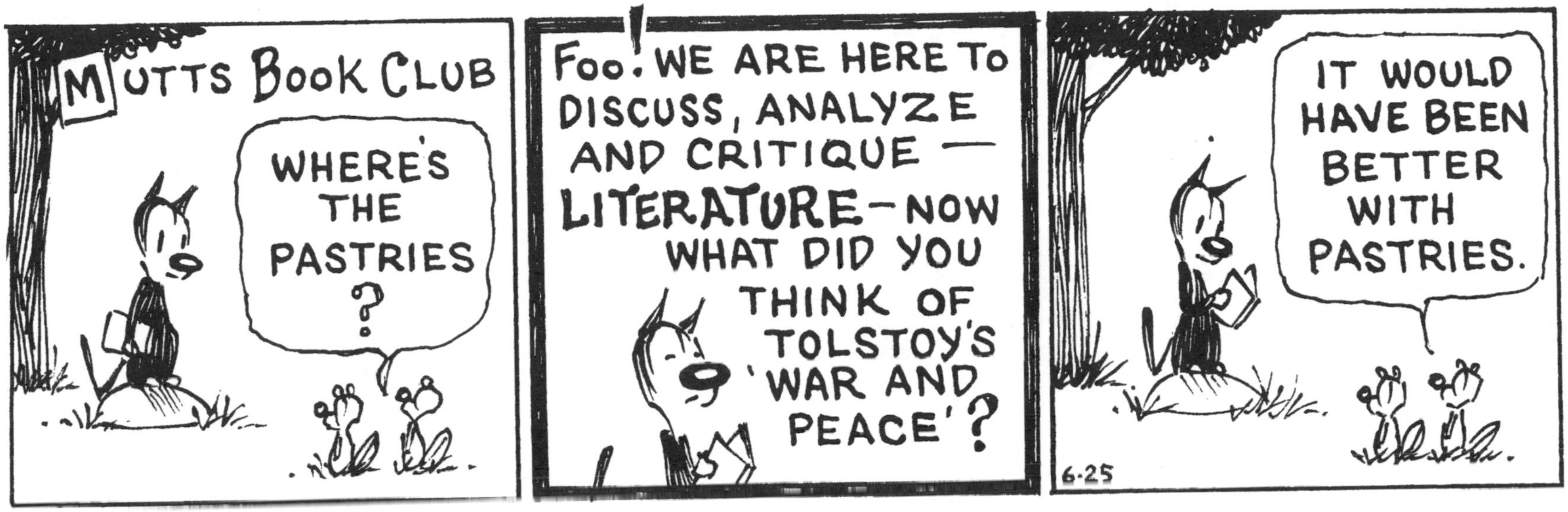
MUTTS BOOK CLUB
WHERE'S THE PASTRIES?
FOO! WE ARE HERE TO DISCUSS, ANALYZE AND CRITIQUE — LITERATURE — NOW WHAT DID YOU THINK OF TOLSTOY'S 'WAR AND PEACE'?
IT WOULD HAVE BEEN BETTER WITH PASTRIES.
6·25

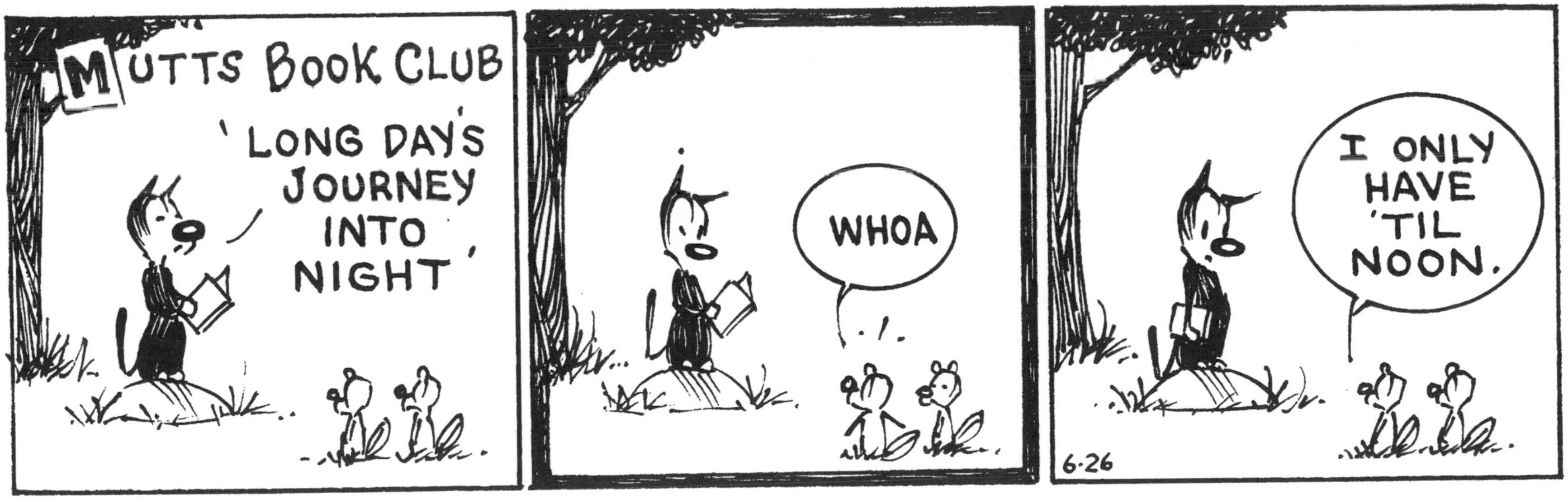
MUTTS BOOK CLUB
'LONG DAY'S JOURNEY INTO NIGHT'
WHOA
I ONLY HAVE 'TIL NOON.
6·26

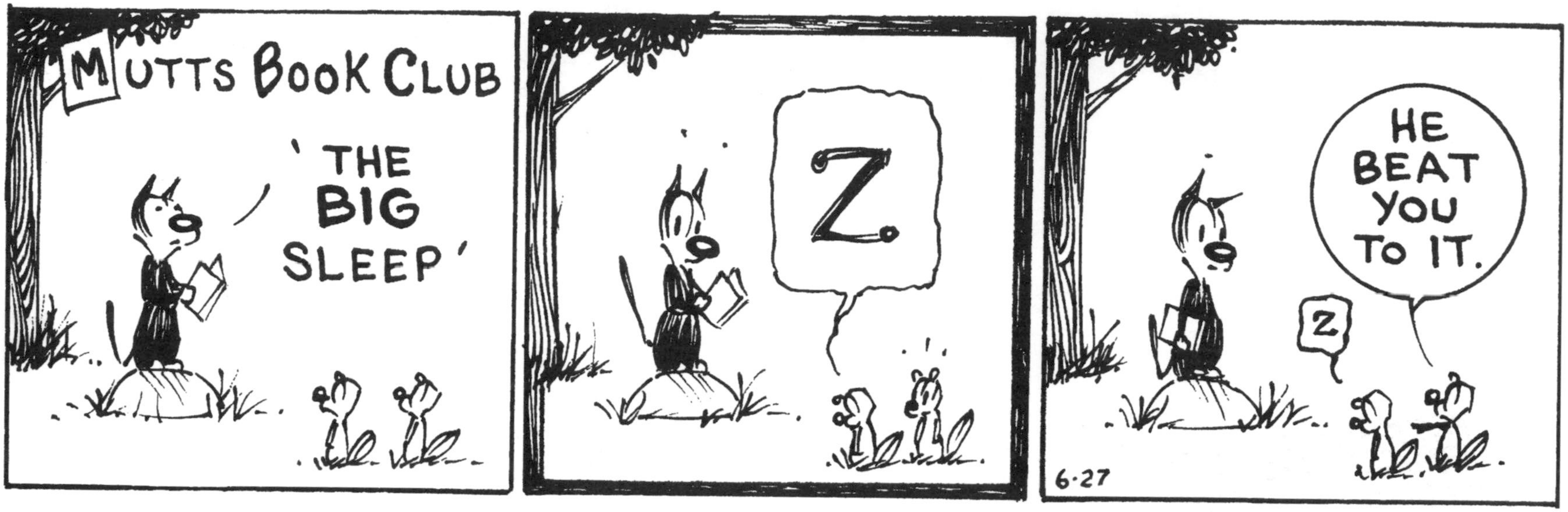
MUTTS BOOK CLUB
'THE BIG SLEEP'
Z.
Z
HE BEAT YOU TO IT.
6·27

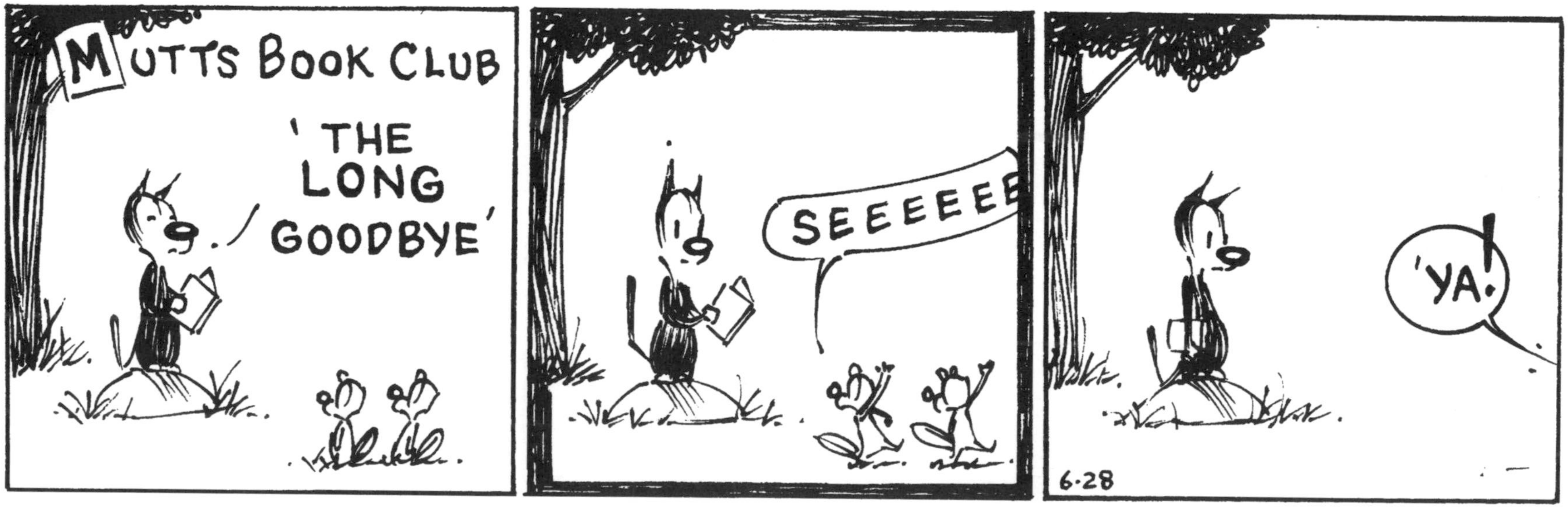
MUTTS BOOK CLUB
'THE LONG GOODBYE'
SEEEEEEE
'YA!
6·28

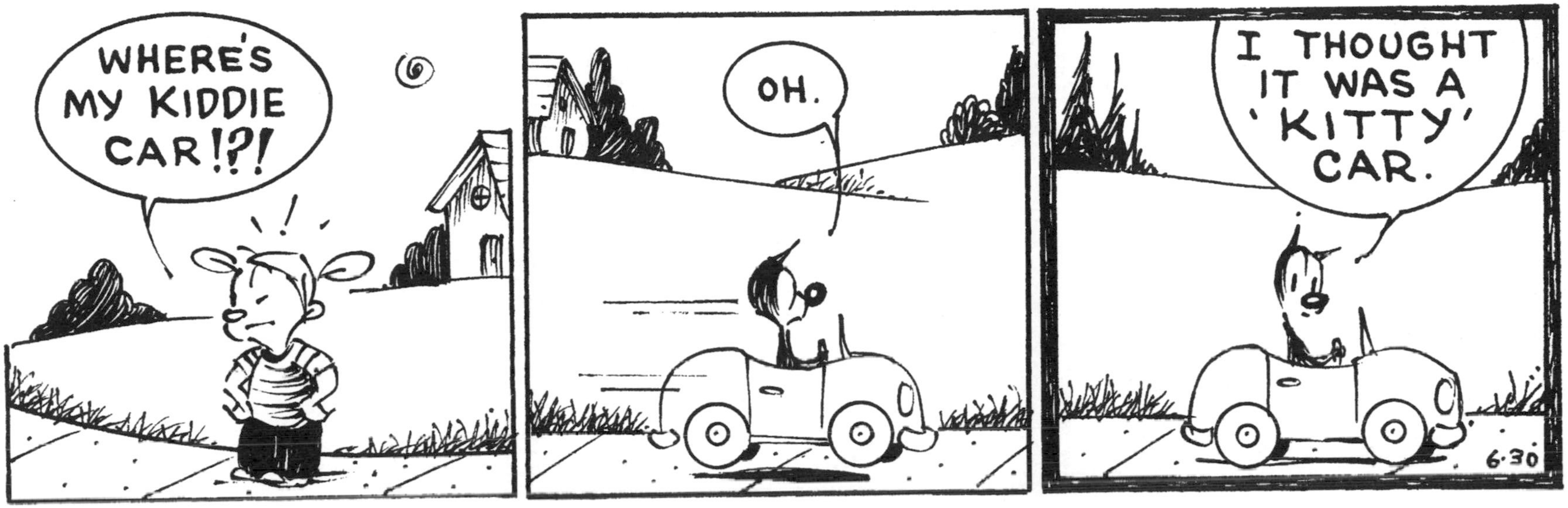
WHERE'S MY KIDDIE CAR!?!
OH.
I THOUGHT IT WAS A 'KITTY' CAR.
6·30

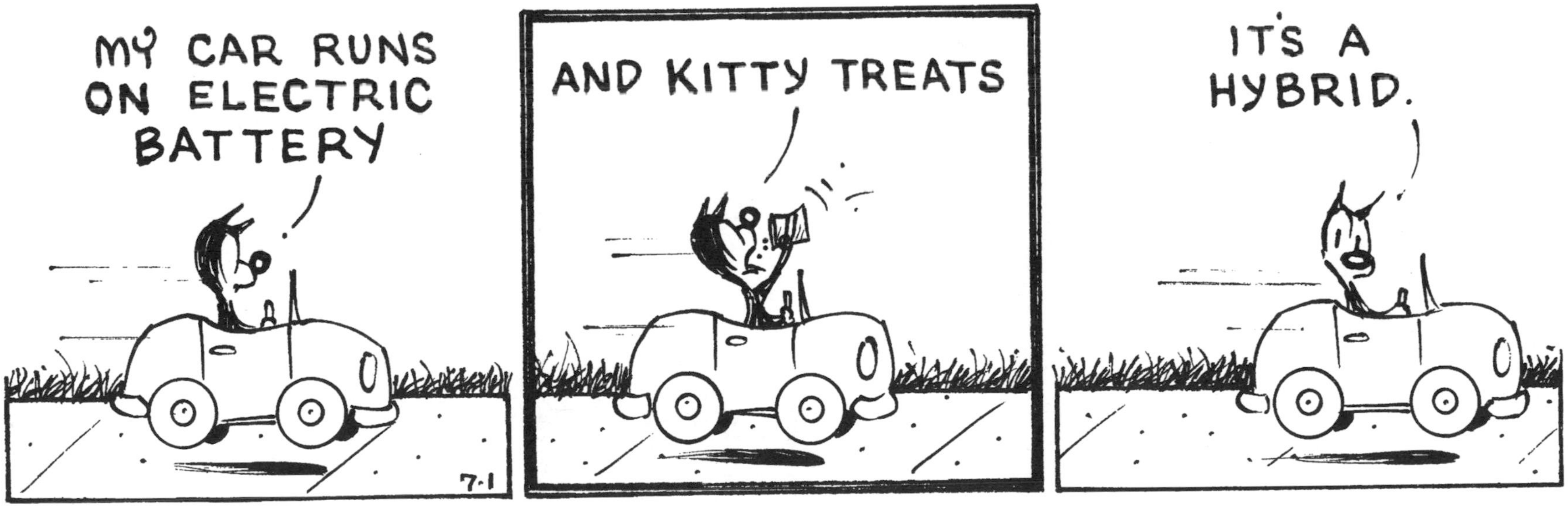
MY CAR RUNS ON ELECTRIC BATTERY
AND KITTY TREATS
IT'S A HYBRID.
7·1

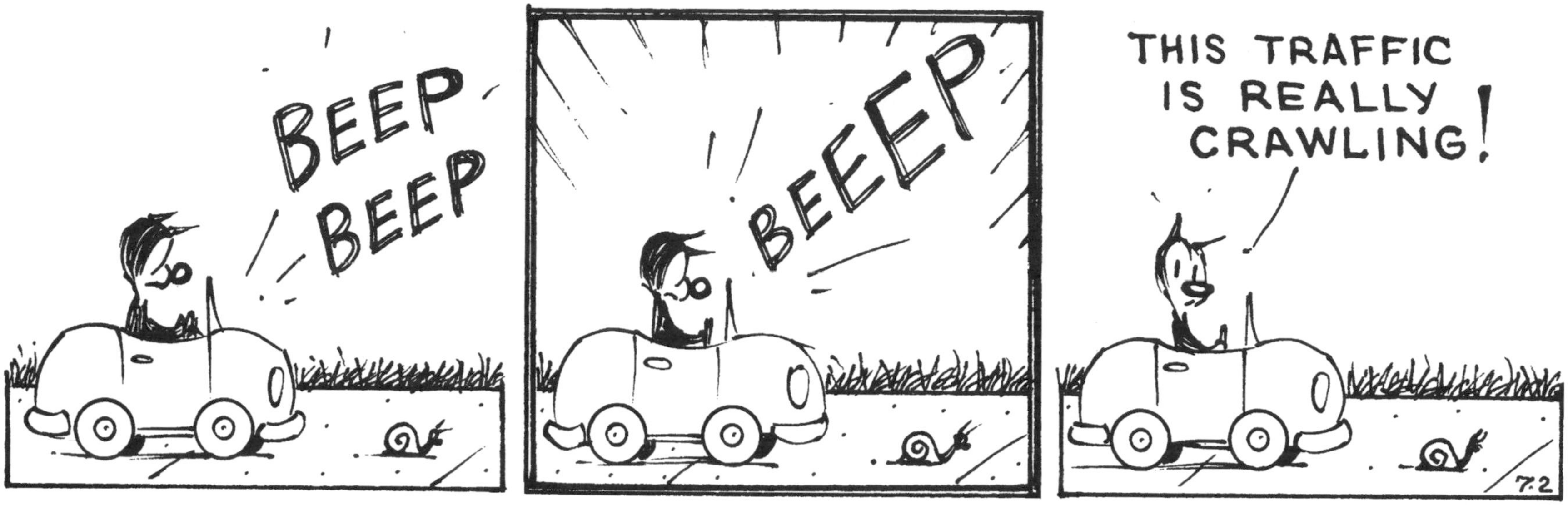
BEEP BEEP
BEEEP
THIS TRAFFIC IS REALLY CRAWLING!
7-2

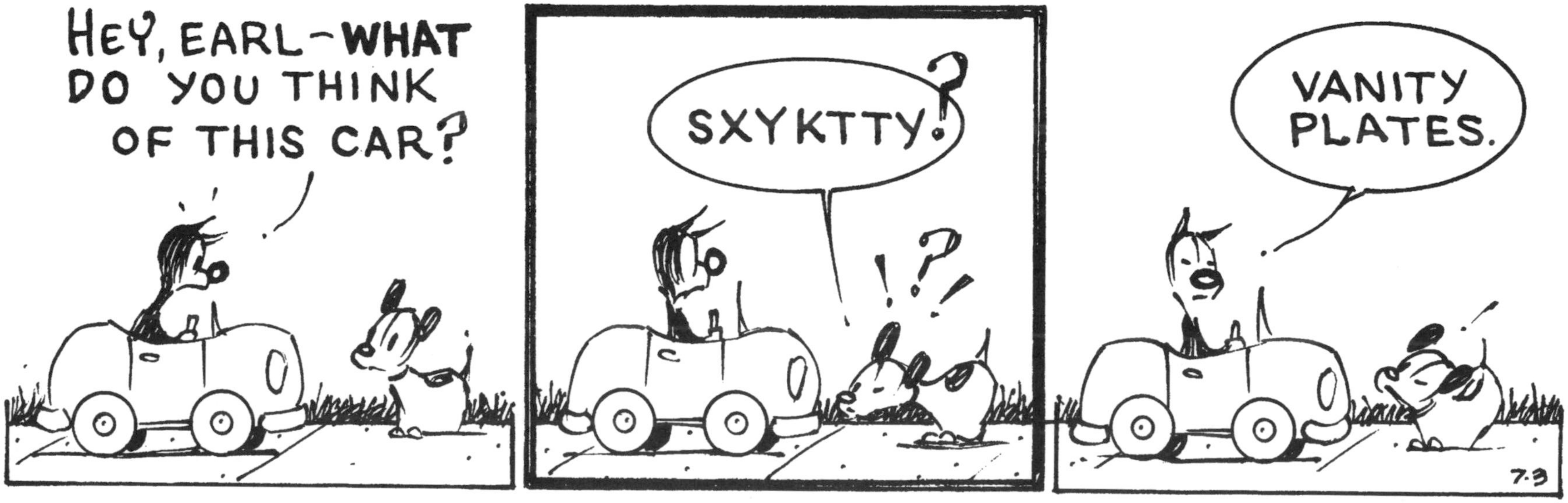
HEY, EARL–**WHAT** DO YOU THINK OF THIS CAR?
SXYKTTY?!
!?!
VANITY PLATES.
7-3

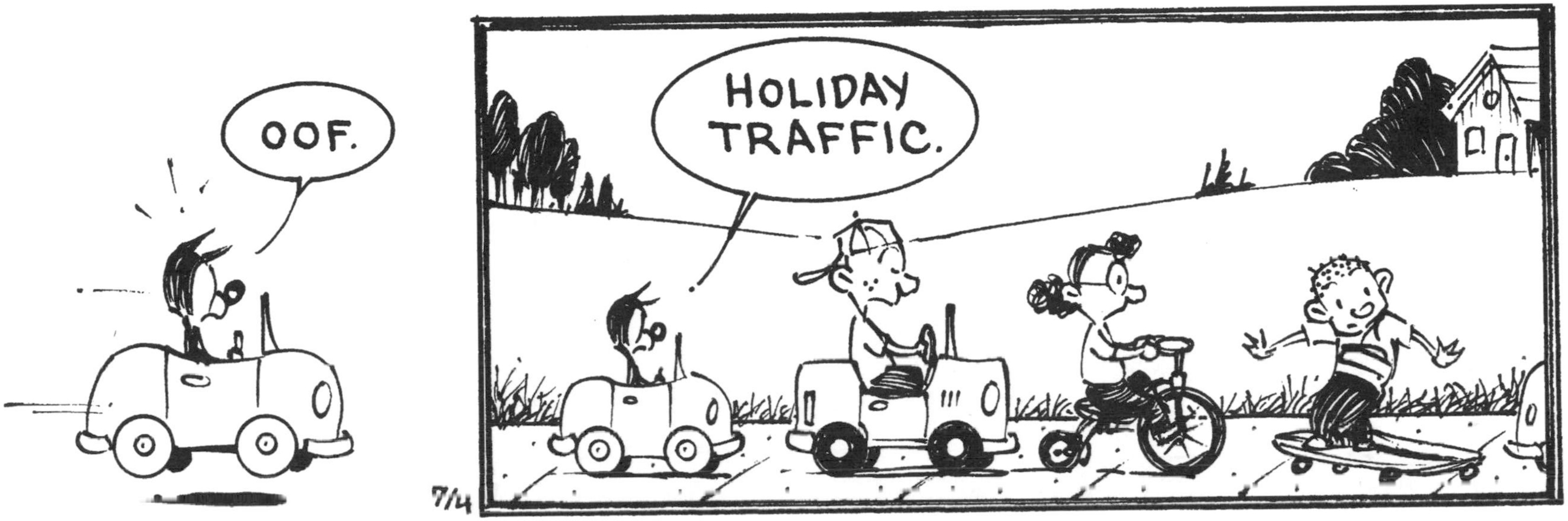
OOF.
HOLIDAY TRAFFIC.
7/4

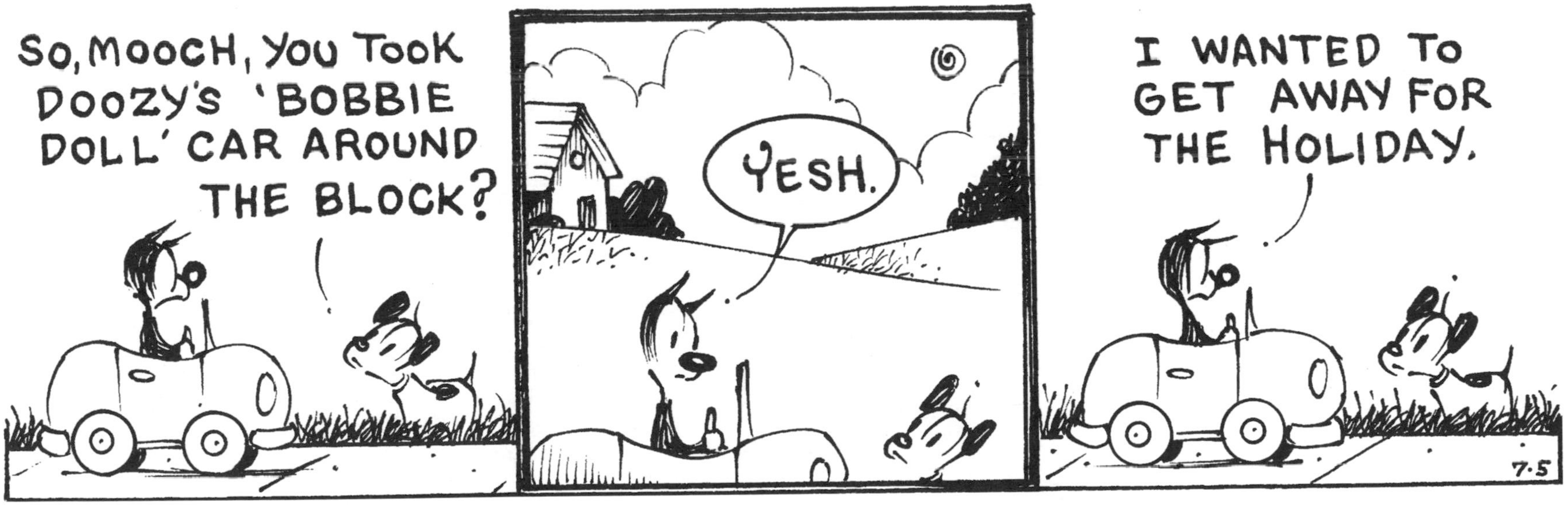
SO, MOOCH, YOU TOOK DOOZY'S 'BOBBIE DOLL' CAR AROUND THE BLOCK?
YESH.
I WANTED TO GET AWAY FOR THE HOLIDAY.
7·5

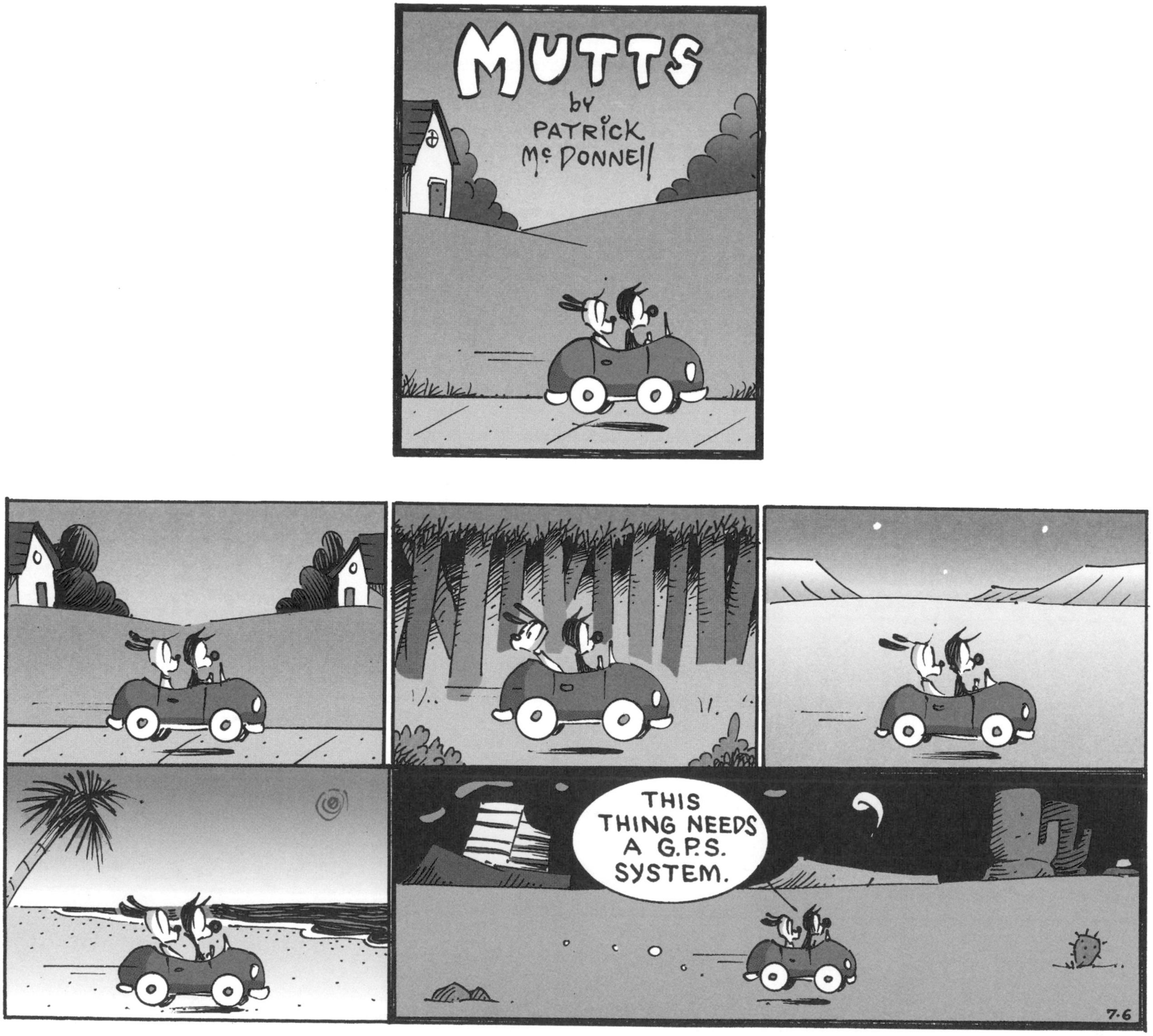
MUTTS
by PATRICK McDONNELL
THIS THING NEEDS A G.P.S. SYSTEM.
7-6

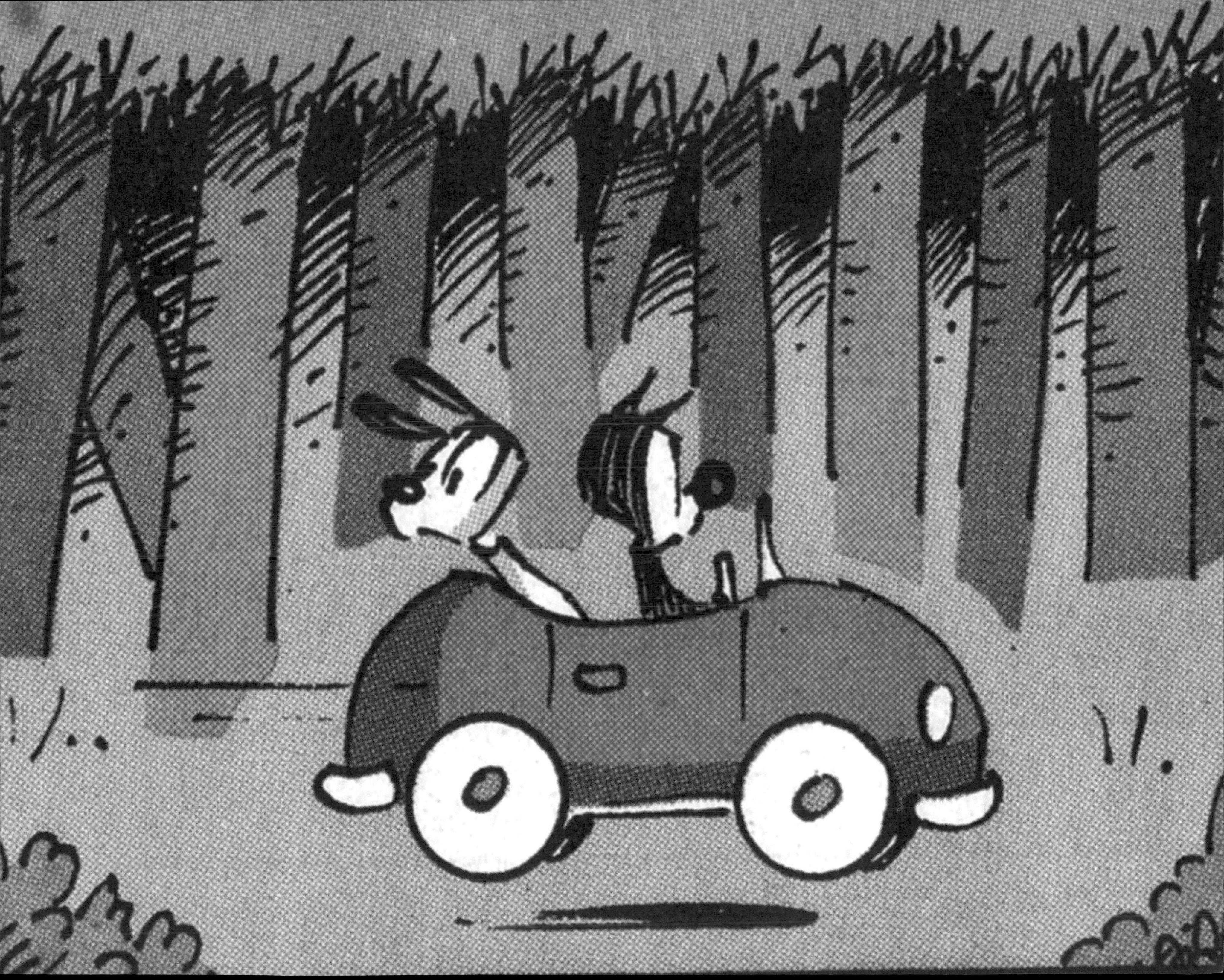

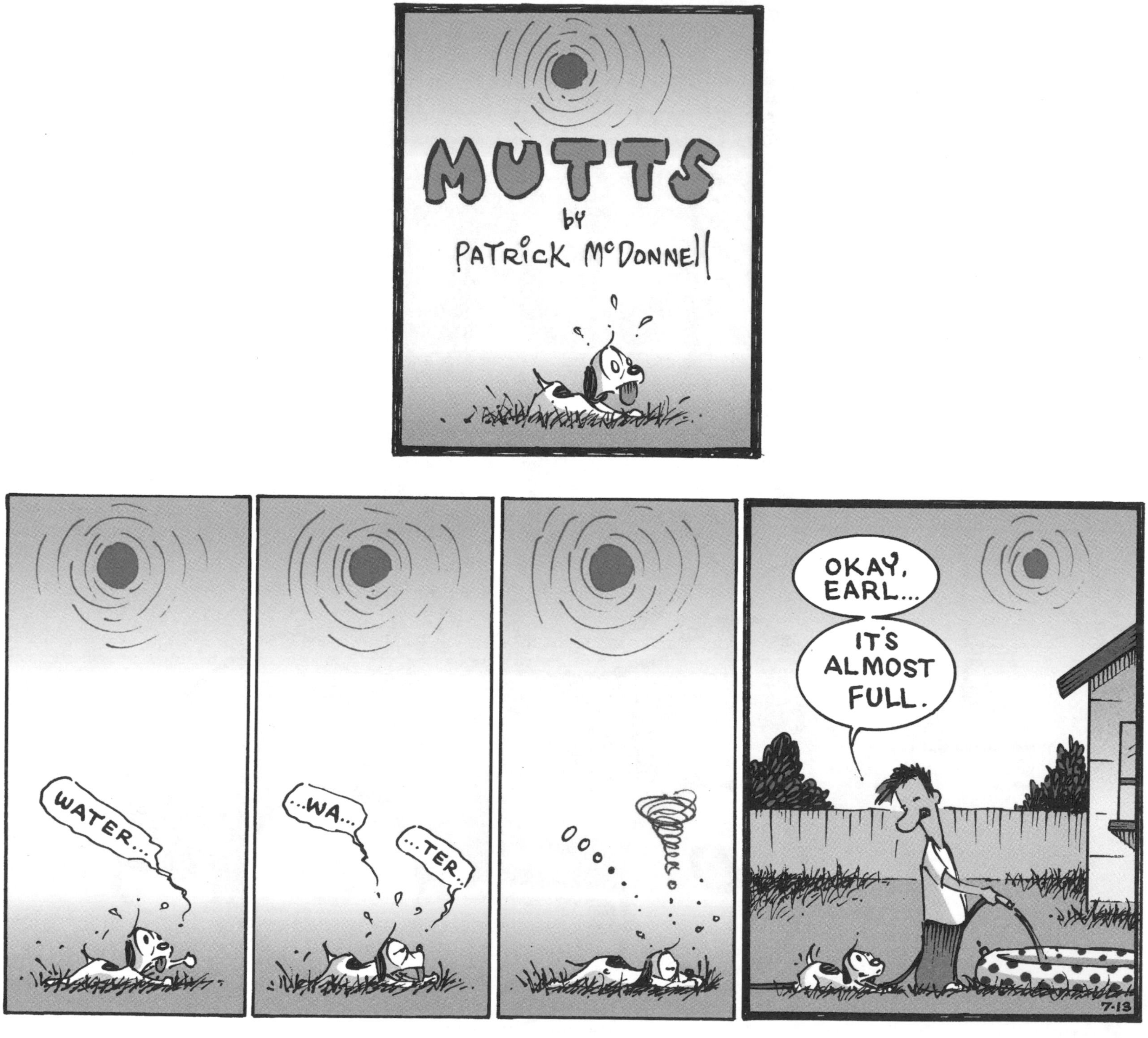
MUTTS
by
PATRICK McDONNELL
WATER....
...WA...
...TER...
OKAY, EARL...
IT'S ALMOST FULL.
7-13

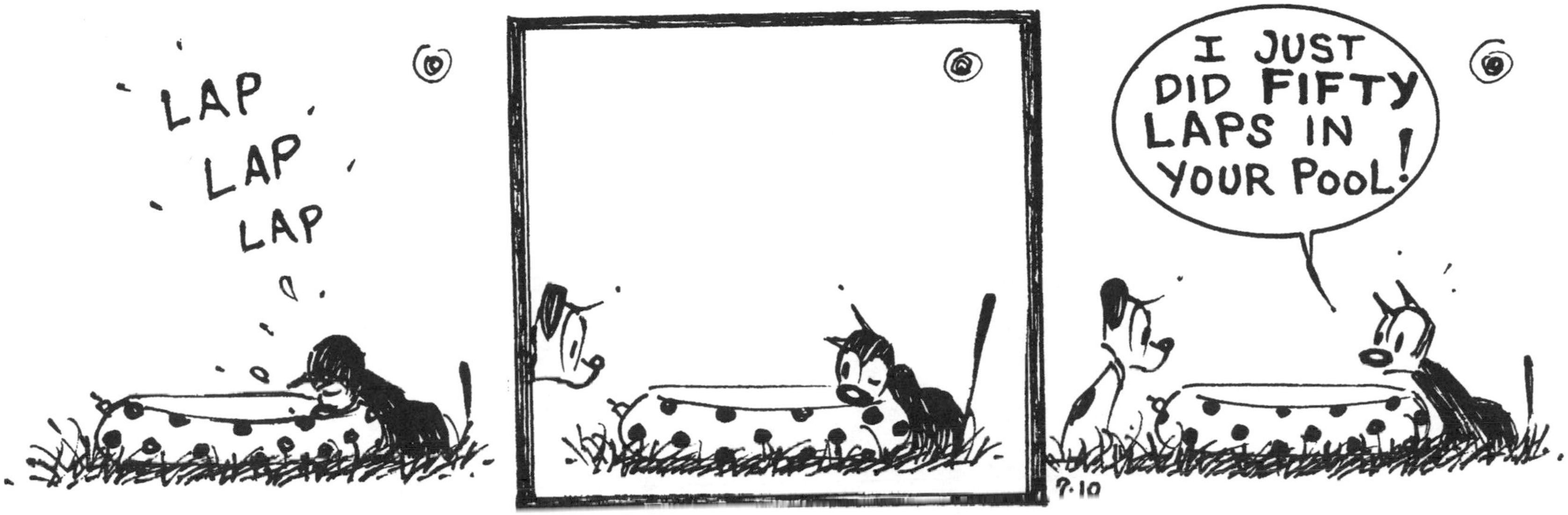
LAP
LAP
LAP
I JUST DID FIFTY LAPS IN YOUR POOL!
7-10

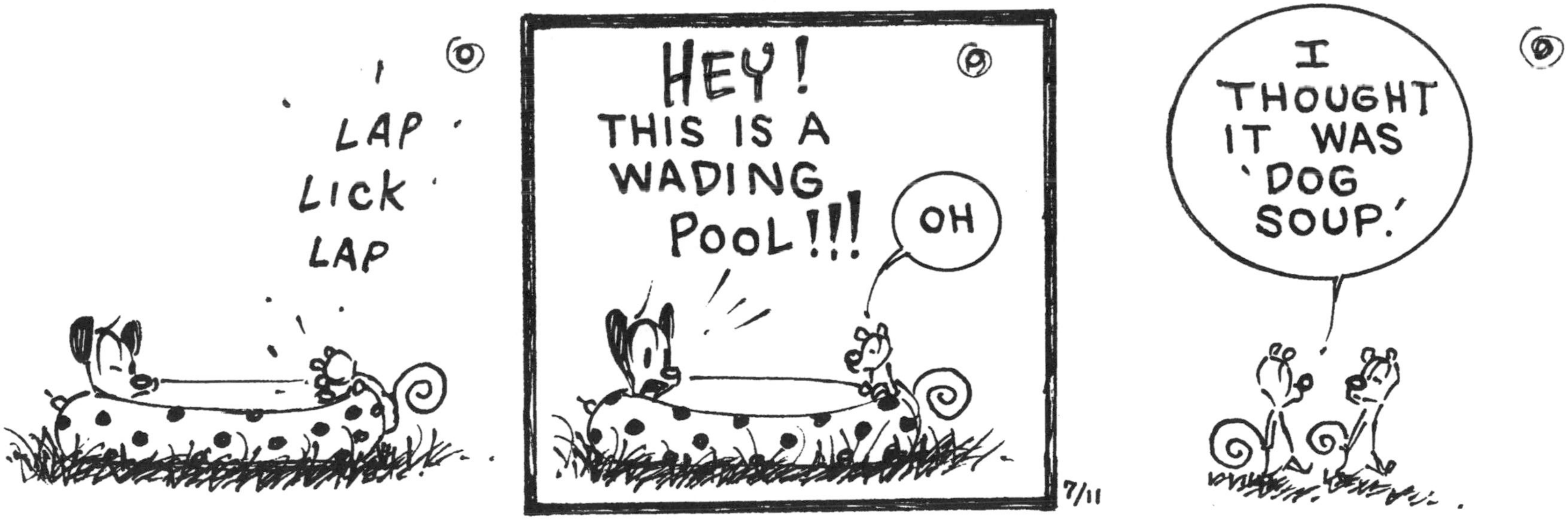
LAP
LICK
LAP
HEY! THIS IS A WADING POOL!!!
OH
7/11
I THOUGHT IT WAS 'DOG SOUP.'

Z Z Z Z
I NEED TO TURN MY LIFE AROUND!
7-20
Z Z Z Z

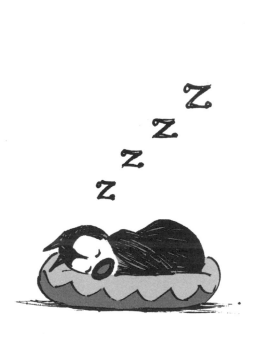

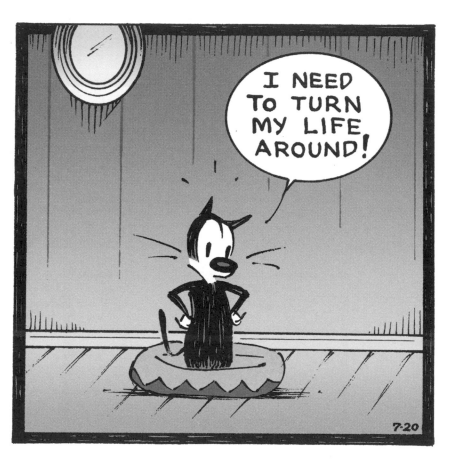

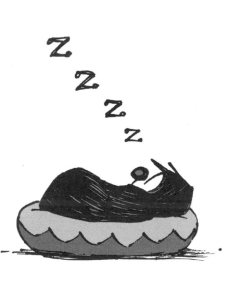

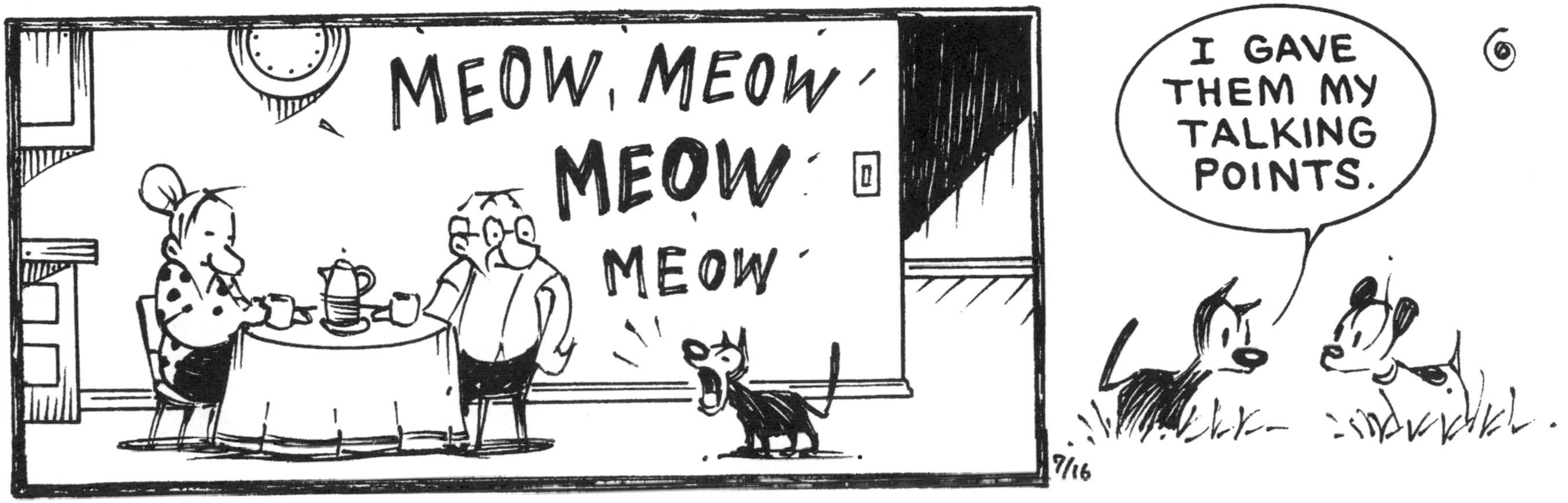
MEOW, MEOW
MEOW
MEOW
I GAVE THEM MY TALKING POINTS.
7/16

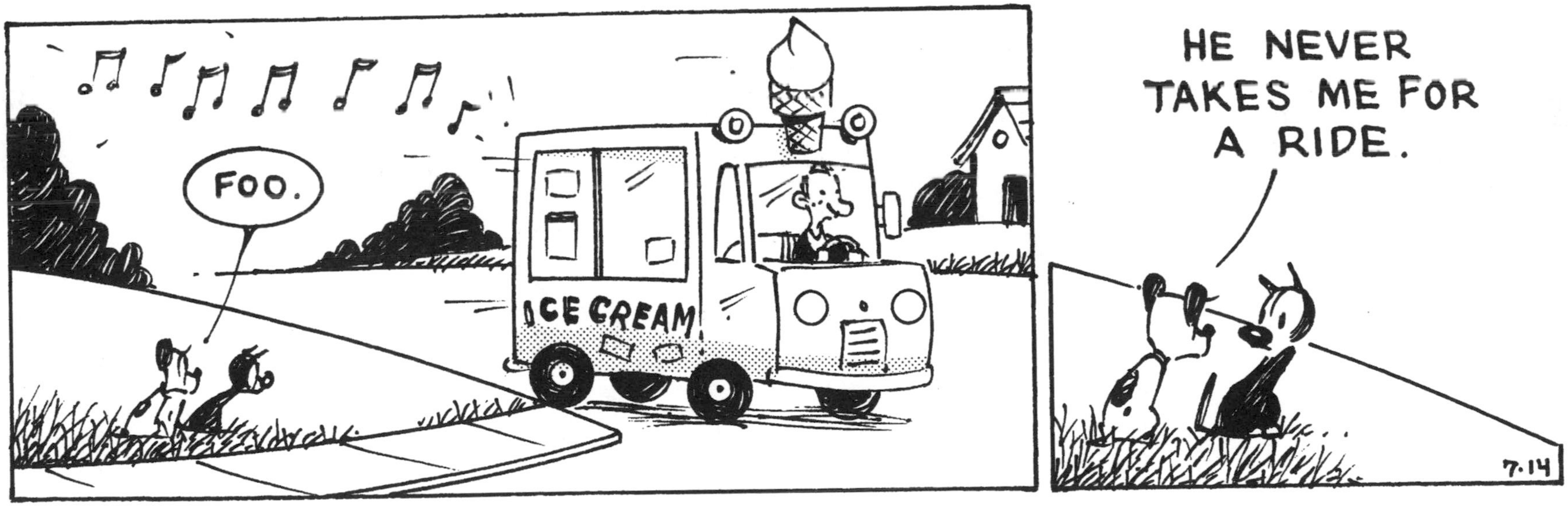
FOO.
ICE CREAM
HE NEVER TAKES ME FOR A RIDE.
7.14

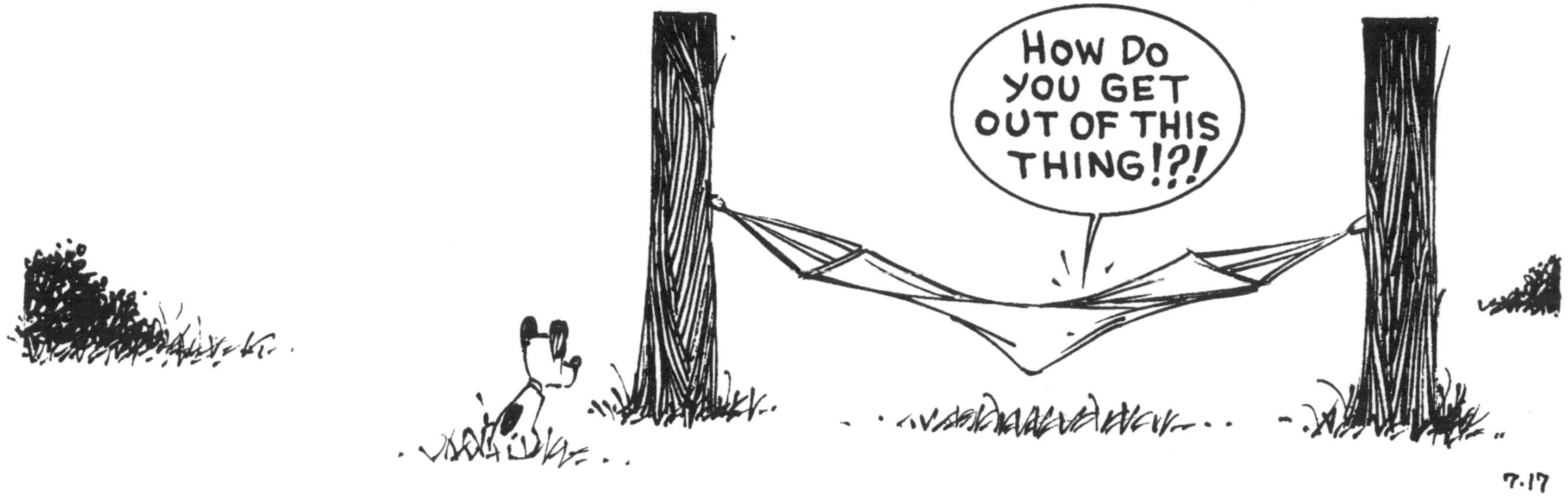
HOW DO YOU GET OUT OF THIS THING!?!
7.17

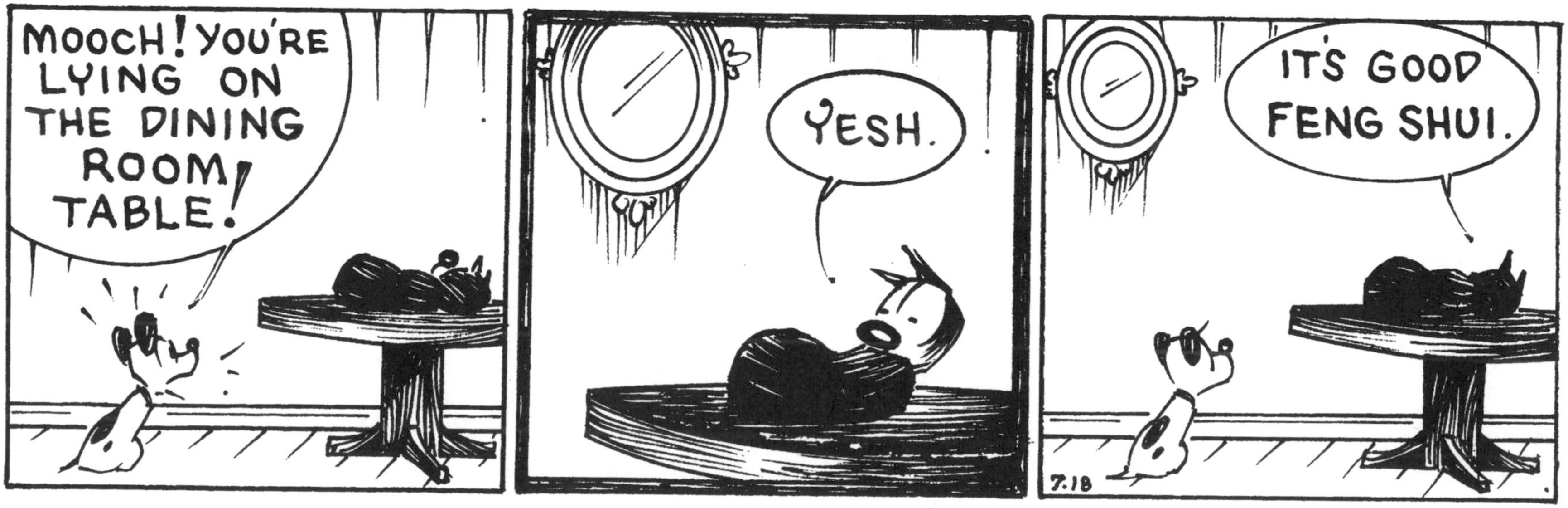
MOOCH! YOU'RE LYING ON THE DINING ROOM TABLE!
YESH.
IT'S GOOD FENG SHUI.
7.18

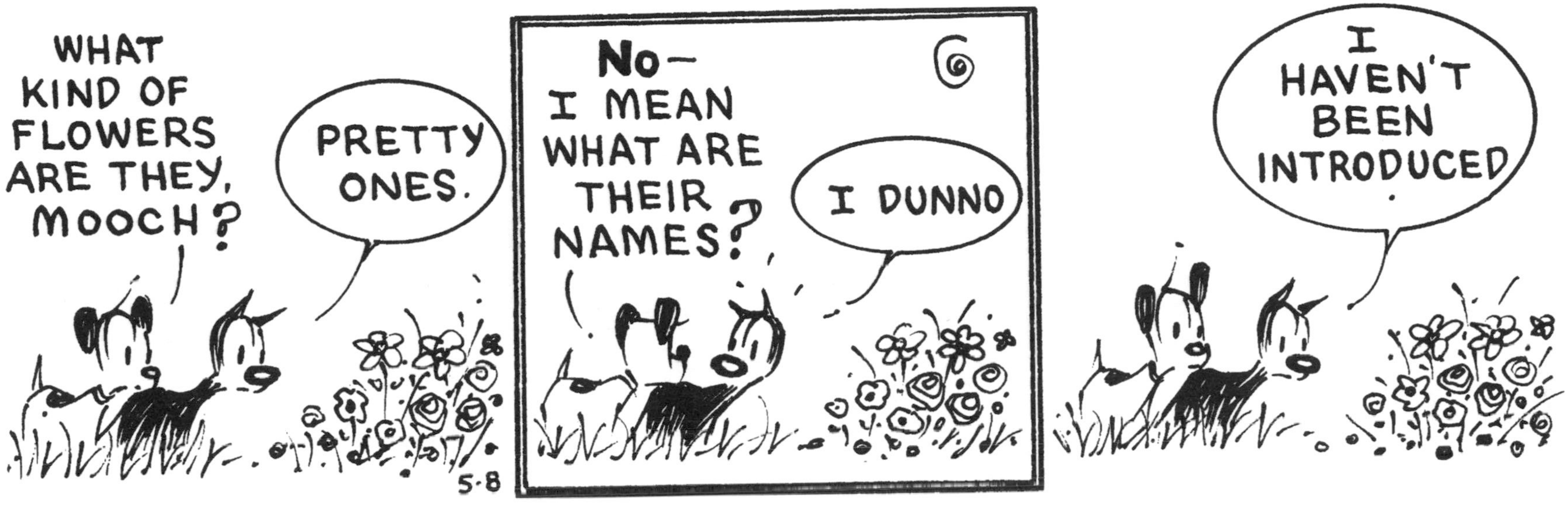
WHAT KIND OF FLOWERS ARE THEY, MOOCH?
PRETTY ONES.
5·8
No— I MEAN WHAT ARE THEIR NAMES?
I DUNNO
I HAVEN'T BEEN INTRODUCED.

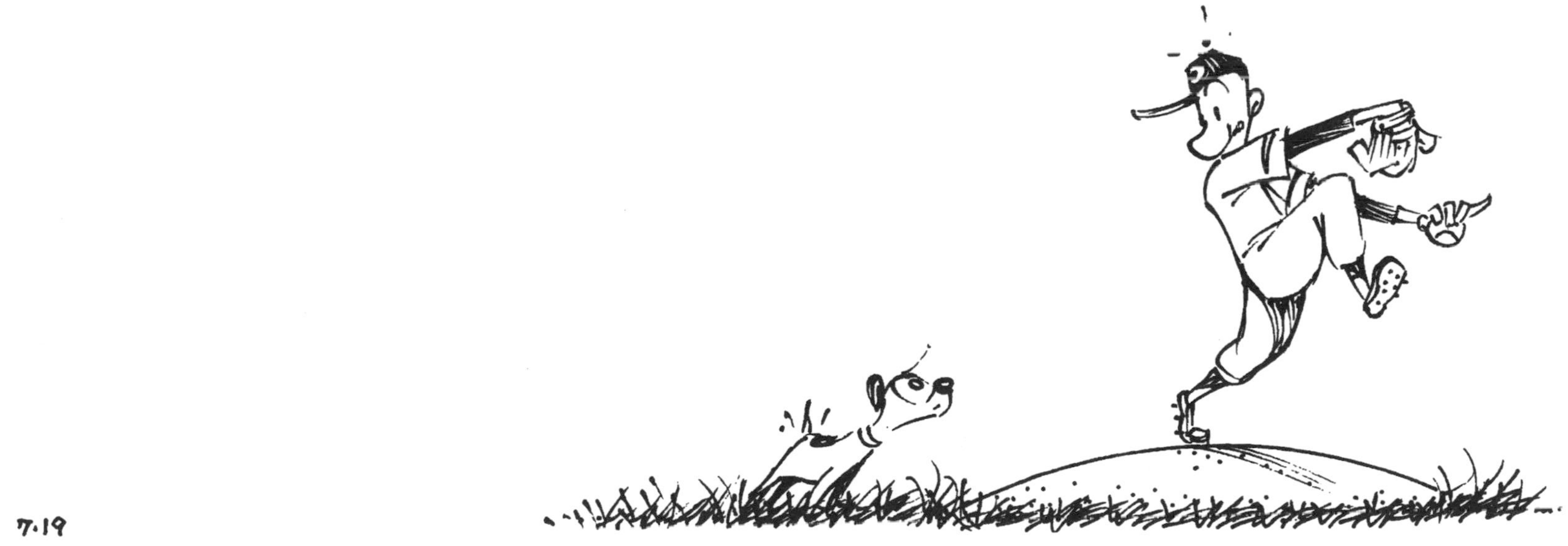
7·19

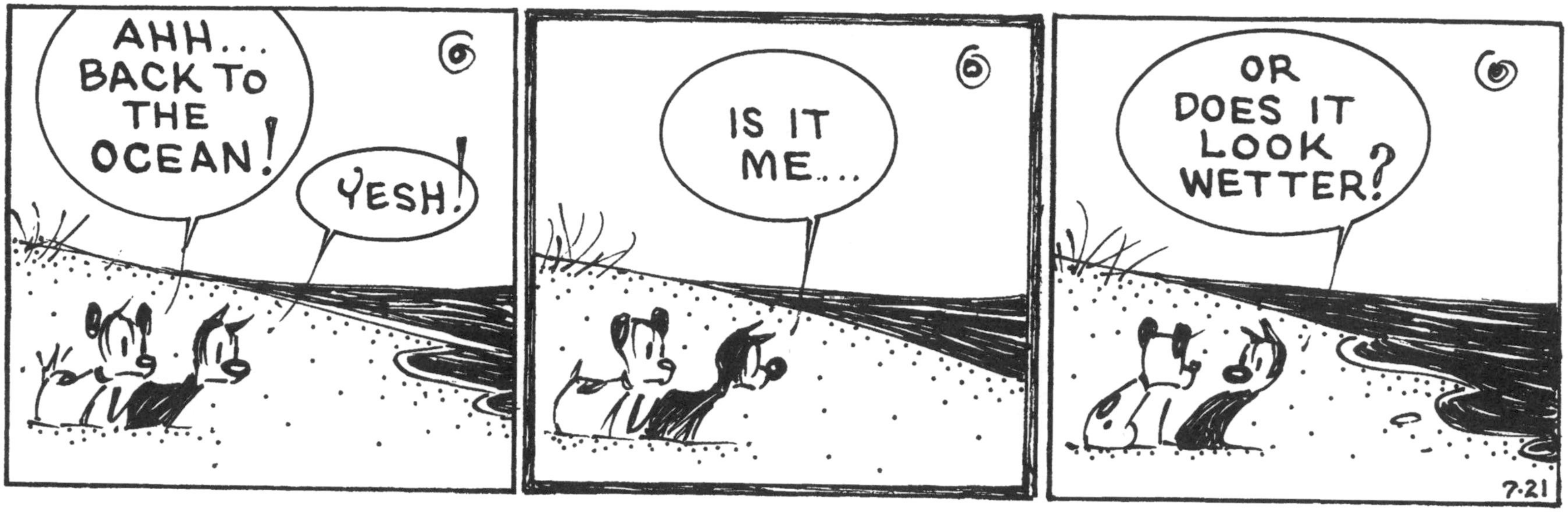
AHH... BACK TO THE OCEAN!
YESH!
IS IT ME...
OR DOES IT LOOK WETTER?
7·21

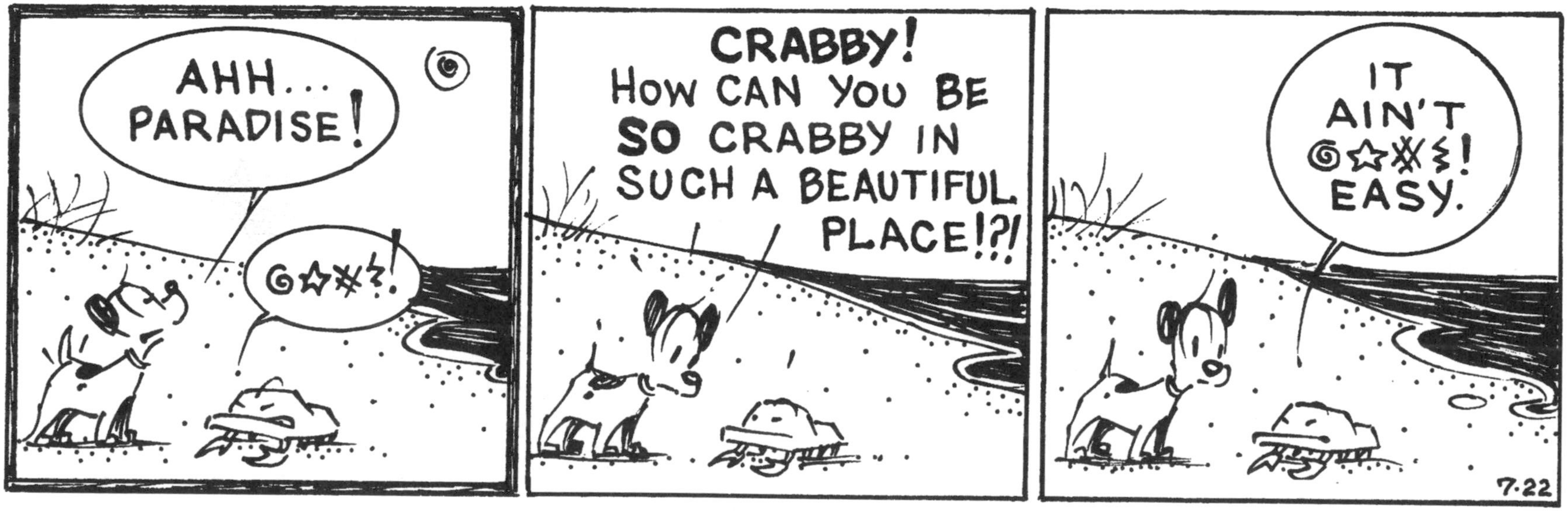
AHH... PARADISE!
CRABBY! HOW CAN YOU BE SO CRABBY IN SUCH A BEAUTIFUL PLACE!?!
IT AIN'T
EASY.
7·22

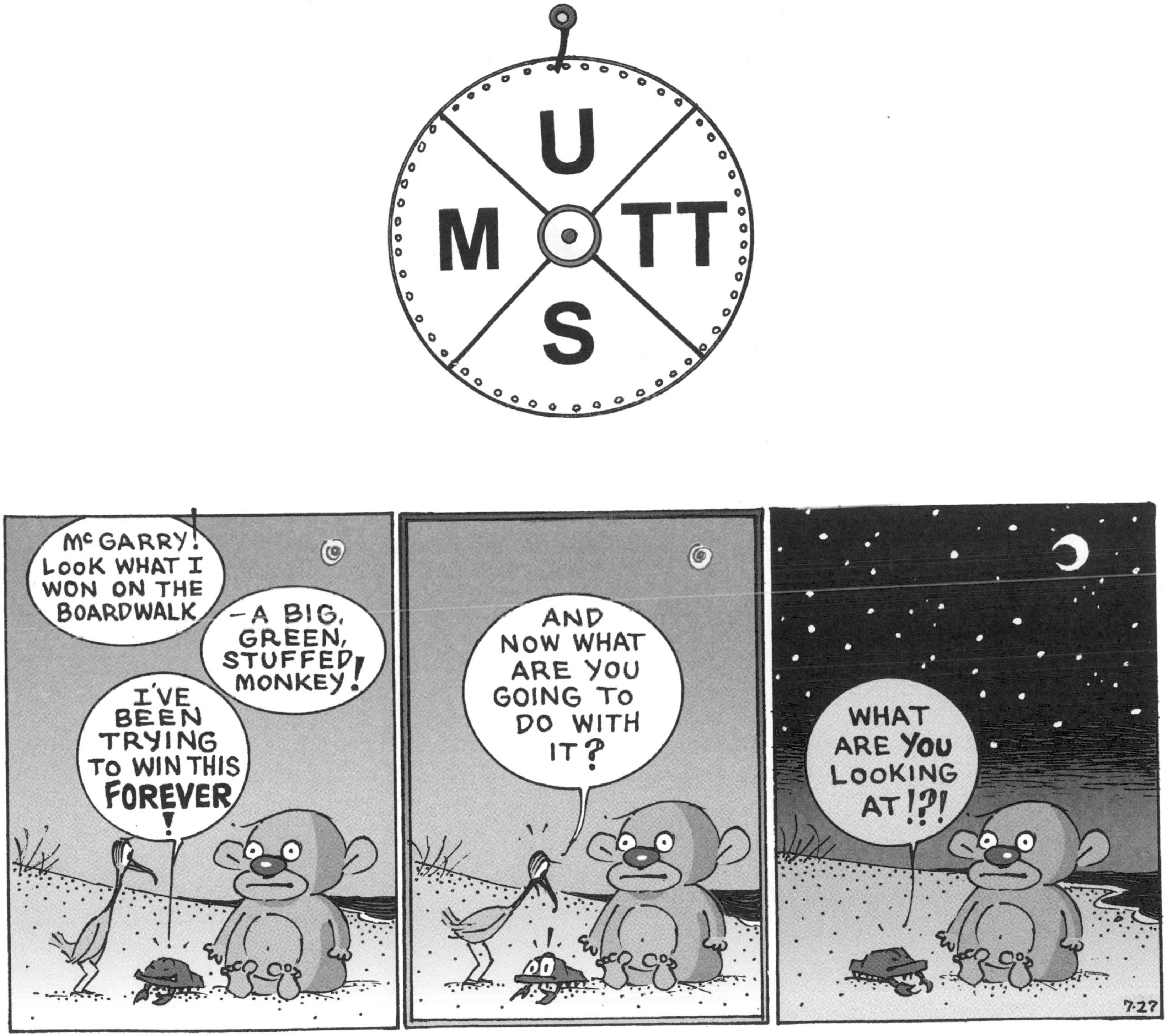
MUTTS
McGARRY! LOOK WHAT I WON ON THE BOARDWALK
—A BIG, GREEN, STUFFED MONKEY!
I'VE BEEN TRYING TO WIN THIS FOREVER!
AND NOW WHAT ARE YOU GOING TO DO WITH IT?
WHAT ARE YOU LOOKING AT!?!
7·27

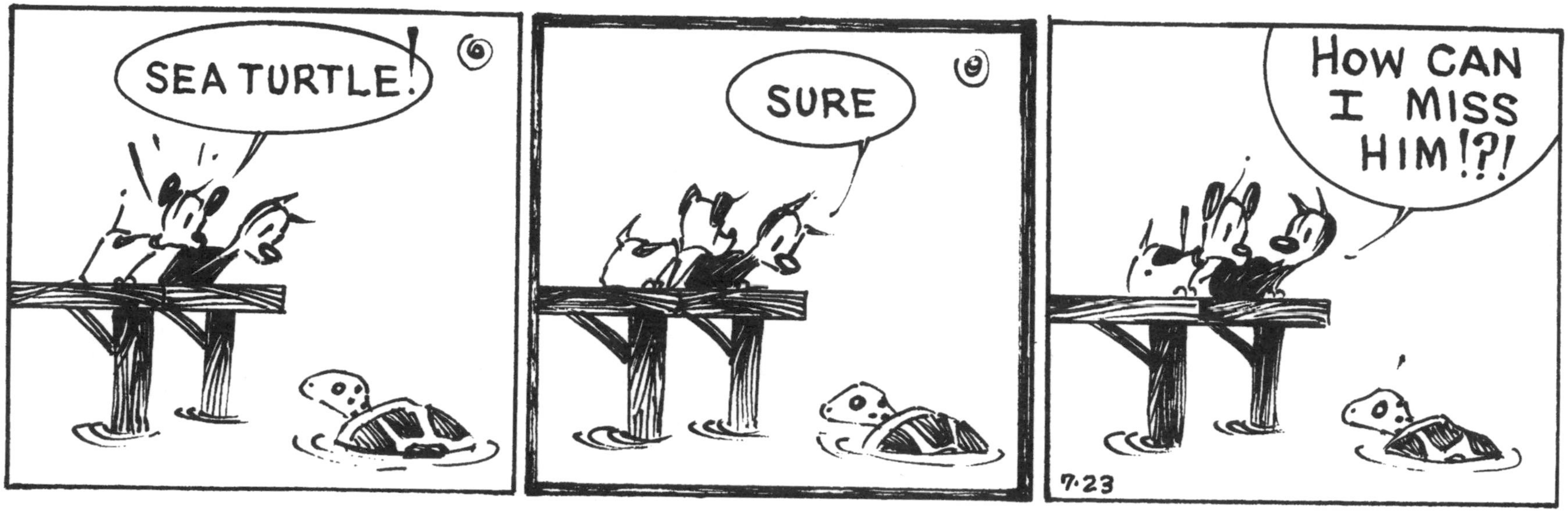
SEA TURTLE!
SURE
HOW CAN I MISS HIM!?!
7·23

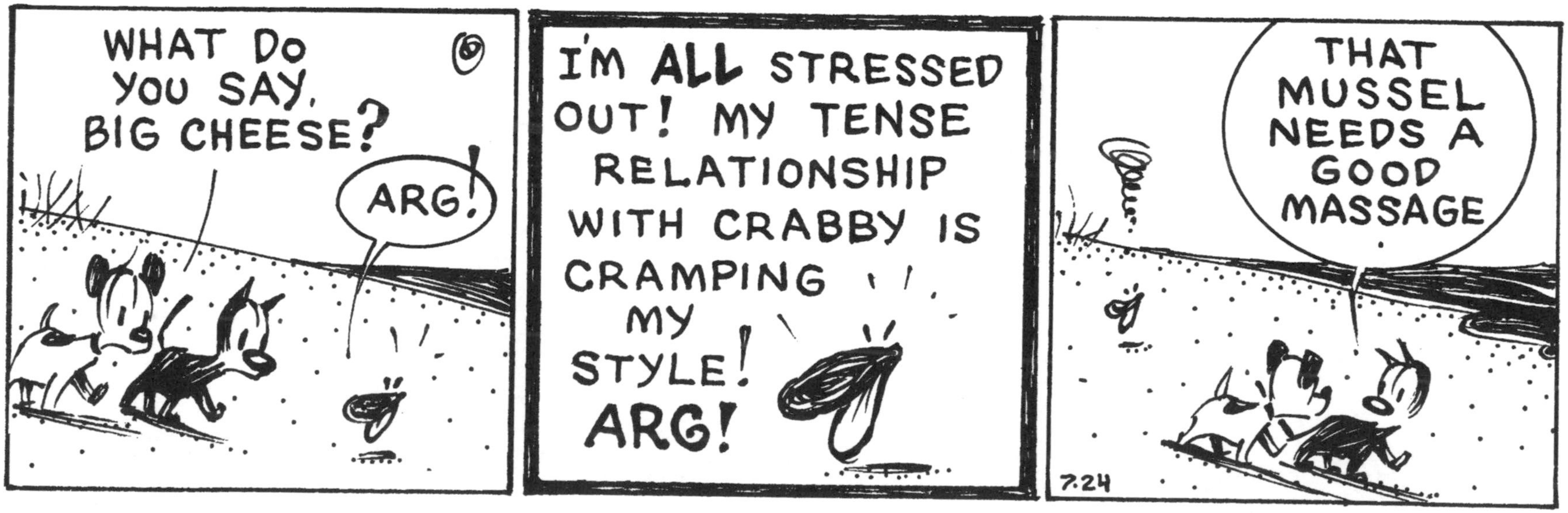
WHAT DO YOU SAY, BIG CHEESE?
ARG!
I'M ALL STRESSED OUT! MY TENSE RELATIONSHIP WITH CRABBY IS CRAMPING MY STYLE! ARG!
THAT MUSSEL NEEDS A GOOD MASSAGE
7·24

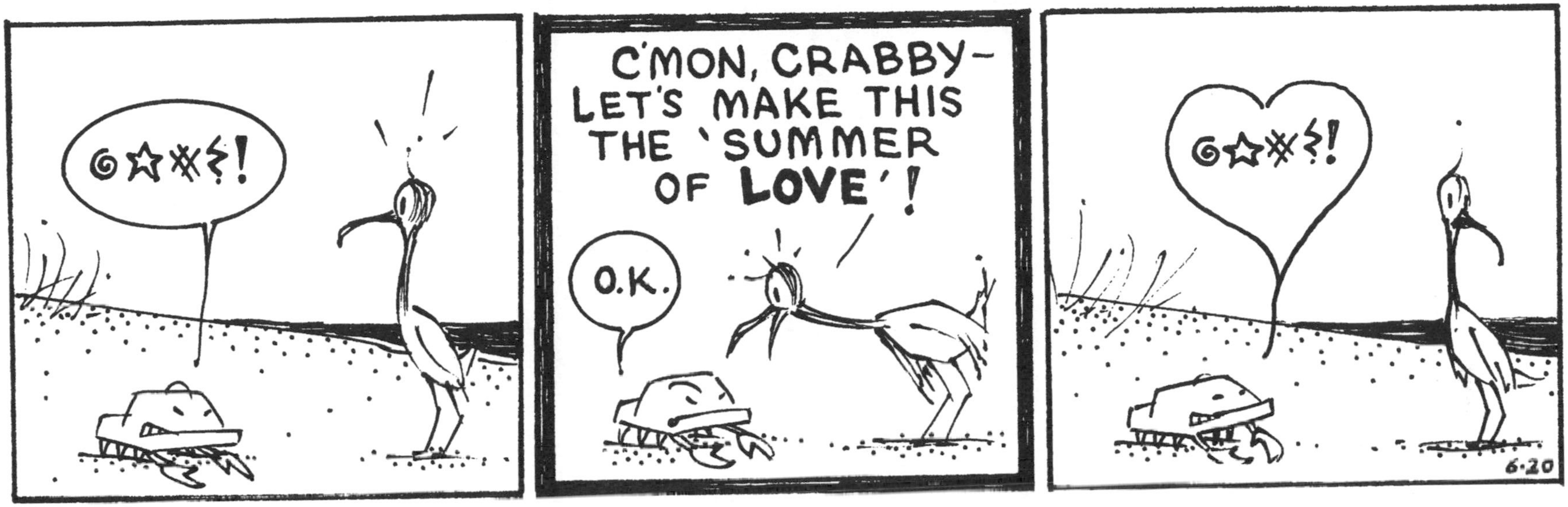
C'MON, CRABBY-
LET'S MAKE THIS
THE 'SUMMER
OF **LOVE**'!
O.K.
6·20

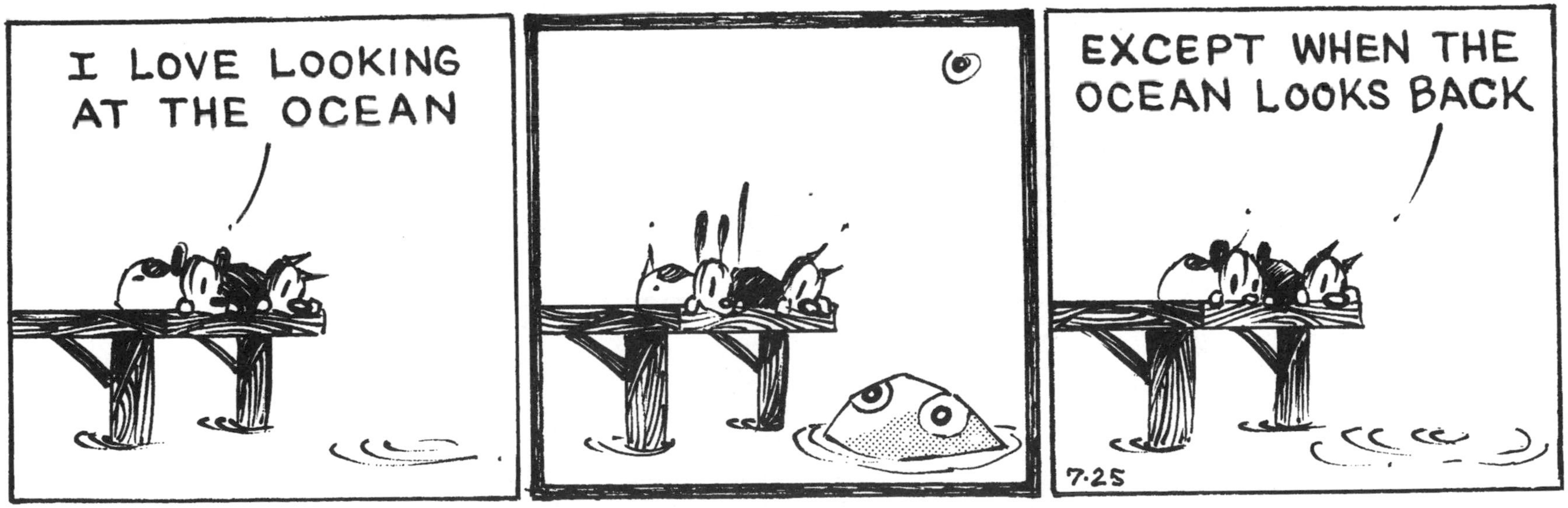
I LOVE LOOKING
AT THE OCEAN
EXCEPT WHEN THE
OCEAN LOOKS BACK
7·25

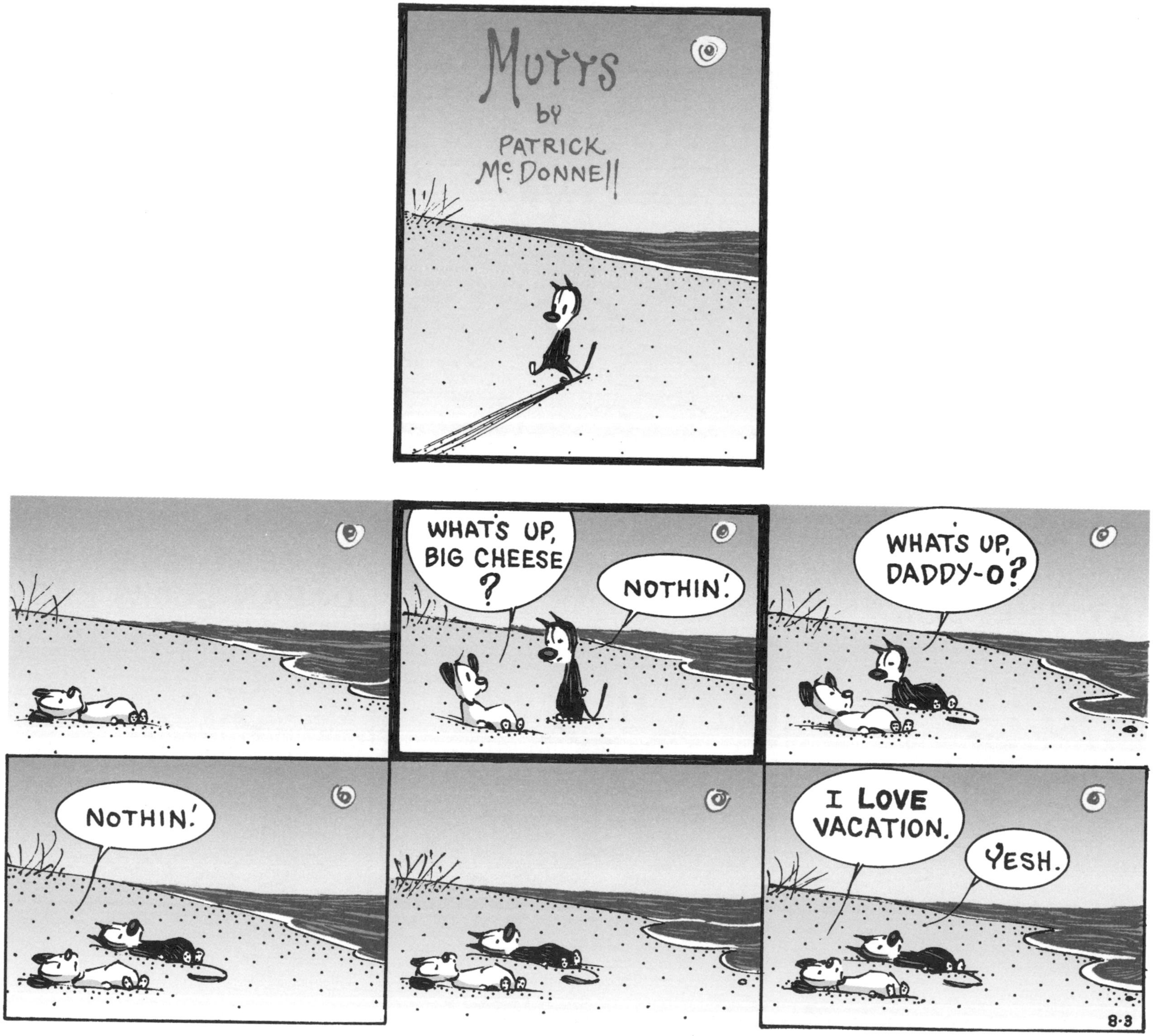

MUTTS
by
PATRICK
McDONNELL
WHAT'S UP, BIG CHEESE?
NOTHIN'.
WHATS UP, DADDY-O?
NOTHIN'.
I LOVE VACATION.
YESH.
8·3

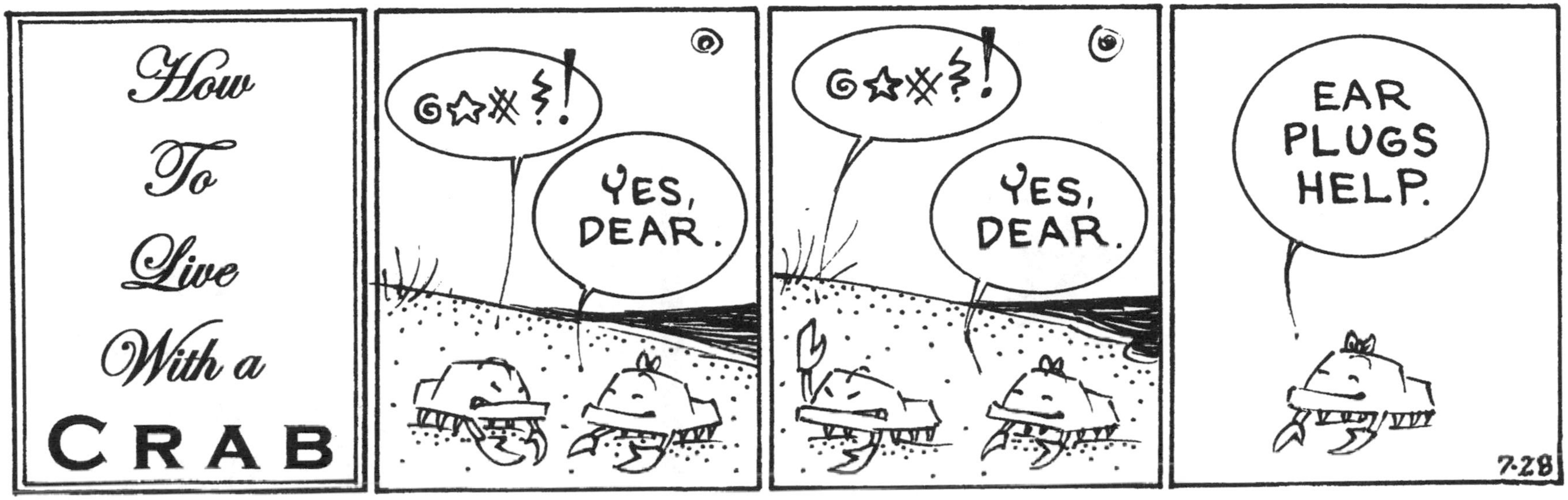
How To Live With a CRAB
YES, DEAR.
YES, DEAR.
EAR PLUGS HELP.
7-28

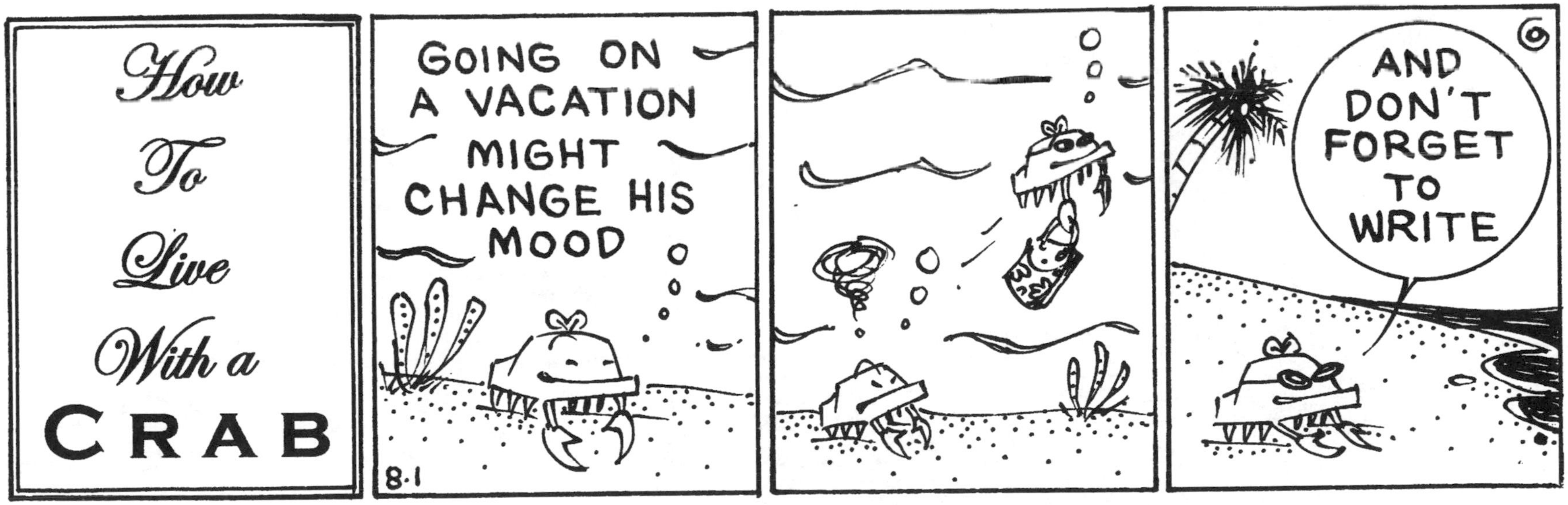
How To Live With a CRAB
GOING ON A VACATION MIGHT CHANGE HIS MOOD
8-1
AND DON'T FORGET TO WRITE

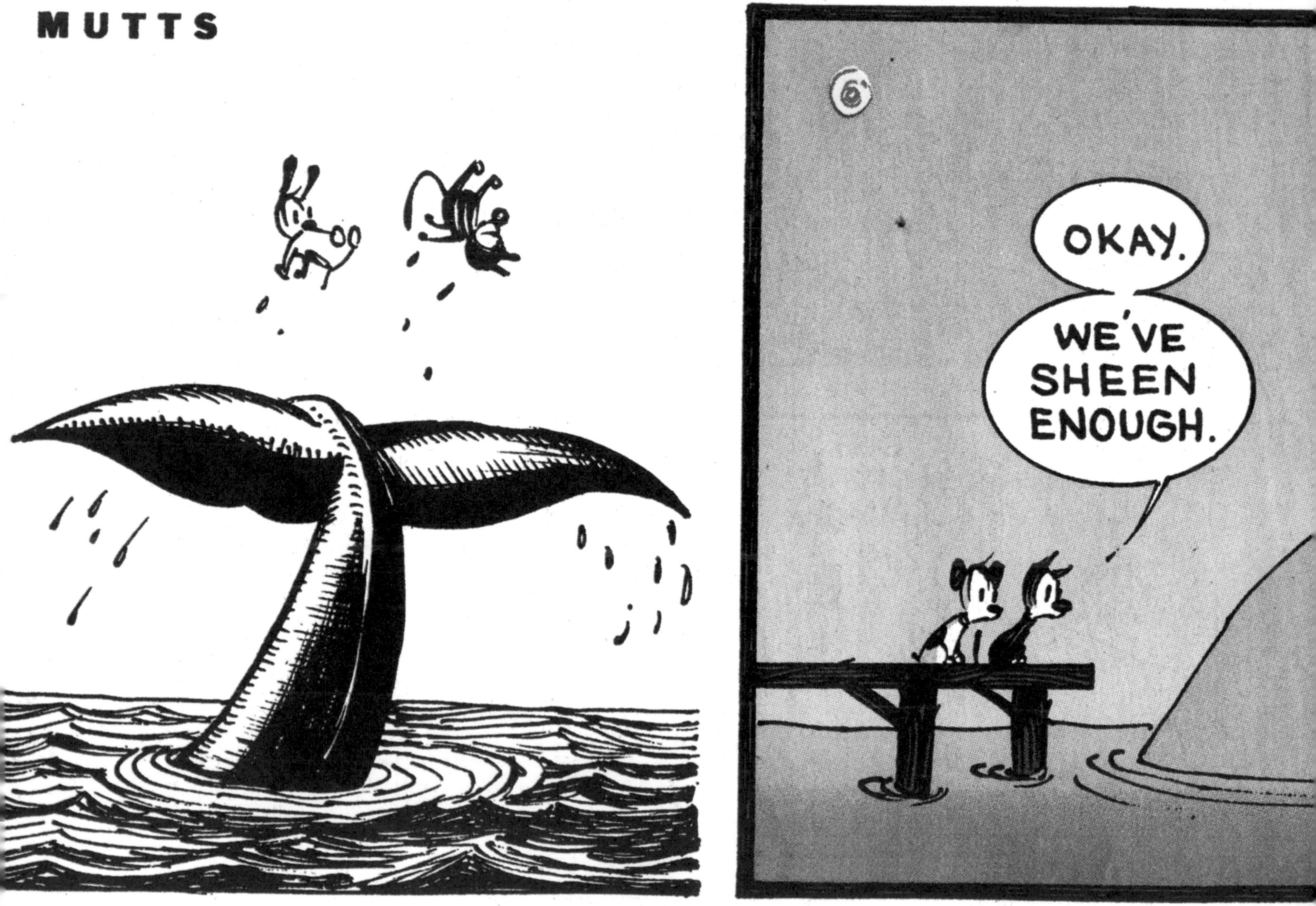
MUTTS
OKAY.
WE'VE SHEEN ENOUGH.

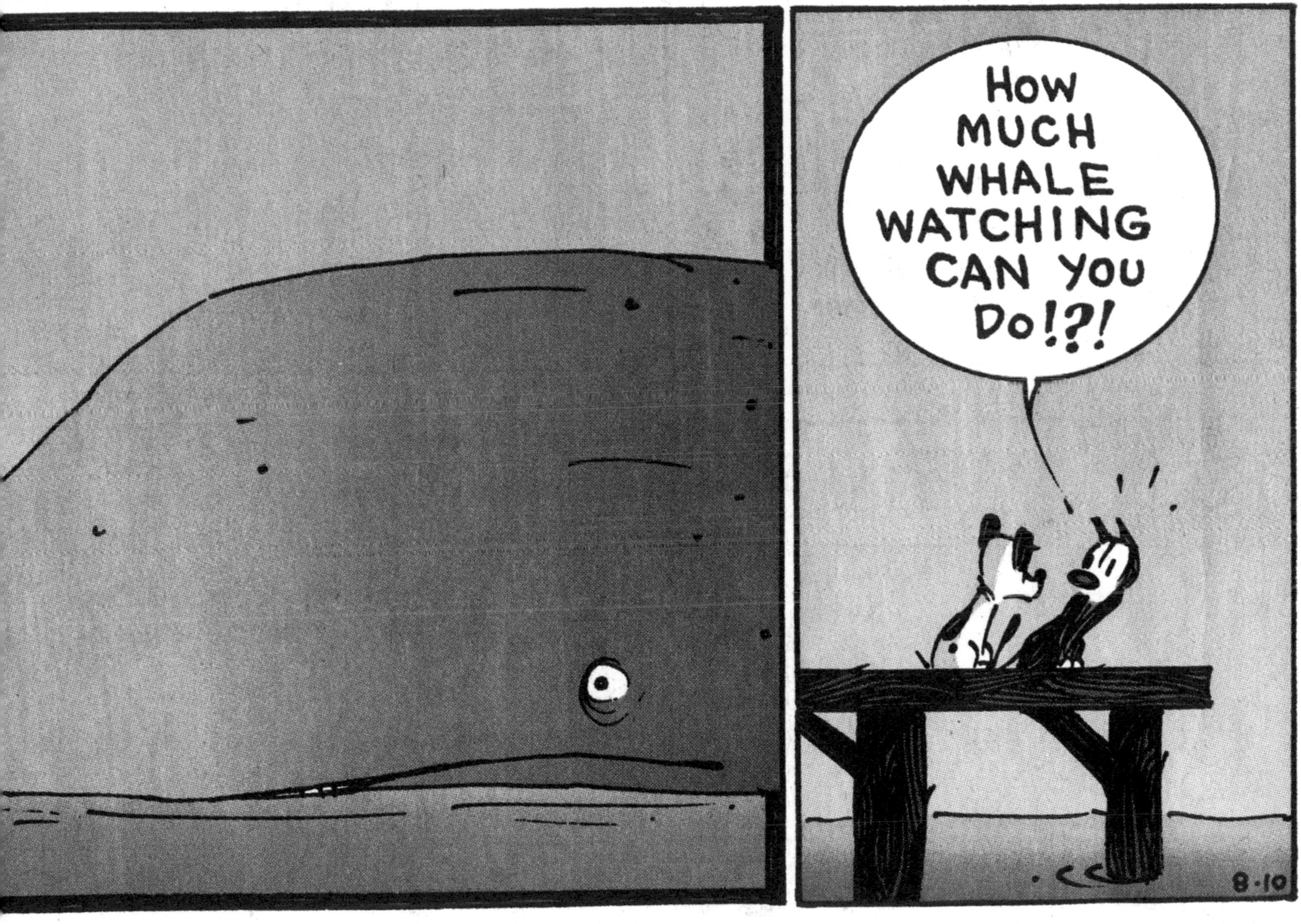
HOW MUCH WHALE WATCHING CAN YOU DO!?!
8-10

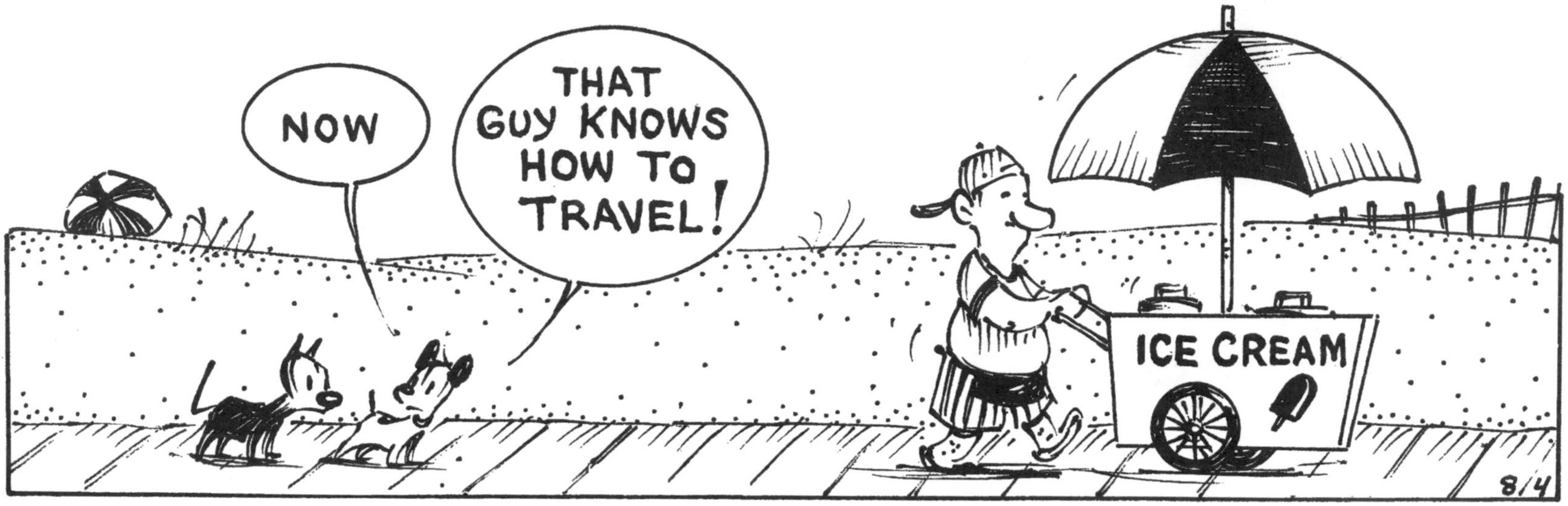
NOW
THAT GUY KNOWS HOW TO TRAVEL!
ICE CREAM
8/4

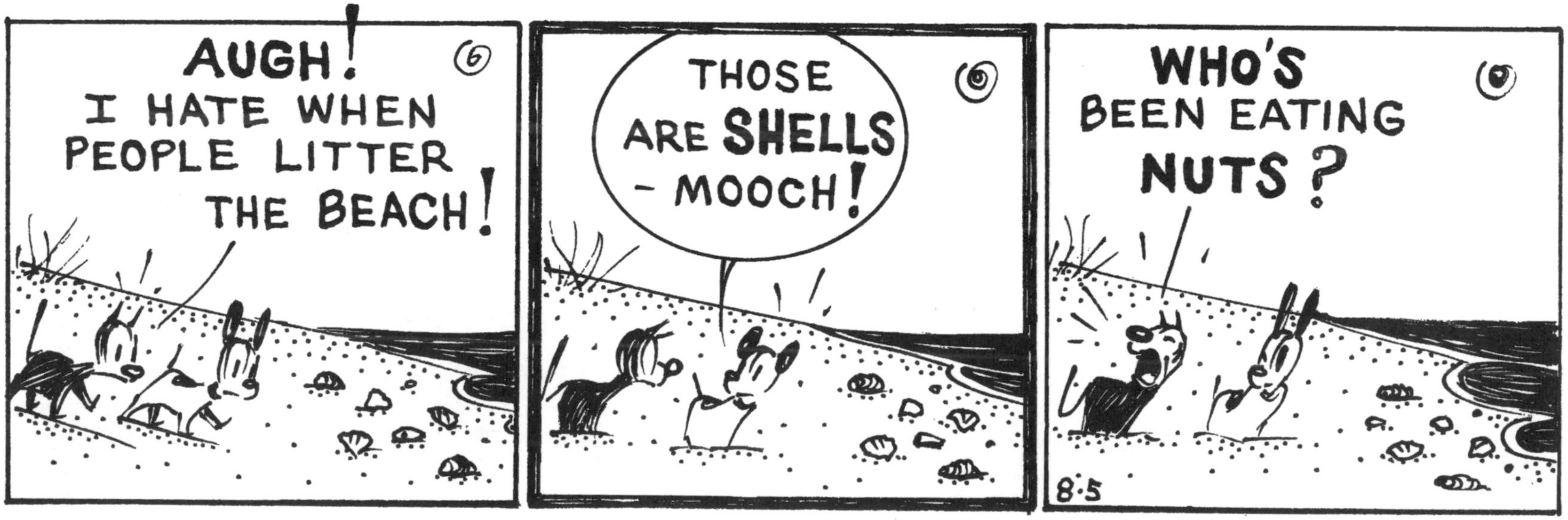
AUGH! I HATE WHEN PEOPLE LITTER THE BEACH!
THOSE ARE SHELLS - MOOCH!
WHO'S BEEN EATING NUTS?
8·5

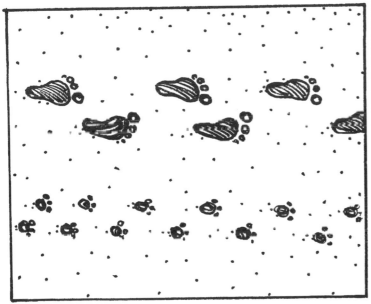

8·8

117

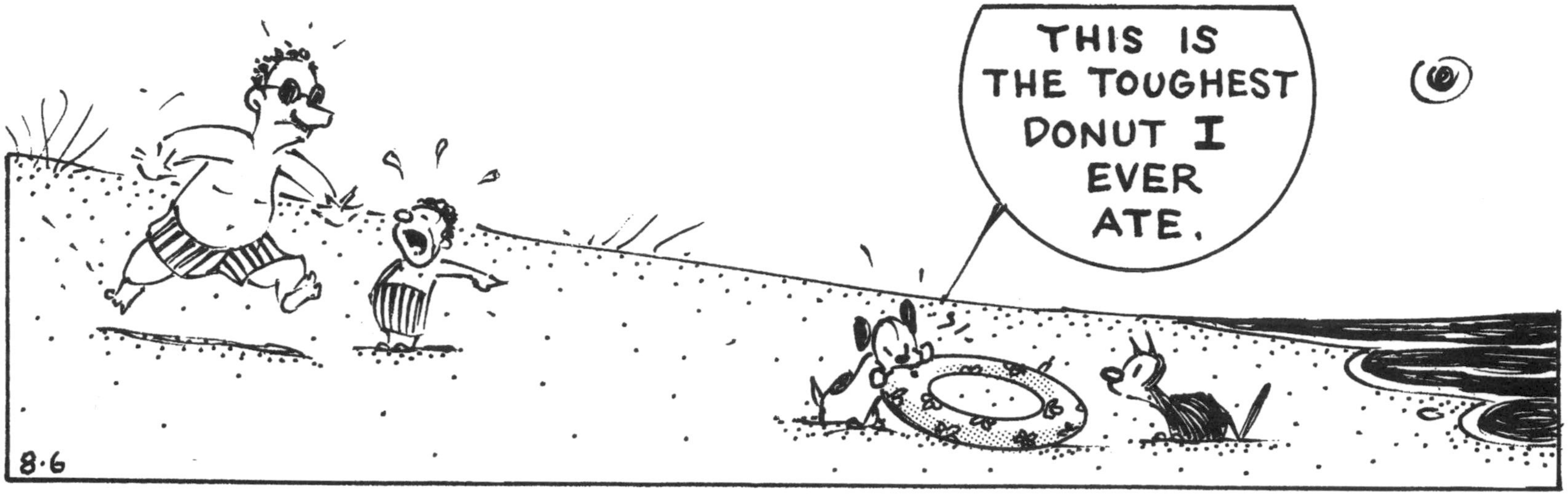
THIS IS THE TOUGHEST DONUT I EVER ATE.
8·6

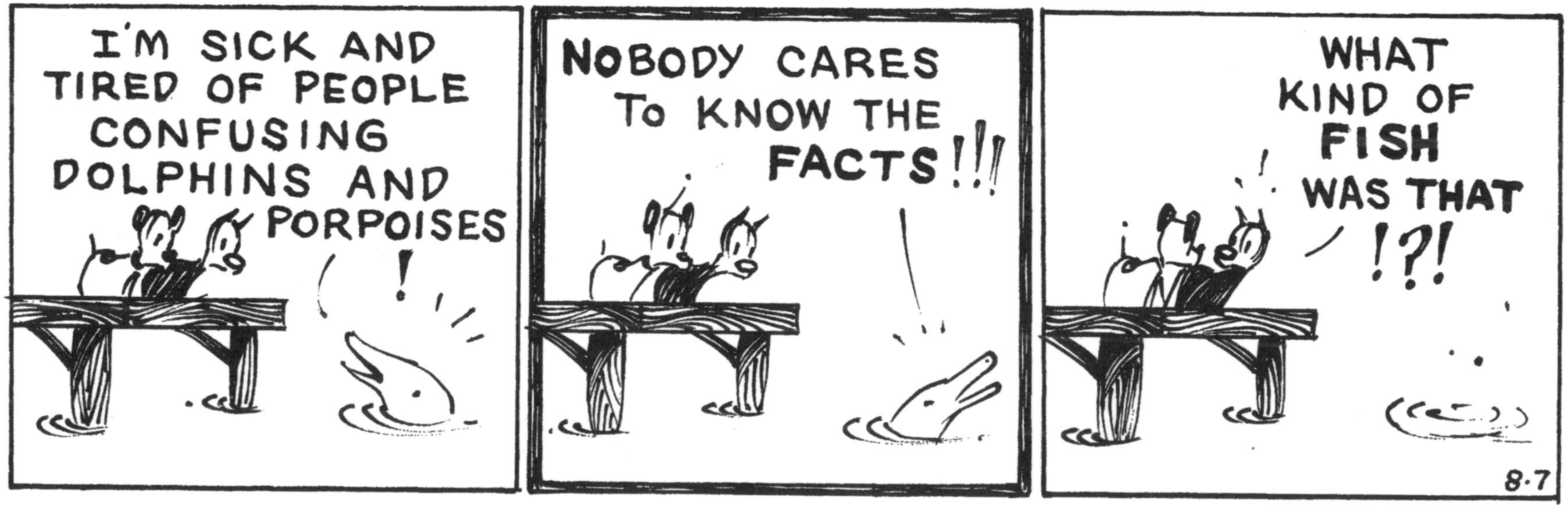
I'M SICK AND TIRED OF PEOPLE CONFUSING DOLPHINS AND PORPOISES
NOBODY CARES TO KNOW THE FACTS!!!
WHAT KIND OF FISH WAS THAT !?!
8·7

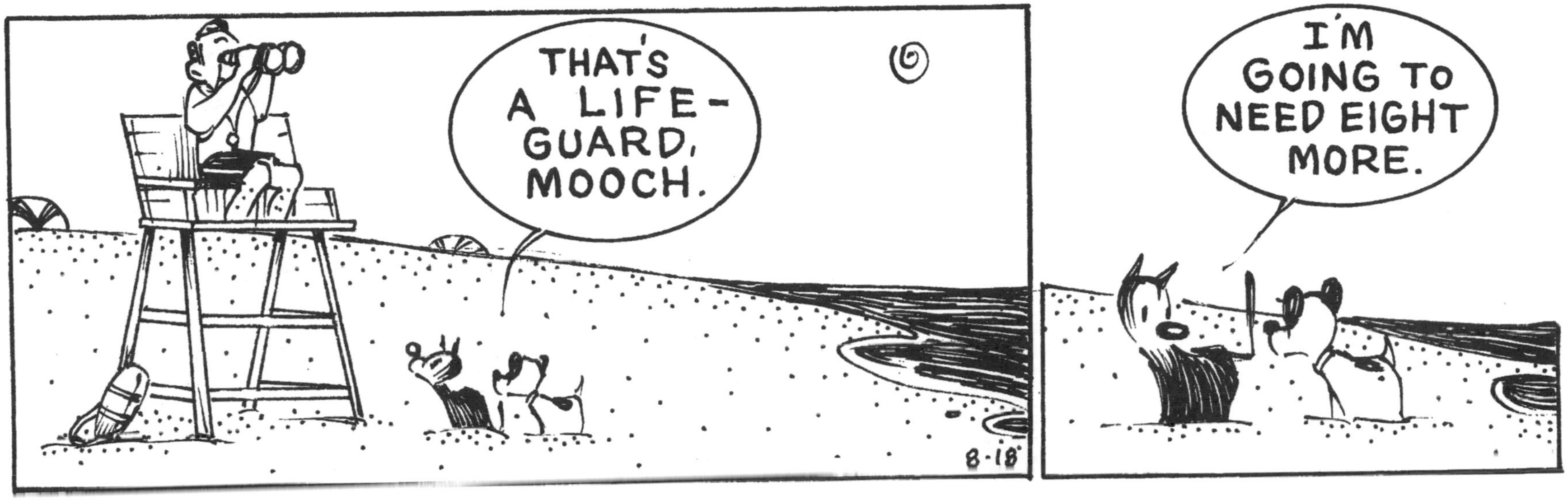
THAT'S A LIFE-GUARD, MOOCH.
I'M GOING TO NEED EIGHT MORE.
8-18

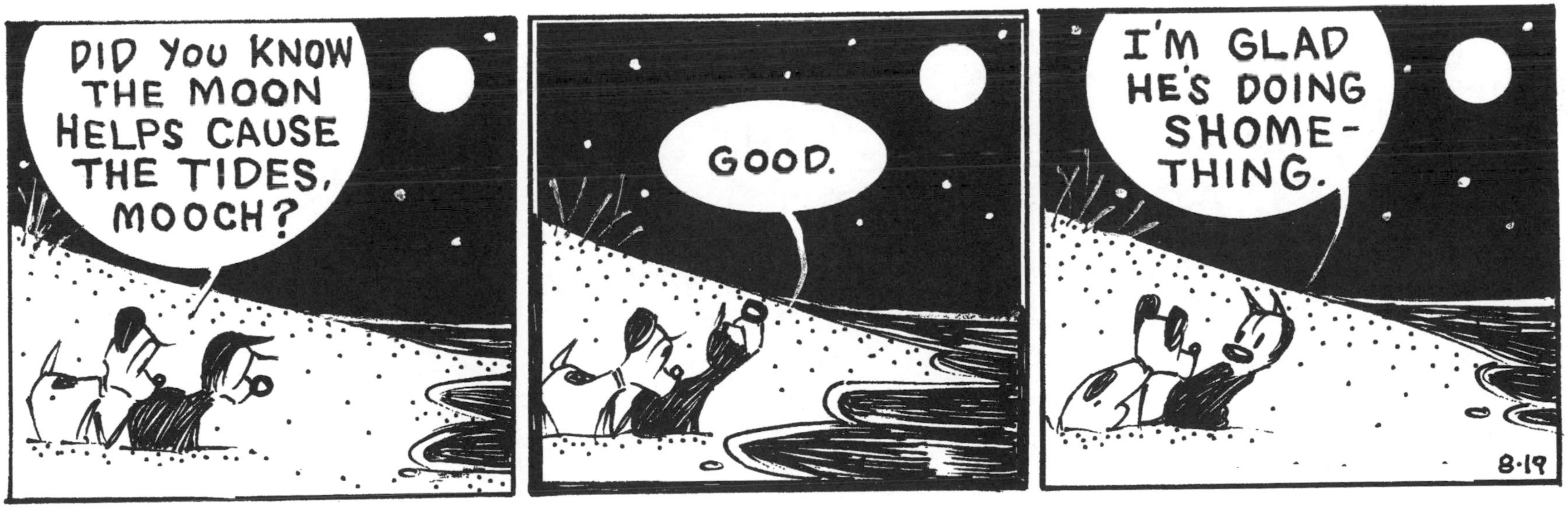
DID YOU KNOW THE MOON HELPS CAUSE THE TIDES, MOOCH?
GOOD.
I'M GLAD HE'S DOING SHOME-THING.
8-19

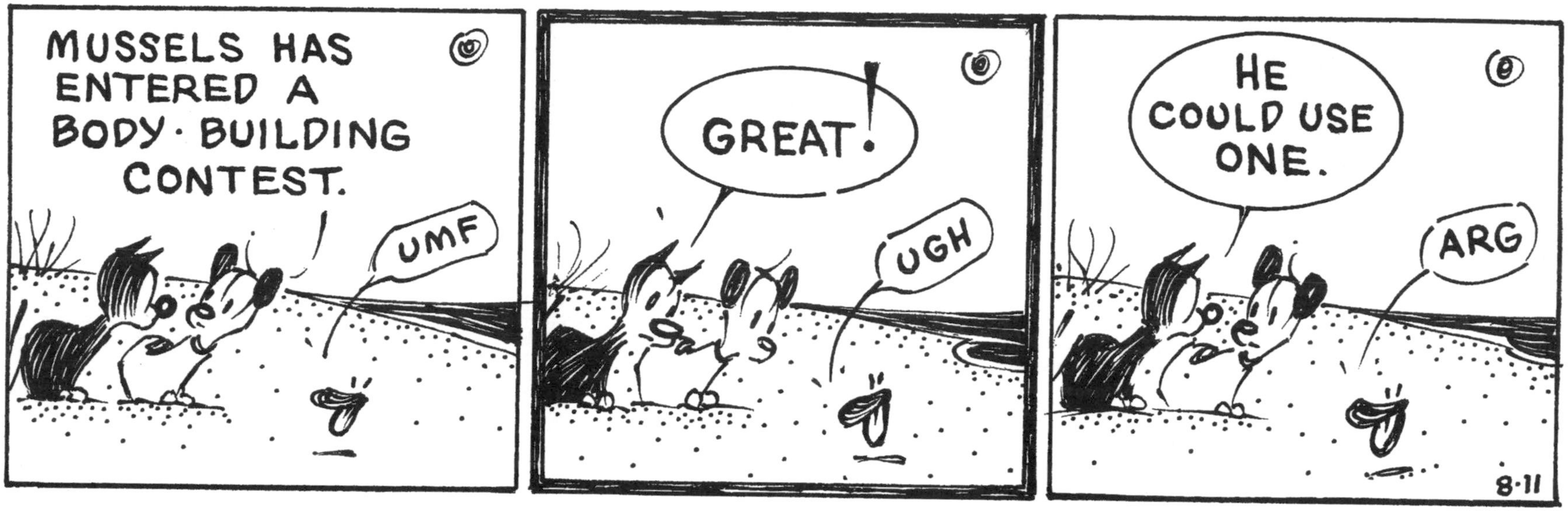
MUSSELS HAS ENTERED A BODY · BUILDING CONTEST.
UMF
GREAT!
UGH
HE COULD USE ONE.
ARG
8·11

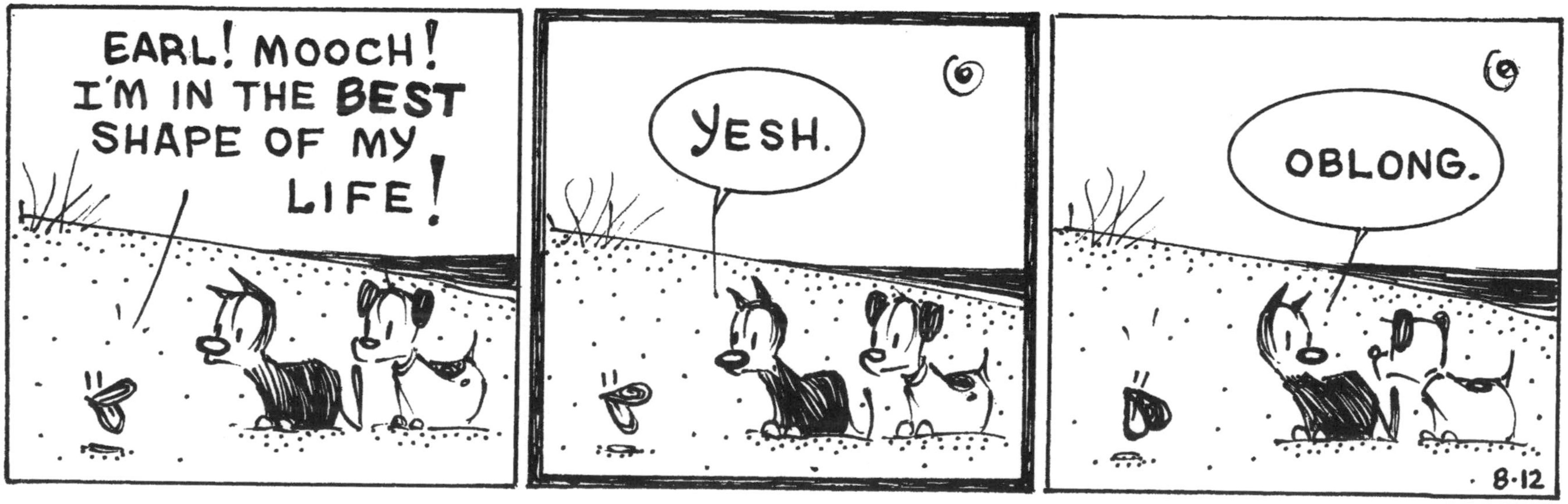
EARL! MOOCH! I'M IN THE BEST SHAPE OF MY LIFE!
YESH.
OBLONG.
8·12

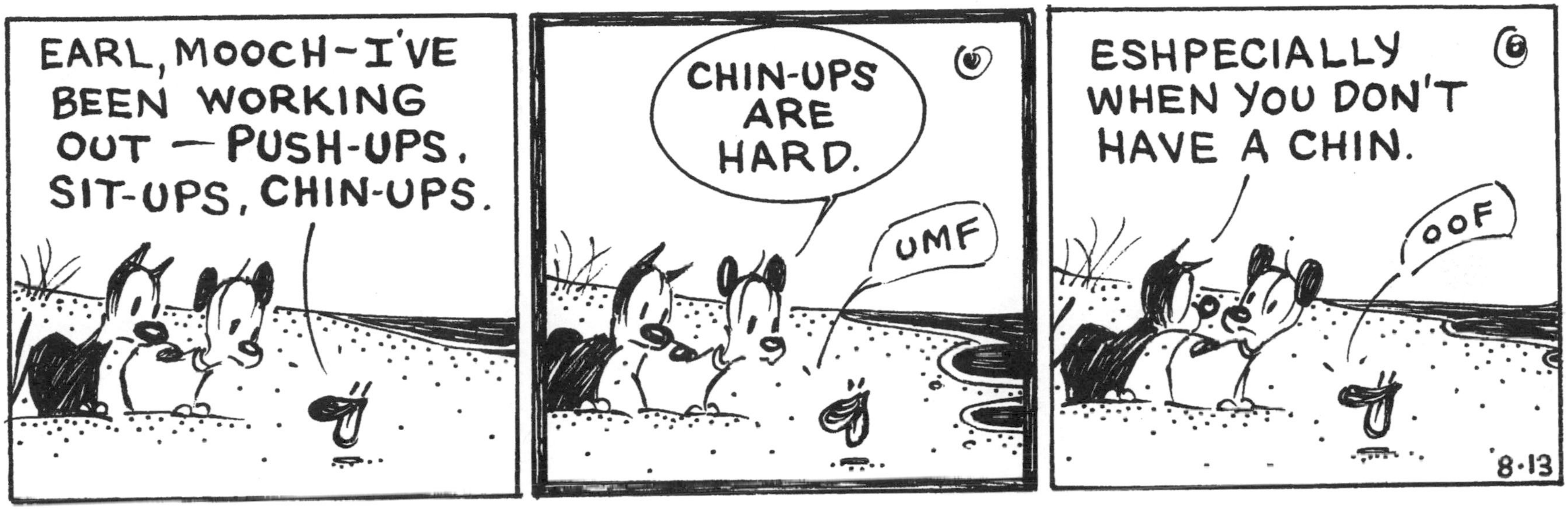
EARL, MOOCH–I'VE BEEN WORKING OUT — PUSH-UPS, SIT-UPS, CHIN-UPS.
CHIN-UPS ARE HARD.
UMF
ESHPECIALLY WHEN YOU DON'T HAVE A CHIN.
OOF
8·13

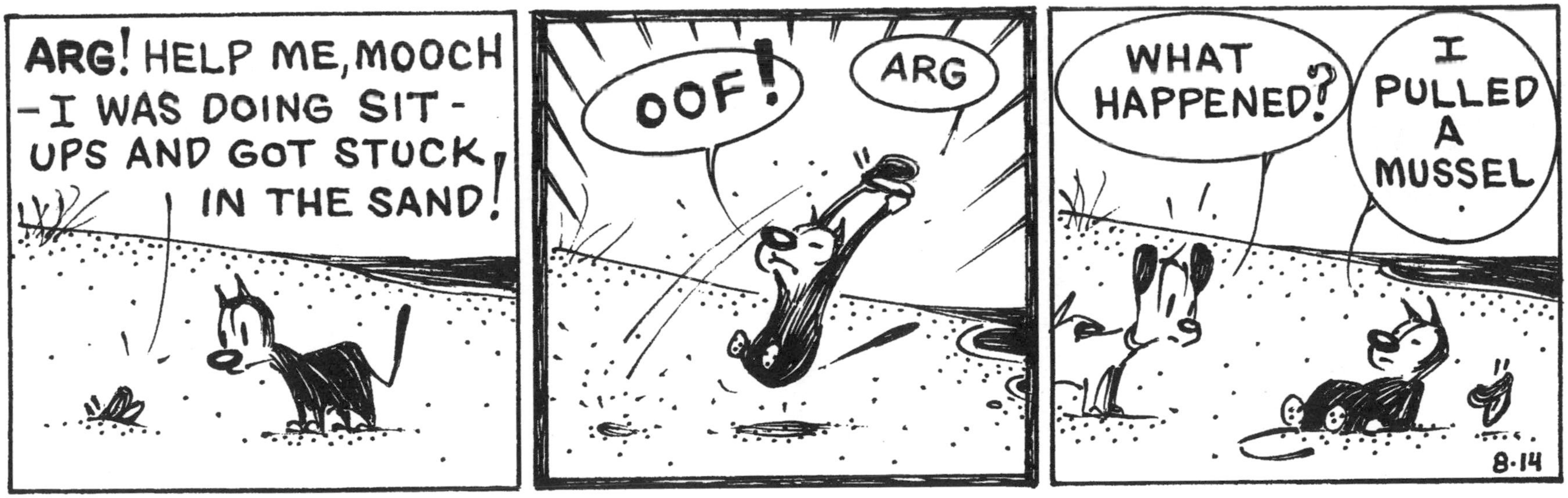
ARG! HELP ME, MOOCH –I WAS DOING SIT-UPS AND GOT STUCK IN THE SAND!
OOF!
ARG
WHAT HAPPENED?
I PULLED A MUSSEL.
8·14

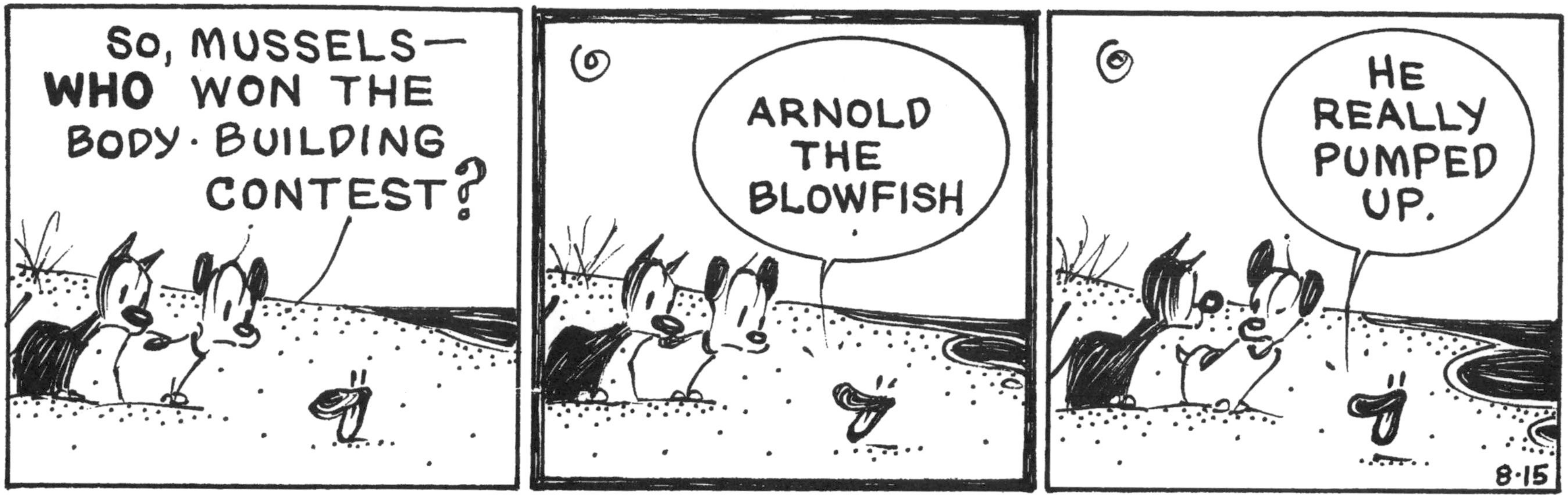
SO, MUSSELS—**WHO** WON THE BODY·BUILDING CONTEST?
ARNOLD THE BLOWFISH
HE REALLY PUMPED UP.
8·15

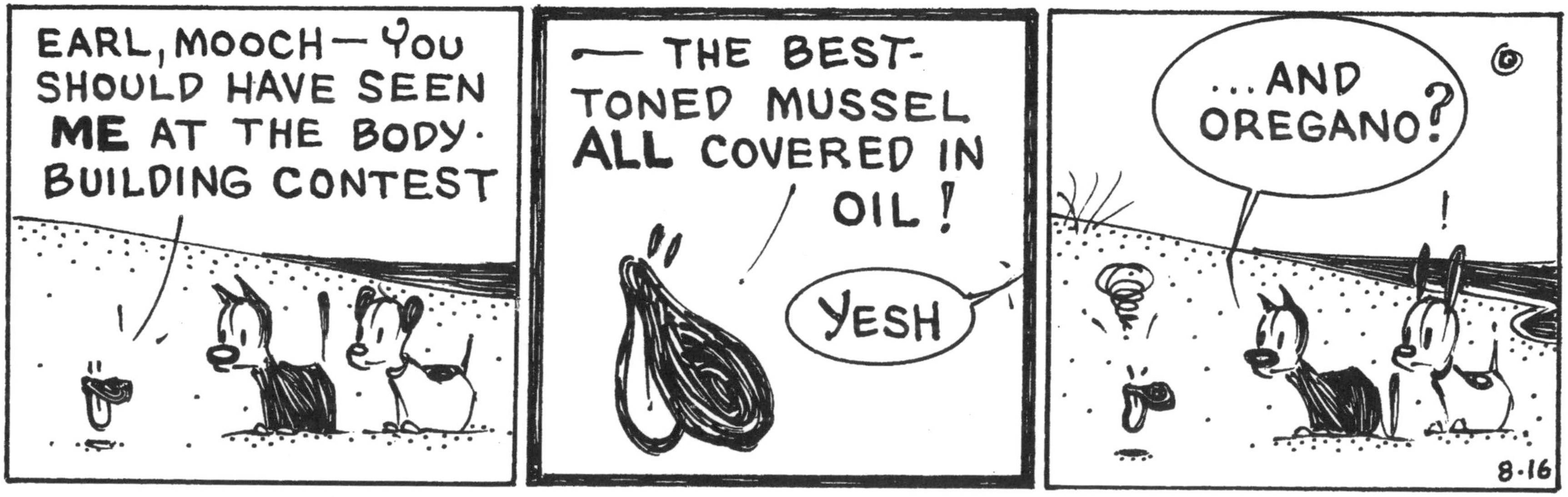
EARL, MOOCH—YOU SHOULD HAVE SEEN **ME** AT THE BODY·BUILDING CONTEST
—THE BEST-TONED MUSSEL **ALL** COVERED IN OIL!
YESH
...AND OREGANO?
8·16

MUSSEL
MAGAZINE
MUTTS

ACK! ACK! THERE'S A WHALE ON THE BEACH!
I'LL HANDLE THIS!
NOBODY MUSCLES IN ON MY TURF!
HEY, YOU! THIS BEACH AIN'T BIG ENOUGH FOR THE TWO OF US!
ARG!
SO BEAT IT!
UMF
THANKS, PAL.
THAT'S ONE @☆#$! TOUGH MUSSEL
8·17

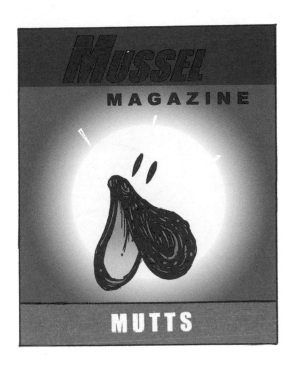

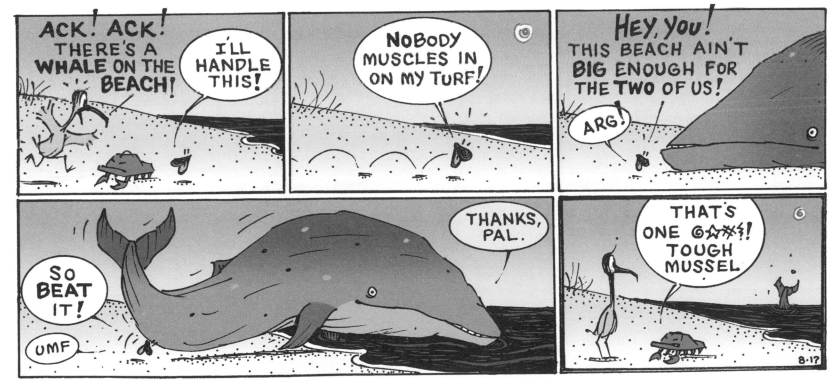

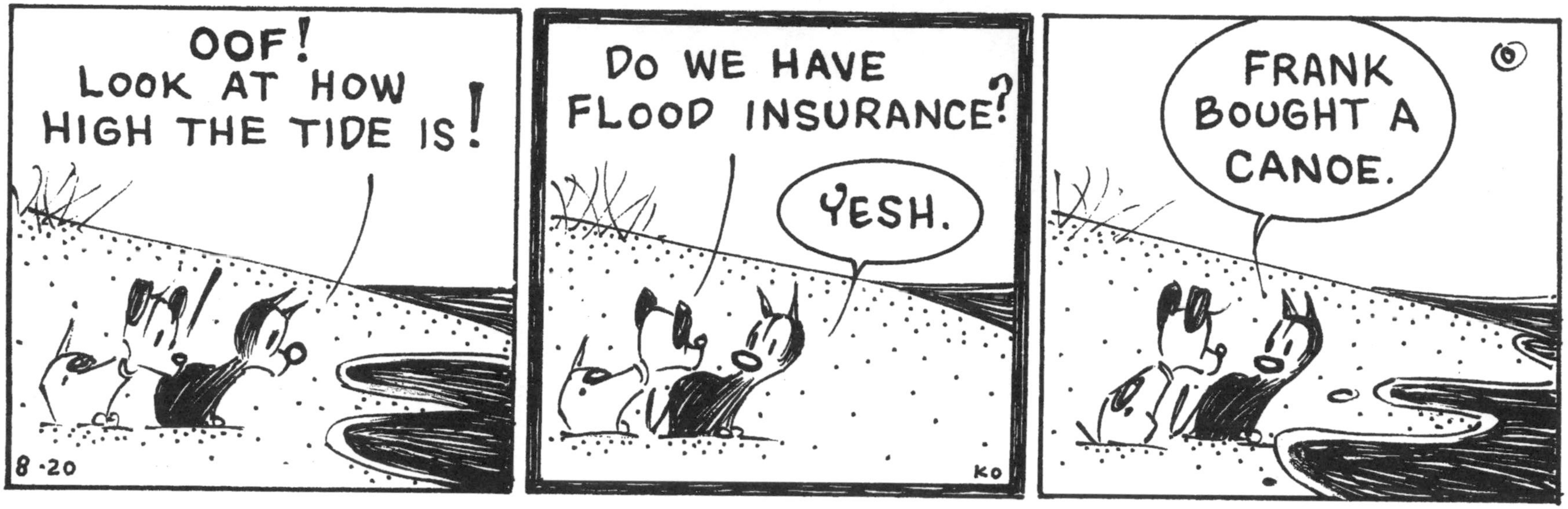
OOF! LOOK AT HOW HIGH THE TIDE IS!
8-20
DO WE HAVE FLOOD INSURANCE?
YESH.
KO
FRANK BOUGHT A CANOE.

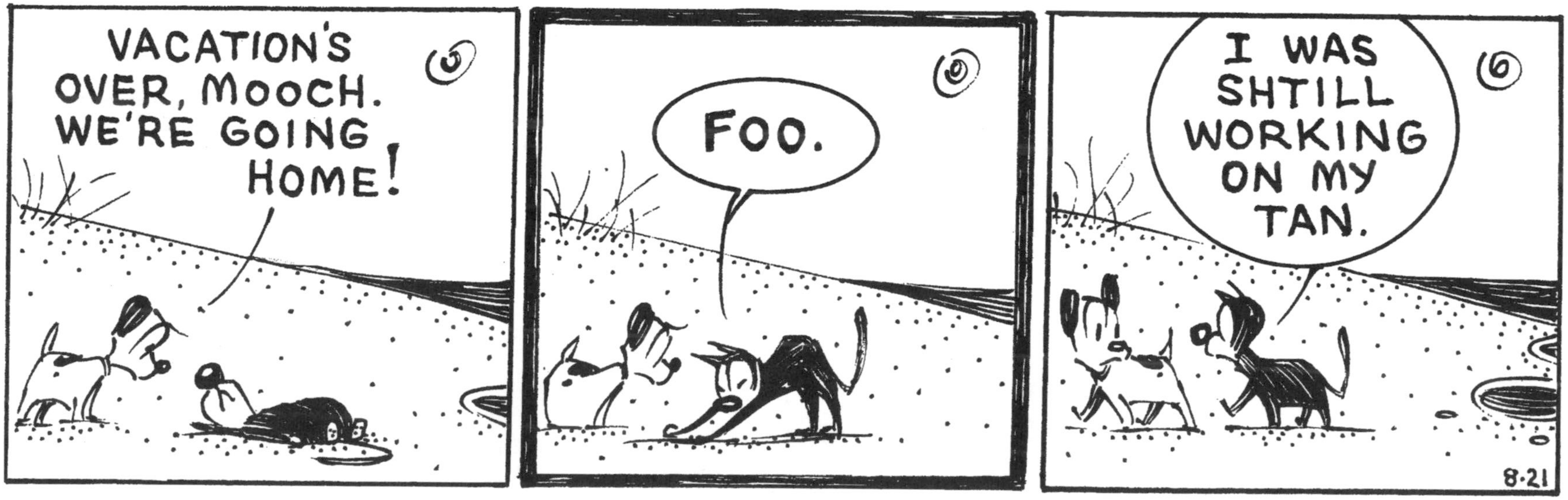
VACATION'S OVER, MOOCH. WE'RE GOING HOME!
FOO.
I WAS SHTILL WORKING ON MY TAN.
8-21

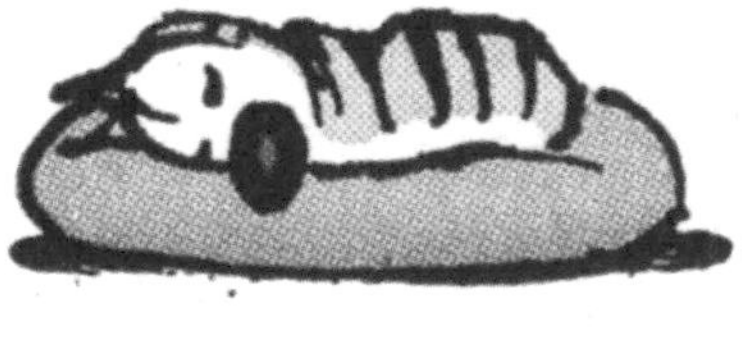

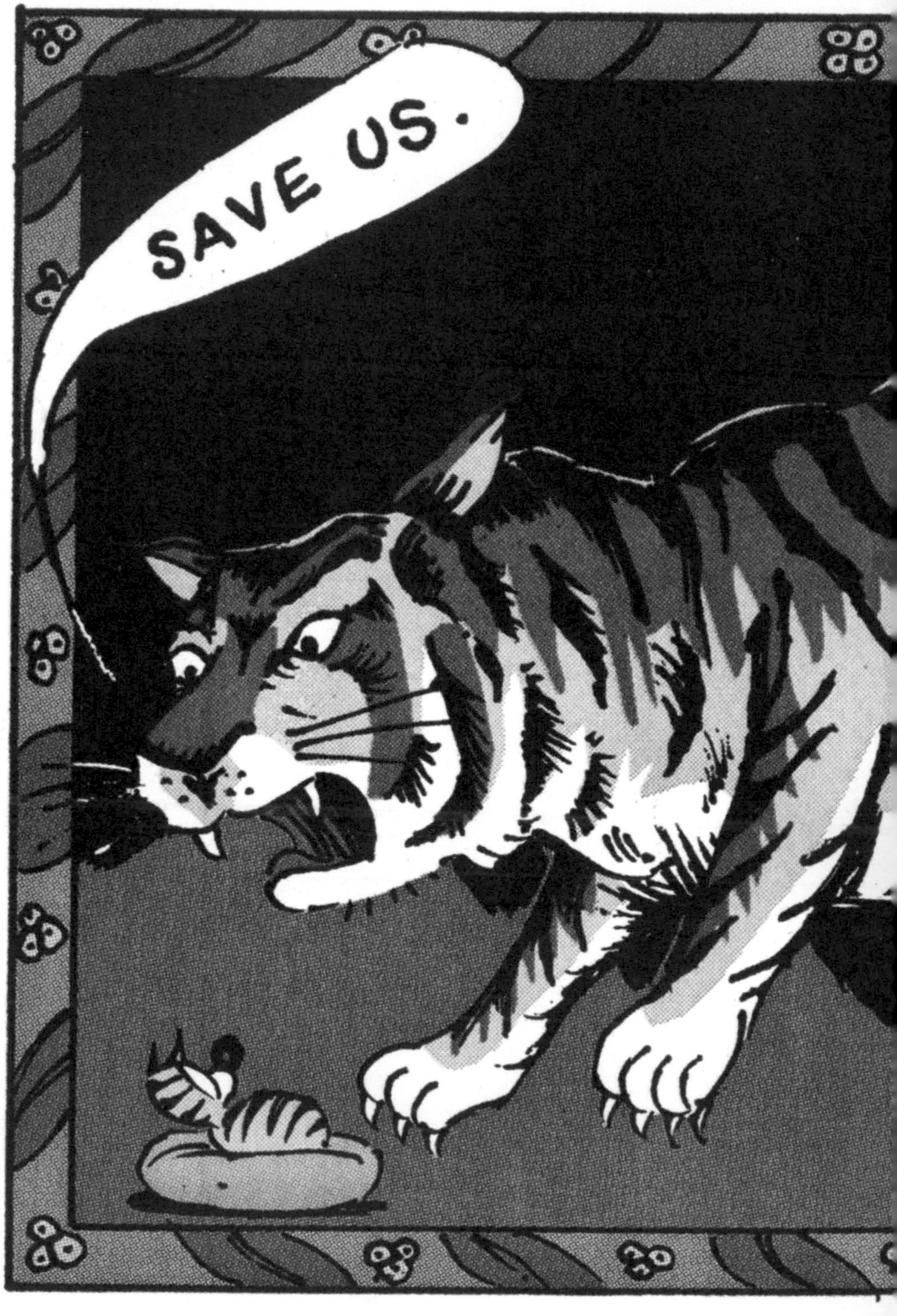
SAVE US.

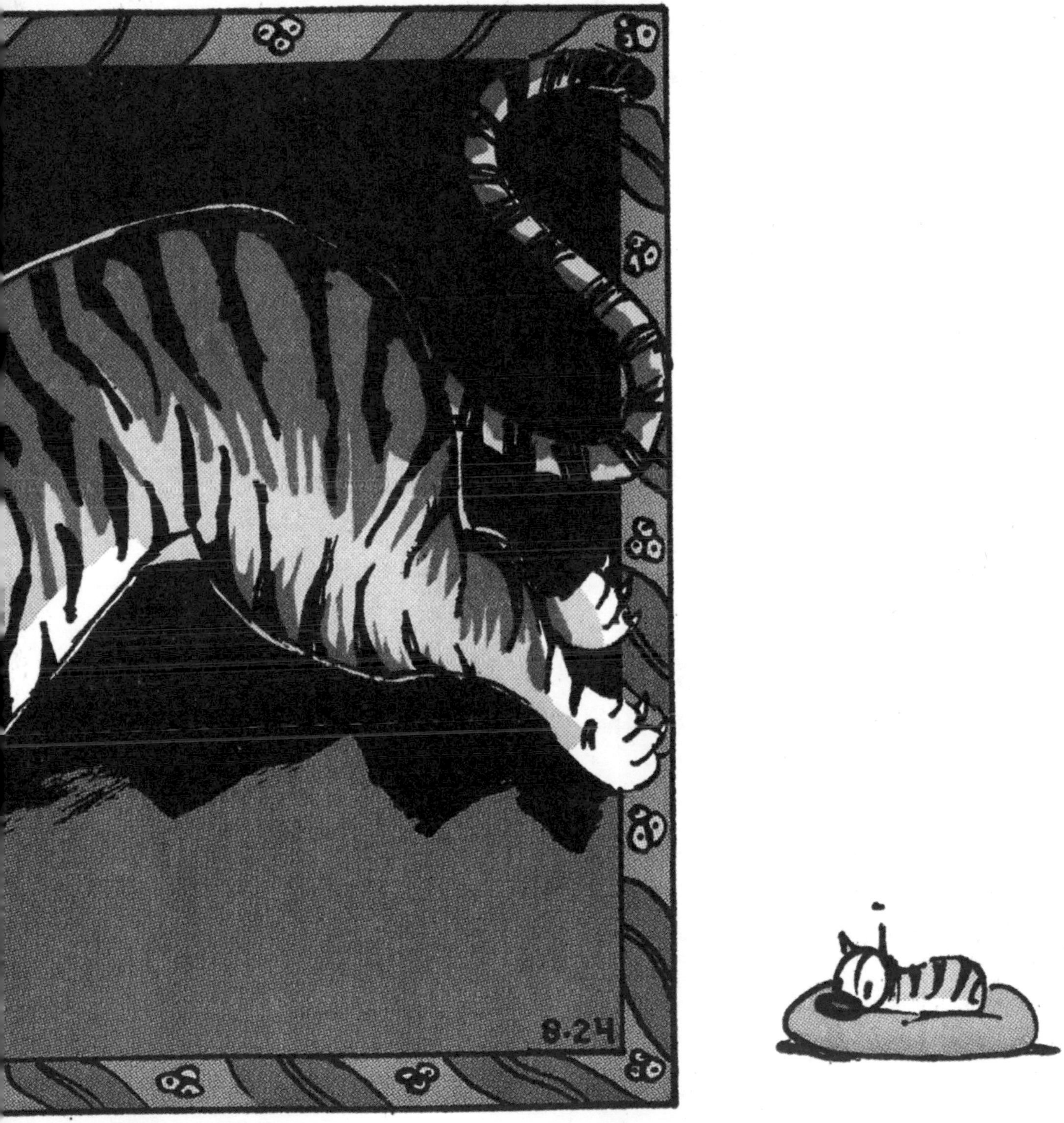
8·24

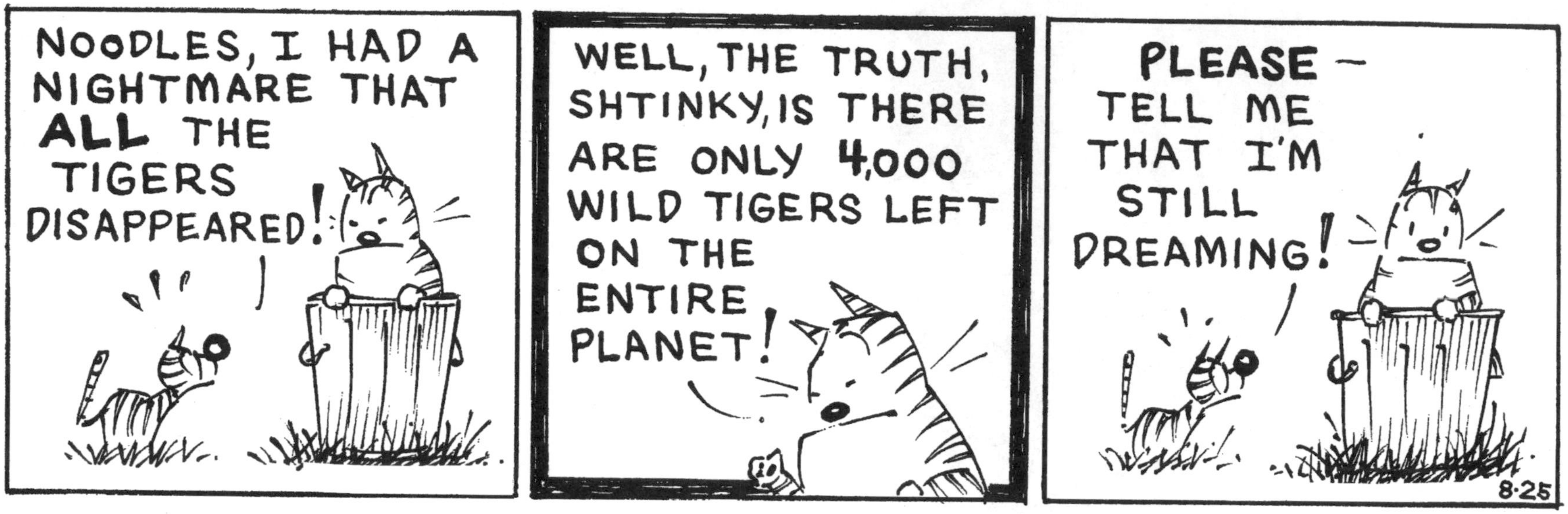
NOODLES, I HAD A NIGHTMARE THAT ALL THE TIGERS DISAPPEARED!
WELL, THE TRUTH, SHTINKY, IS THERE ARE ONLY 4,000 WILD TIGERS LEFT ON THE ENTIRE PLANET!
PLEASE - TELL ME THAT I'M STILL DREAMING!
8·25

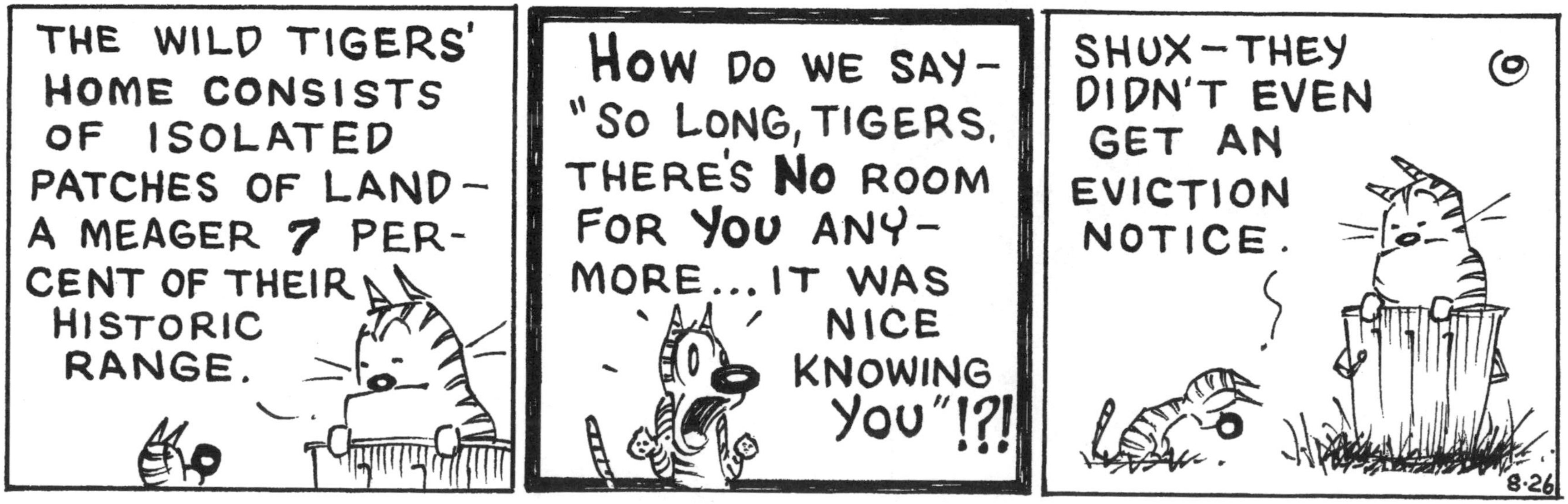
THE WILD TIGERS' HOME CONSISTS OF ISOLATED PATCHES OF LAND - A MEAGER 7 PERCENT OF THEIR HISTORIC RANGE.
HOW DO WE SAY - "SO LONG, TIGERS. THERE'S NO ROOM FOR YOU ANYMORE... IT WAS NICE KNOWING YOU"!?!
SHUX - THEY DIDN'T EVEN GET AN EVICTION NOTICE.
8·26

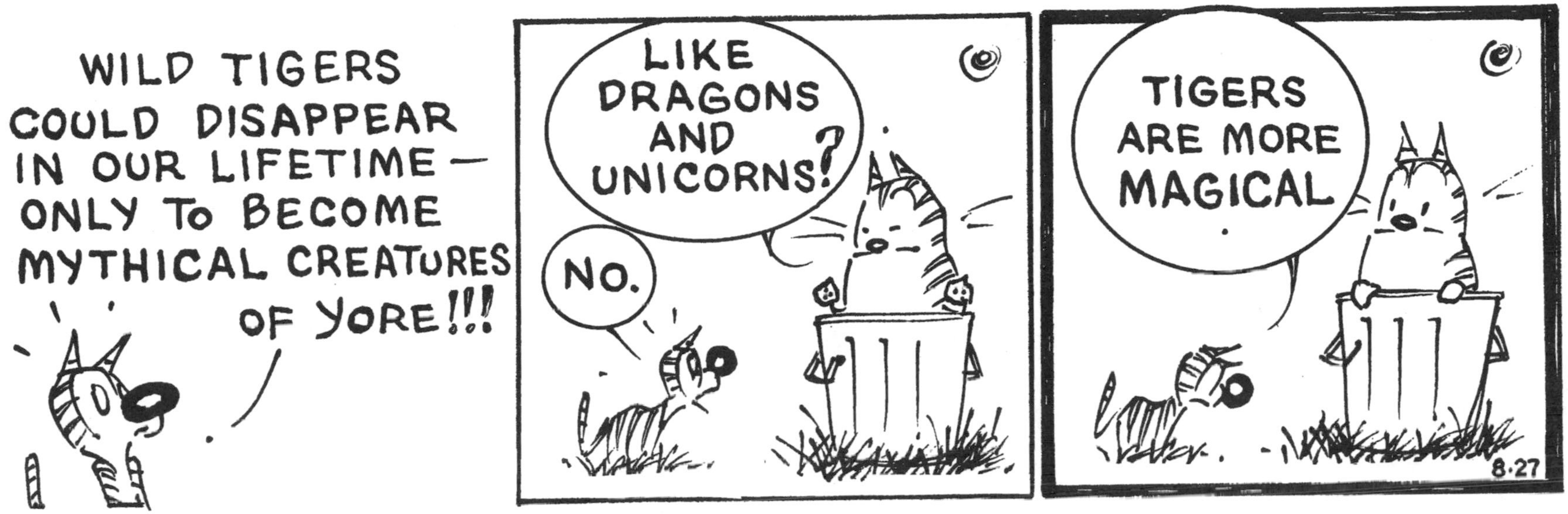
WILD TIGERS COULD DISAPPEAR IN OUR LIFETIME— ONLY To BECOME MYTHICAL CREATURES OF YORE!!!
LIKE DRAGONS AND UNICORNS?
NO.
TIGERS ARE MORE MAGICAL.
8·27

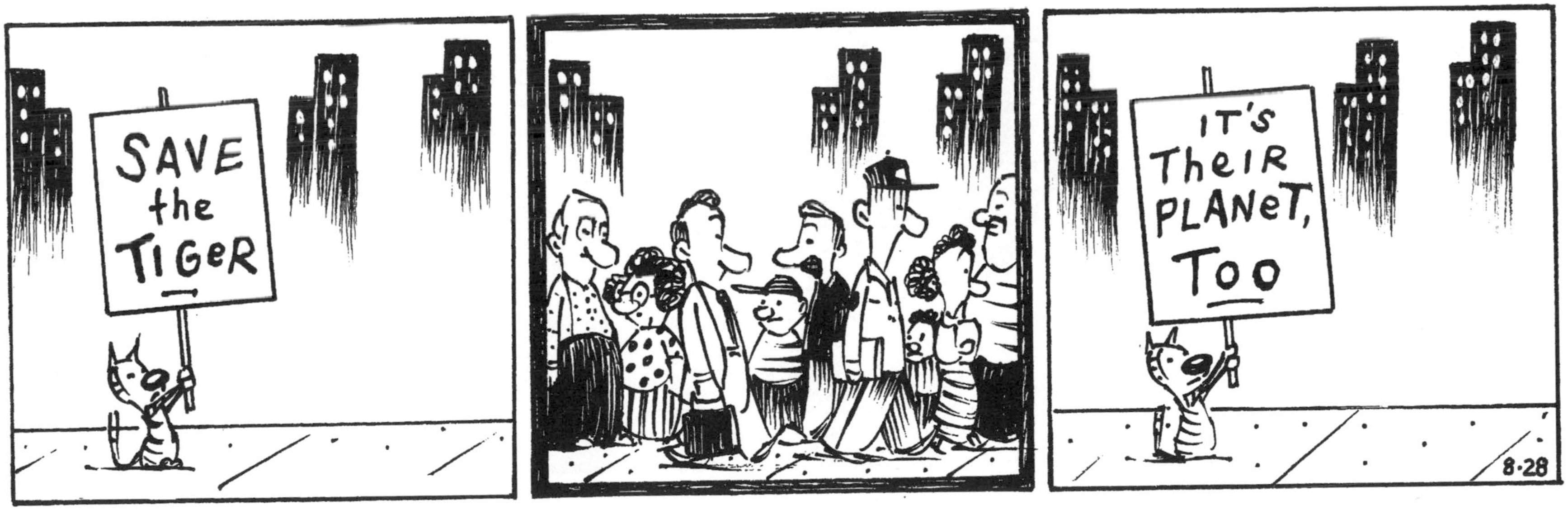
SAVE the TIGER
IT'S Their PLANET, TOO
8·28

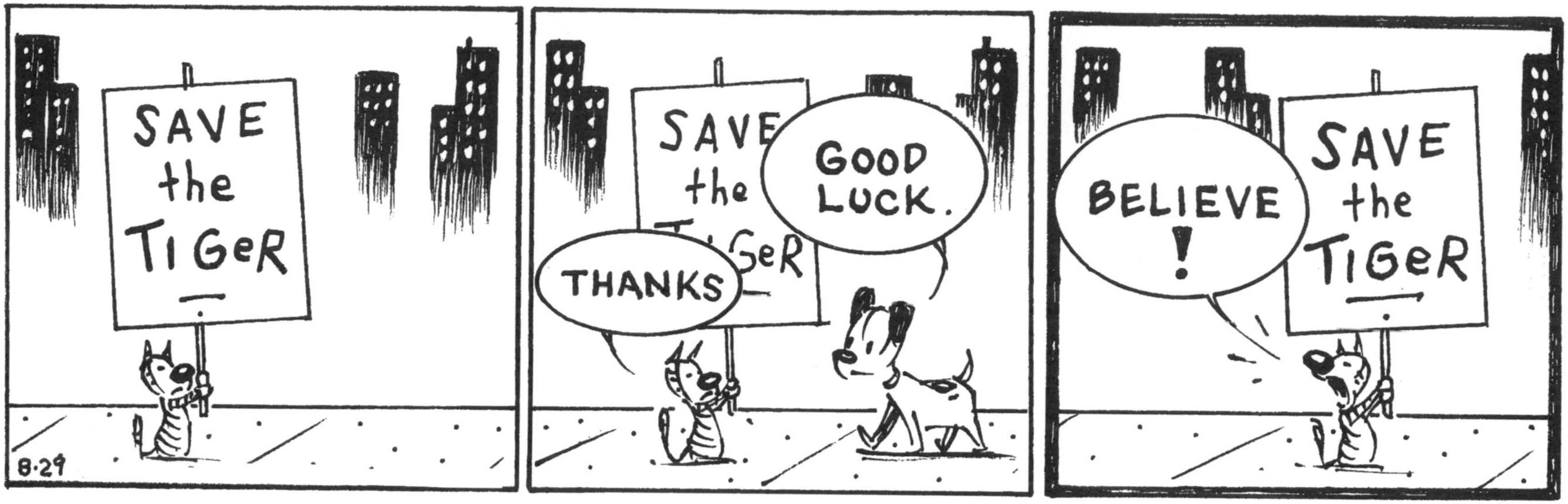
SAVE the TIGER
8·29
SAVE the TIGER
THANKS
GOOD LUCK.
BELIEVE!
SAVE the TIGER

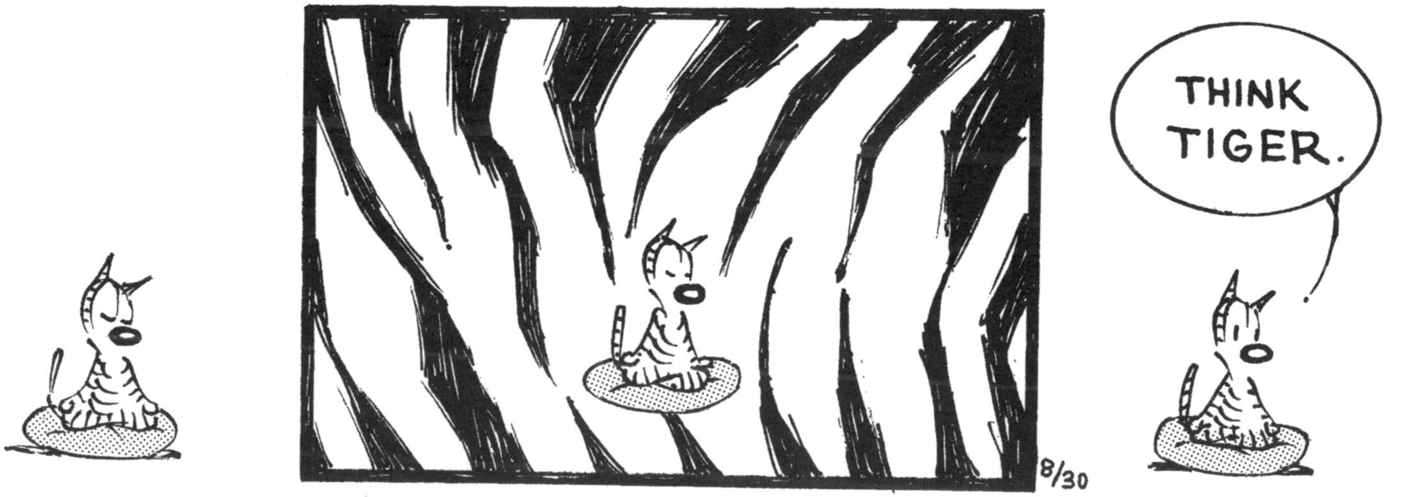
8/30
THINK TIGER.

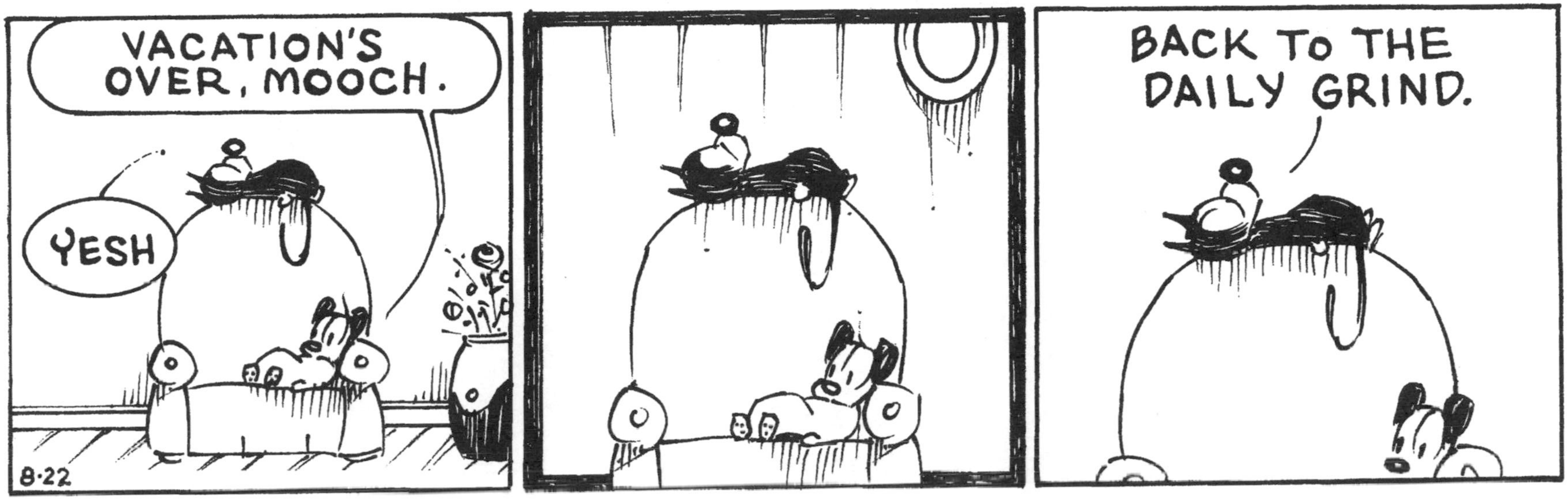
VACATION'S OVER, MOOCH.
YESH
8·22
BACK To THE DAILY GRIND.

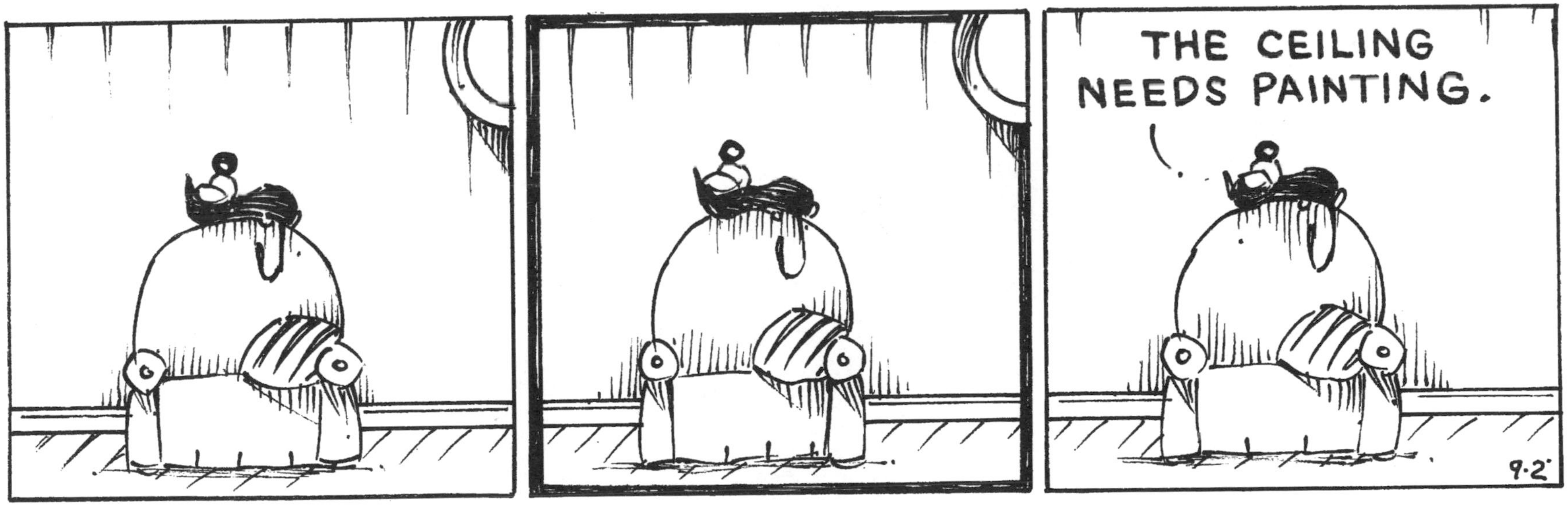
THE CEILING NEEDS PAINTING.
9·2

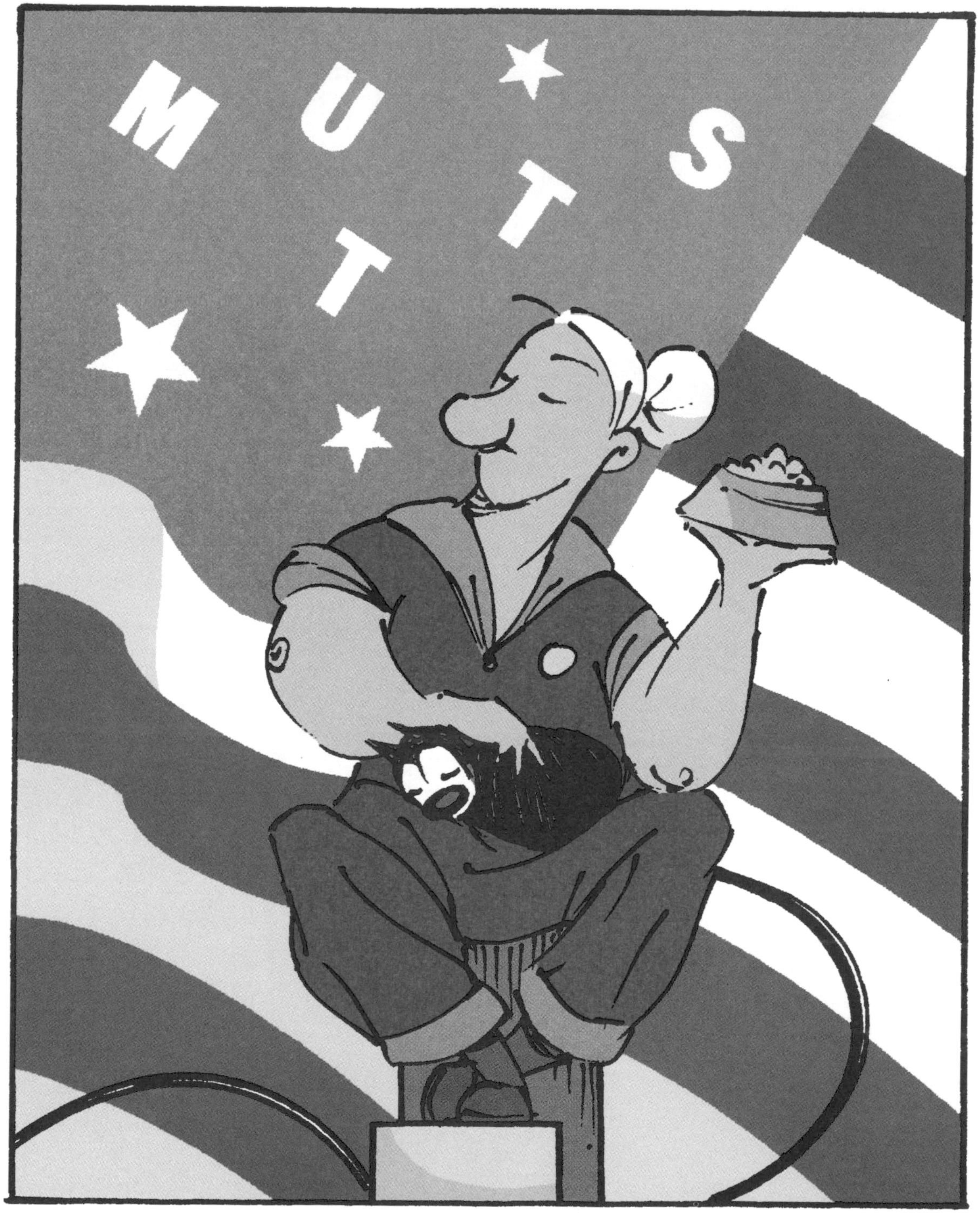
MUTTS

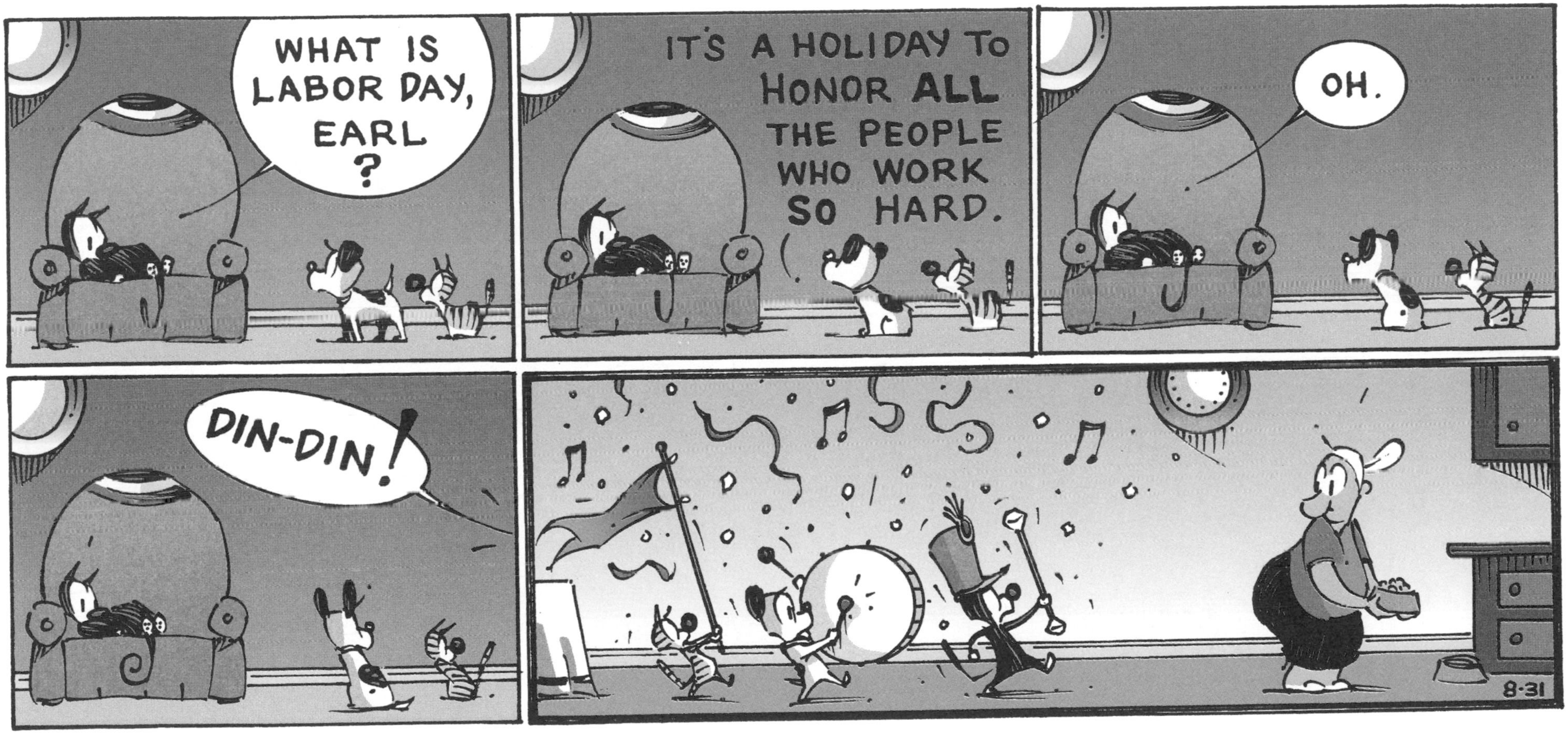
WHAT IS LABOR DAY, EARL ?
IT'S A HOLIDAY TO HONOR ALL THE PEOPLE WHO WORK SO HARD.
OH.
DIN-DIN!
8-31

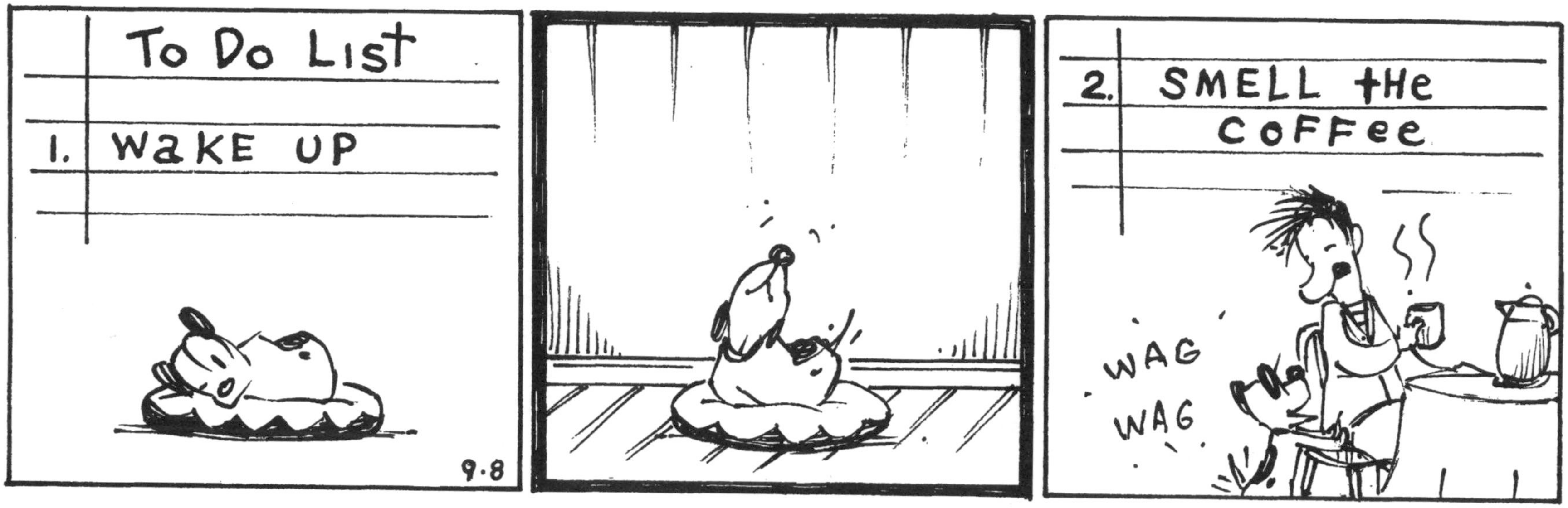
To Do List
1. WaKE UP
9·8
2. SMELL tHe COFFee
WAG
WAG

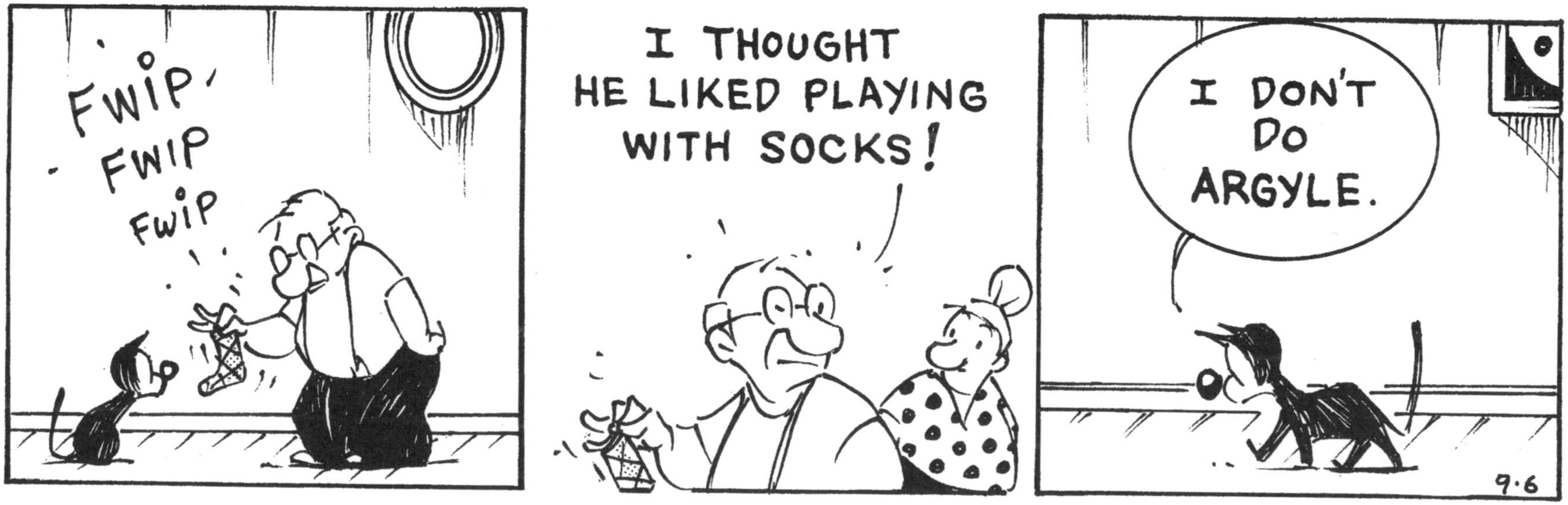
FWIP
FWIP
FWIP
I THOUGHT HE LIKED PLAYING WITH SOCKS!
I DON'T DO ARGYLE.
9·6

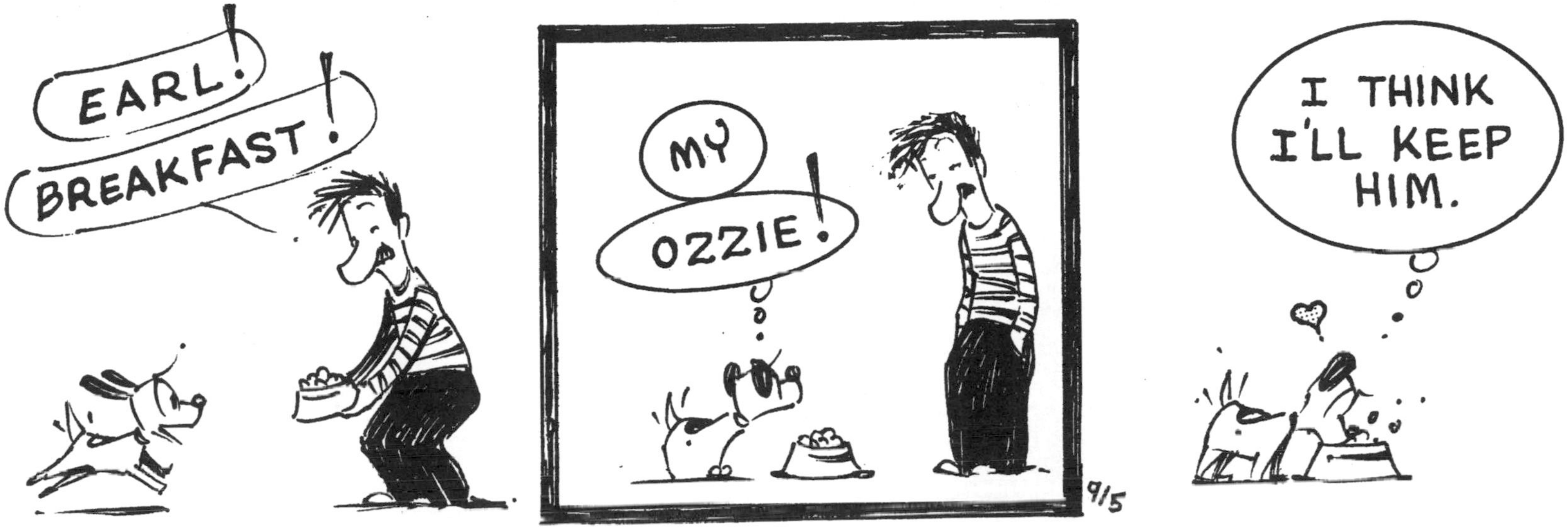
EARL!
BREAKFAST!
MY
OZZIE!
I THINK I'LL KEEP HIM.
9/5

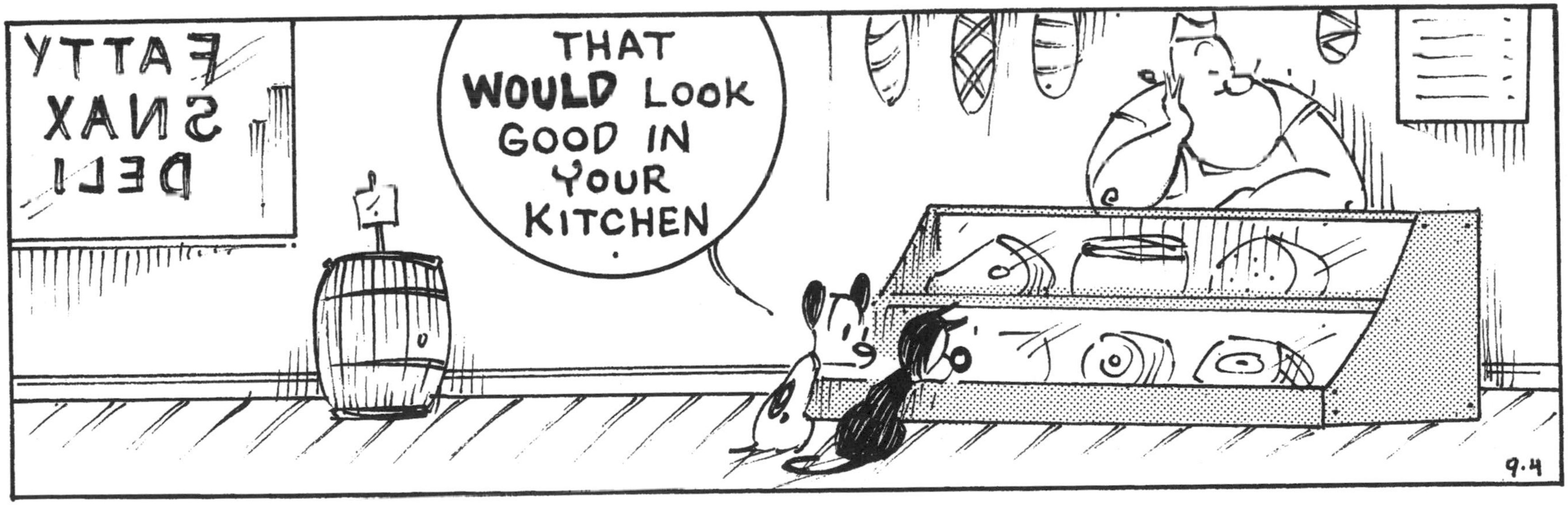
FATTY SNAX DELI
THAT WOULD LOOK GOOD IN YOUR KITCHEN
9.4

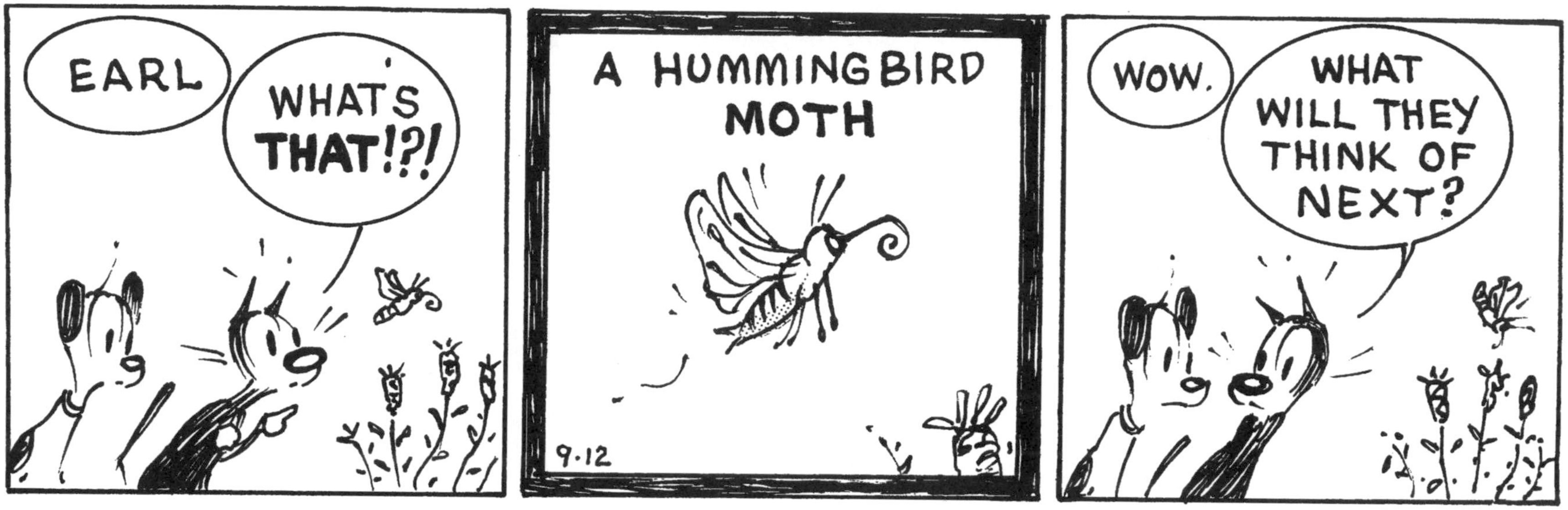
EARL
WHAT'S **THAT**!?!
A HUMMINGBIRD **MOTH**
9.12
WOW.
WHAT WILL THEY THINK OF NEXT?

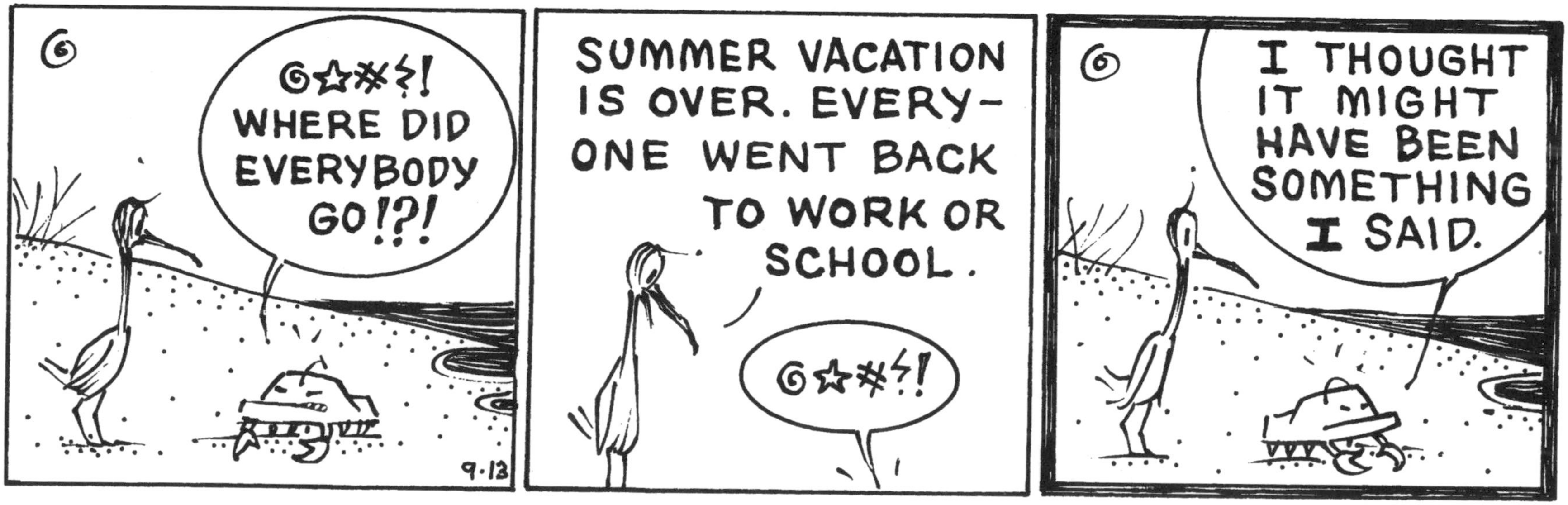
@☆#?! WHERE DID EVERYBODY GO!?!
9.13
SUMMER VACATION IS OVER. EVERY-ONE WENT BACK TO WORK OR SCHOOL.
@☆#?!
I THOUGHT IT MIGHT HAVE BEEN SOMETHING **I** SAID.

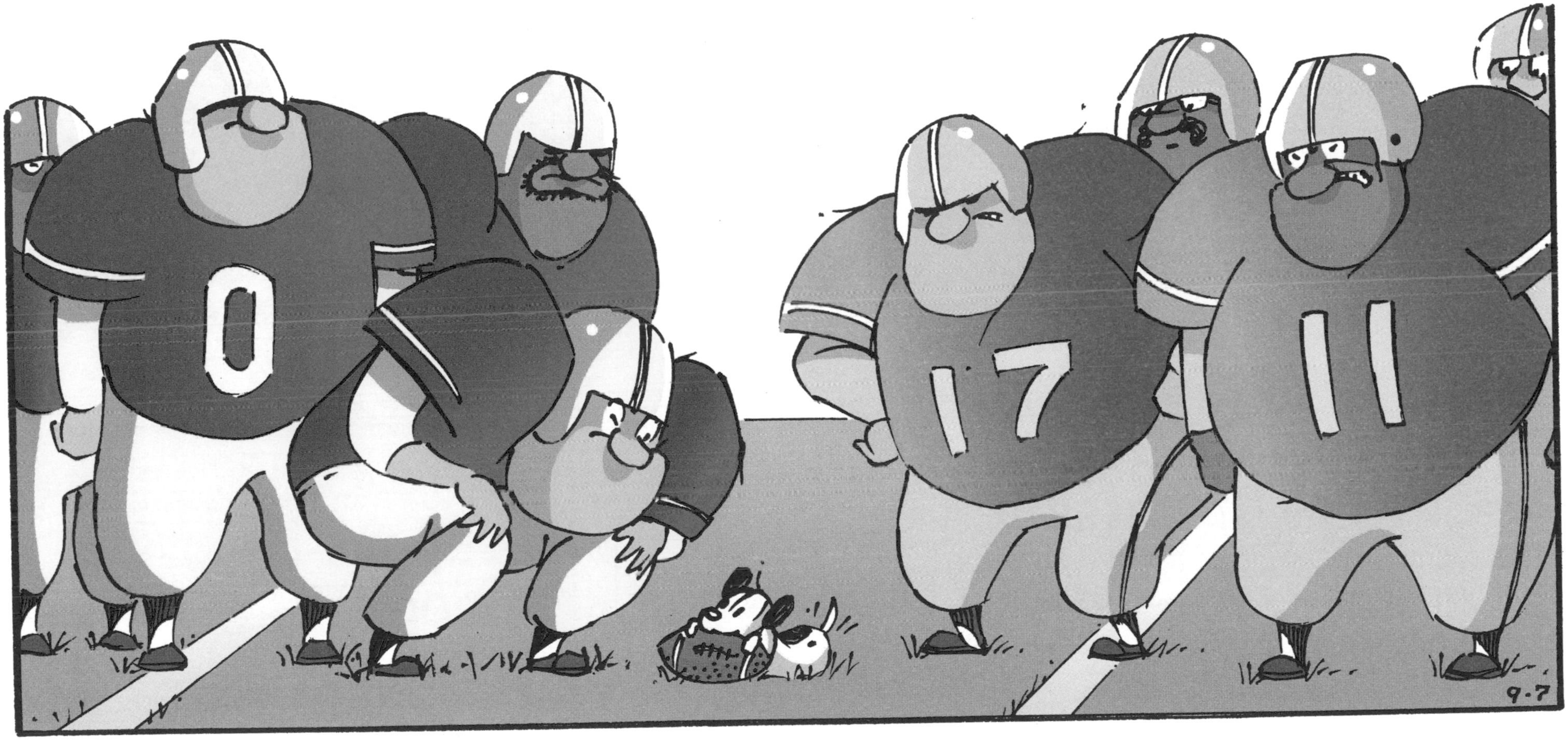
0
17
11
9-7

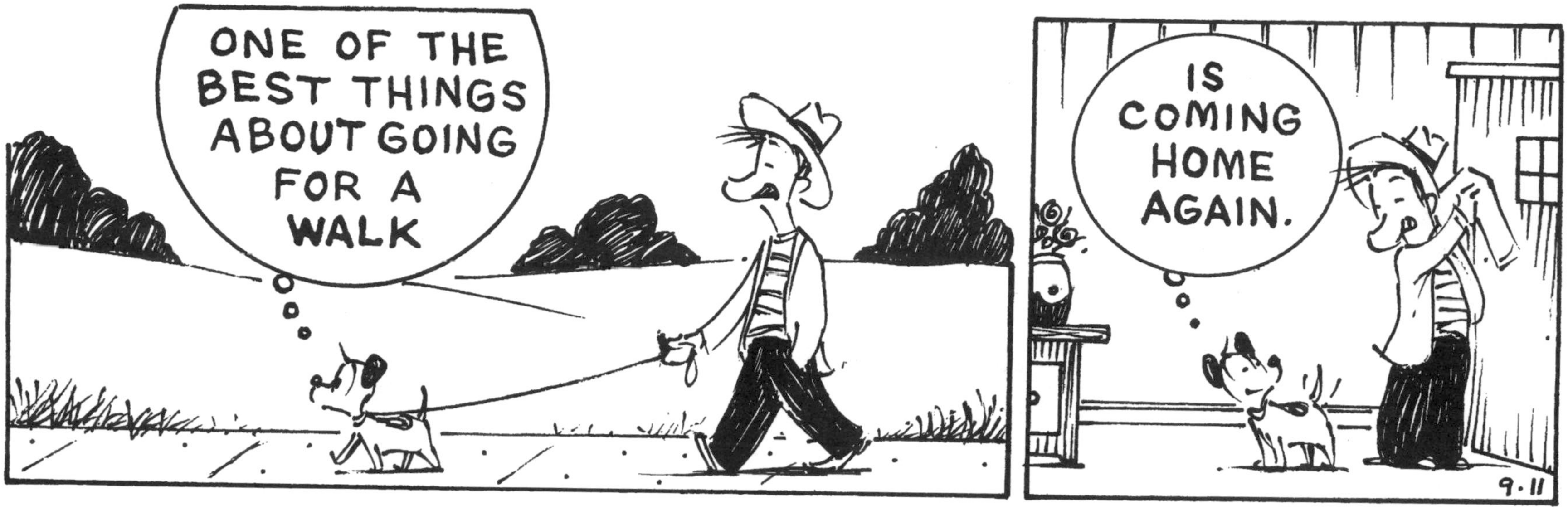
ONE OF THE BEST THINGS ABOUT GOING FOR A WALK
IS COMING HOME AGAIN.
9·11

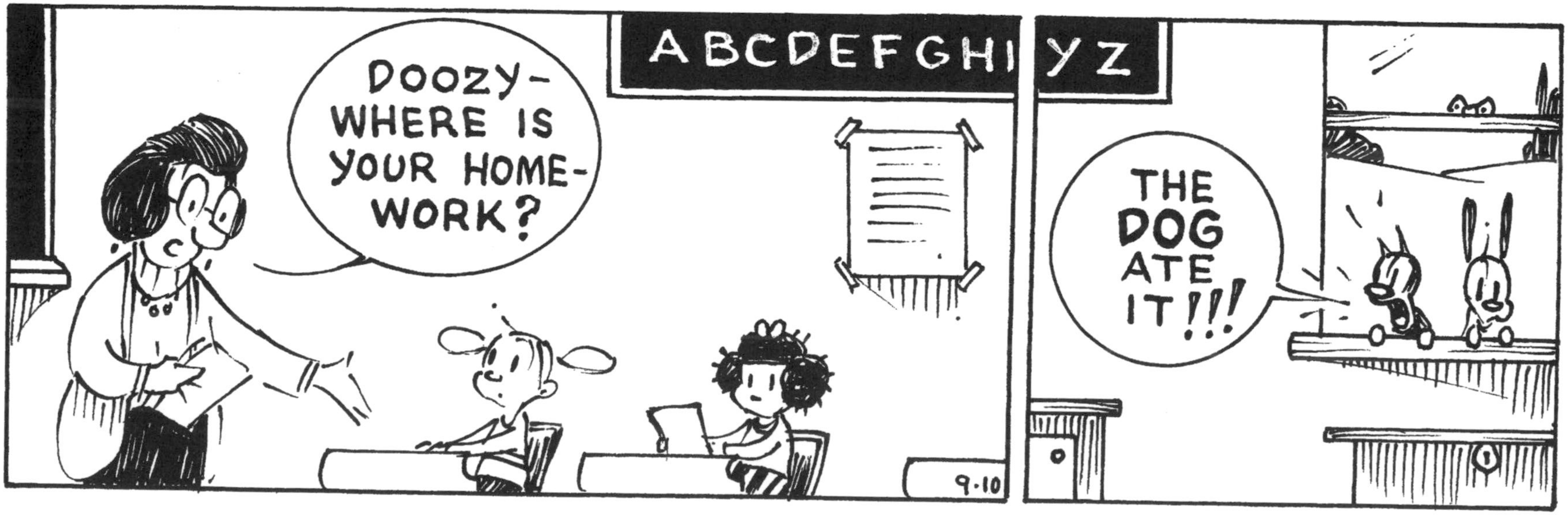
ABCDEFGHI YZ
DOOZY- WHERE IS YOUR HOME-WORK?
9·10
THE DOG ATE IT!!!

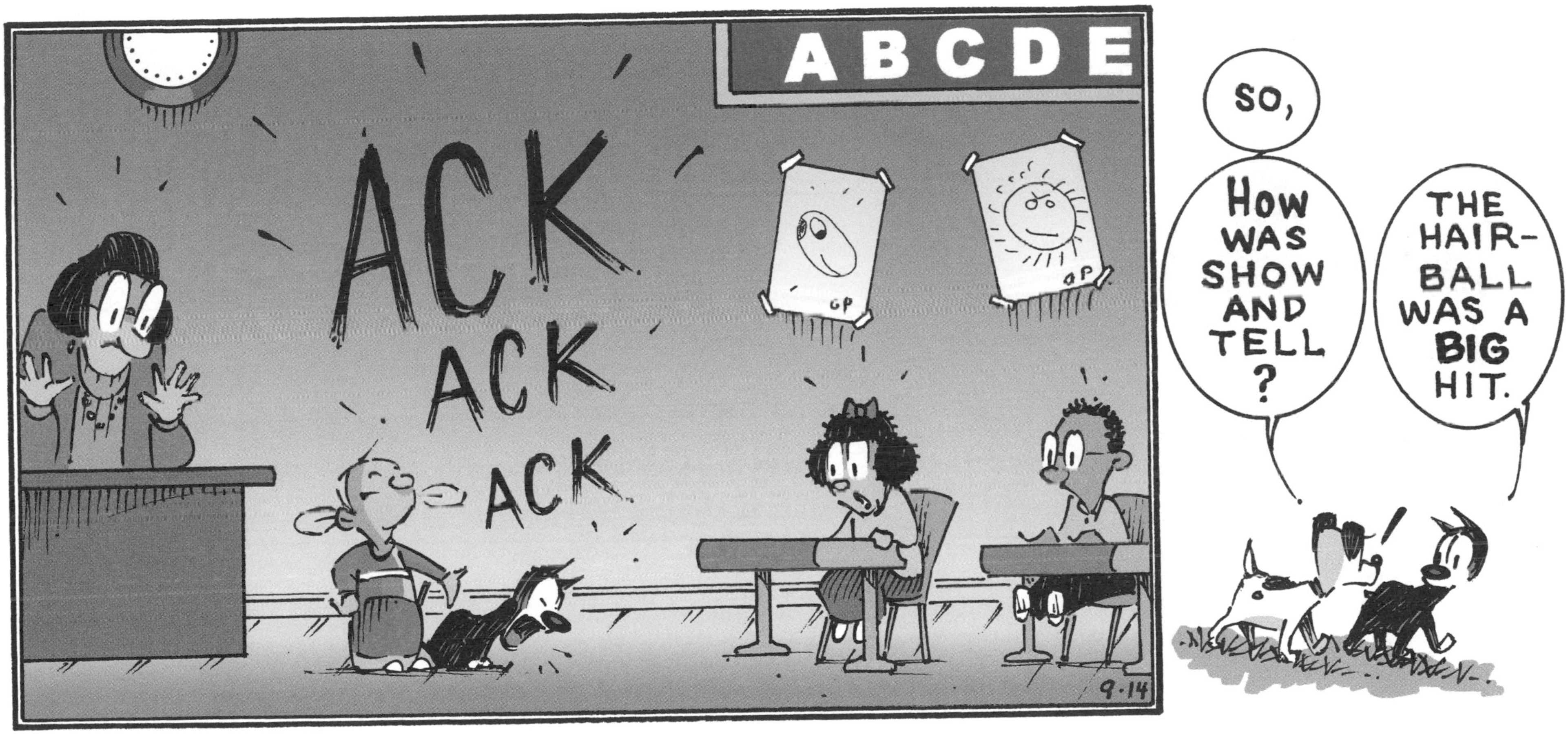
ABCDE
ACK
ACK
ACK
9-14
SO,
HOW WAS SHOW AND TELL?
THE HAIR-BALL WAS A BIG HIT.

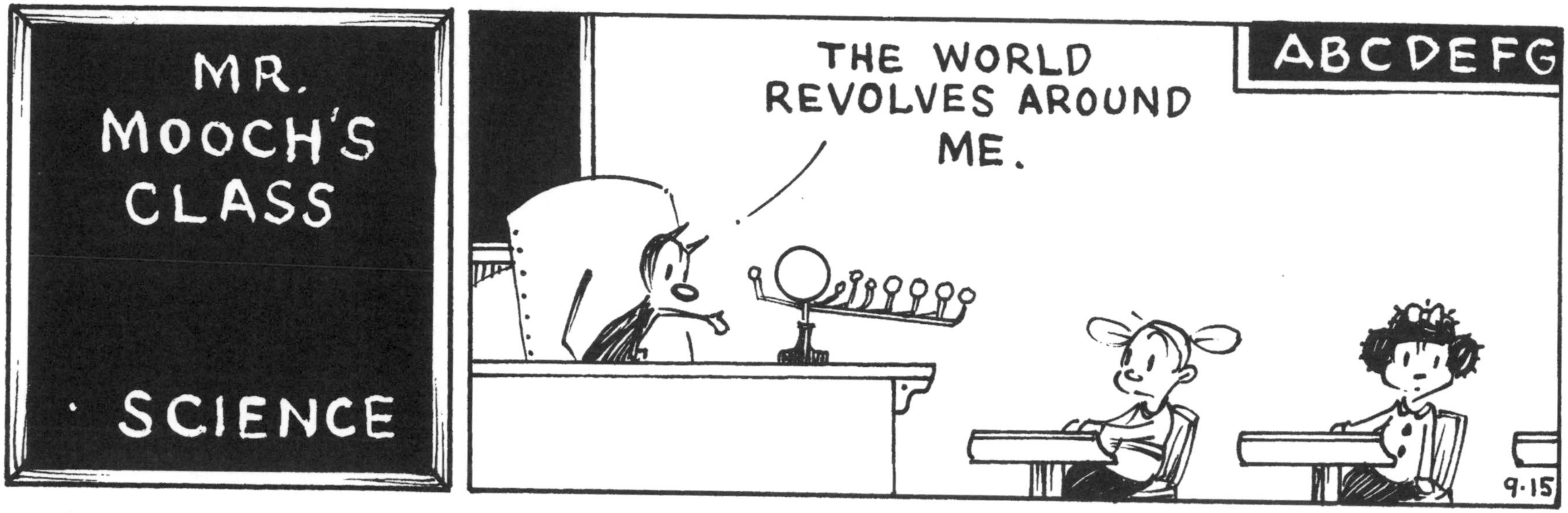
MR. MOOCH'S CLASS
· SCIENCE
THE WORLD REVOLVES AROUND ME.
ABCDEFG
9·15

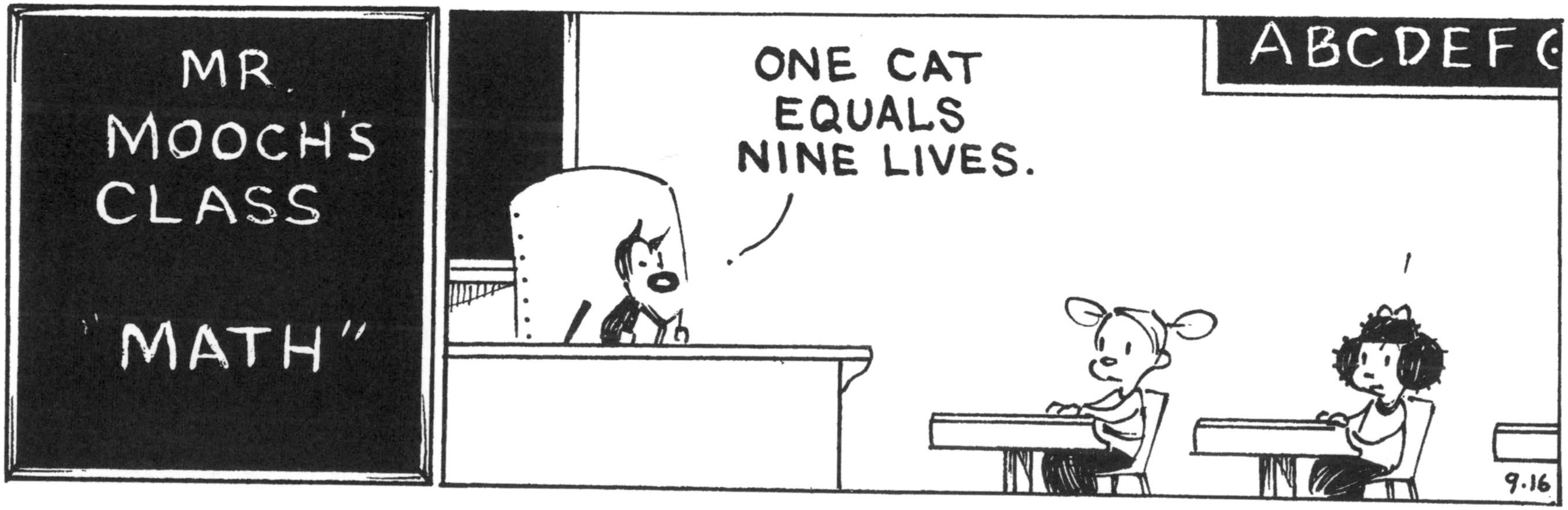
MR. MOOCH'S CLASS
"MATH"
ONE CAT EQUALS NINE LIVES.
ABCDEFG
9·16

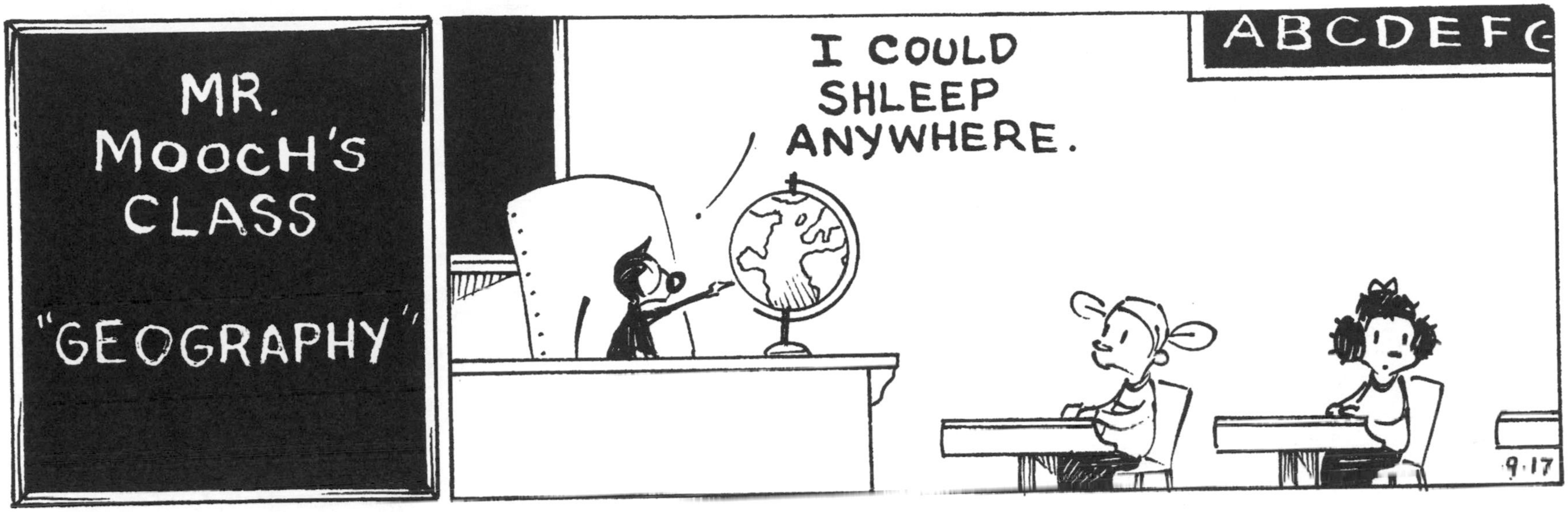
MR. MOOCH'S CLASS
"GEOGRAPHY"
ABCDEFG
I COULD SHLEEP ANYWHERE.
9·17

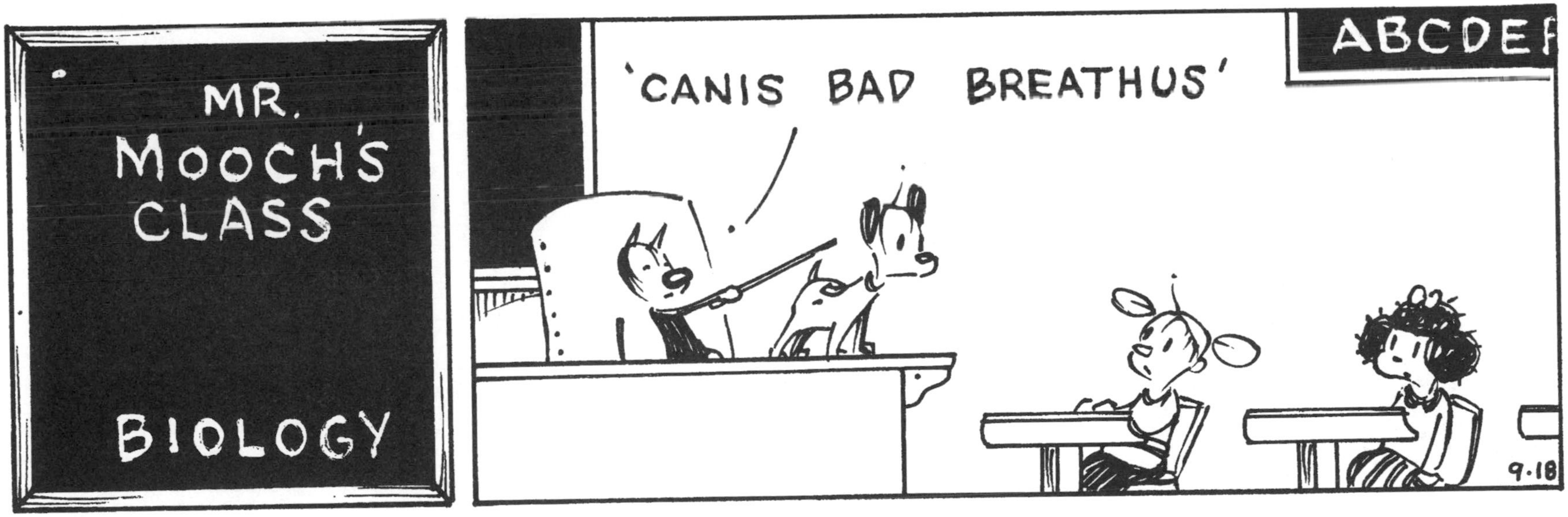
MR. MOOCH'S CLASS
BIOLOGY
ABCDEF
'CANIS BAD BREATHUS'
9·18

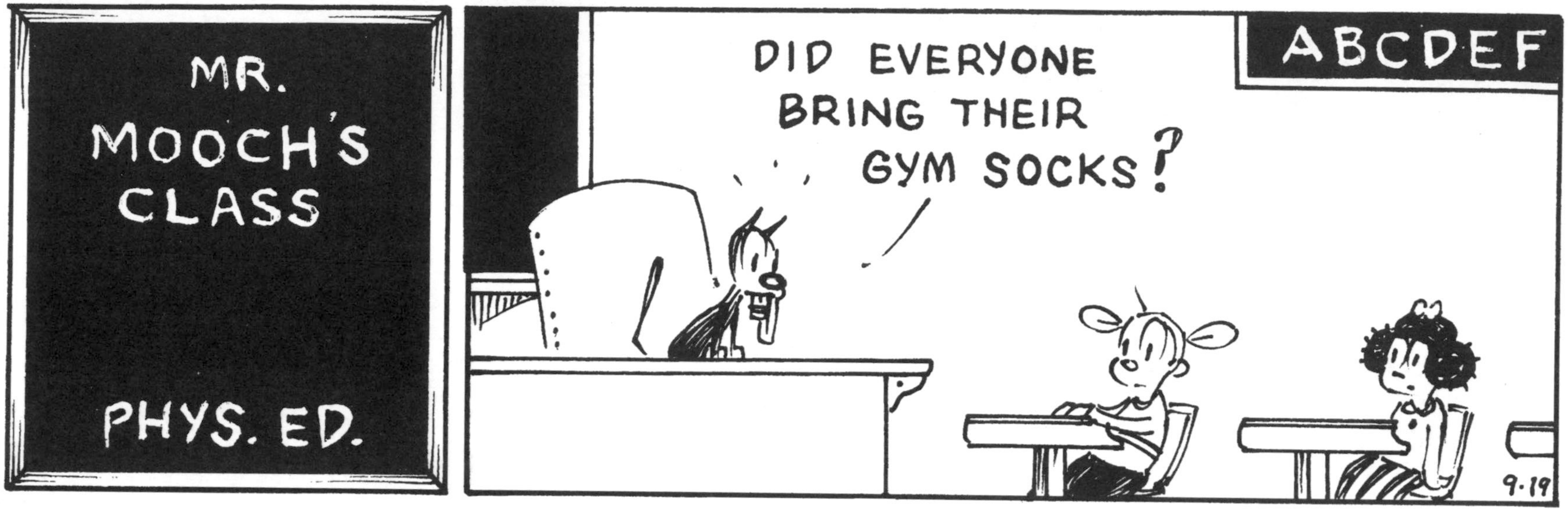
MR. MOOCH'S CLASS
PHYS. ED.
ABCDEF
DID EVERYONE BRING THEIR GYM SOCKS?
9·19

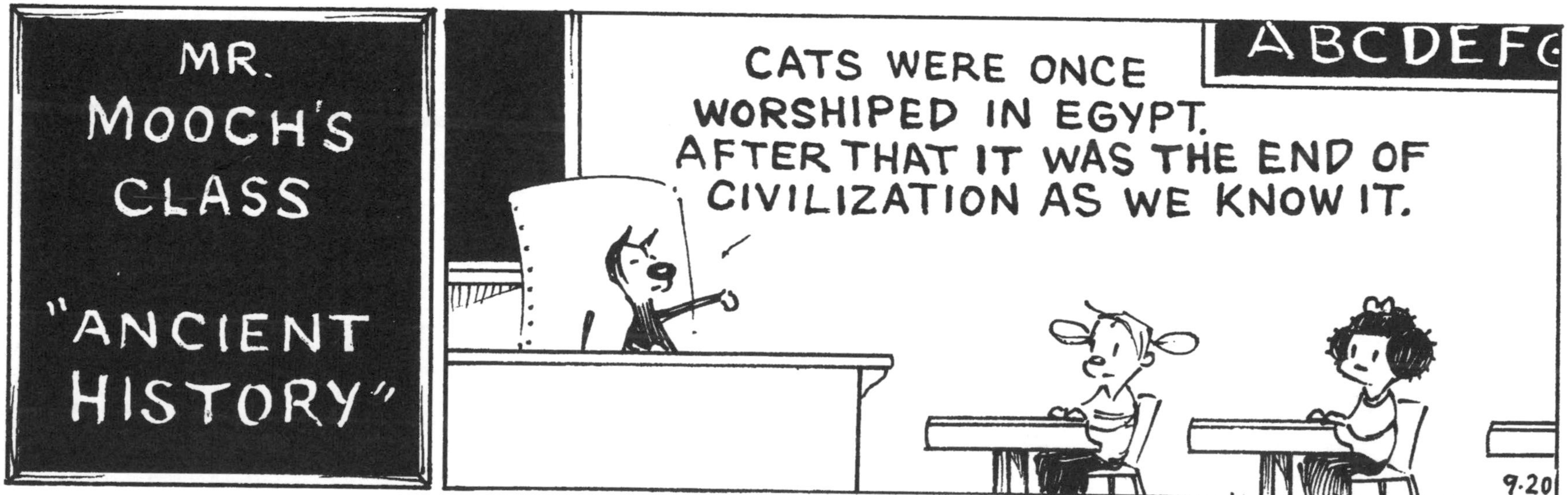
MR. MOOCH'S CLASS
"ANCIENT HISTORY"
ABCDEFG
CATS WERE ONCE WORSHIPED IN EGYPT. AFTER THAT IT WAS THE END OF CIVILIZATION AS WE KNOW IT.
9·20

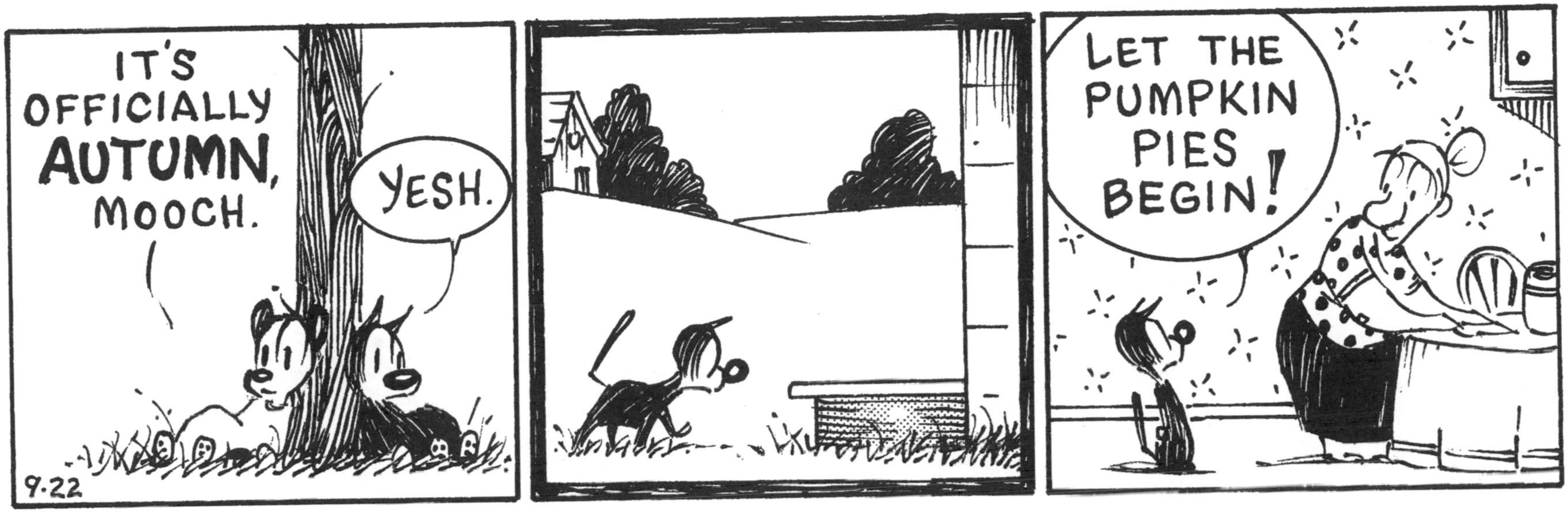
IT'S OFFICIALLY AUTUMN, MOOCH.
YESH.
9·22
LET THE PUMPKIN PIES BEGIN!

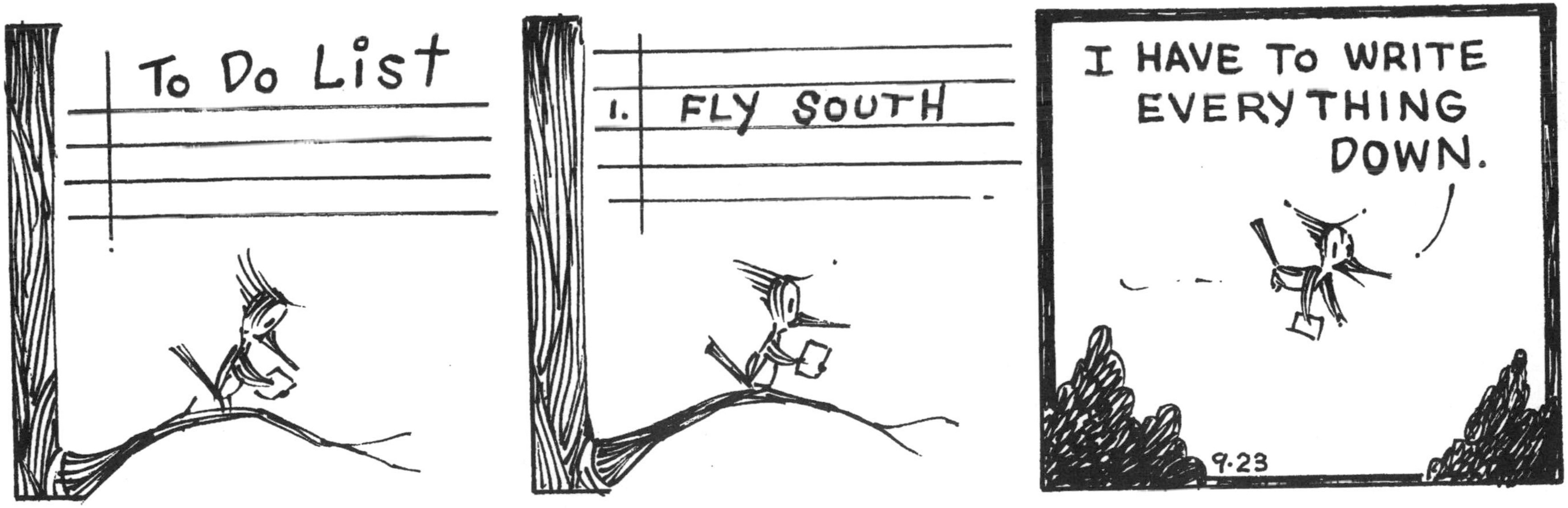
To Do List
1. FLY SOUTH
I HAVE TO WRITE EVERYTHING DOWN.
9·23

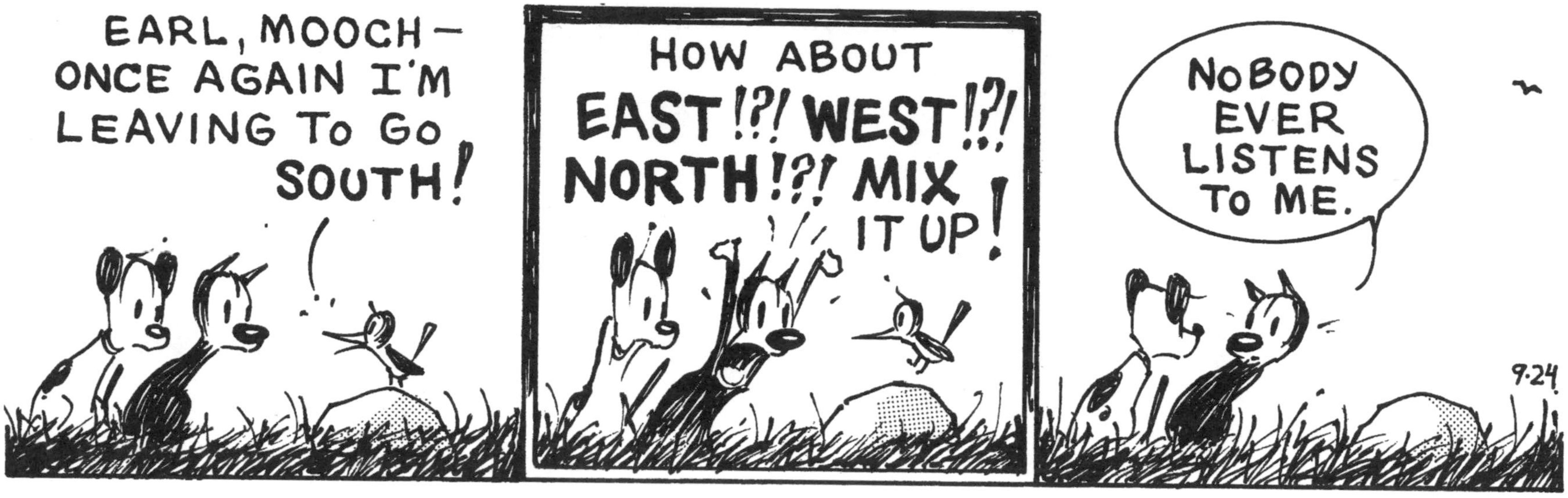
EARL, MOOCH — ONCE AGAIN I'M LEAVING TO GO SOUTH!
HOW ABOUT EAST!?! WEST!?! NORTH!?! MIX IT UP!
NOBODY EVER LISTENS TO ME.
9·24

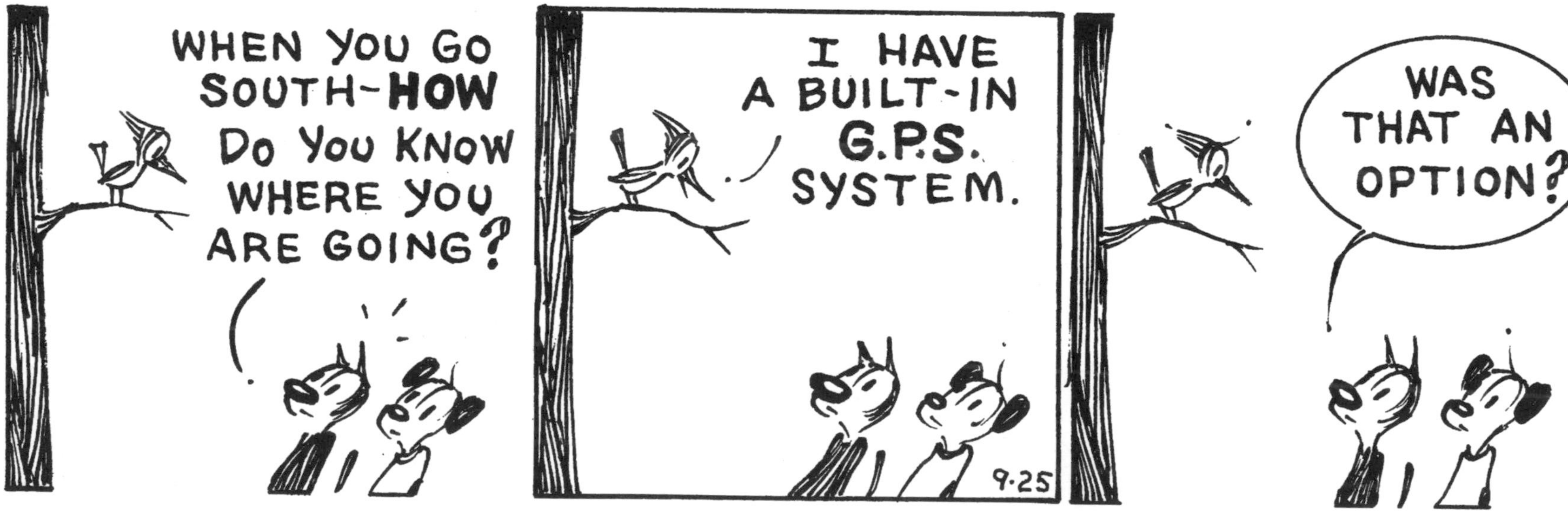
WHEN YOU GO SOUTH–HOW DO YOU KNOW WHERE YOU ARE GOING?
I HAVE A BUILT-IN G.P.S. SYSTEM.
9·25
WAS THAT AN OPTION?

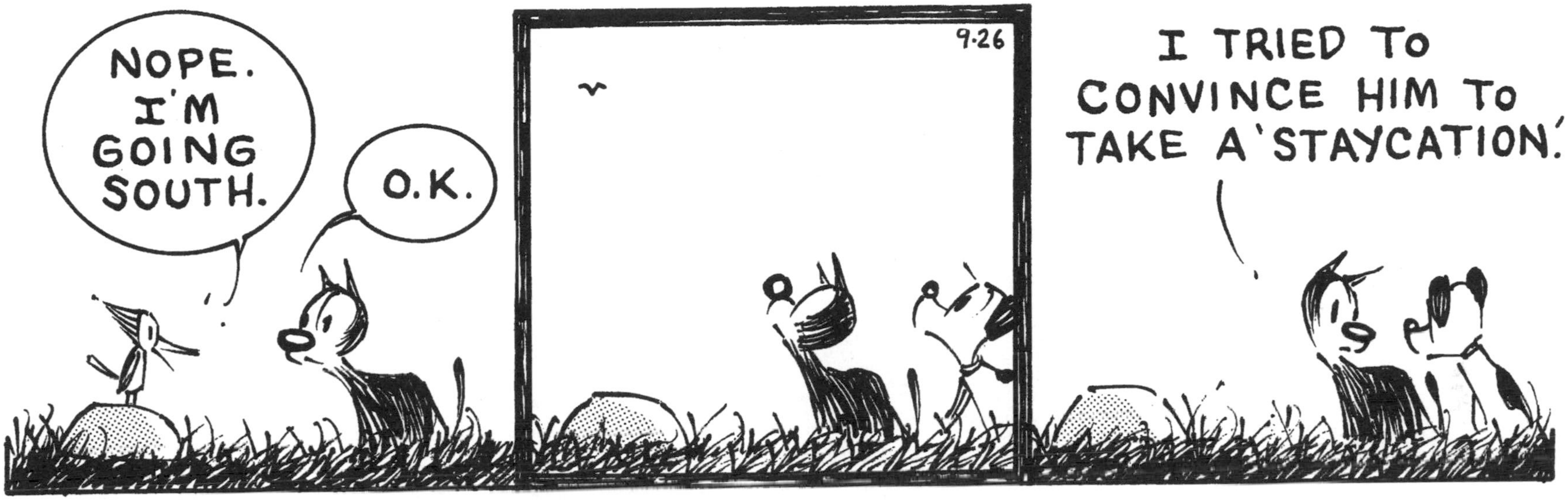
NOPE. I'M GOING SOUTH.
O.K.
9·26
I TRIED TO CONVINCE HIM TO TAKE A 'STAYCATION.'

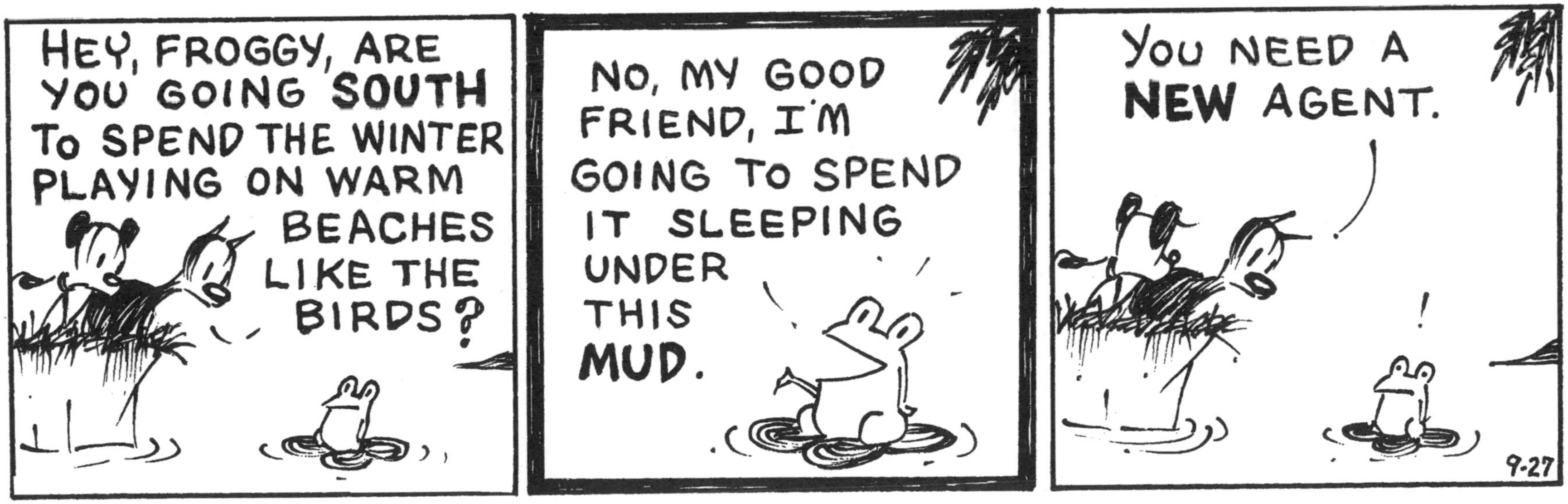
HEY, FROGGY, ARE YOU GOING **SOUTH** TO SPEND THE WINTER PLAYING ON WARM BEACHES LIKE THE BIRDS?
NO, MY GOOD FRIEND, I'M GOING TO SPEND IT SLEEPING UNDER THIS **MUD**.
YOU NEED A **NEW** AGENT.
!
9·27

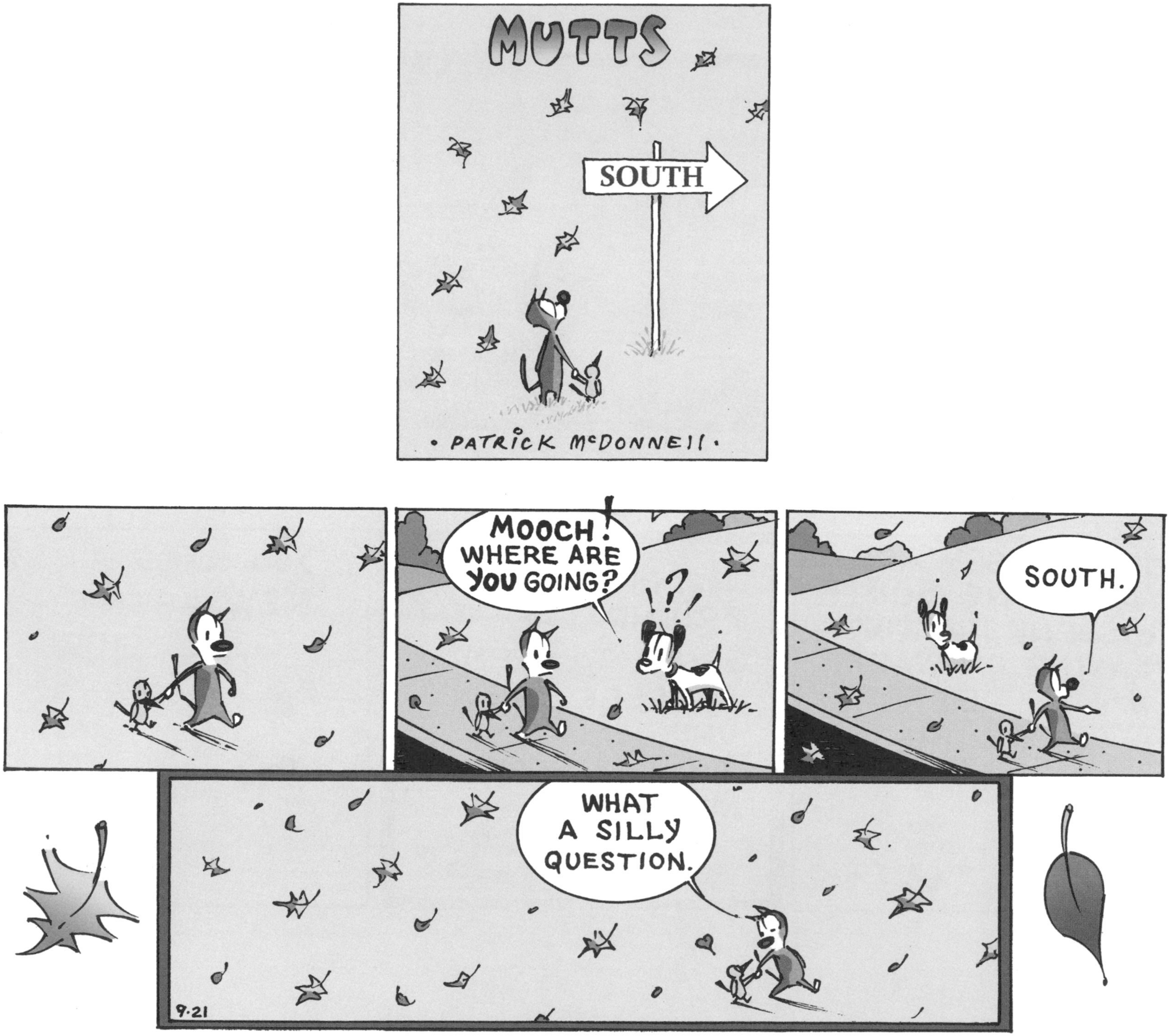
MUTTS
SOUTH
• PATRICK McDONNELL •
MOOCH! WHERE ARE YOU GOING?
!?!
SOUTH.
WHAT A SILLY QUESTION.
9.21

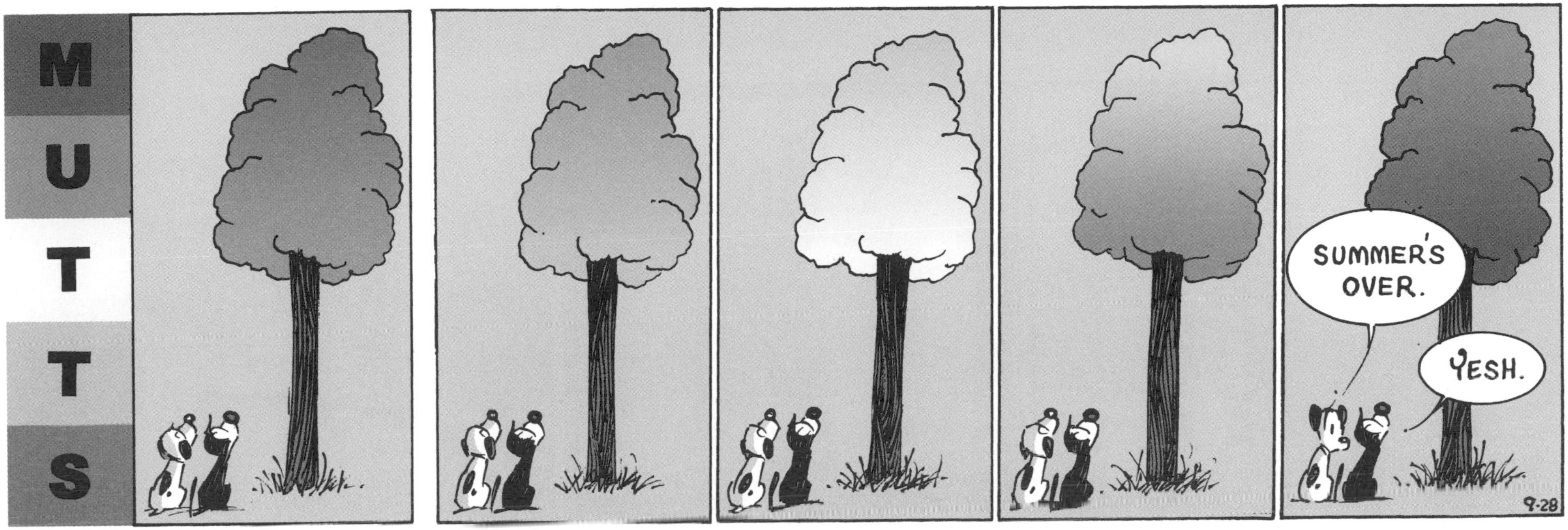
MUTTS
SUMMER'S OVER.
YESH.
9·28

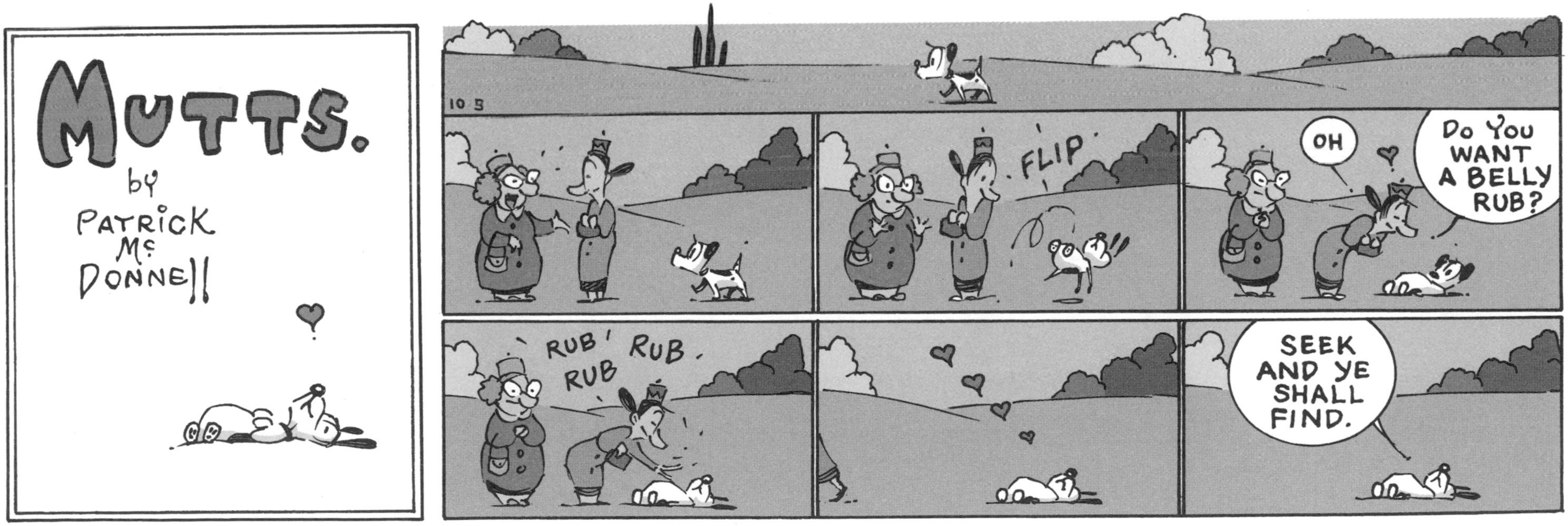
MUTTS.
by PATRICK McDONNELL
10 5
FLIP
OH
DO YOU WANT A BELLY RUB?
RUB RUB RUB
SEEK AND YE SHALL FIND.

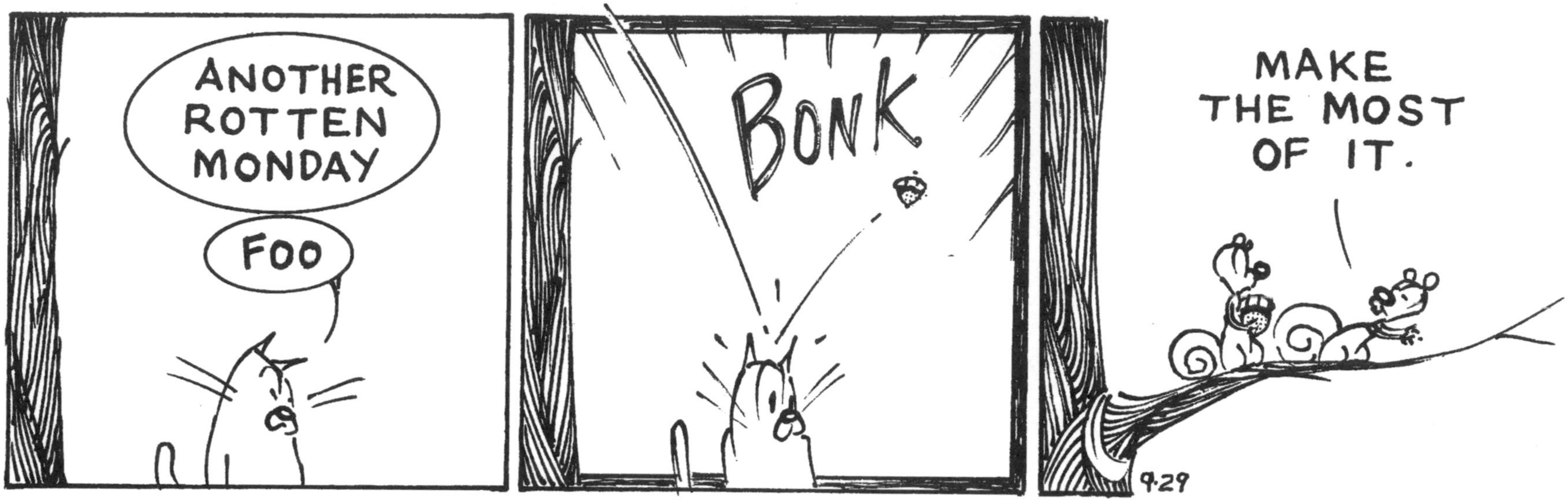
ANOTHER ROTTEN MONDAY
FOO
BONK
MAKE THE MOST OF IT.
9·29

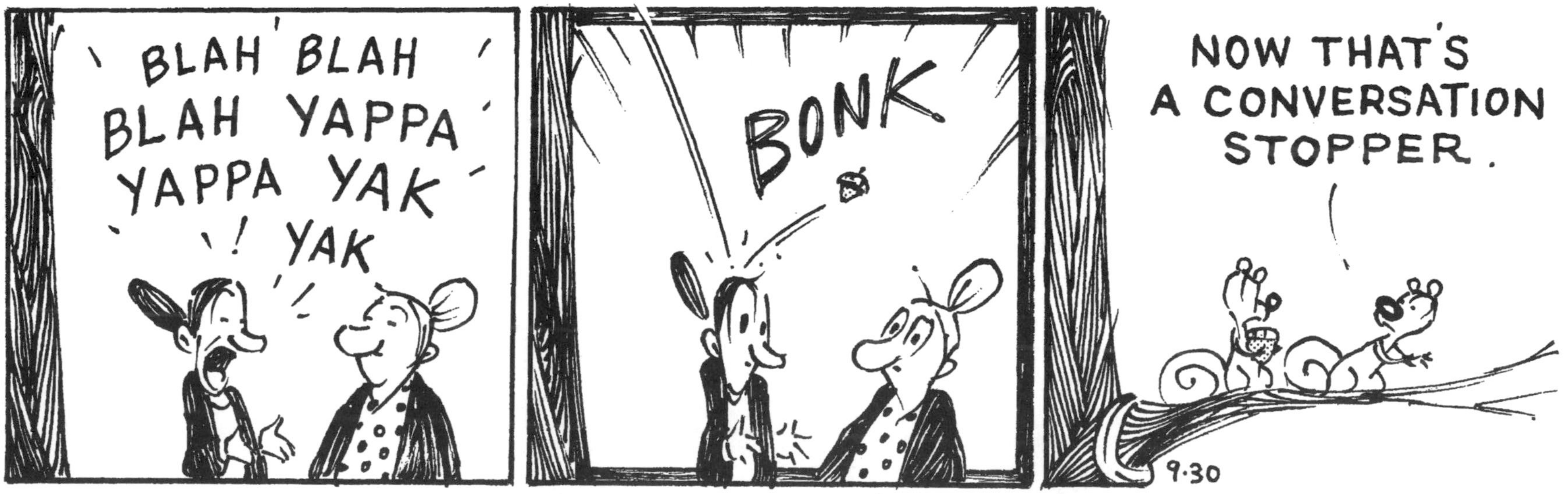
BLAH BLAH BLAH YAPPA YAPPA YAPPA YAK YAK
BONK
NOW THAT'S A CONVERSATION STOPPER.
9·30

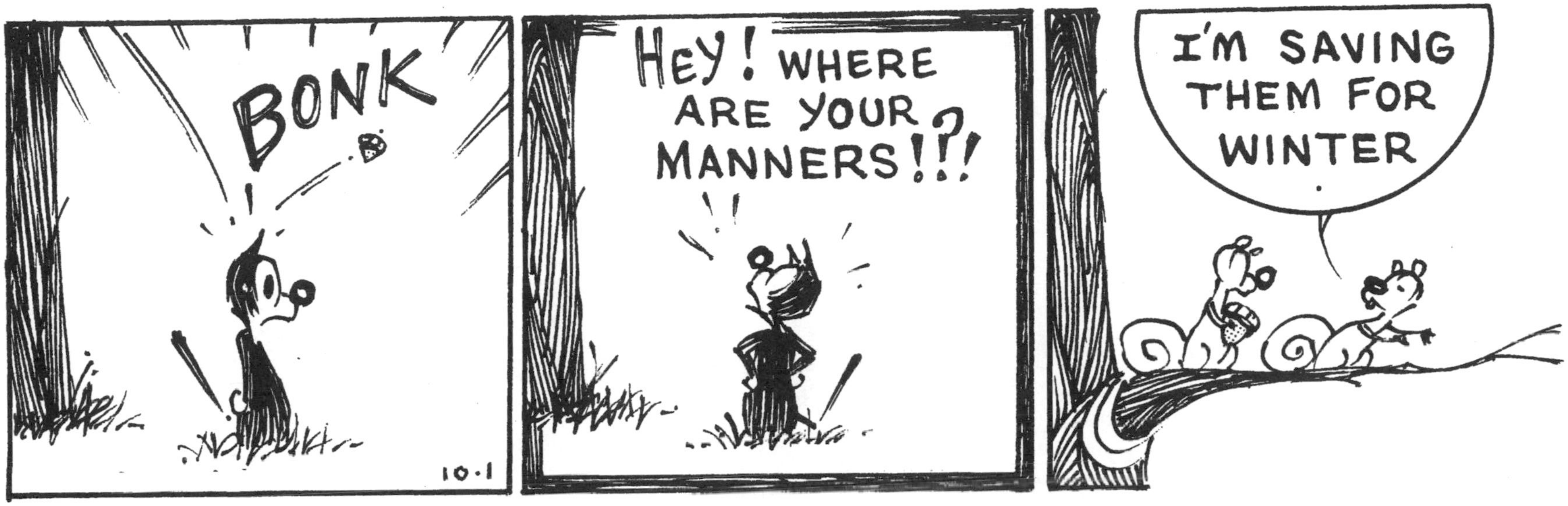
BONK
10·1
HEY! WHERE ARE YOUR MANNERS!?!
I'M SAVING THEM FOR WINTER

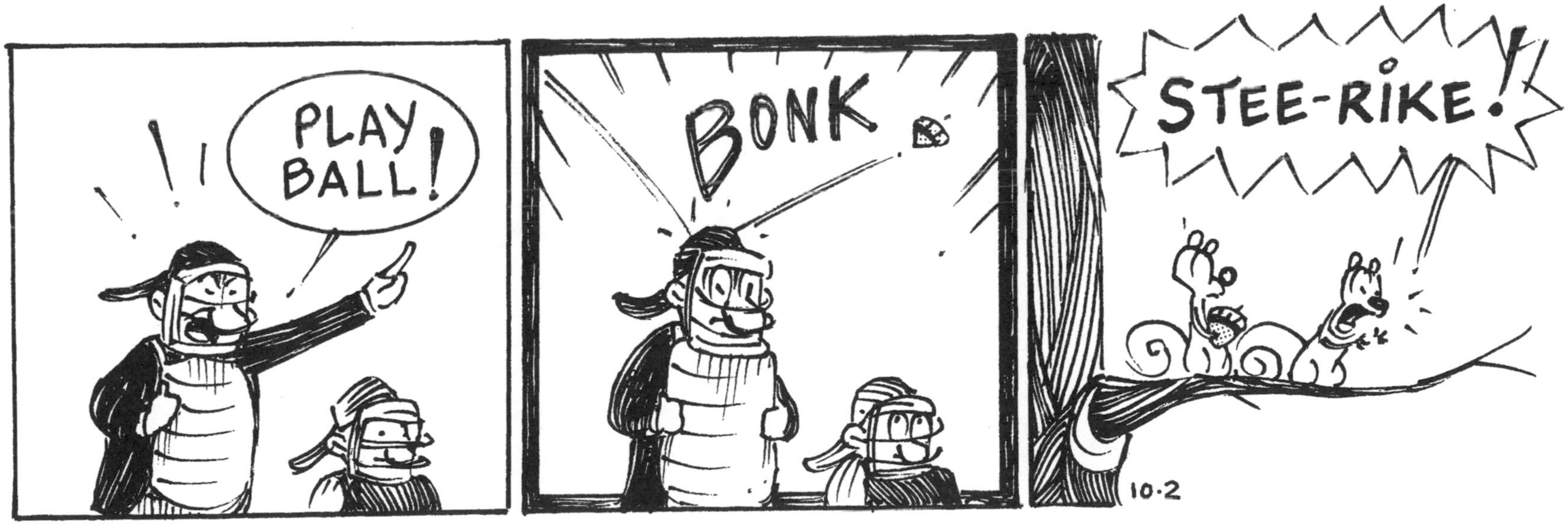
PLAY BALL!
BONK
STEE-RIKE!
10·2

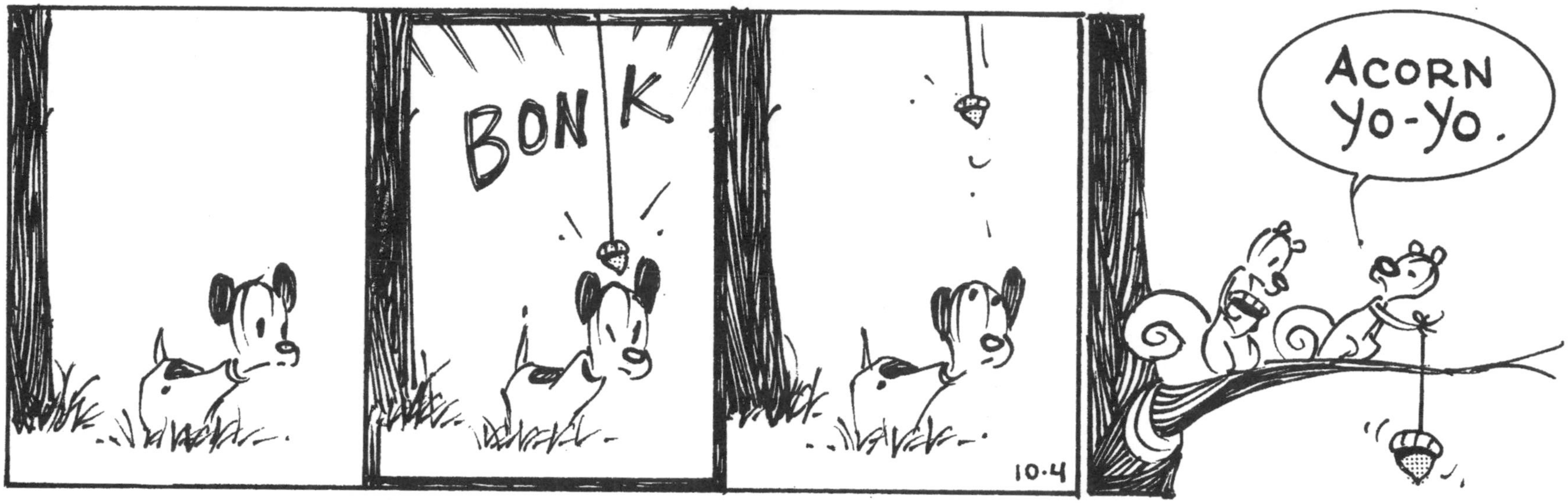
BONK
10·4
ACORN YO-YO.

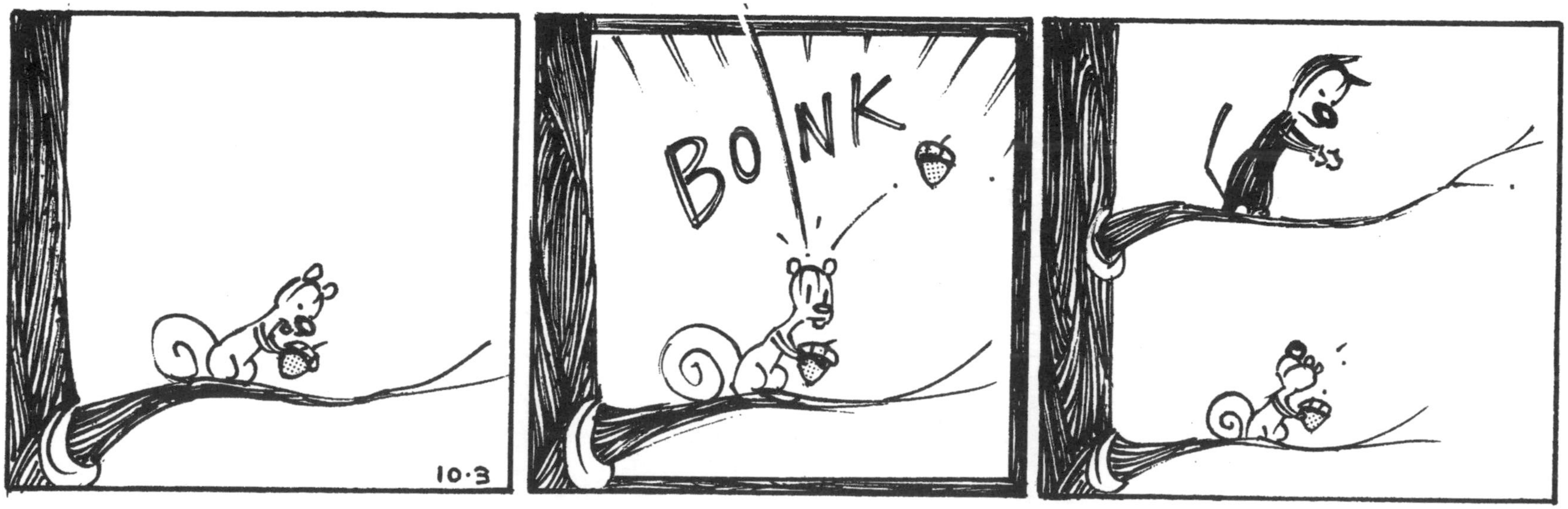
10·3
BONK

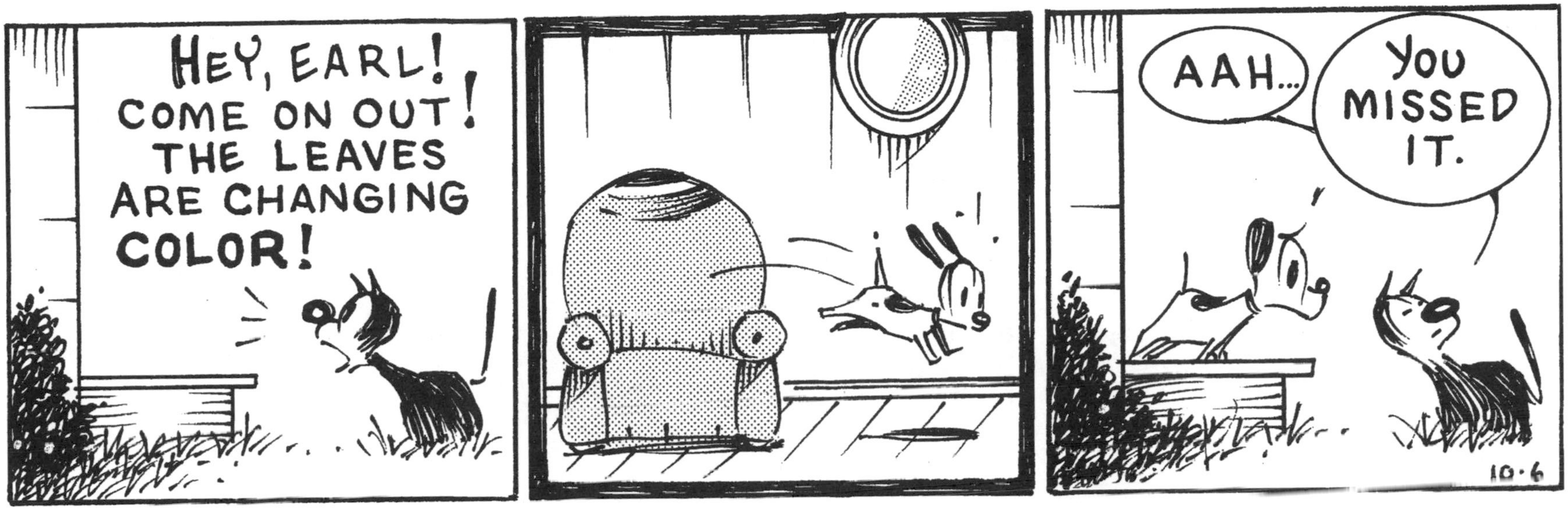
HEY, EARL! COME ON OUT! THE LEAVES ARE CHANGING COLOR!
AAH...
YOU MISSED IT.
10·6

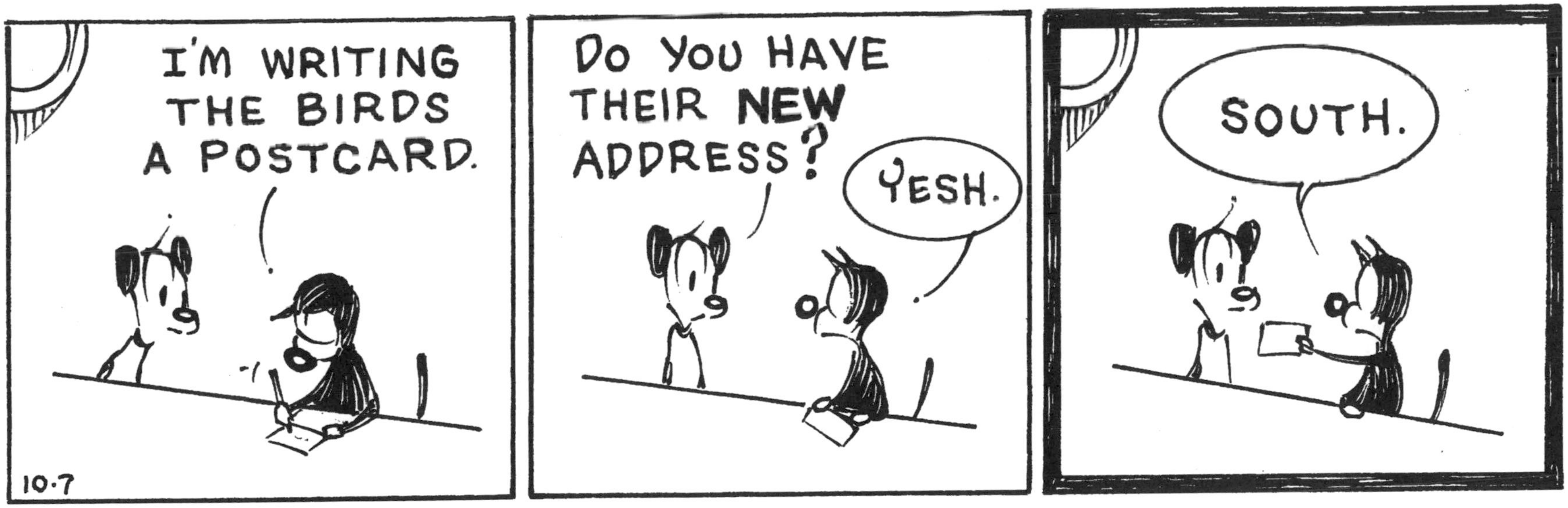
I'M WRITING THE BIRDS A POSTCARD.
10·7
DO YOU HAVE THEIR NEW ADDRESS?
YESH.
SOUTH.

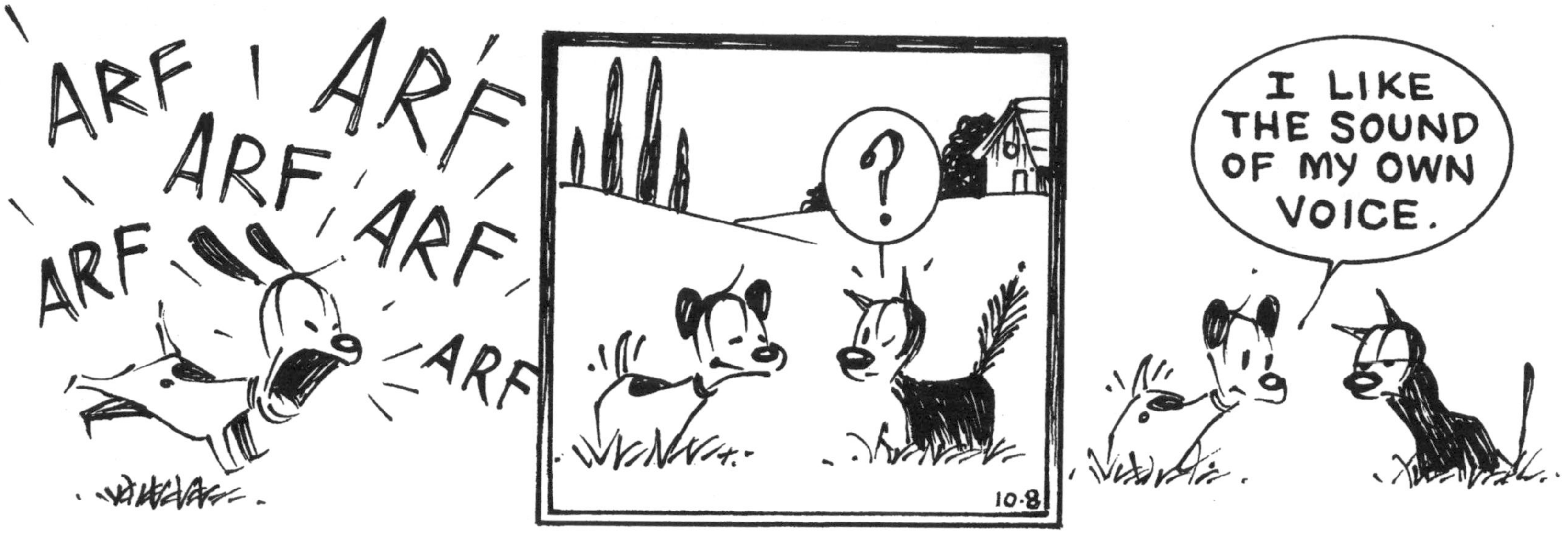
ARF
ARF
ARF
ARF
ARF
ARF
?
I LIKE THE SOUND OF MY OWN VOICE.
10·8

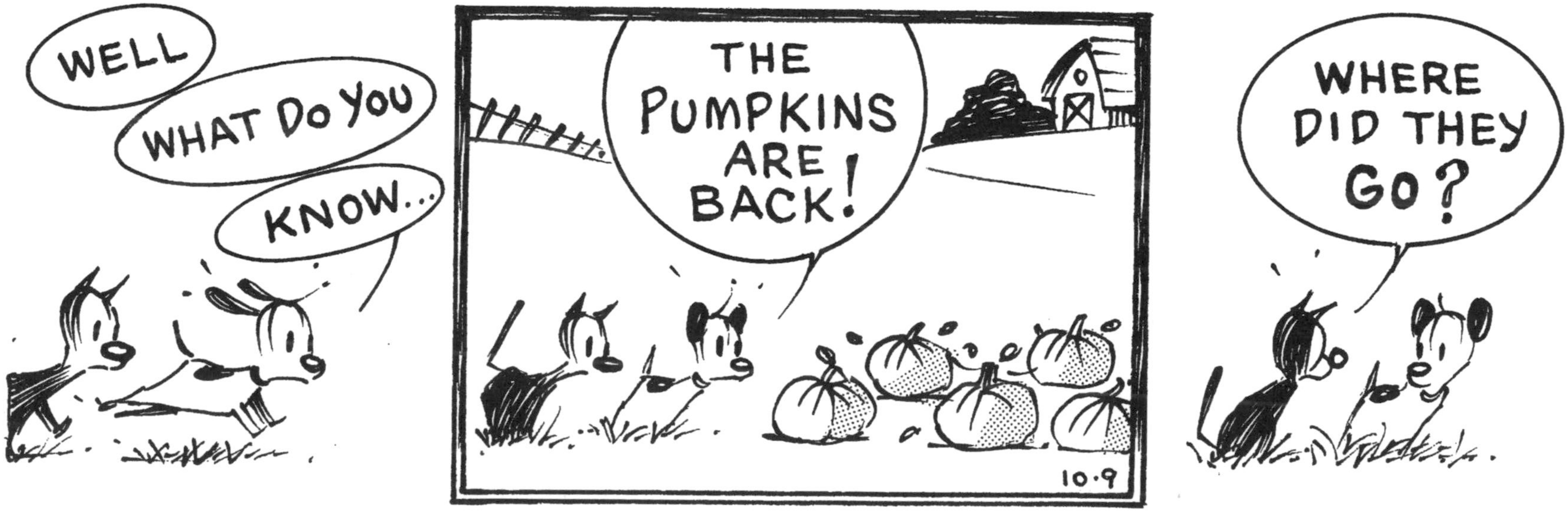
WELL
WHAT DO YOU
KNOW...
THE PUMPKINS ARE BACK!
WHERE DID THEY GO?
10·9

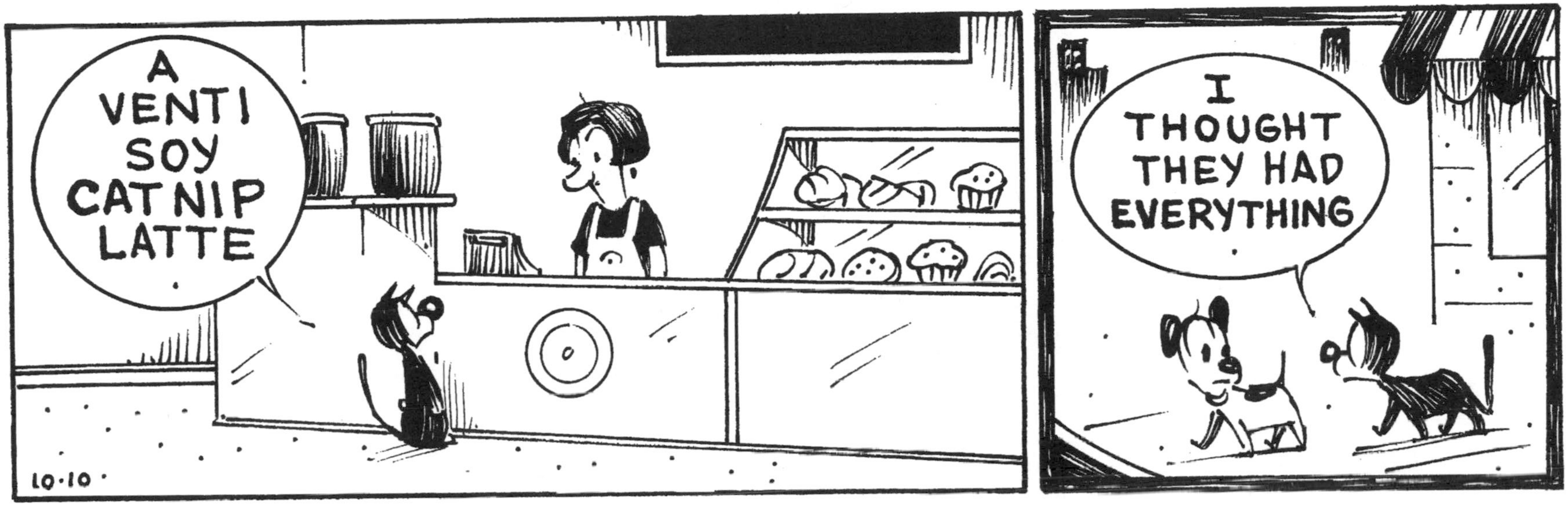
A VENTI SOY CATNIP LATTE
10·10
I THOUGHT THEY HAD EVERYTHING

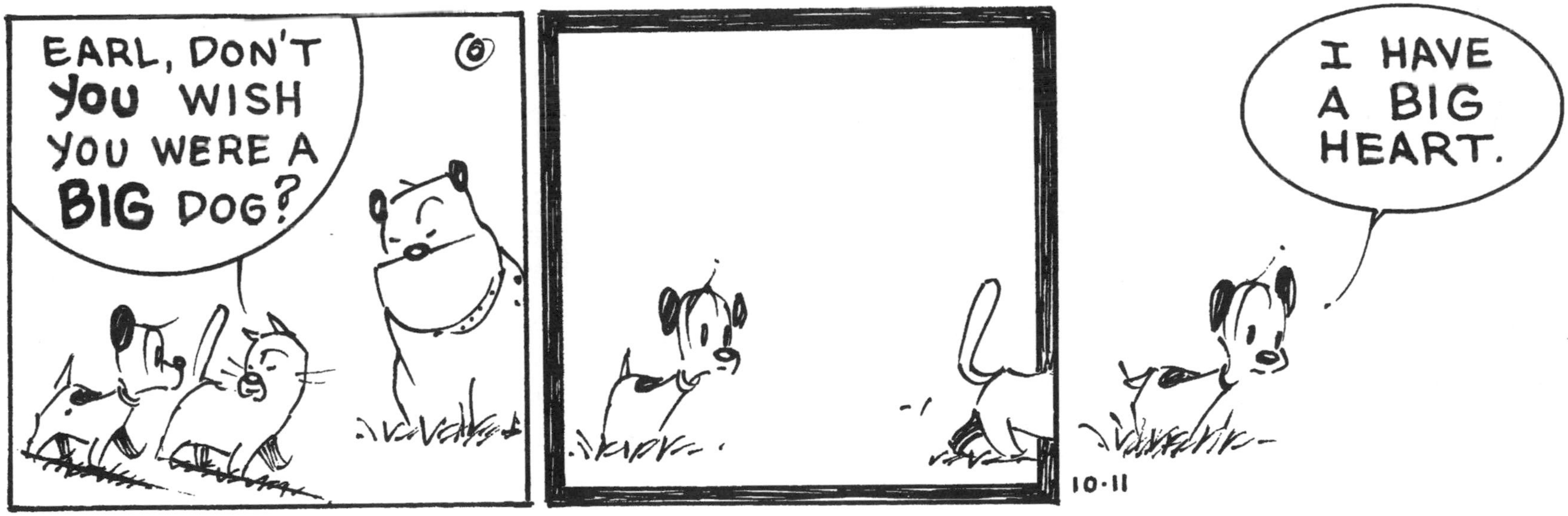
EARL, DON'T YOU WISH YOU WERE A BIG DOG?
I HAVE A BIG HEART.
10·11

MUTTS

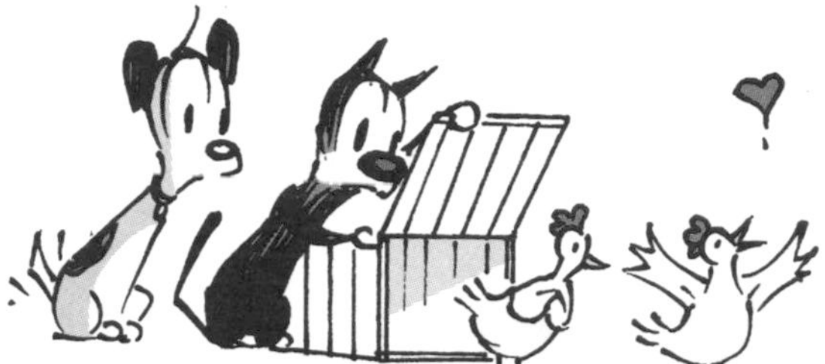

PATRICK McDONNELL

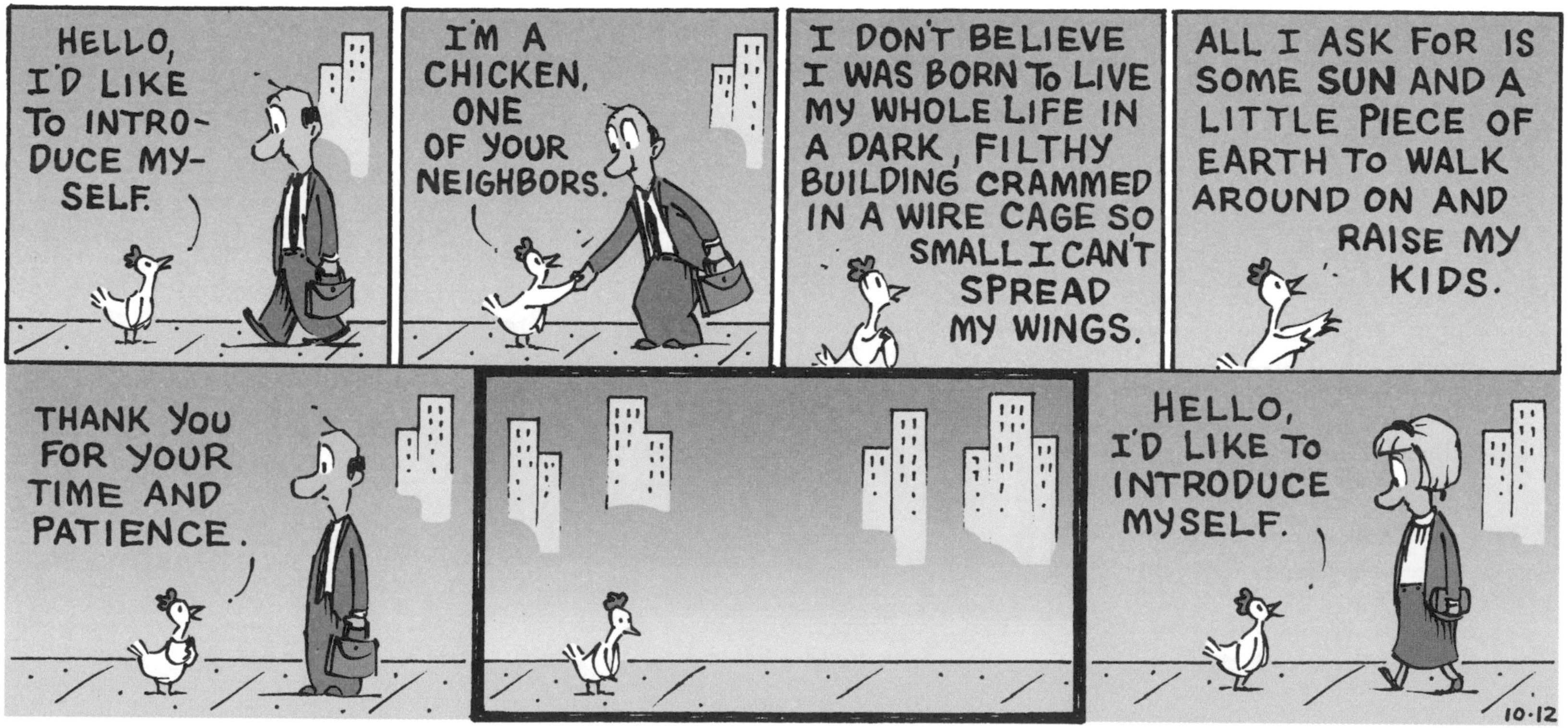
HELLO, I'D LIKE TO INTRO-DUCE MY-SELF.
I'M A CHICKEN, ONE OF YOUR NEIGHBORS.
I DON'T BELIEVE I WAS BORN TO LIVE MY WHOLE LIFE IN A DARK, FILTHY BUILDING CRAMMED IN A WIRE CAGE SO SMALL I CAN'T SPREAD MY WINGS.
ALL I ASK FOR IS SOME SUN AND A LITTLE PIECE OF EARTH TO WALK AROUND ON AND RAISE MY KIDS.
THANK YOU FOR YOUR TIME AND PATIENCE.
HELLO, I'D LIKE TO INTRODUCE MYSELF.
10·12

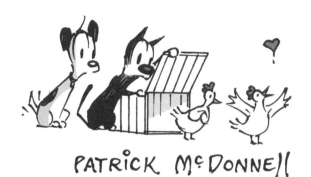

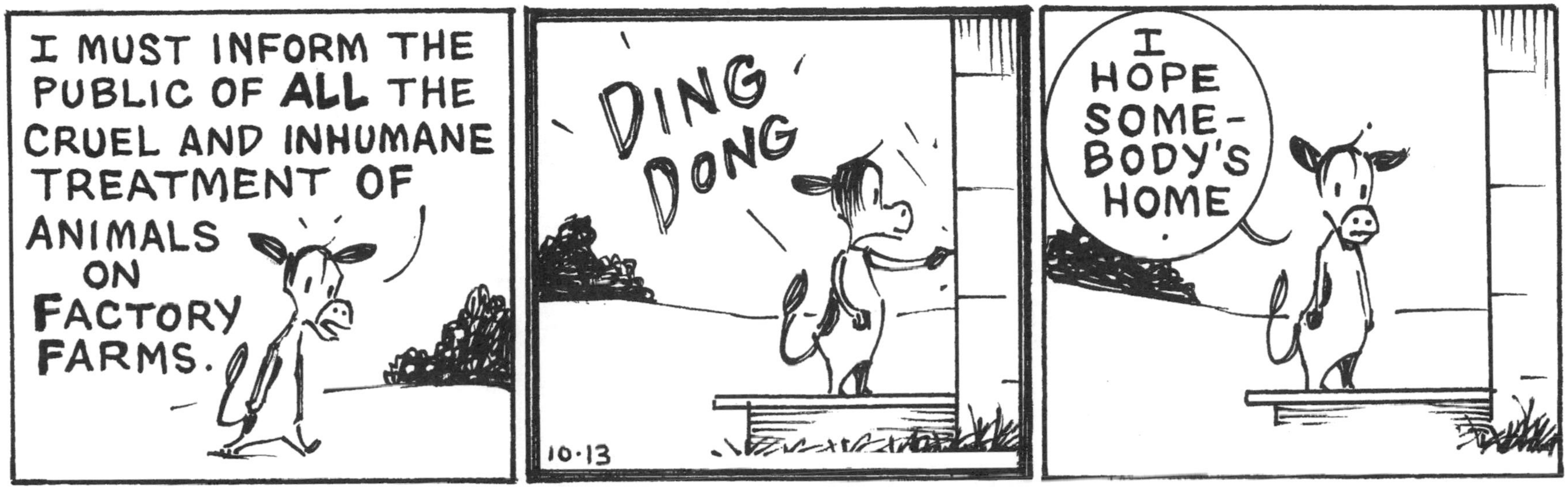
I MUST INFORM THE PUBLIC OF **ALL** THE CRUEL AND INHUMANE TREATMENT OF ANIMALS ON FACTORY FARMS.
DING DONG
10·13
I HOPE SOME-BODY'S HOME.

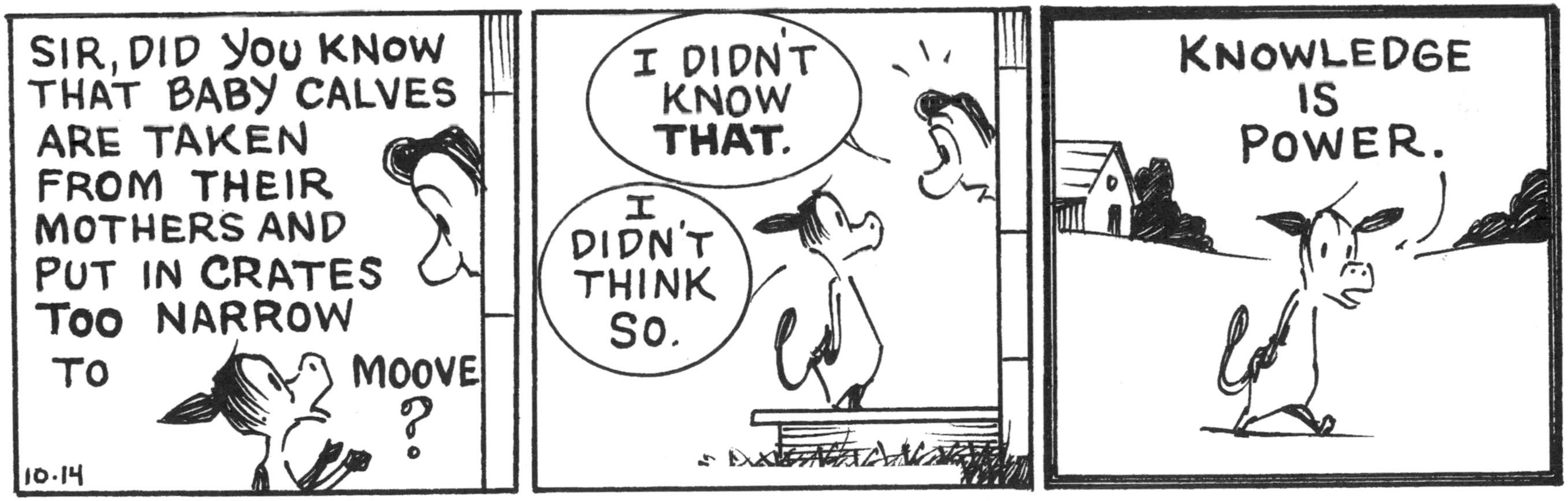
SIR, DID YOU KNOW THAT BABY CALVES ARE TAKEN FROM THEIR MOTHERS AND PUT IN CRATES TOO NARROW TO MOOVE?
10·14
I DIDN'T KNOW **THAT**.
I DIDN'T THINK SO.
KNOWLEDGE IS POWER.

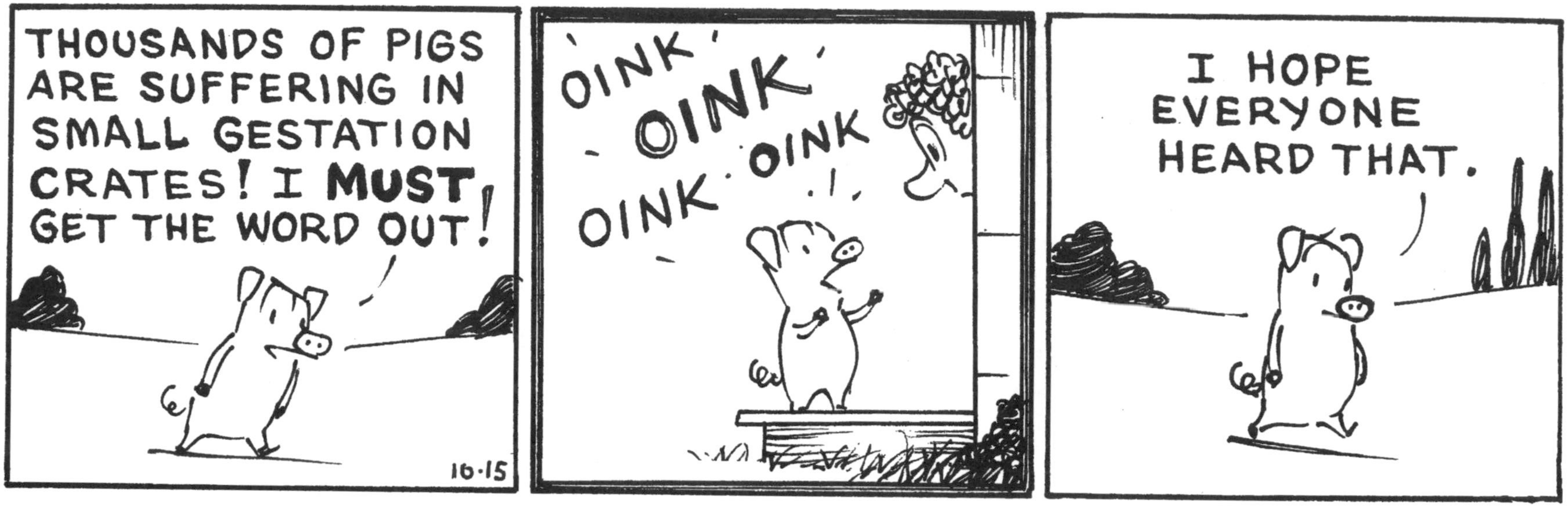
THOUSANDS OF PIGS ARE SUFFERING IN SMALL GESTATION CRATES! I **MUST** GET THE WORD OUT!
10-15
OINK OINK OINK OINK
I HOPE EVERYONE HEARD THAT.

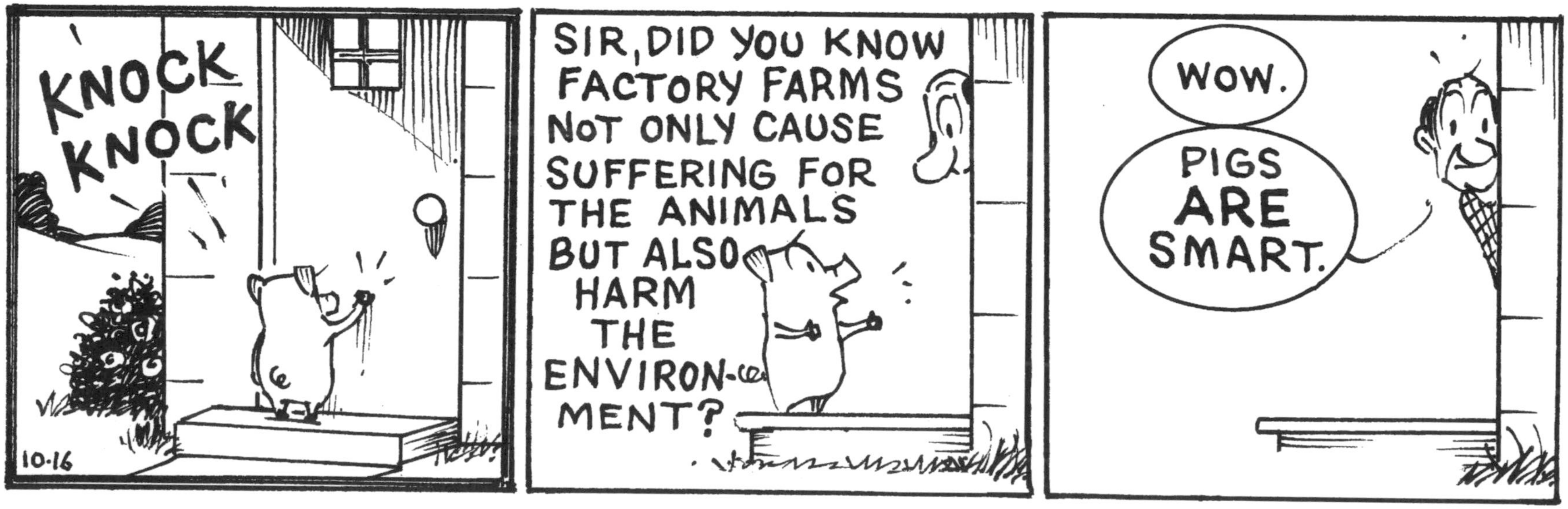
KNOCK KNOCK
10-16
SIR, DID YOU KNOW FACTORY FARMS NOT ONLY CAUSE SUFFERING FOR THE ANIMALS BUT ALSO HARM THE ENVIRONMENT?
WOW.
PIGS **ARE** SMART.

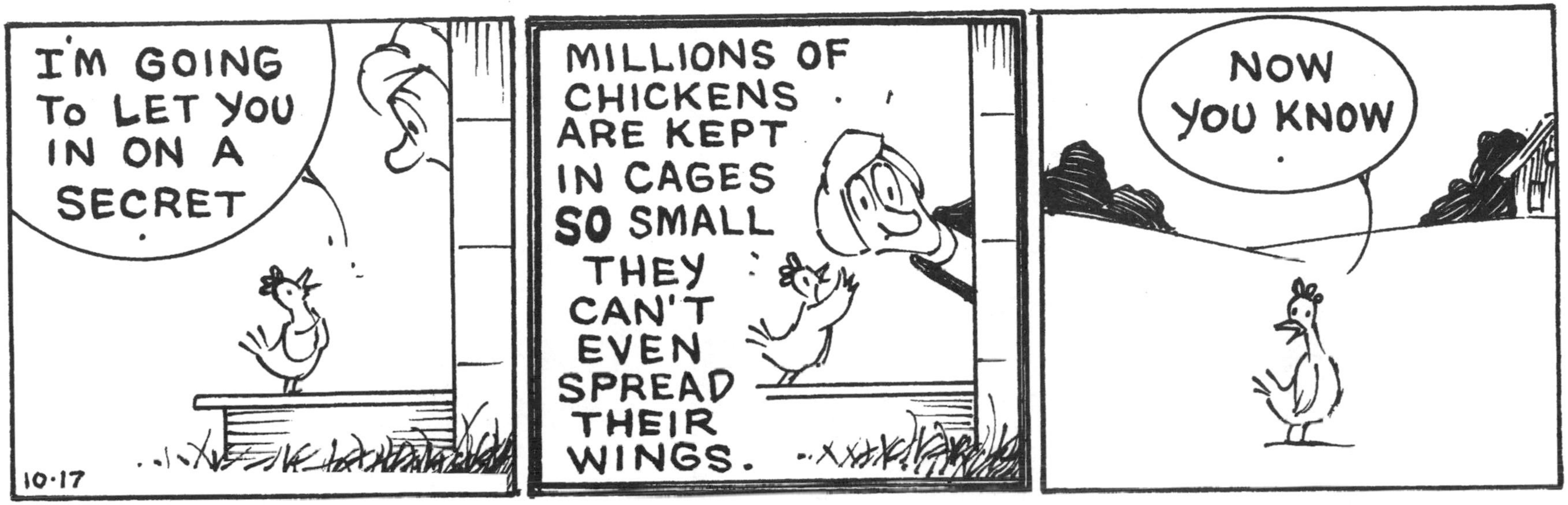
I'M GOING TO LET YOU IN ON A SECRET
MILLIONS OF CHICKENS ARE KEPT IN CAGES SO SMALL THEY CAN'T EVEN SPREAD THEIR WINGS.
NOW YOU KNOW
10·17

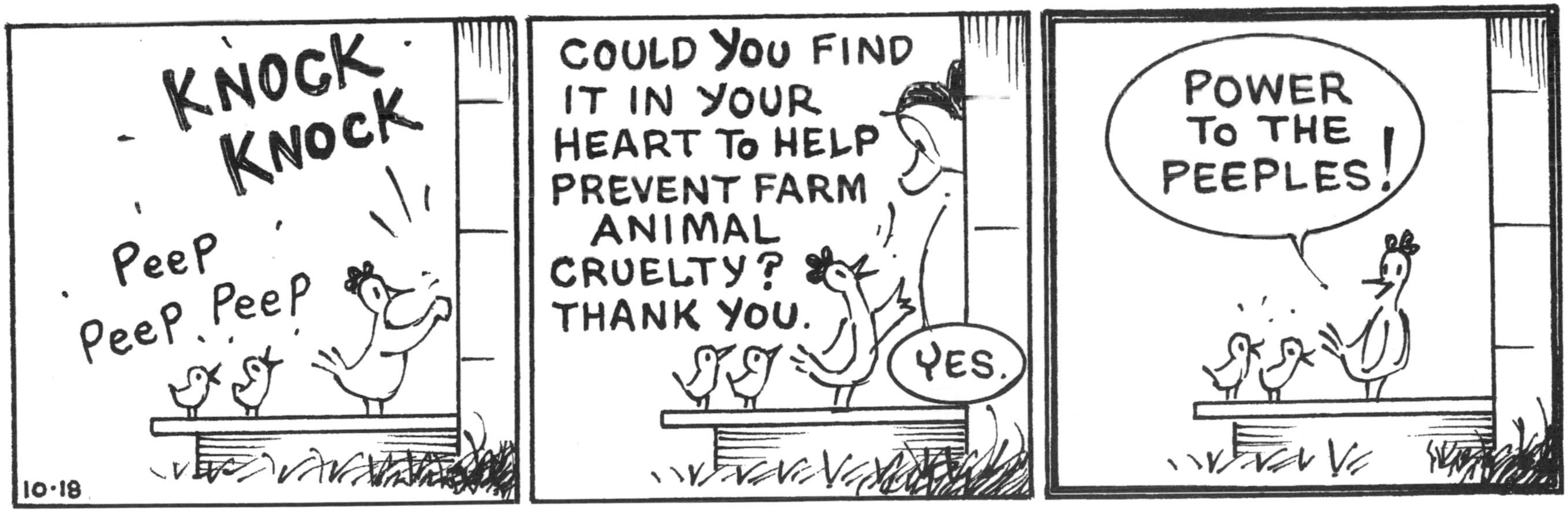
KNOCK KNOCK
Peep Peep Peep
COULD YOU FIND IT IN YOUR HEART TO HELP PREVENT FARM ANIMAL CRUELTY? THANK YOU.
YES.
POWER TO THE PEEPLES!
10·18

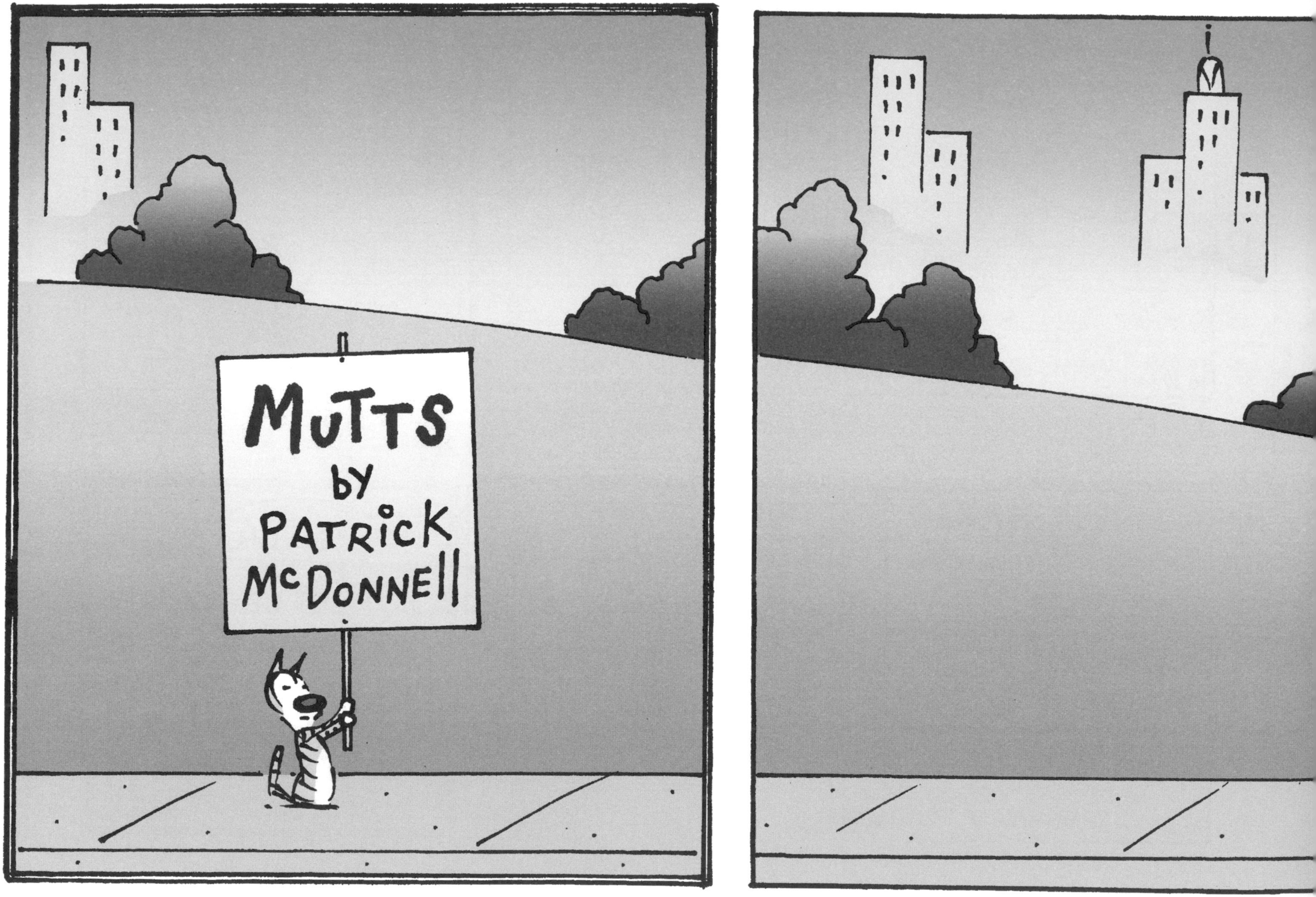
MUTTS
by
PATRICK
McDONNELL

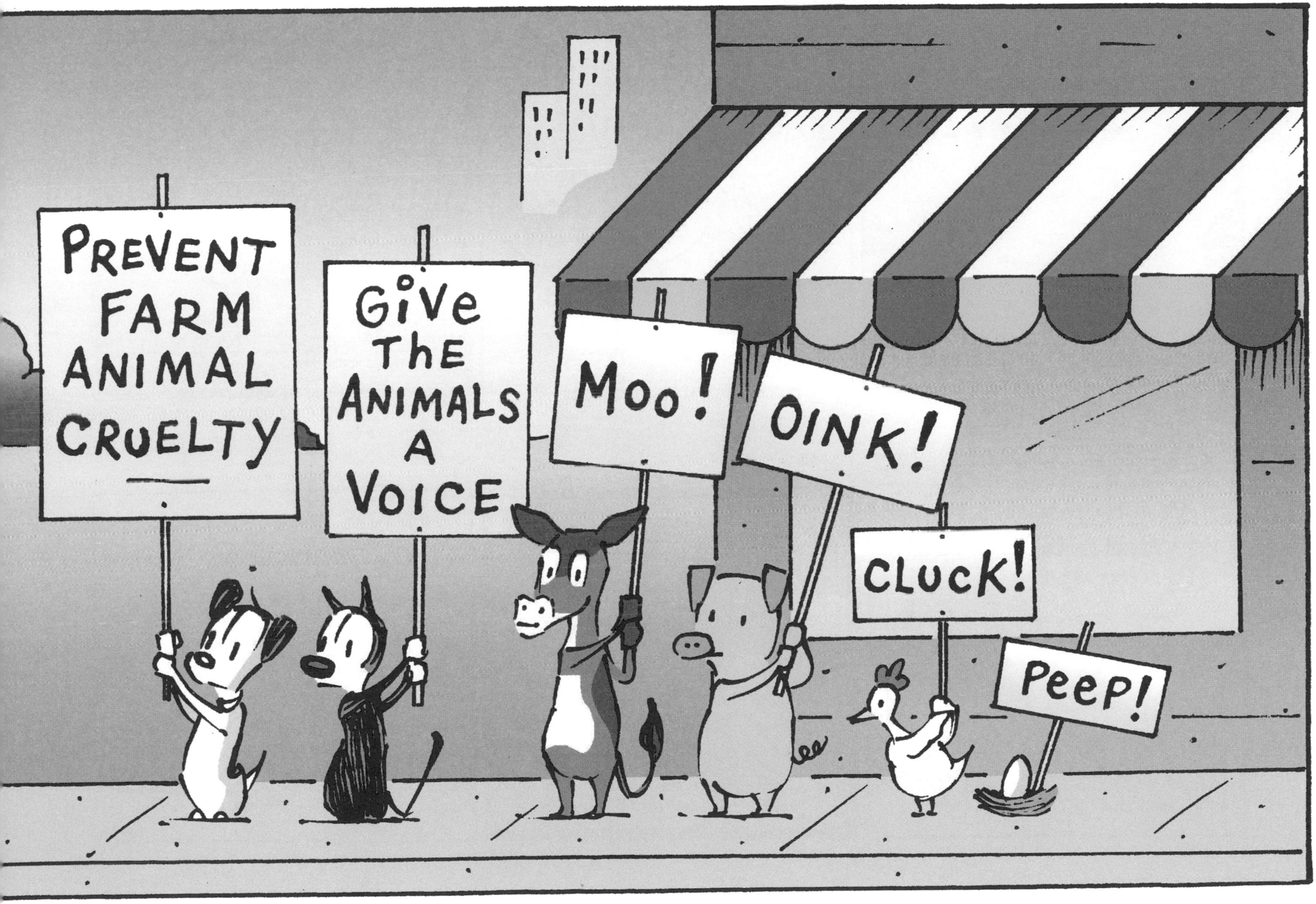
PREVENT FARM ANIMAL CRUELTY
Give The ANIMALS A VOICE
Moo!
OINK!
CLUCK!
Peep!

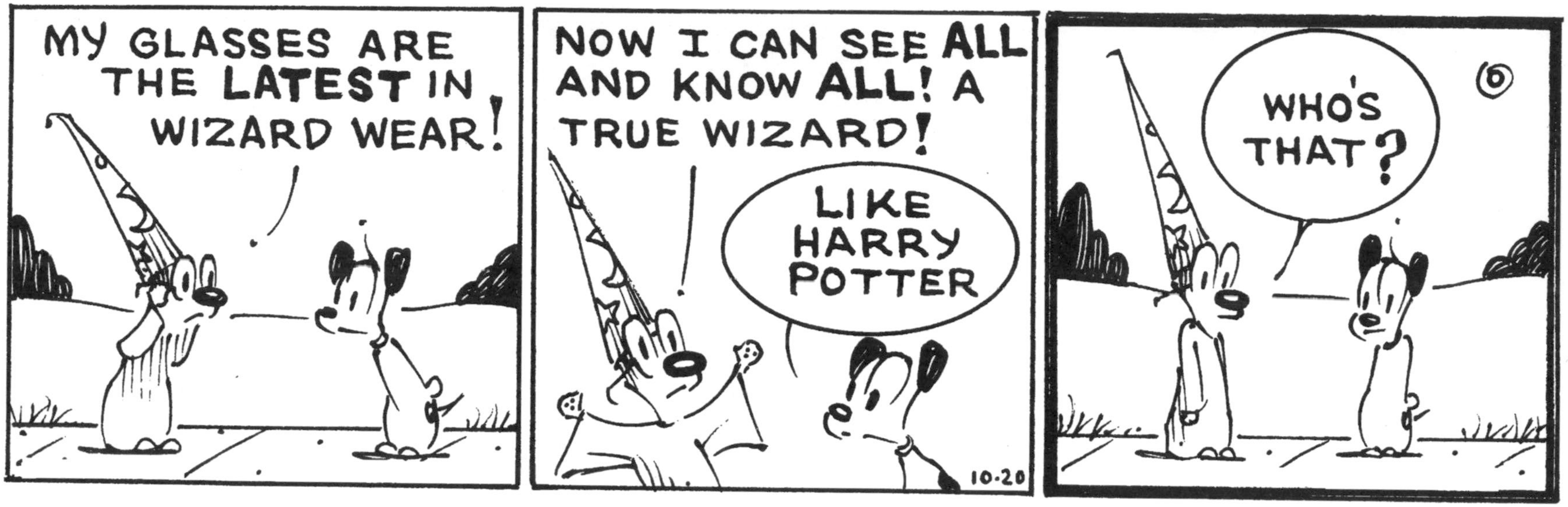
MY GLASSES ARE THE LATEST IN WIZARD WEAR!
NOW I CAN SEE ALL AND KNOW ALL! A TRUE WIZARD!
LIKE HARRY POTTER
10·20
WHO'S THAT?

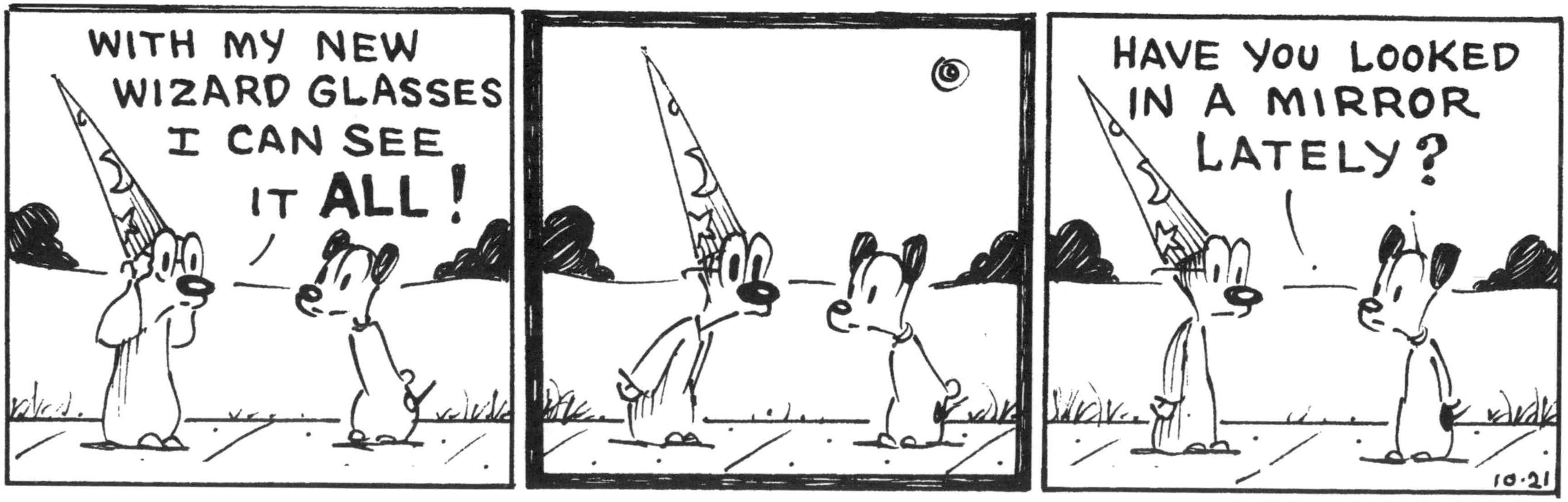
WITH MY NEW WIZARD GLASSES I CAN SEE IT ALL!
HAVE YOU LOOKED IN A MIRROR LATELY?
10·21

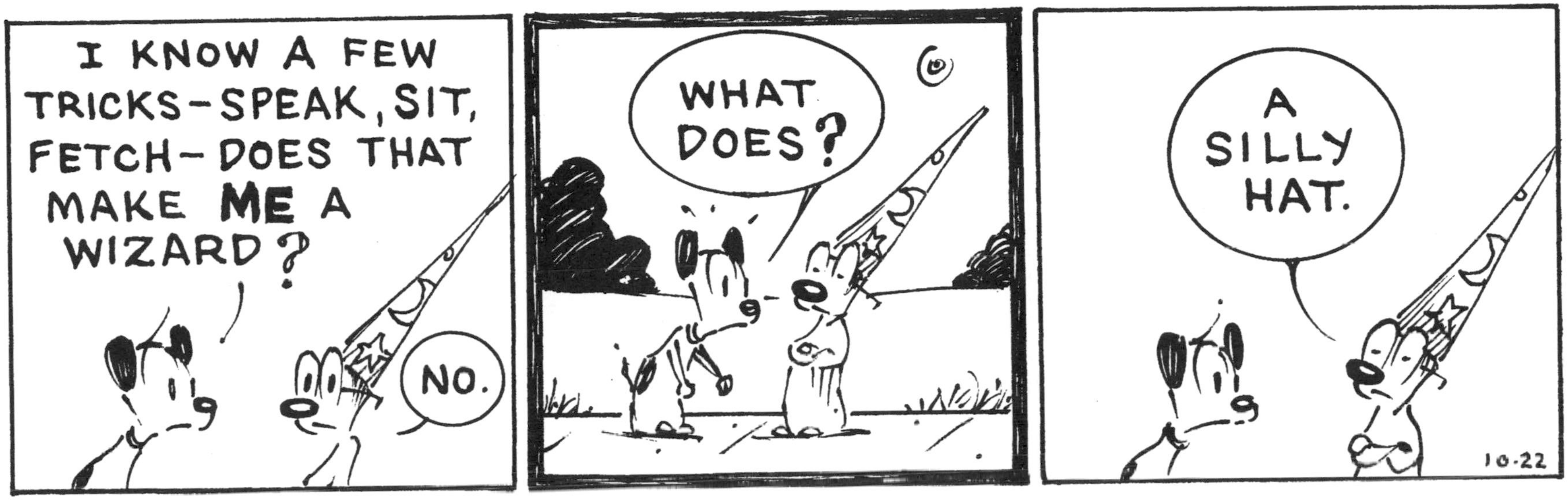
I KNOW A FEW TRICKS-SPEAK, SIT, FETCH-DOES THAT MAKE ME A WIZARD?
NO.
WHAT DOES?
A SILLY HAT.
10-22

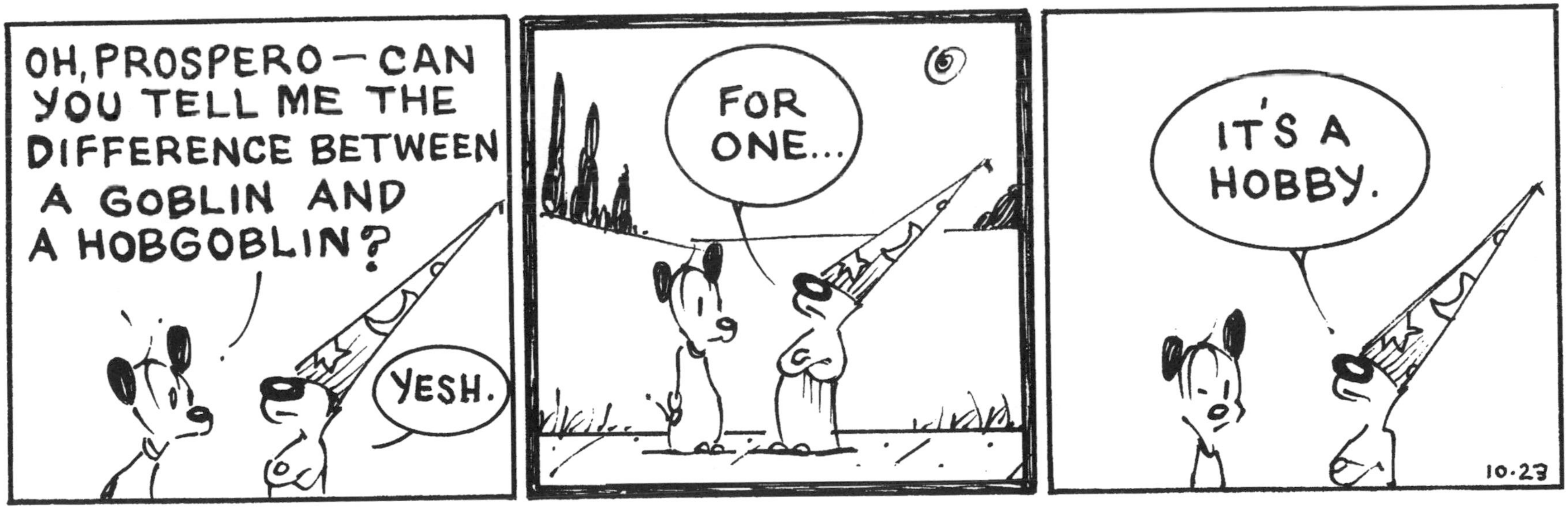
OH, PROSPERO-CAN YOU TELL ME THE DIFFERENCE BETWEEN A GOBLIN AND A HOBGOBLIN?
YESH.
FOR ONE...
IT'S A HOBBY.
10-23

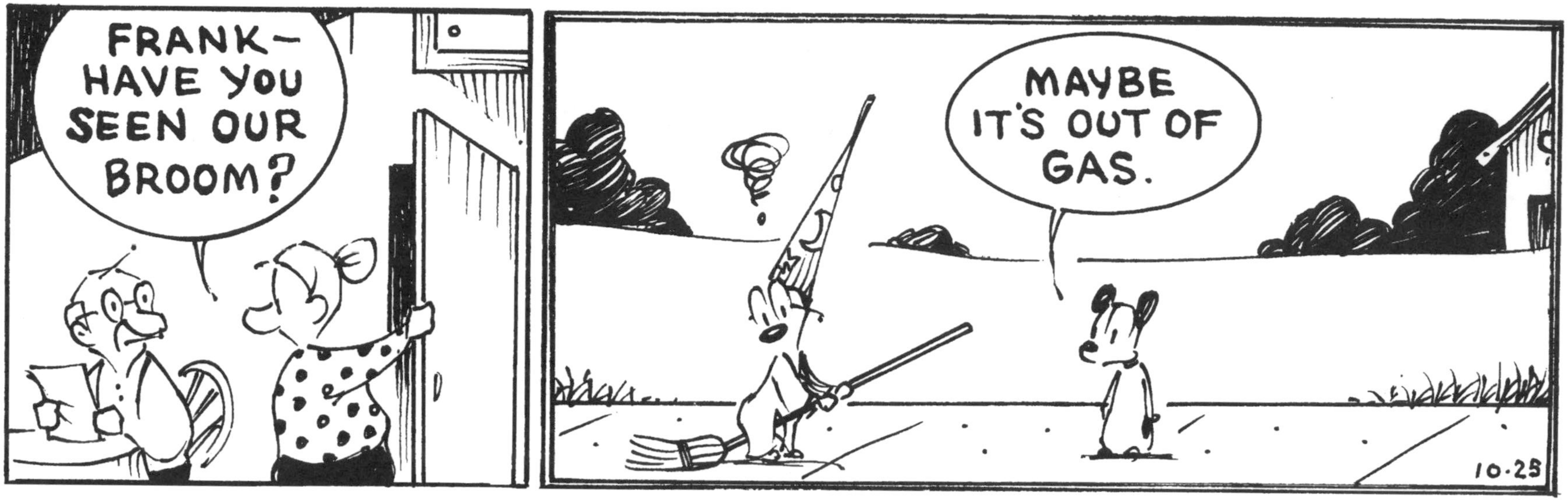
FRANK— HAVE YOU SEEN OUR BROOM?
MAYBE IT'S OUT OF GAS.
10·25

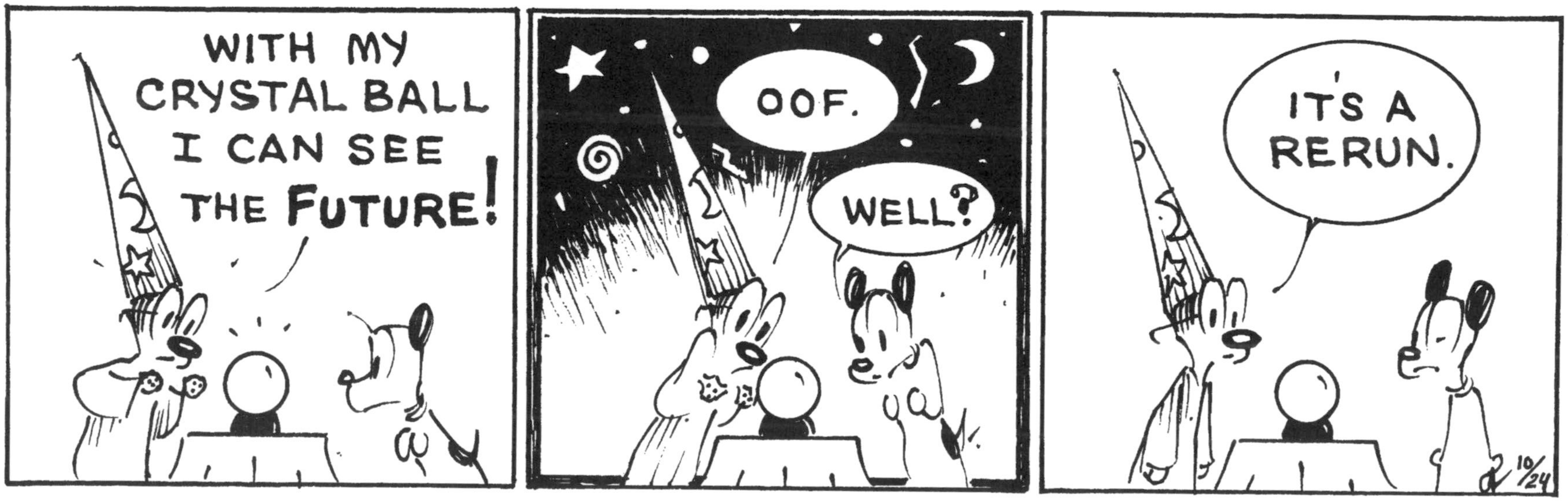
WITH MY CRYSTAL BALL I CAN SEE THE FUTURE!
OOF.
WELL?
IT'S A RERUN.
10/24

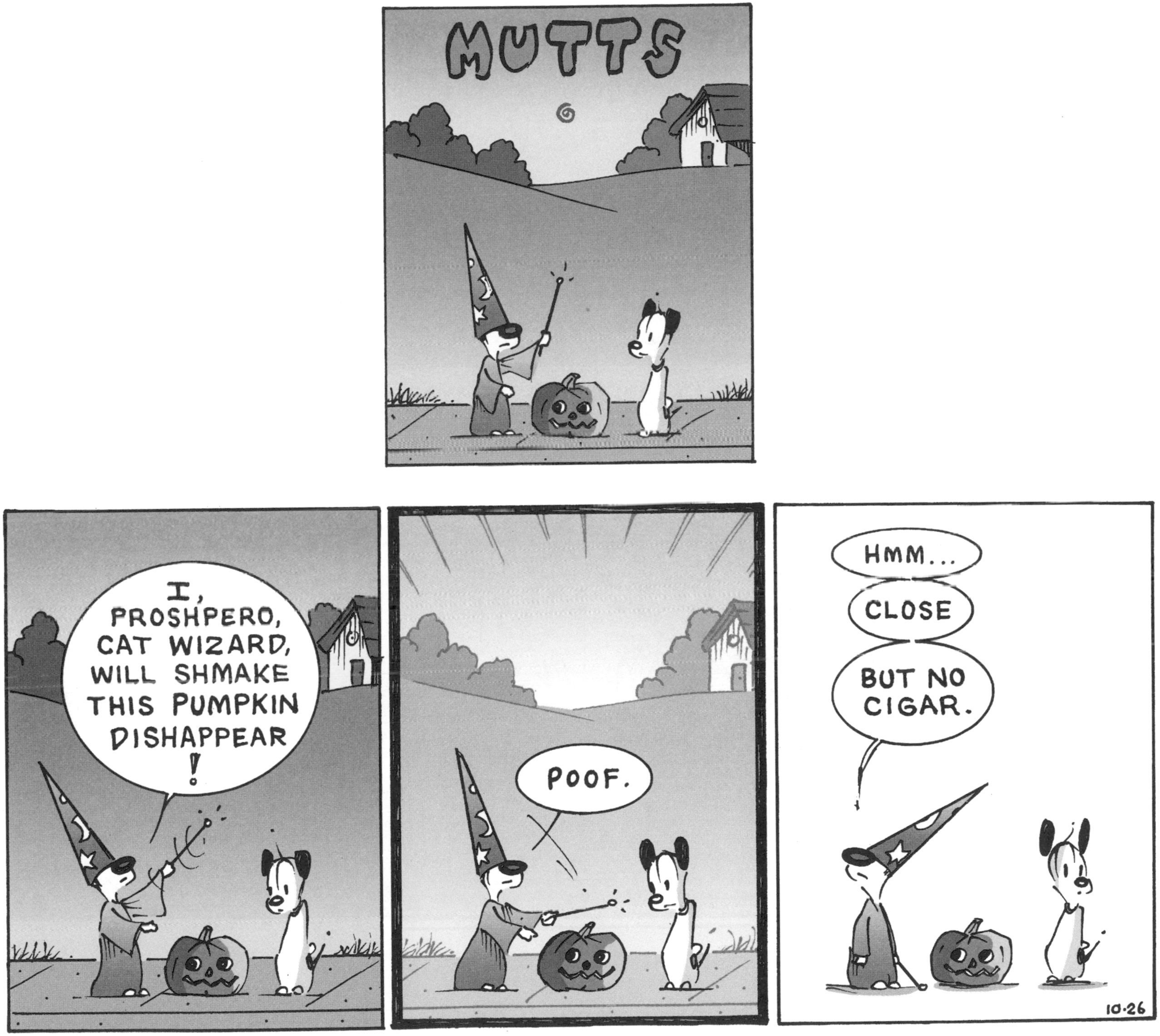
MUTTS
I, PROSHPERO, CAT WIZARD, WILL SHMAKE THIS PUMPKIN DISHAPPEAR !
POOF.
HMM...
CLOSE
BUT NO CIGAR.
10·26

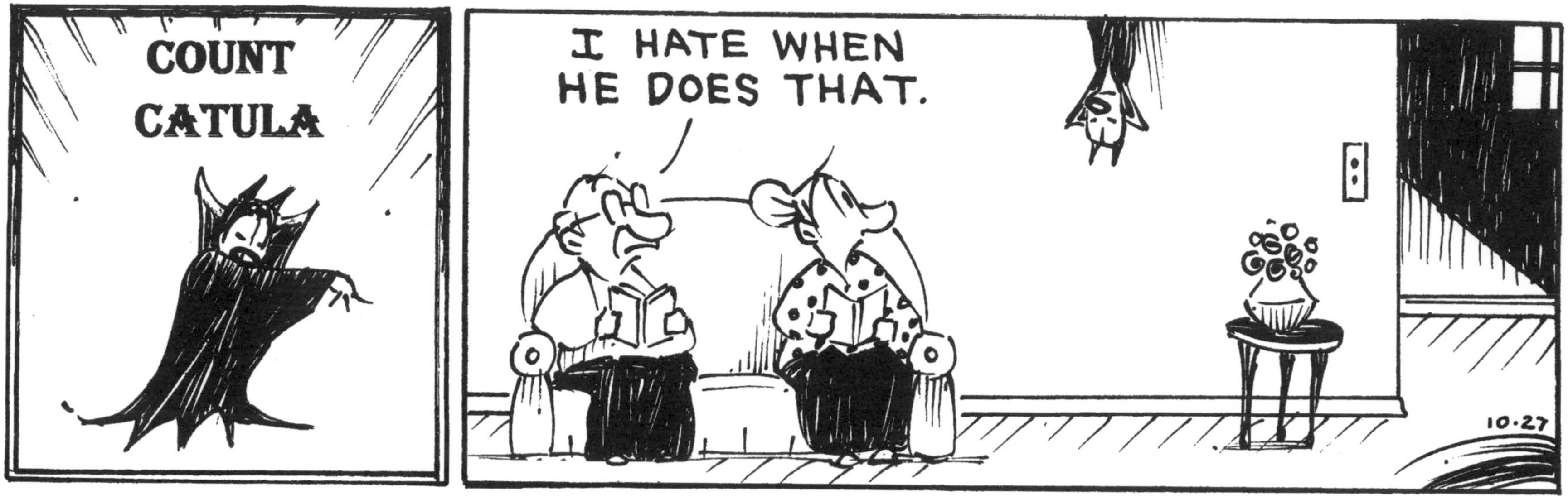
COUNT
CATULA
I HATE WHEN
HE DOES THAT.
10·27

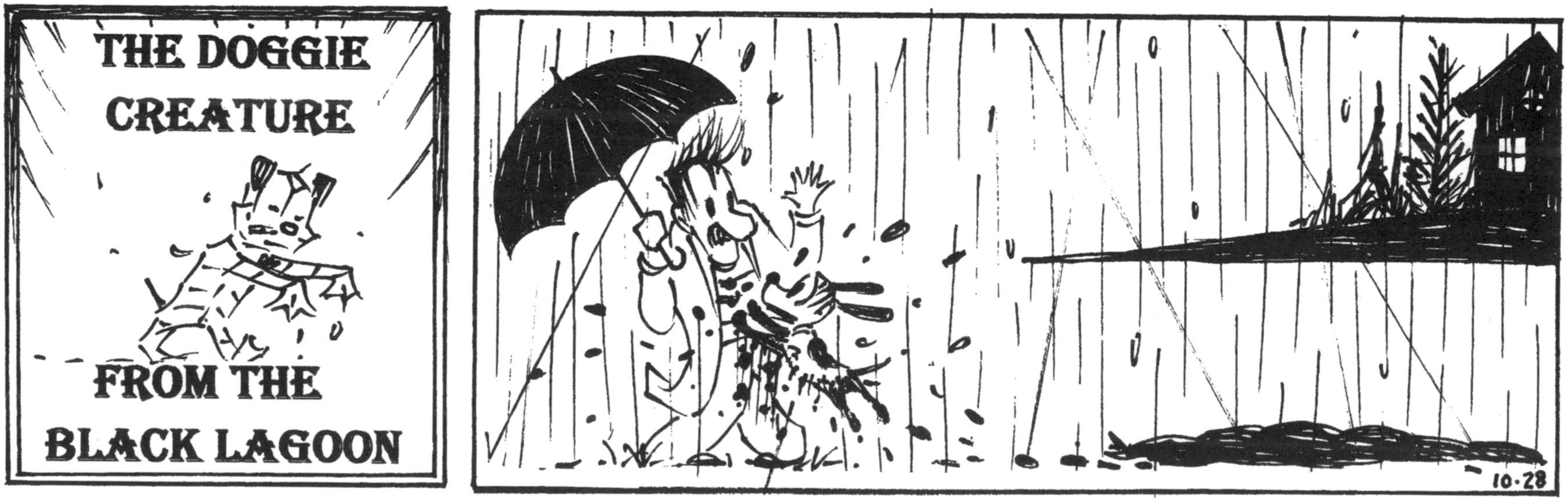
THE DOGGIE
CREATURE
FROM THE
BLACK LAGOON
10·28

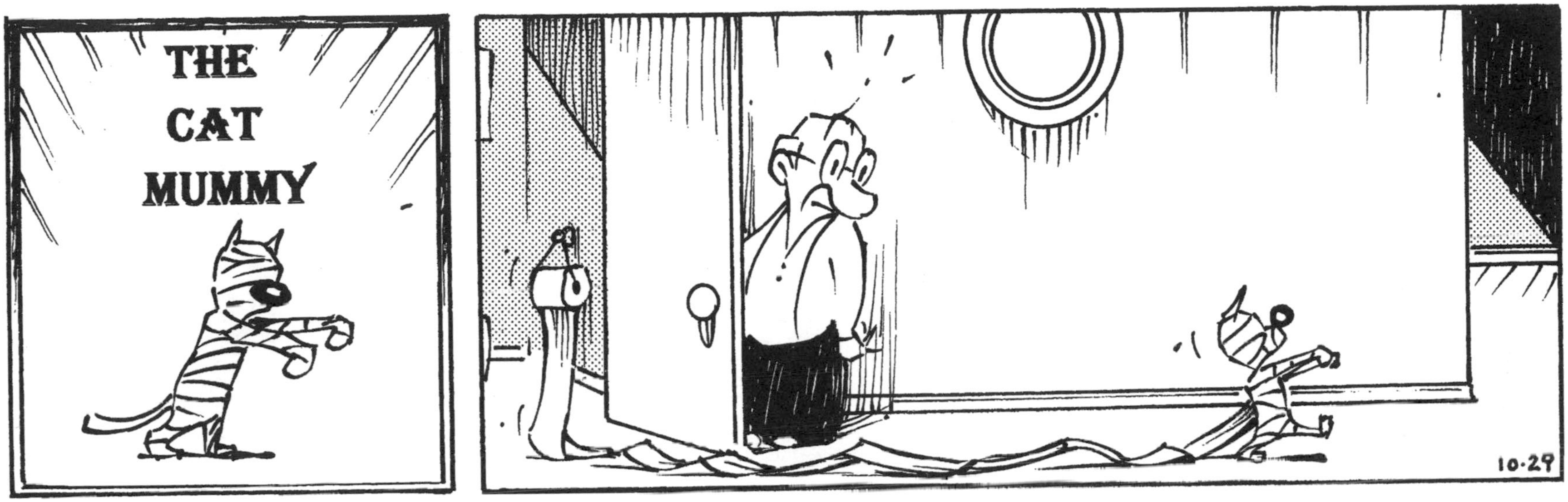
THE CAT MUMMY
10·29

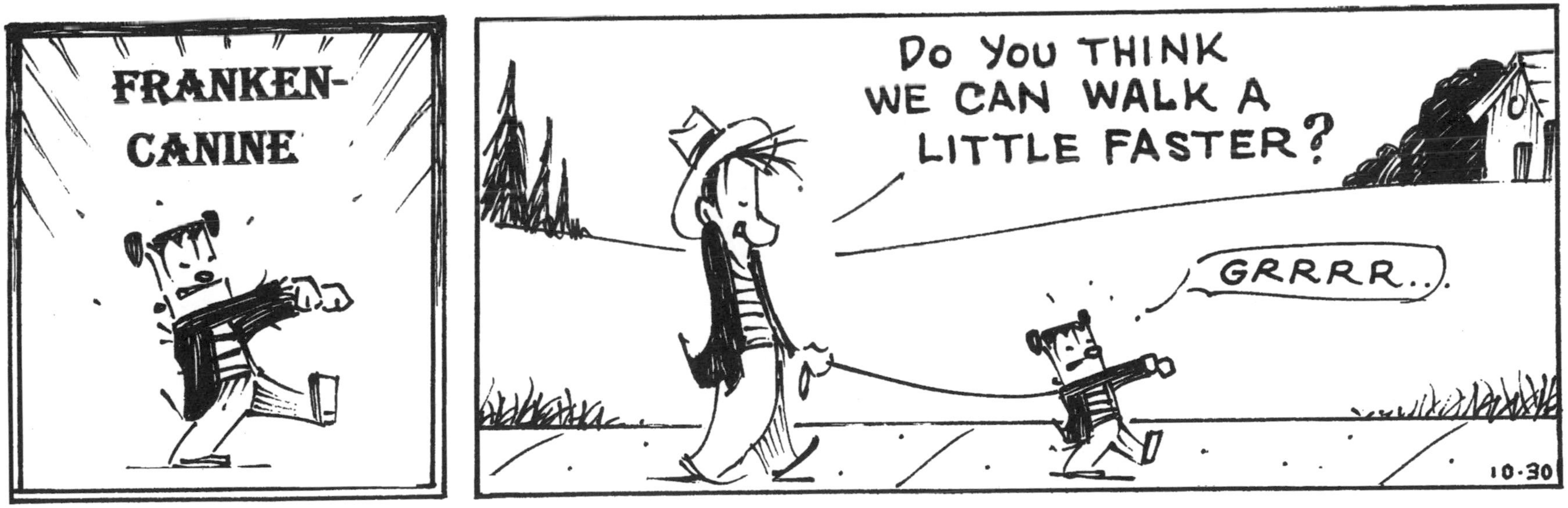
FRANKEN-CANINE
DO YOU THINK WE CAN WALK A LITTLE FASTER?
GRRRR..
10·30

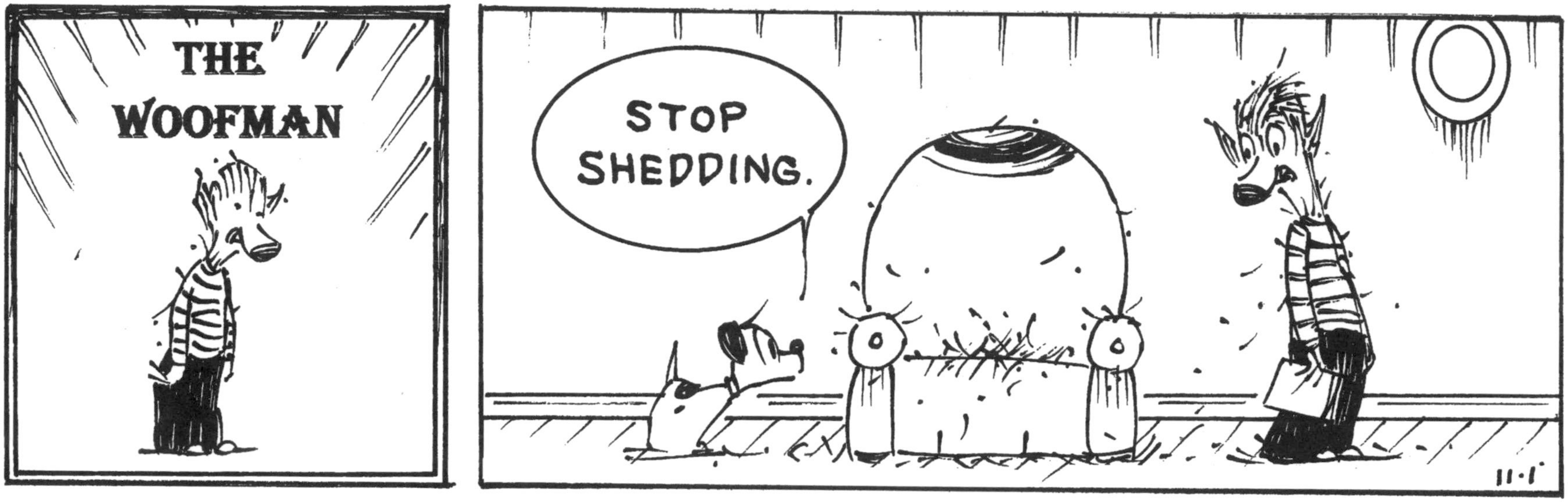
THE WOOFMAN
STOP SHEDDING.
11-1

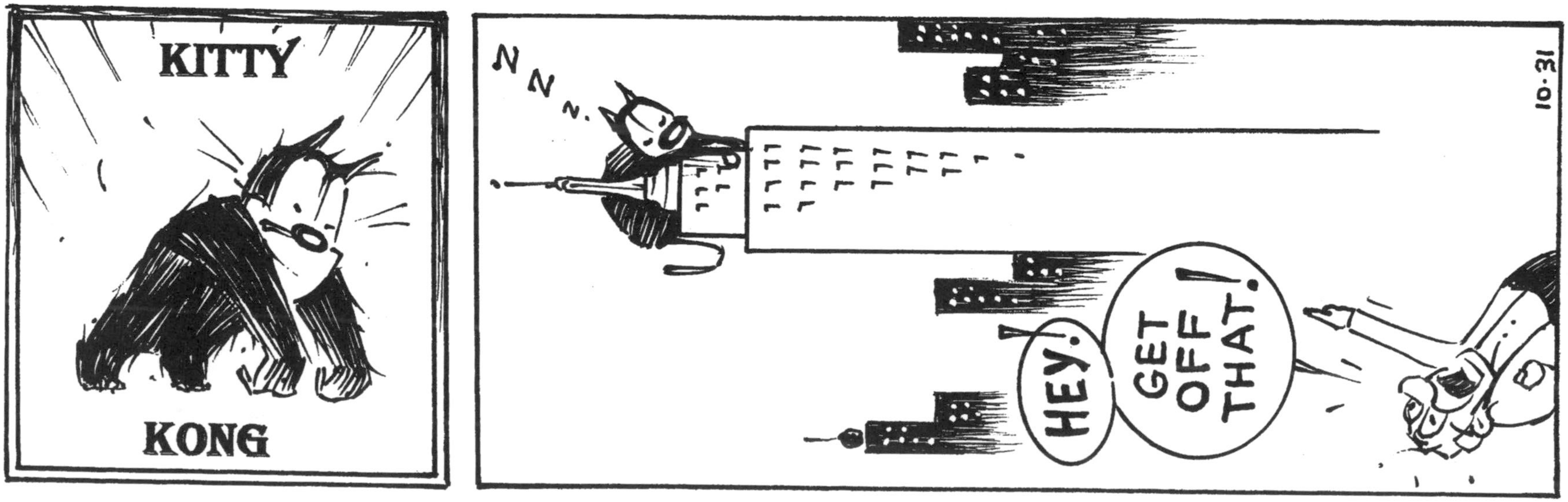
KITTY KONG
NNN.
HEY!
GET OFF THAT!
10-31

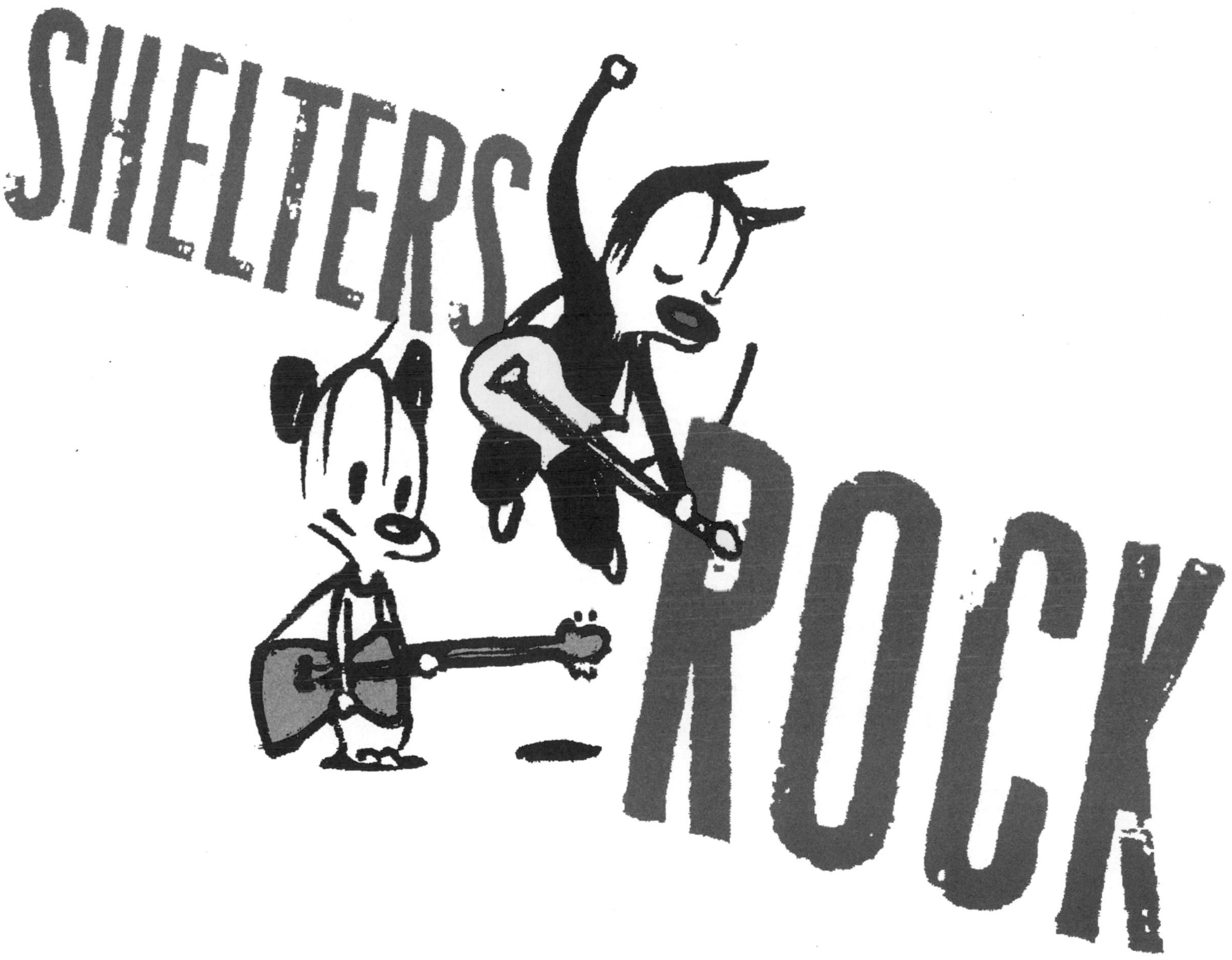
SHELTERS
ROCK

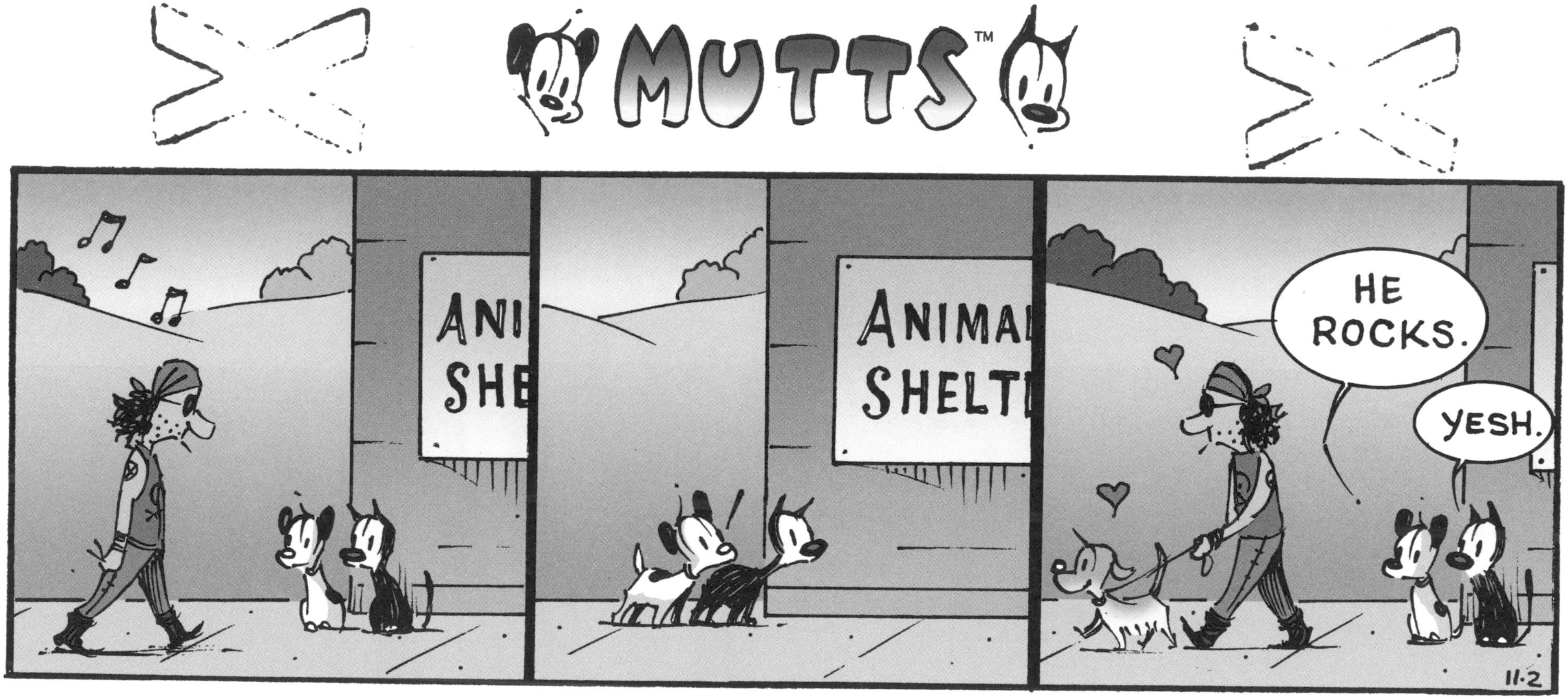
MUTTS™
ANI
SHE
ANIMAL
SHELT
HE ROCKS.
YESH.
11.2

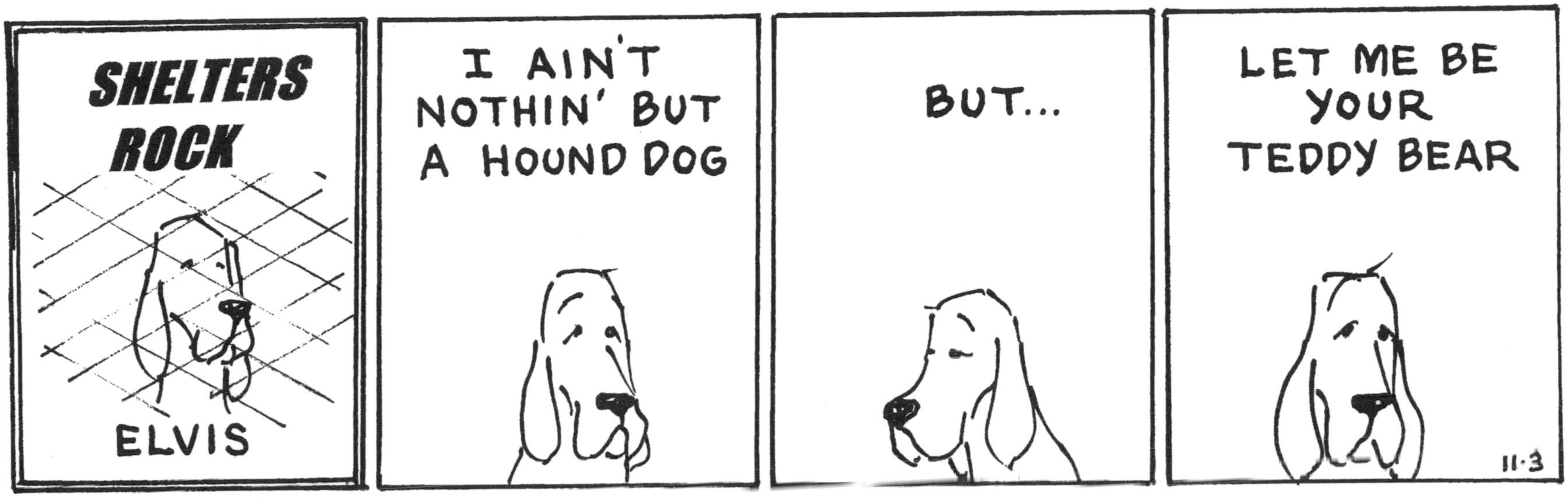
SHELTERS ROCK
ELVIS
I AIN'T NOTHIN' BUT A HOUND DOG
BUT...
LET ME BE YOUR TEDDY BEAR
11·3

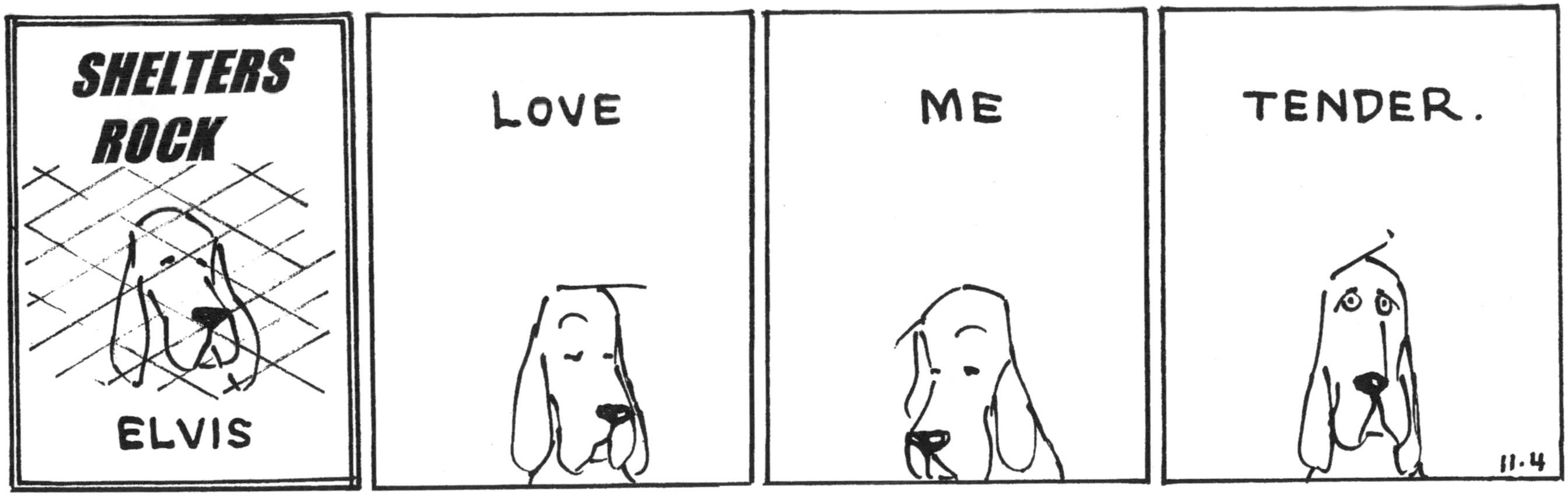
SHELTERS ROCK
ELVIS
LOVE
ME
TENDER.
11·4

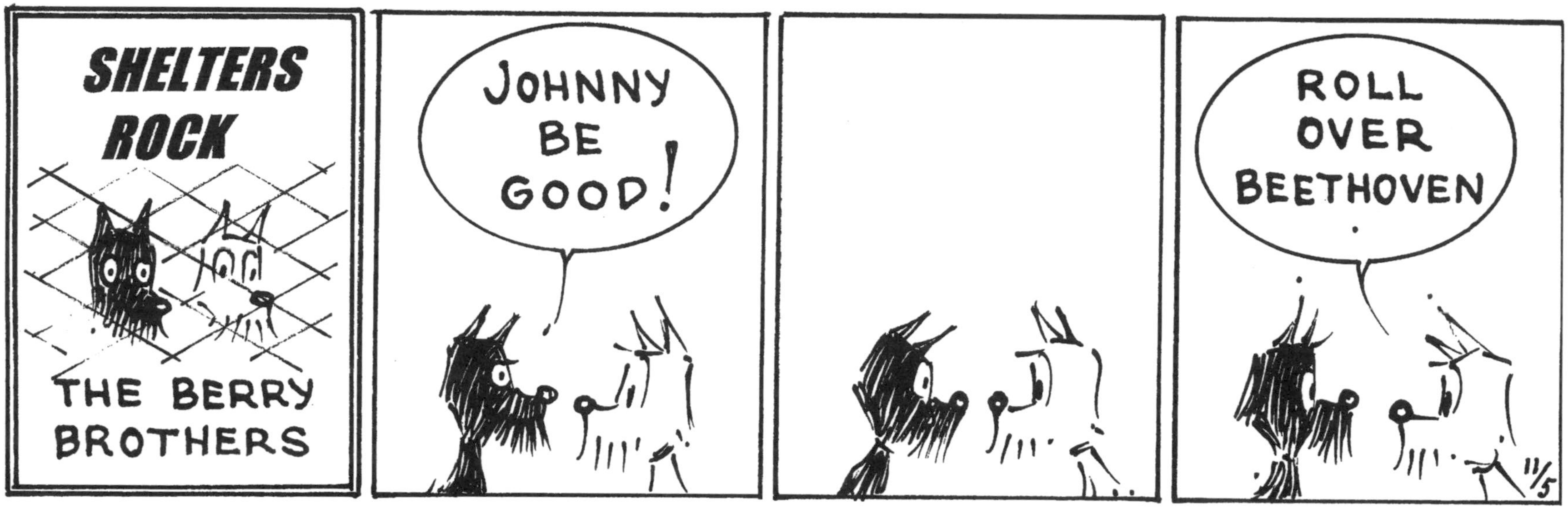
SHELTERS ROCK
THE BERRY BROTHERS
JOHNNY BE GOOD!
ROLL OVER BEETHOVEN
11/5

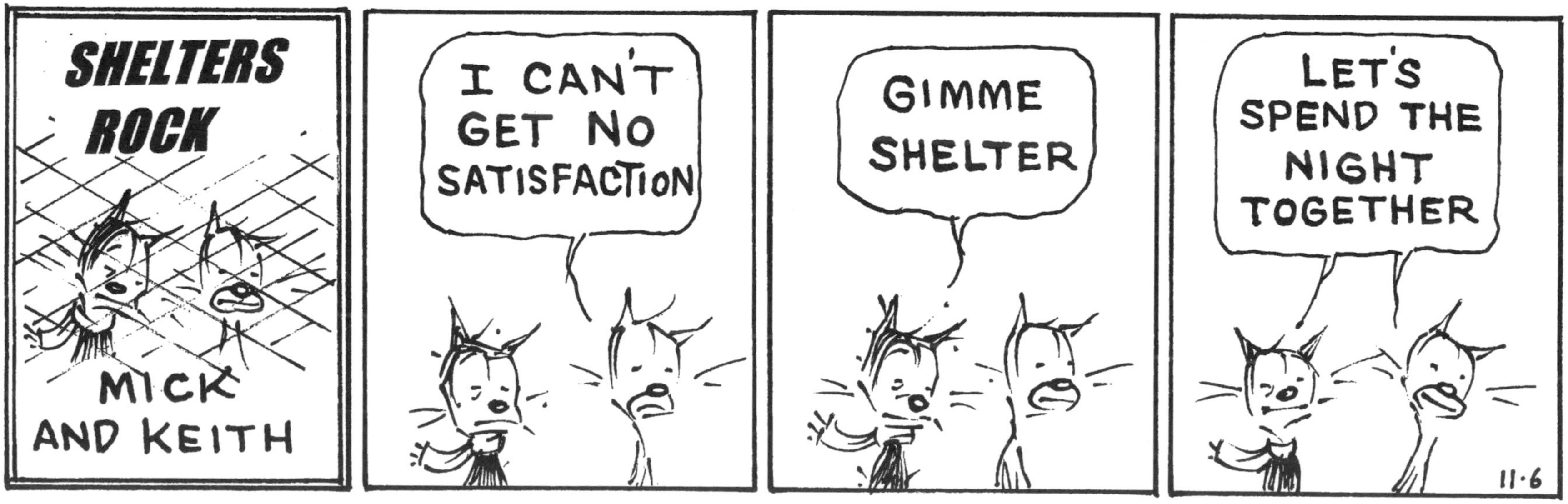
SHELTERS ROCK
MICK AND KEITH
I CAN'T GET NO SATISFACTION
GIMME SHELTER
LET'S SPEND THE NIGHT TOGETHER
11·6

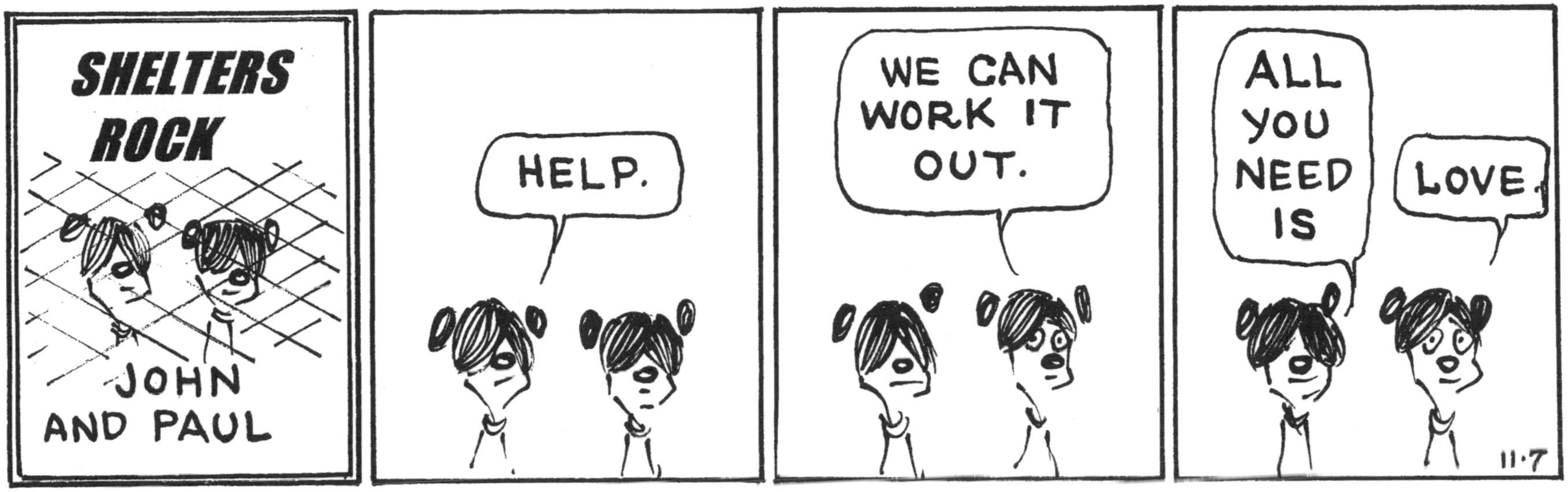
SHELTERS ROCK
JOHN AND PAUL
HELP.
WE CAN WORK IT OUT.
ALL YOU NEED IS
LOVE.
11·7

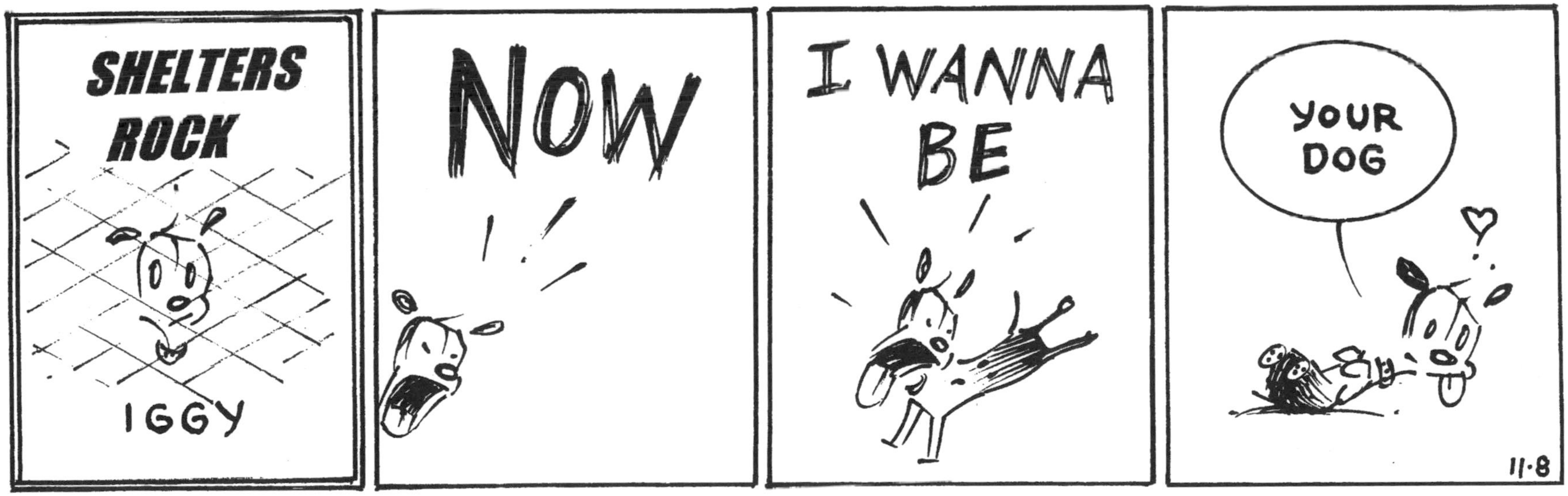
SHELTERS ROCK
IGGY
NOW
I WANNA BE
YOUR DOG
11·8

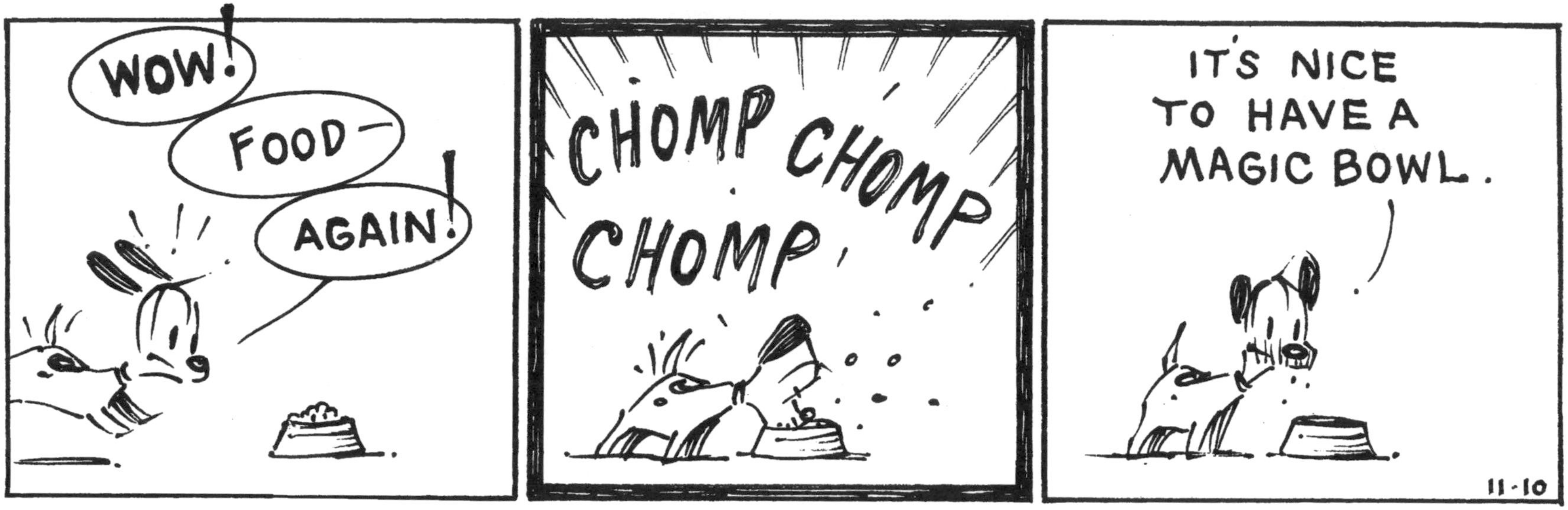
WOW!
FOOD—
AGAIN!
CHOMP CHOMP CHOMP
IT'S NICE TO HAVE A MAGIC BOWL.
11-10

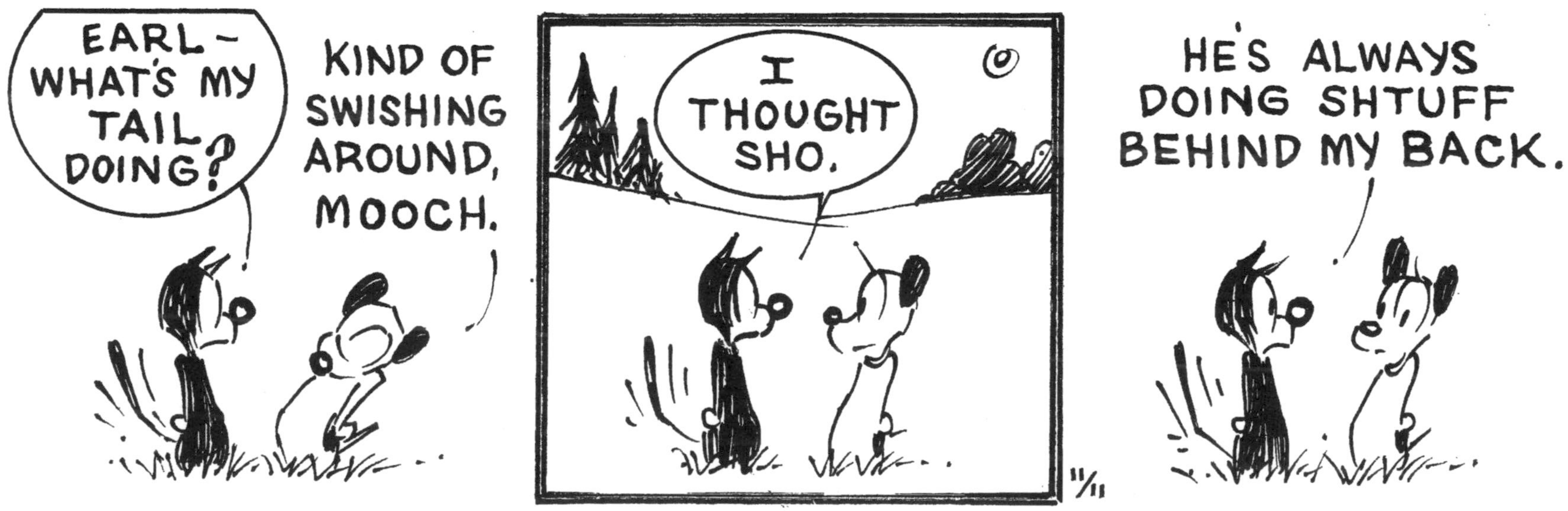
EARL— WHAT'S MY TAIL DOING?
KIND OF SWISHING AROUND, MOOCH.
I THOUGHT SHO.
11/11
HE'S ALWAYS DOING SHTUFF BEHIND MY BACK.

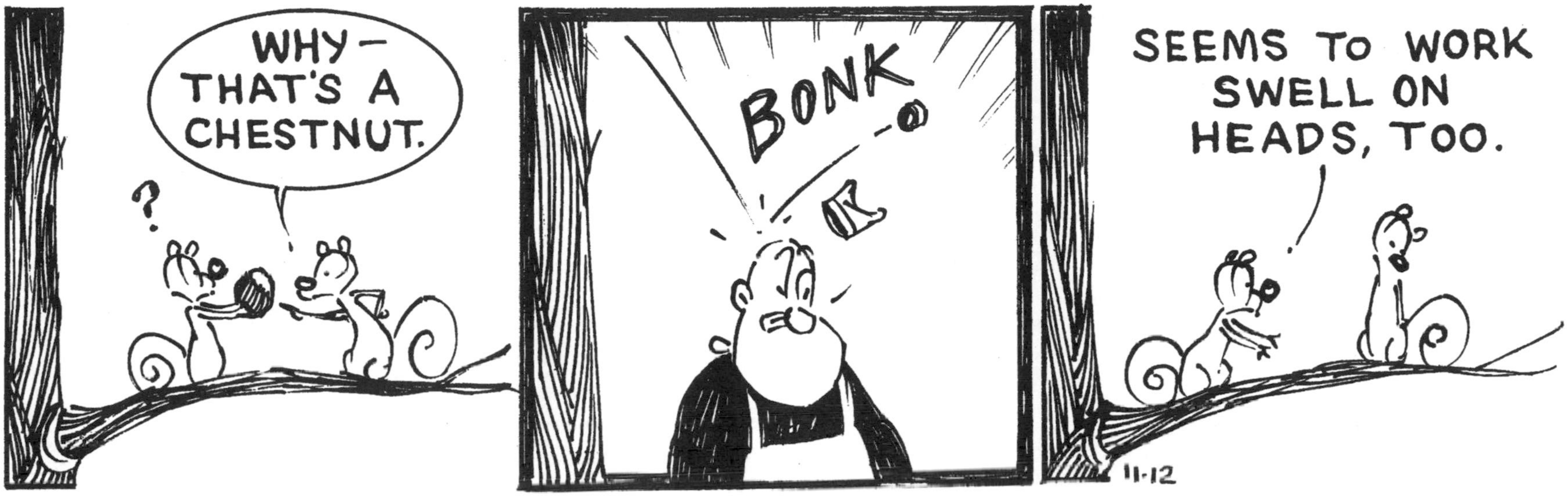
WHY-
THAT'S A
CHESTNUT.
?
BONK
SEEMS TO WORK
SWELL ON
HEADS, TOO.
11-12

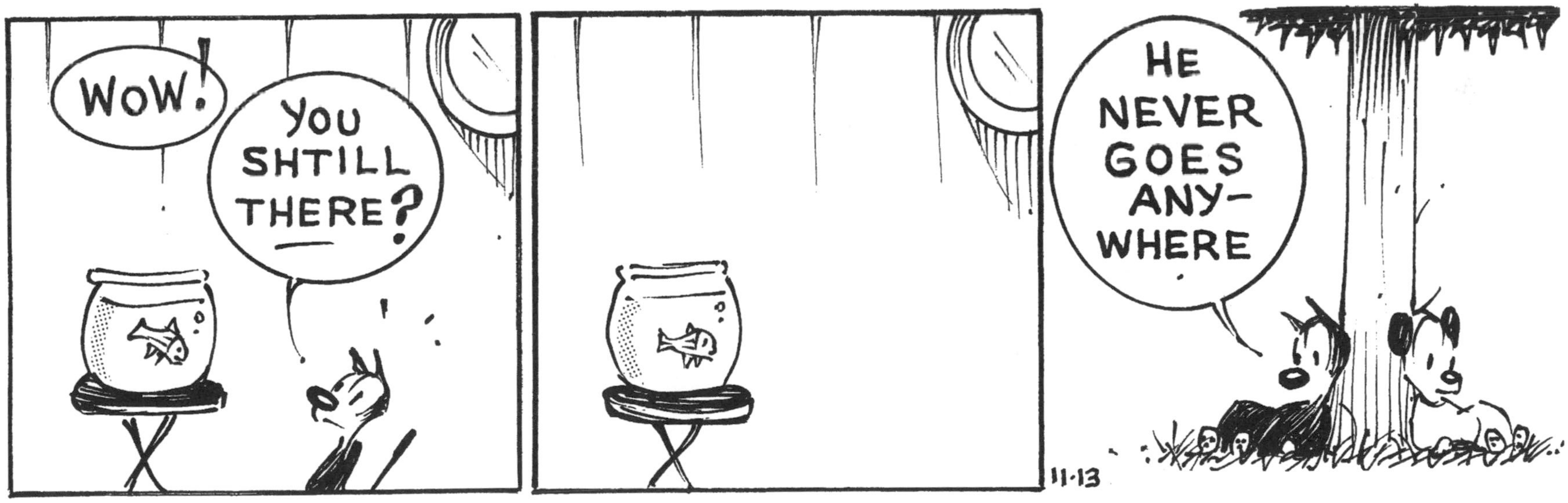
WOW!
YOU
SHTILL
THERE?
HE
NEVER
GOES
ANY-
WHERE
11-13

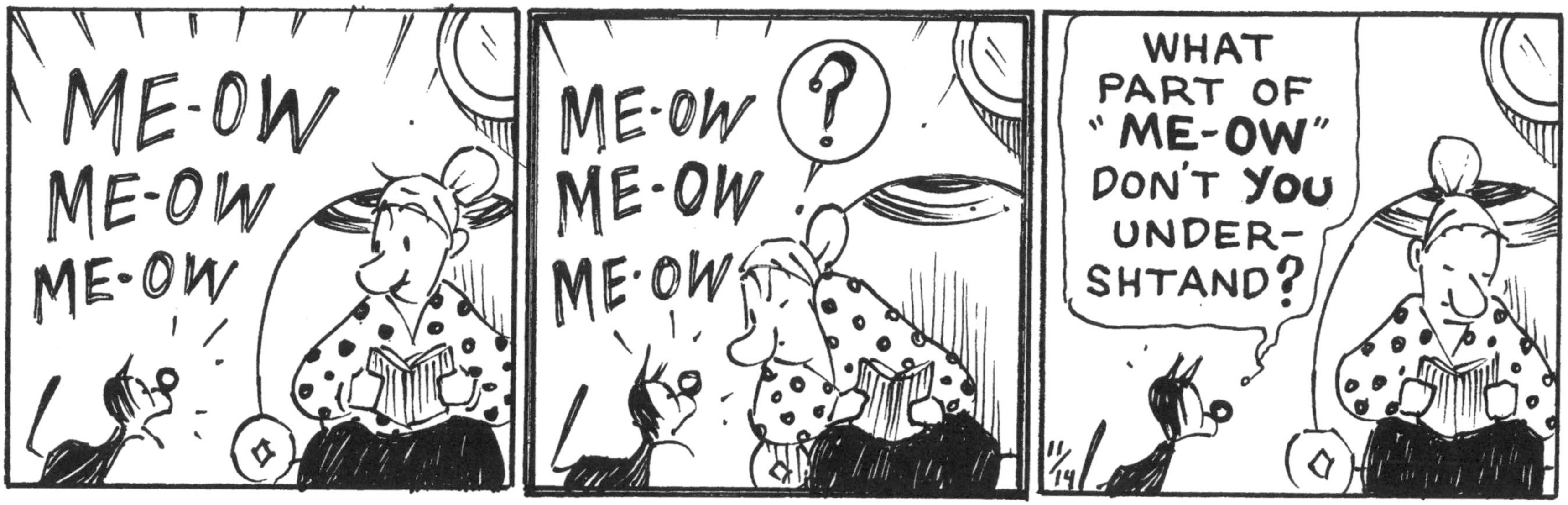
ME-OW
ME-OW
ME-OW
ME-OW
ME-OW
ME-OW
?
WHAT PART OF "ME-OW" DON'T YOU UNDER-SHTAND?
11/14

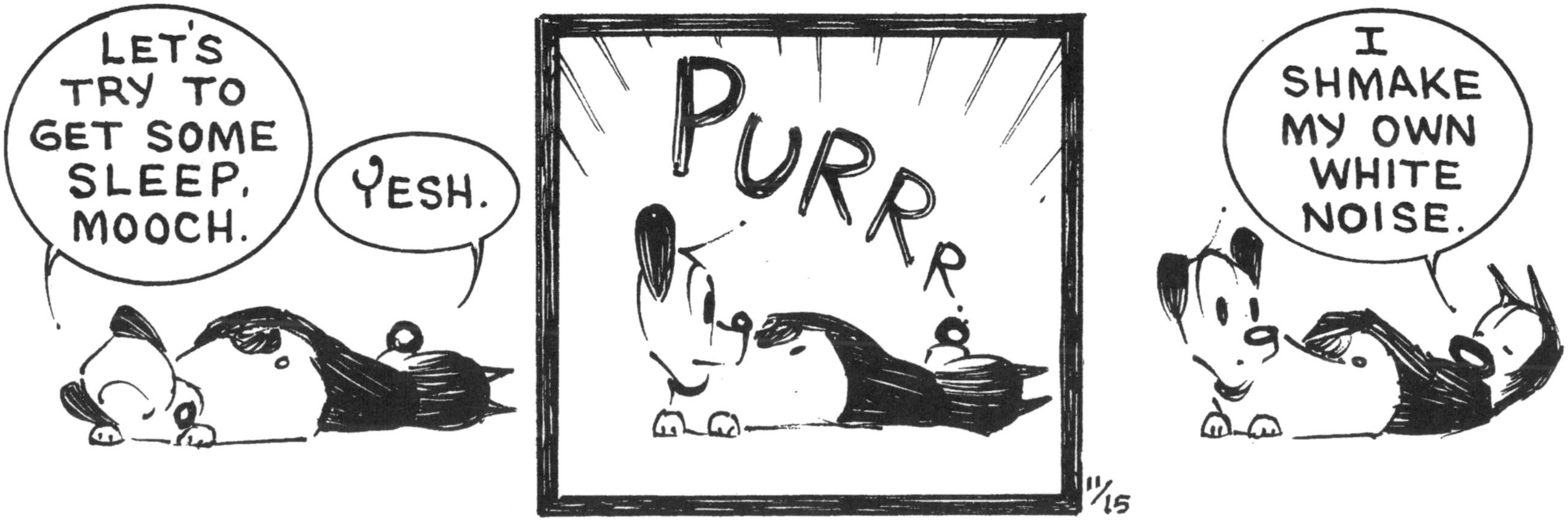
LET'S TRY TO GET SOME SLEEP, MOOCH.
YESH.
PURRR.
I SHMAKE MY OWN WHITE NOISE.
11/15

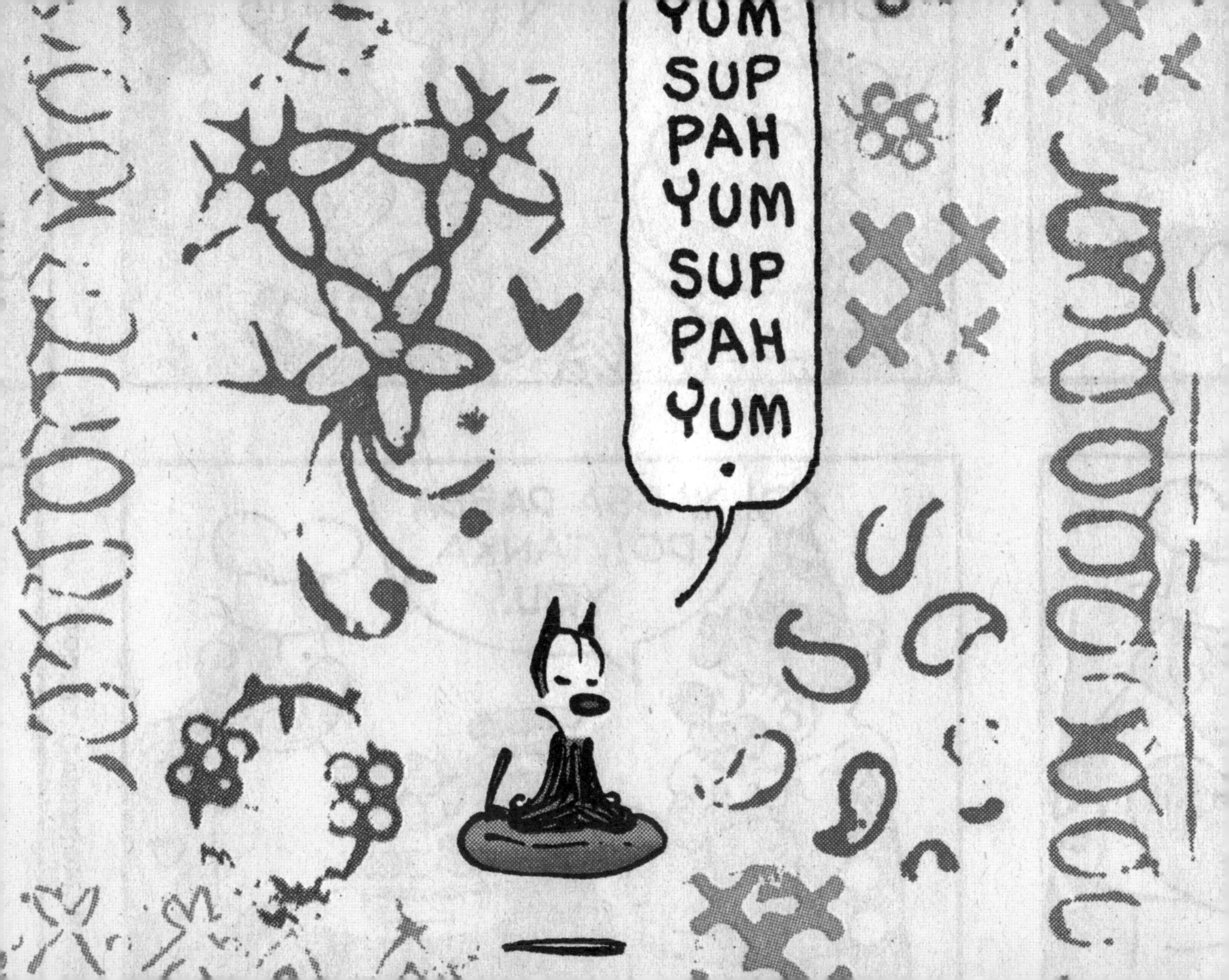
YUM
SUP
PAH
YUM
SUP
PAH
YUM
.

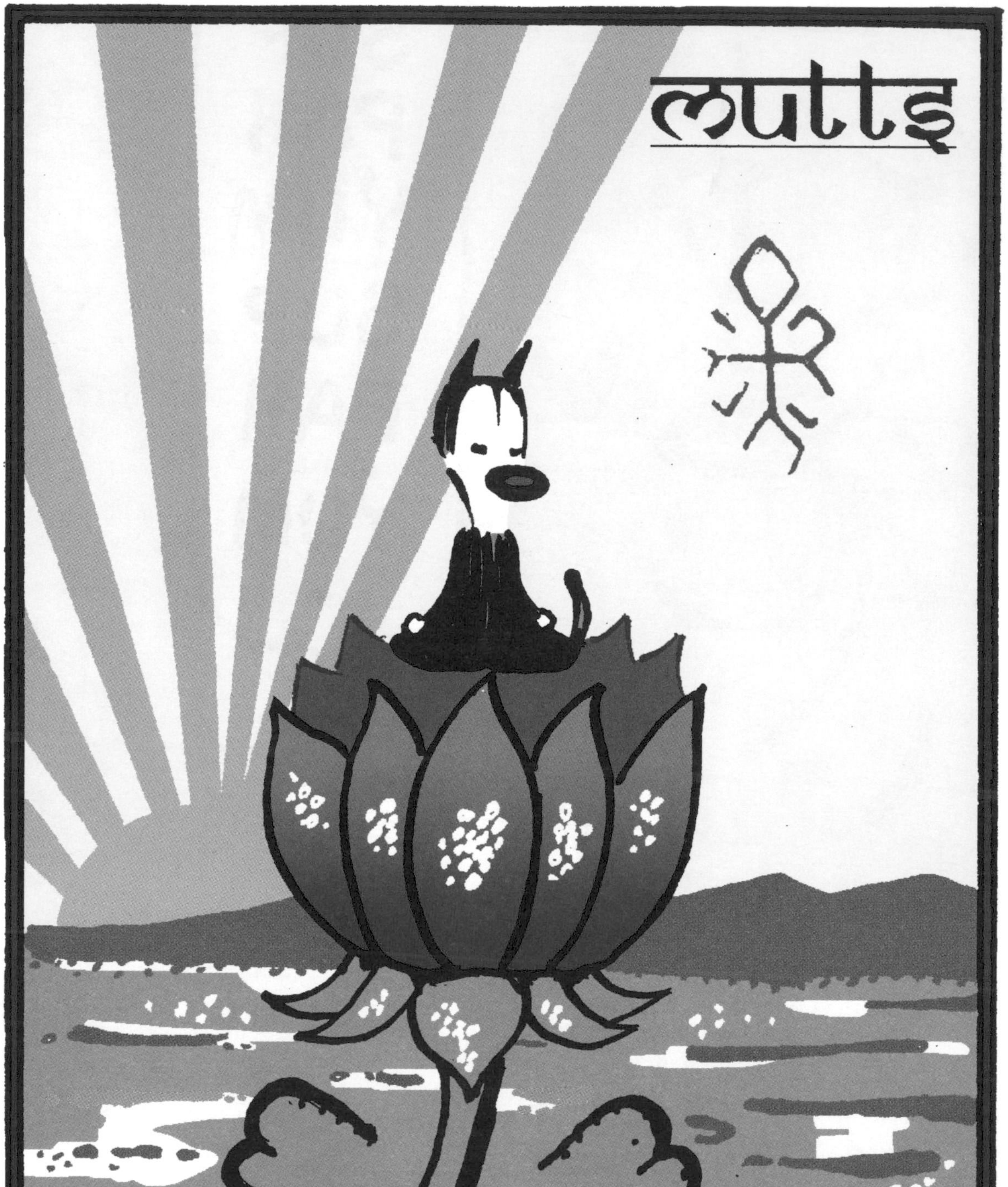
mutts

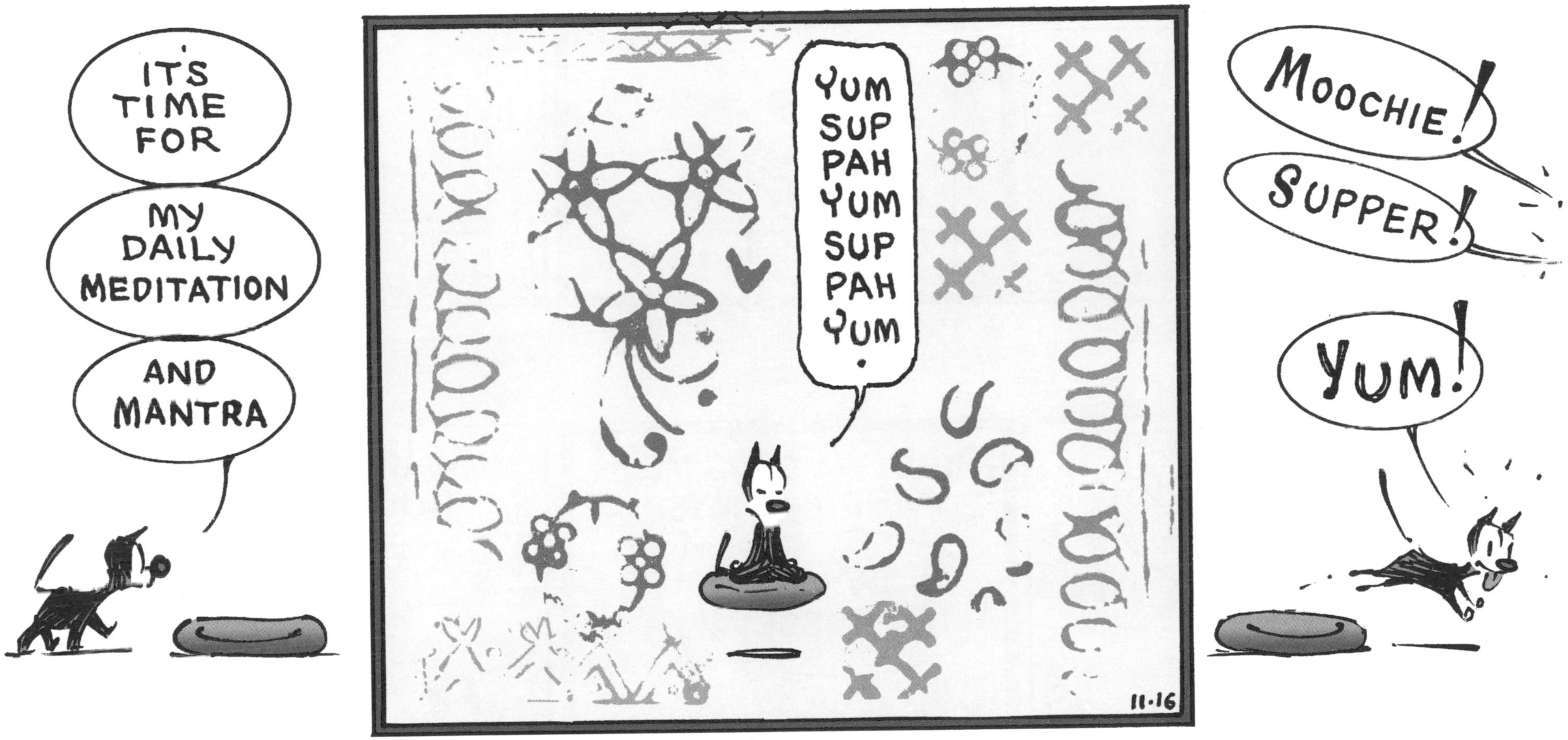
IT'S TIME FOR
MY DAILY MEDITATION
AND MANTRA
YUM SUP PAH YUM SUP PAH YUM.
11·16
MOOCHIE!
SUPPER!
YUM!

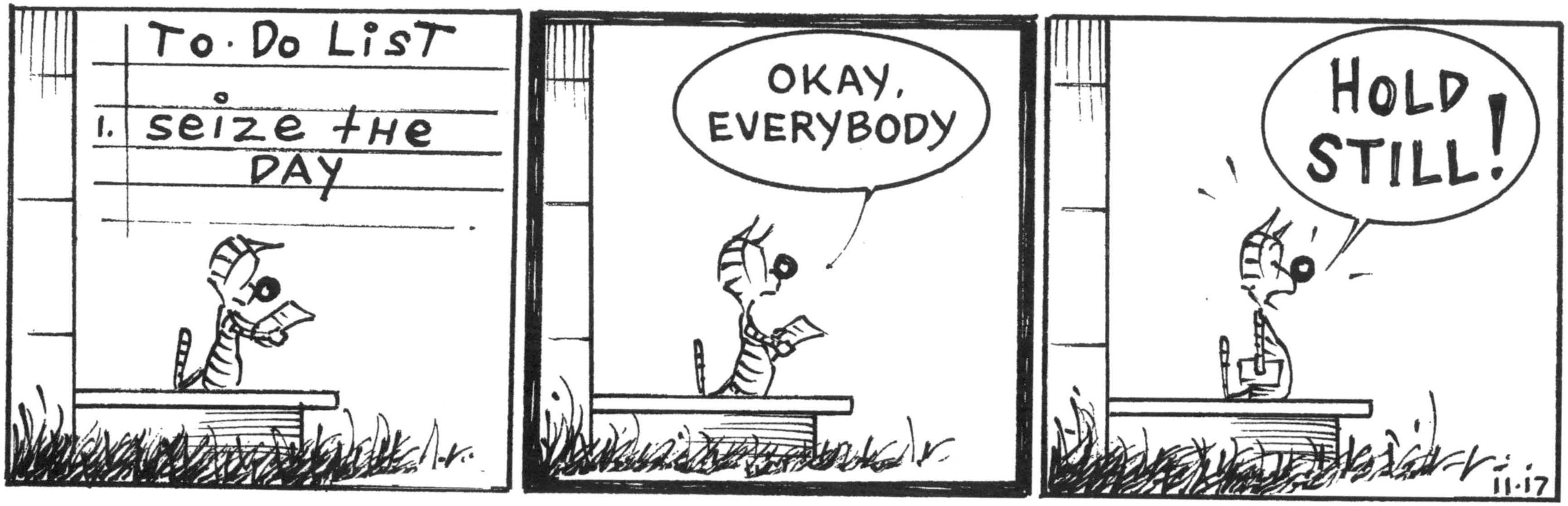
TO·DO LIST
1. seize the DAY
OKAY, EVERYBODY
HOLD STILL!
11-17

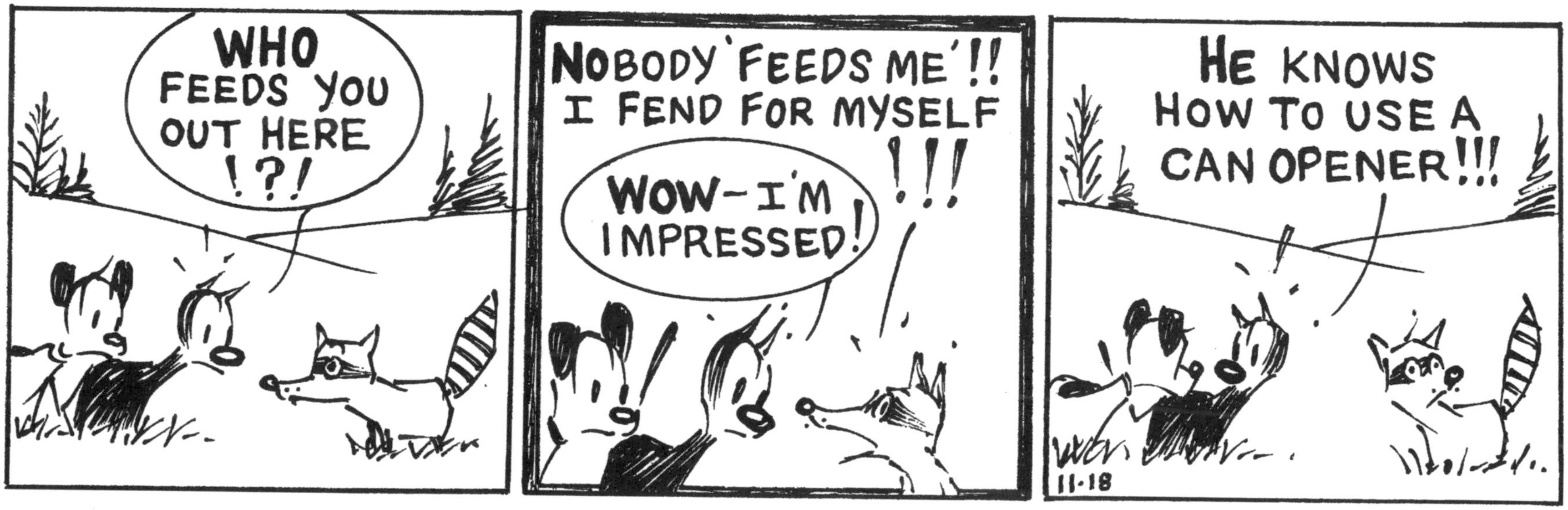
WHO FEEDS YOU OUT HERE !?!
NOBODY FEEDS ME!! I FEND FOR MYSELF !!!
WOW-I'M IMPRESSED!
HE KNOWS HOW TO USE A CAN OPENER!!!
11-18

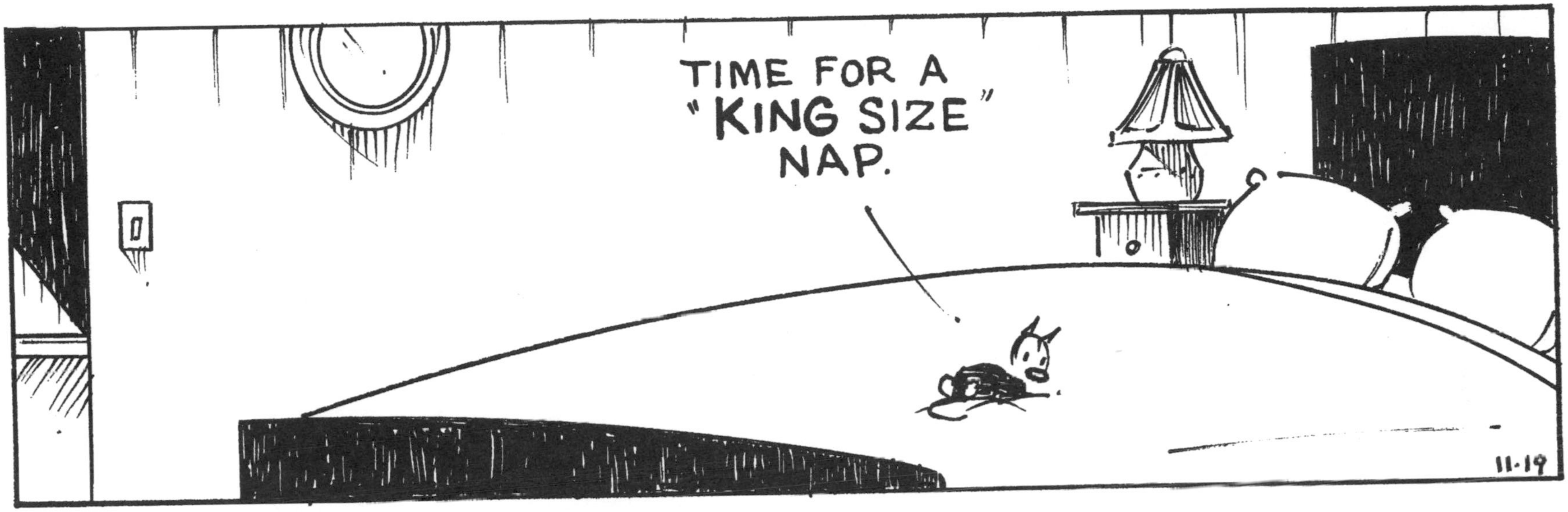
TIME FOR A "KING SIZE" NAP.
11-19

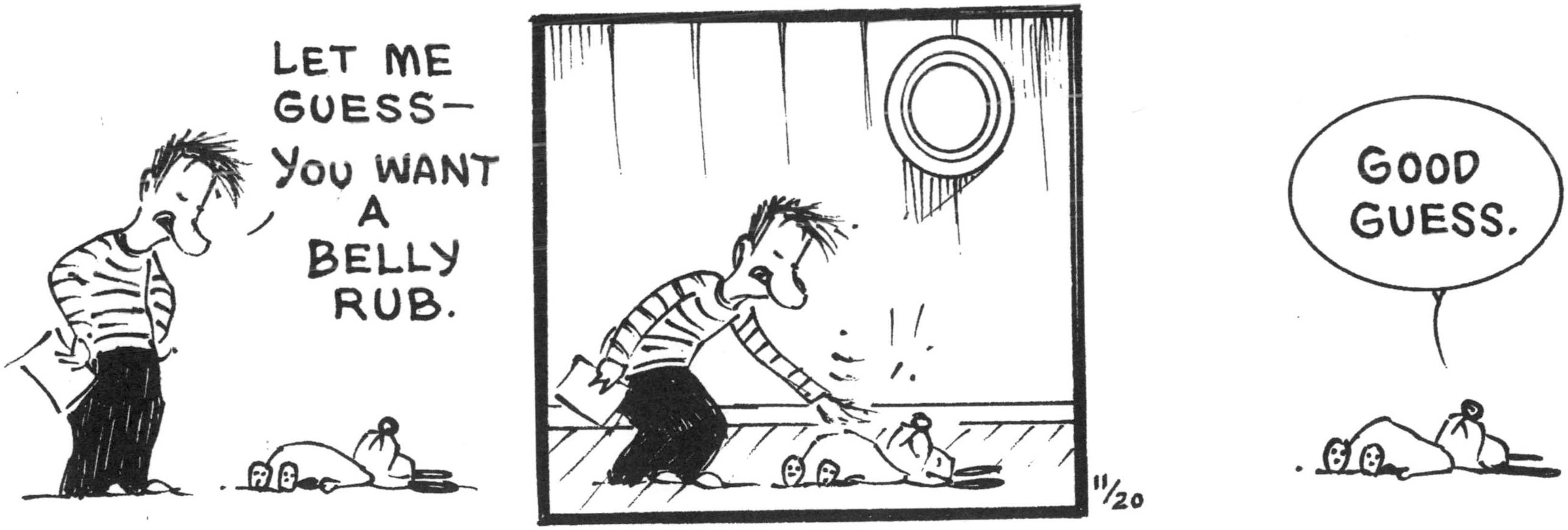
LET ME GUESS— YOU WANT A BELLY RUB.
11/20
GOOD GUESS.

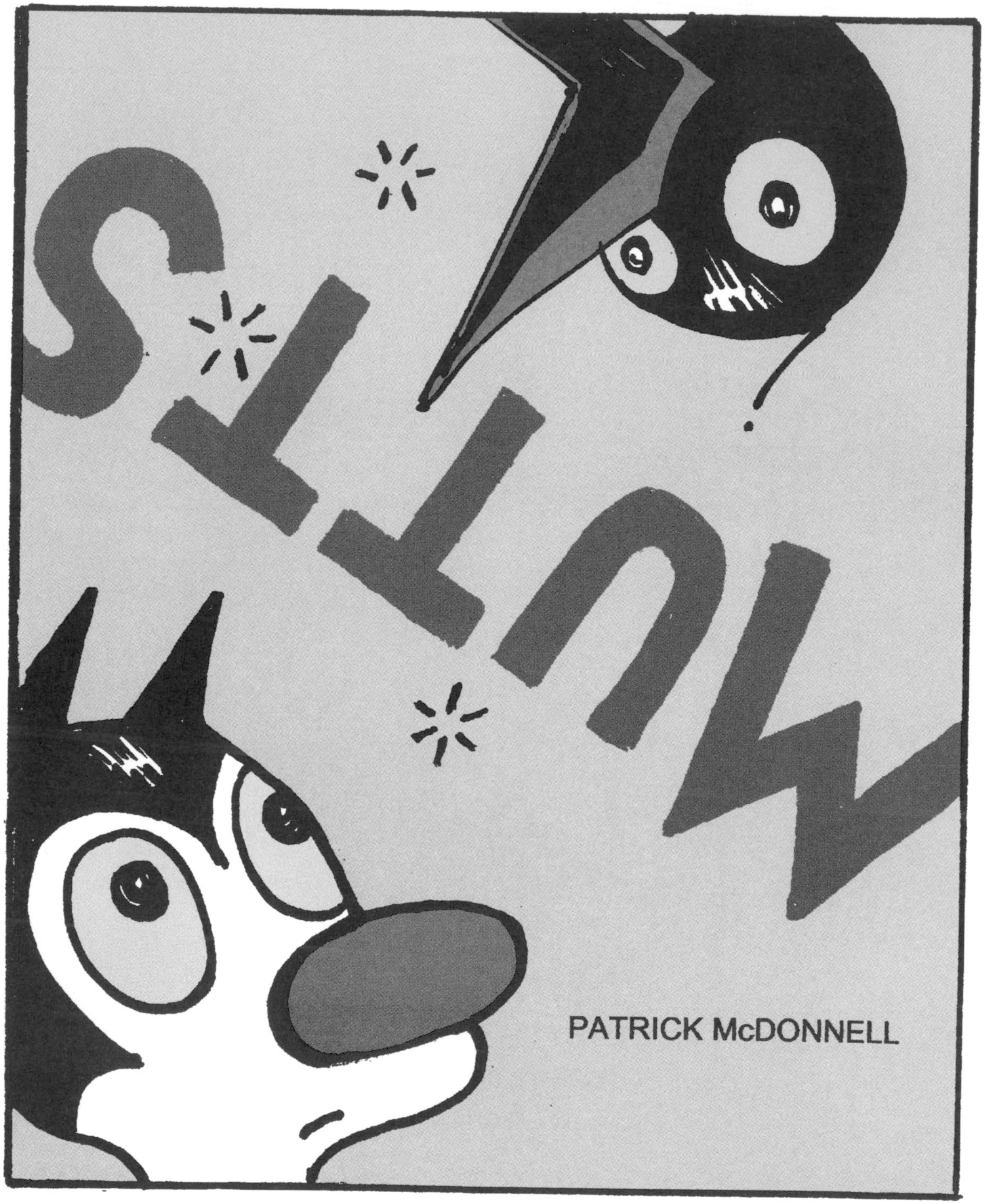
MUTTS
PATRICK McDONNELL

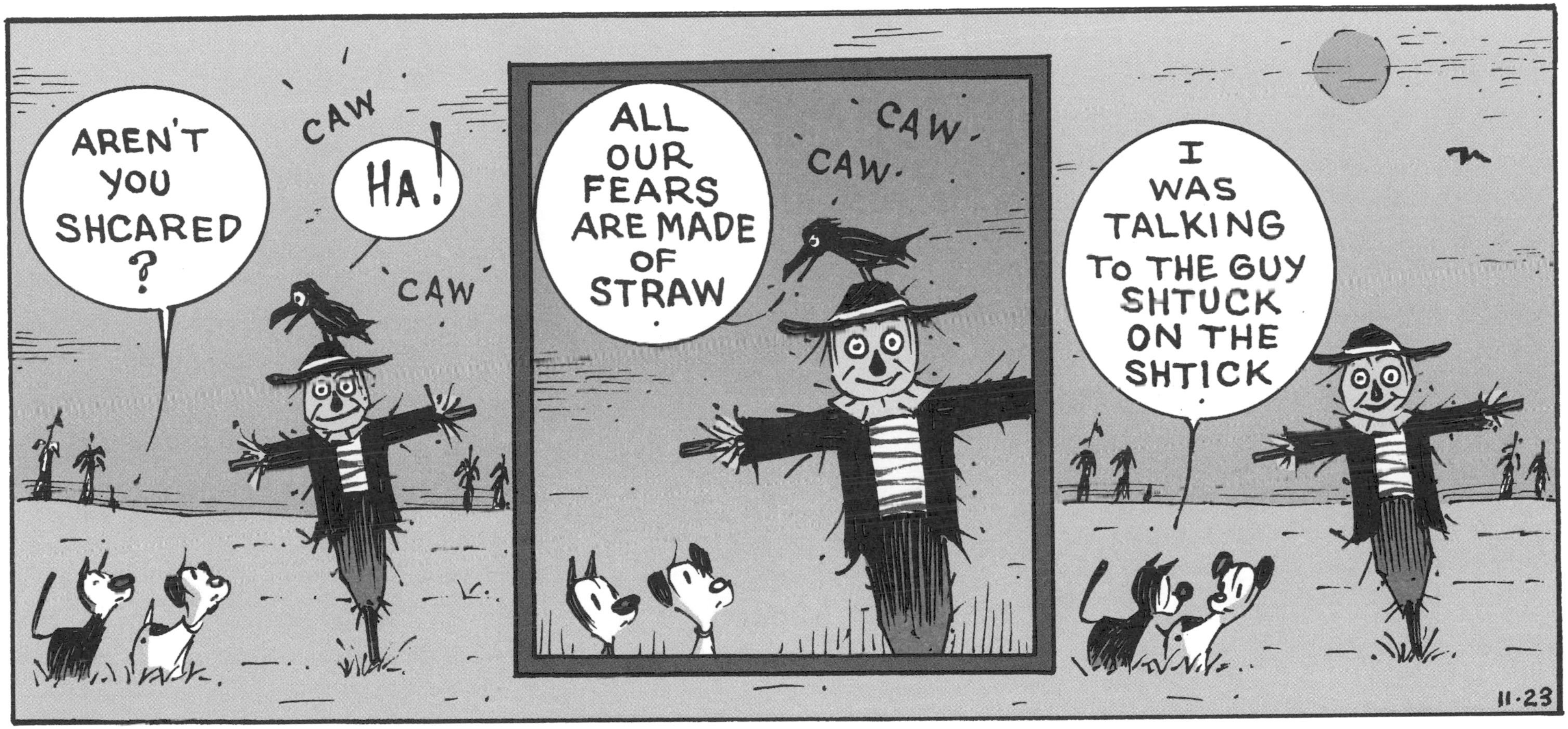
AREN'T YOU SHCARED ?
CAW
HA!
CAW
ALL OUR FEARS ARE MADE OF STRAW
CAW
CAW
I WAS TALKING TO THE GUY SHTUCK ON THE SHTICK
11·23

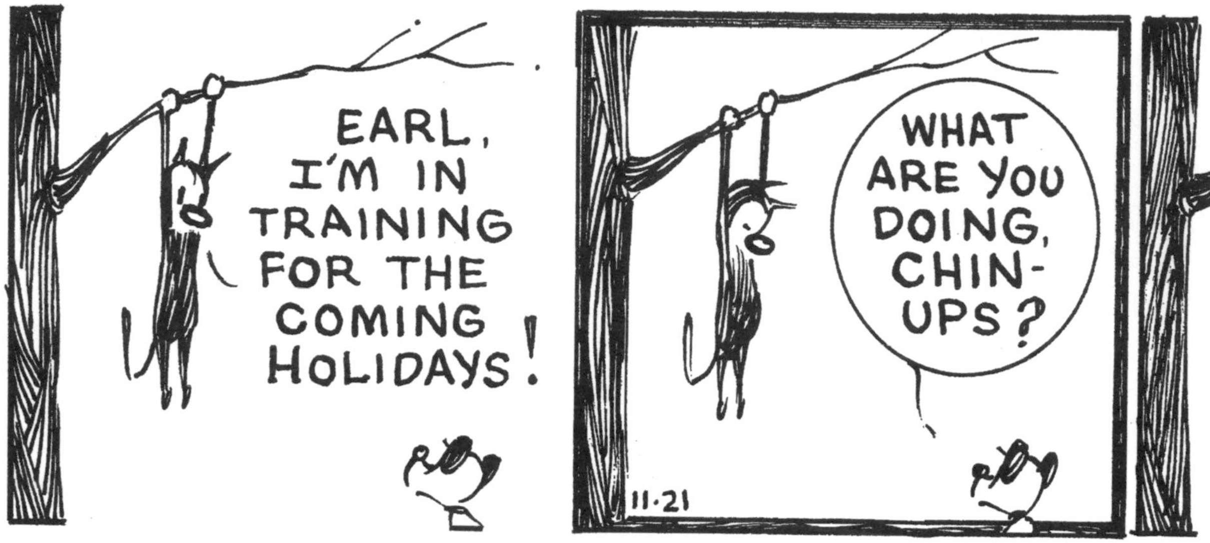
EARL, I'M IN TRAINING FOR THE COMING HOLIDAYS!
WHAT ARE YOU DOING, CHIN-UPS?
BELLY SHTRETCHERS.
11·21

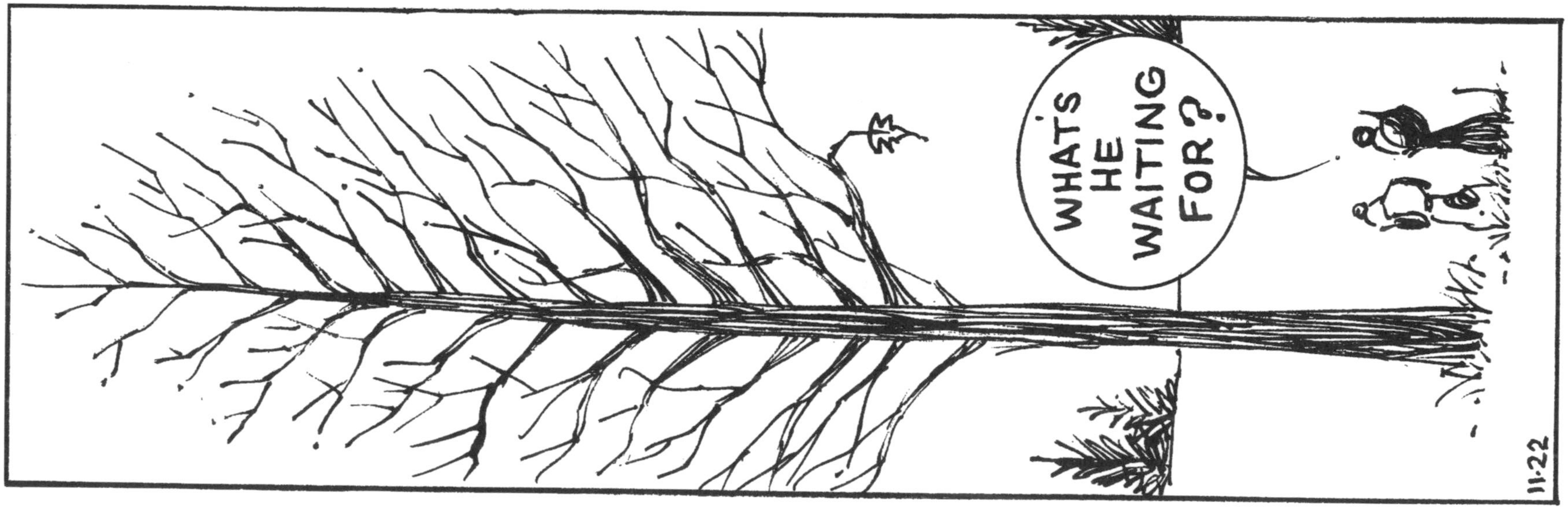
WHAT'S HE WAITING FOR?
11·22

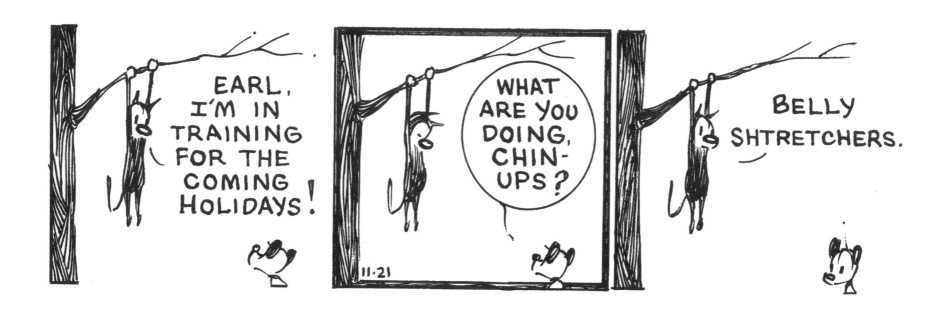

THANKS GIVING

EARL

Nothing is more honorable

than a grateful heart.

~ Seneca

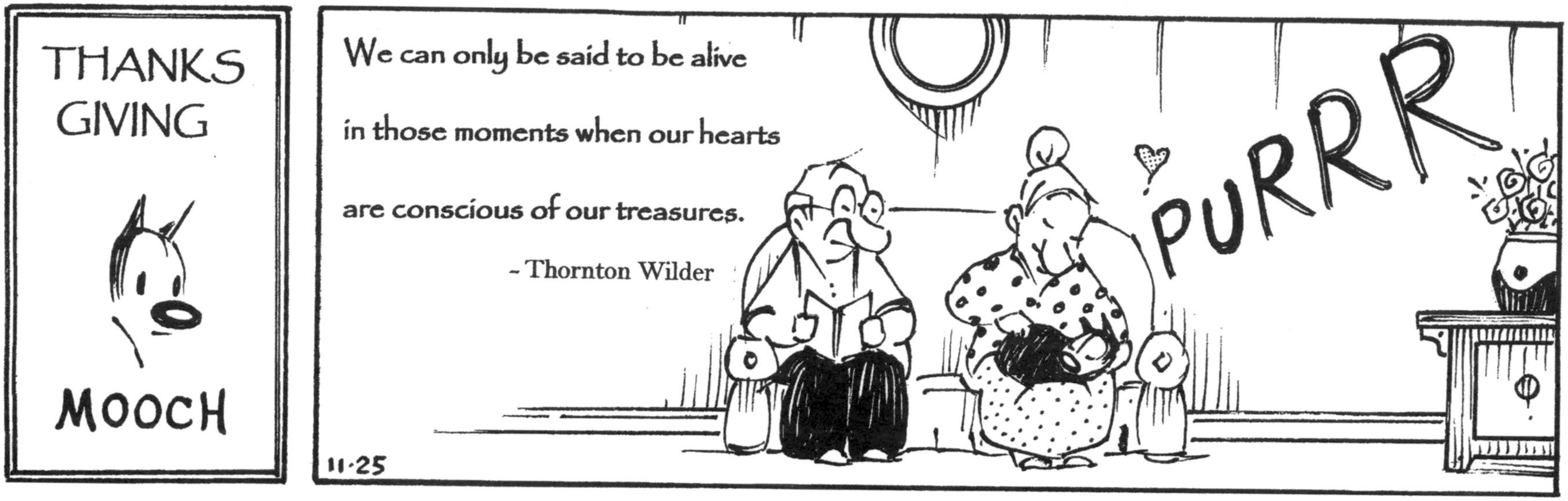
THANKS GIVING
MOOCH
We can only be said to be alive in those moments when our hearts are conscious of our treasures.
- Thornton Wilder
PURRR
11-25

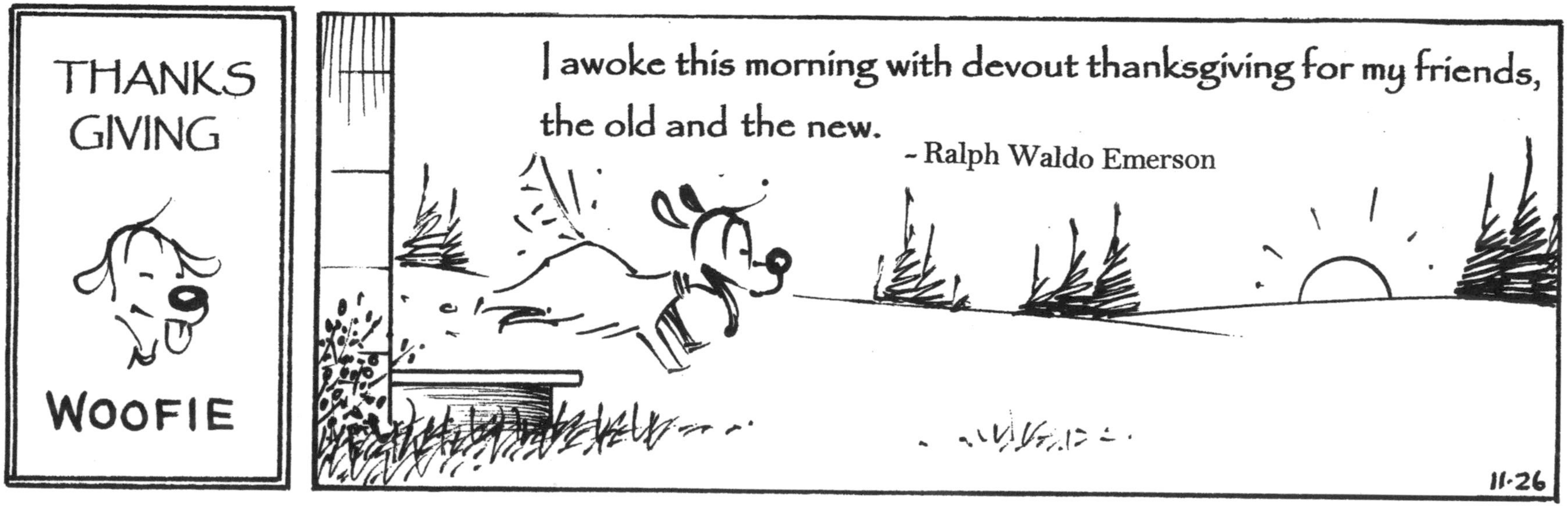
THANKS GIVING
WOOFIE
I awoke this morning with devout thanksgiving for my friends, the old and the new.
- Ralph Waldo Emerson
11-26

THANKS GIVING

JULES

Thanksgiving, after all,

is a word of action.

– W.J. Cameron

11-27

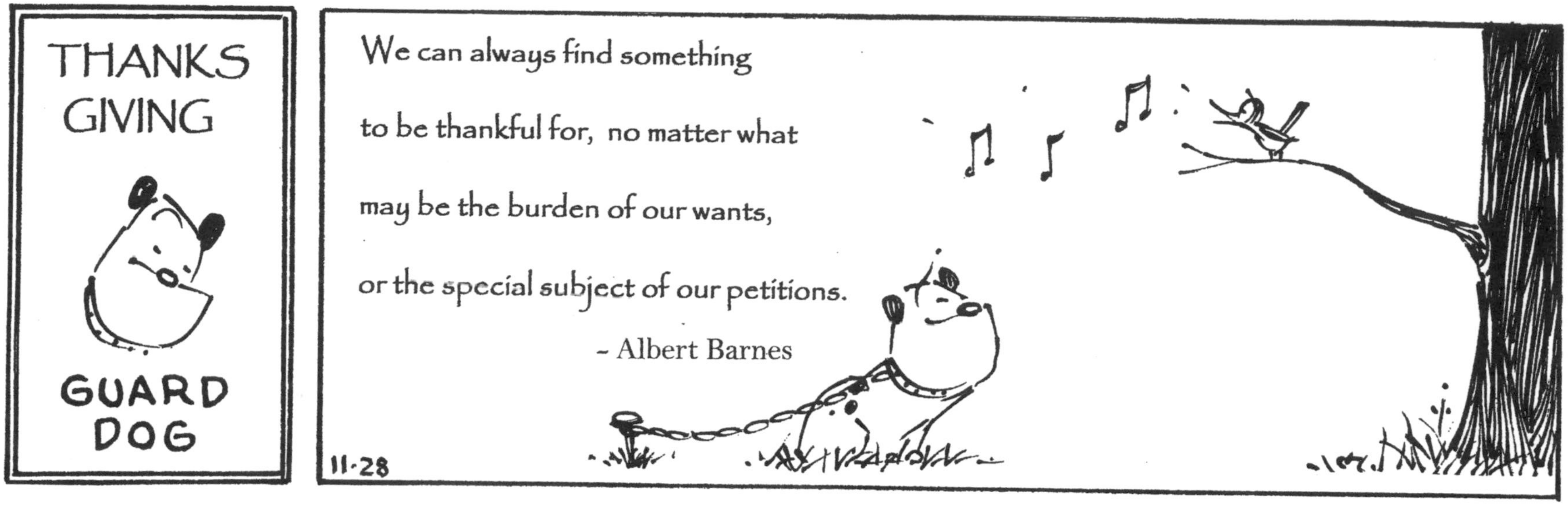
THANKS GIVING
GUARD DOG
We can always find something to be thankful for, no matter what may be the burden of our wants, or the special subject of our petitions.
- Albert Barnes
11-28

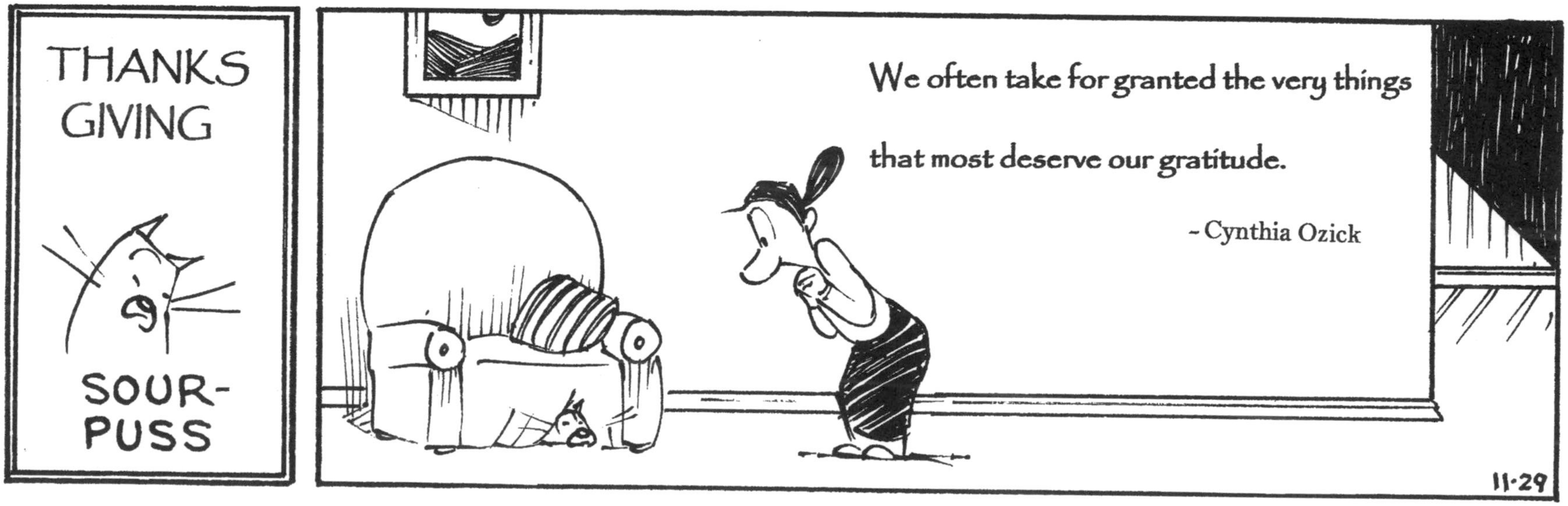
THANKS GIVING
SOUR-PUSS
We often take for granted the very things that most deserve our gratitude.
- Cynthia Ozick
11-29

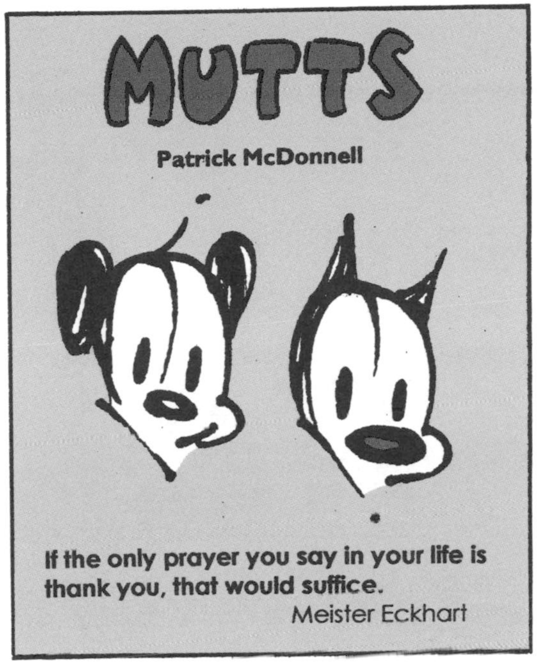
MUTTS
Patrick McDonnell
If the only prayer you say in your life is thank you, that would suffice.
Meister Eckhart

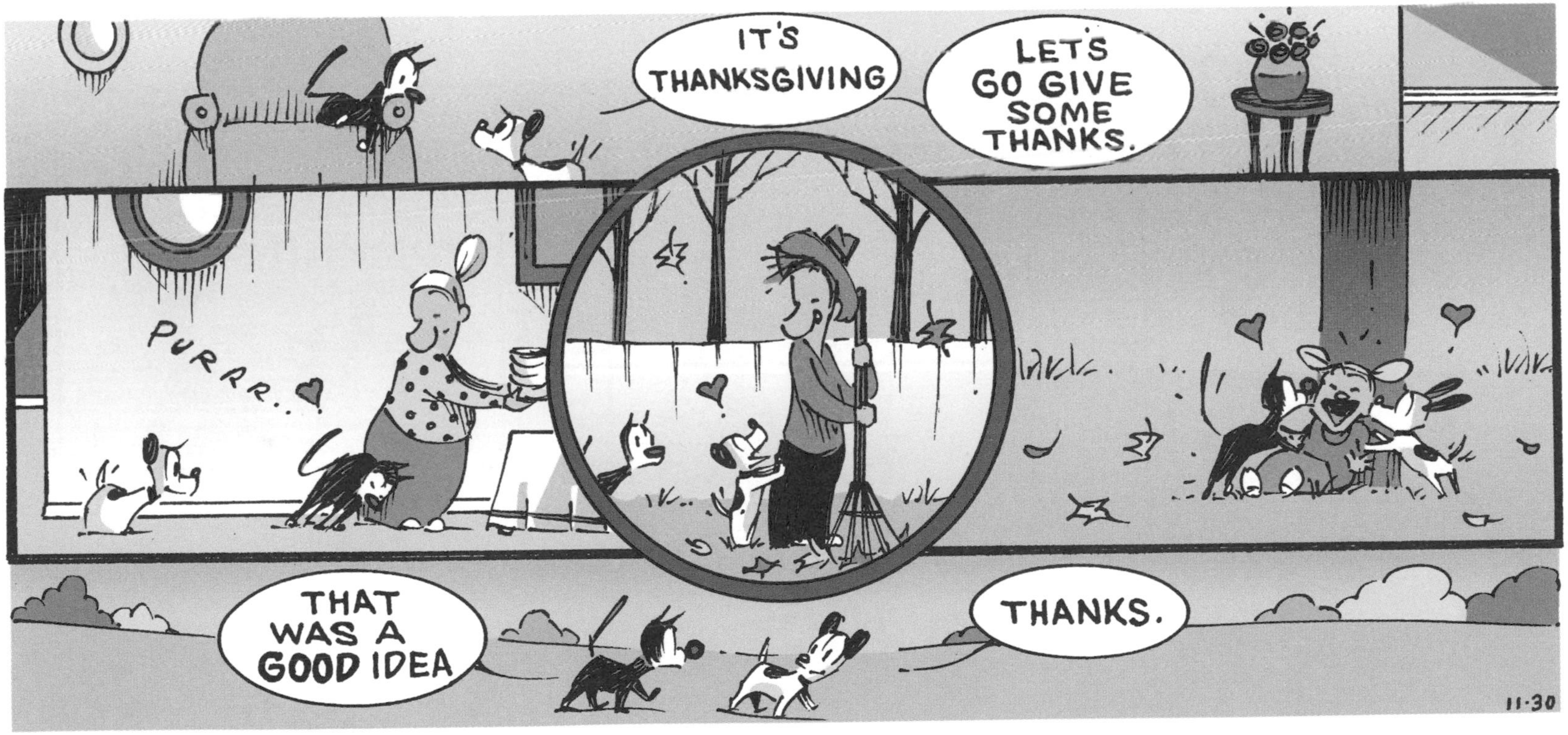
IT'S THANKSGIVING
LET'S GO GIVE SOME THANKS.
PURRR..
THAT WAS A GOOD IDEA
THANKS.
11·30

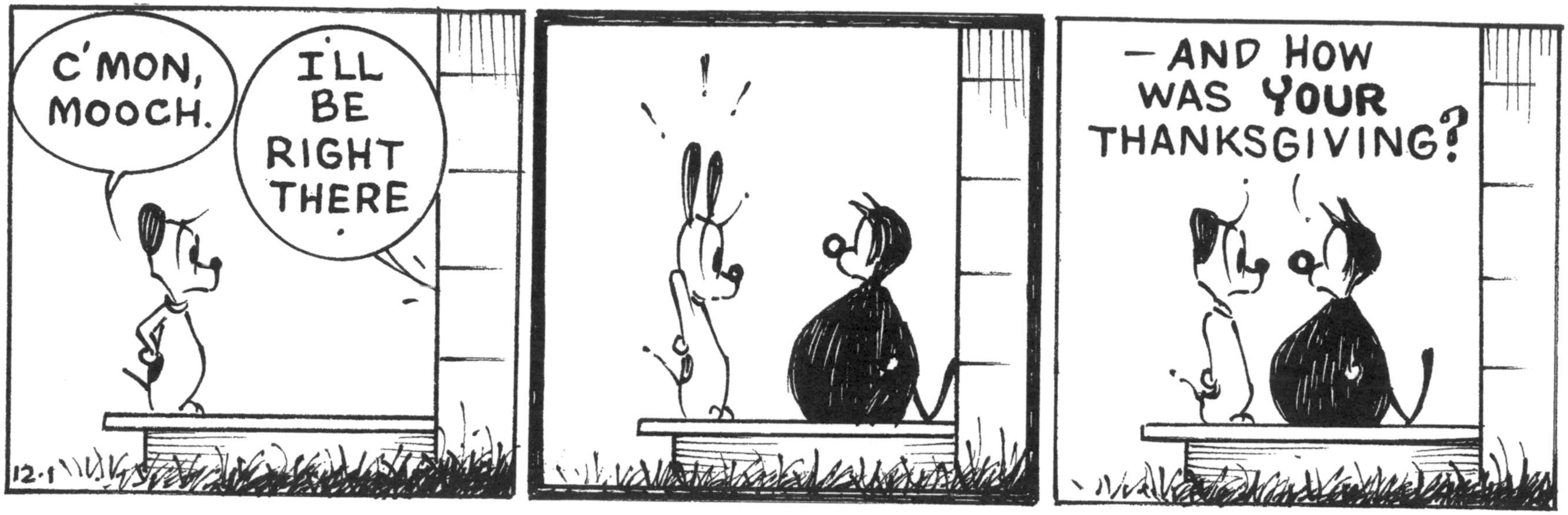
C'MON, MOOCH.
I'LL BE RIGHT THERE
— AND HOW WAS YOUR THANKSGIVING?
12·1

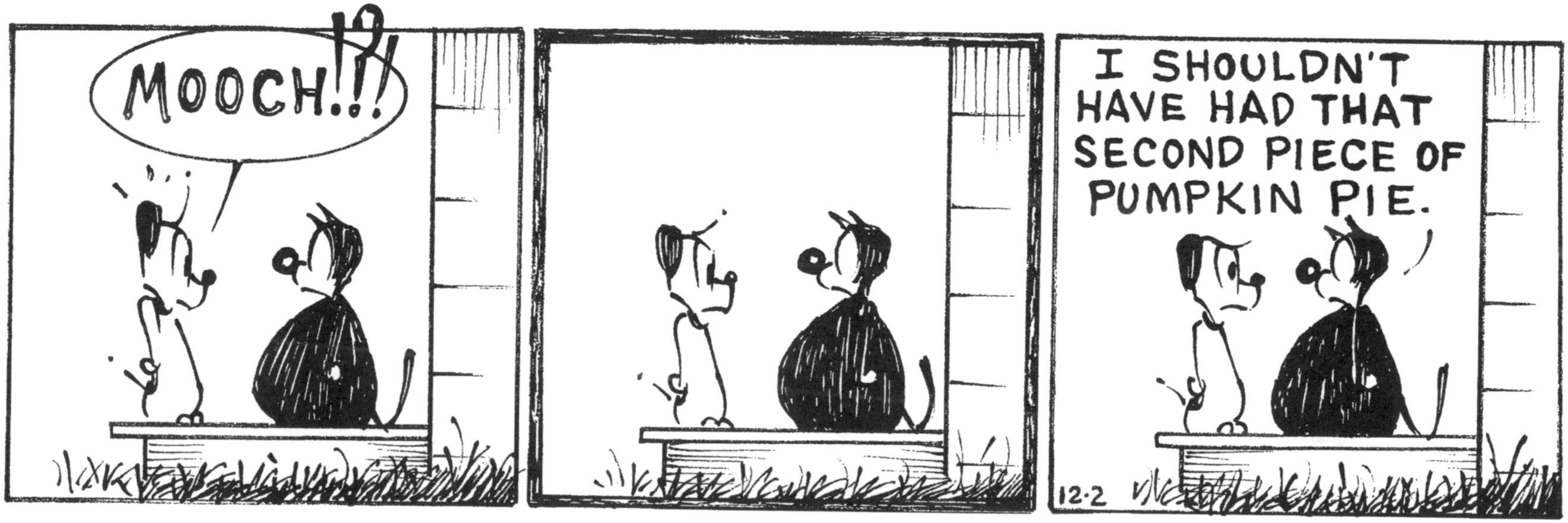
MOOCH!?!
I SHOULDN'T HAVE HAD THAT SECOND PIECE OF PUMPKIN PIE.
12·2

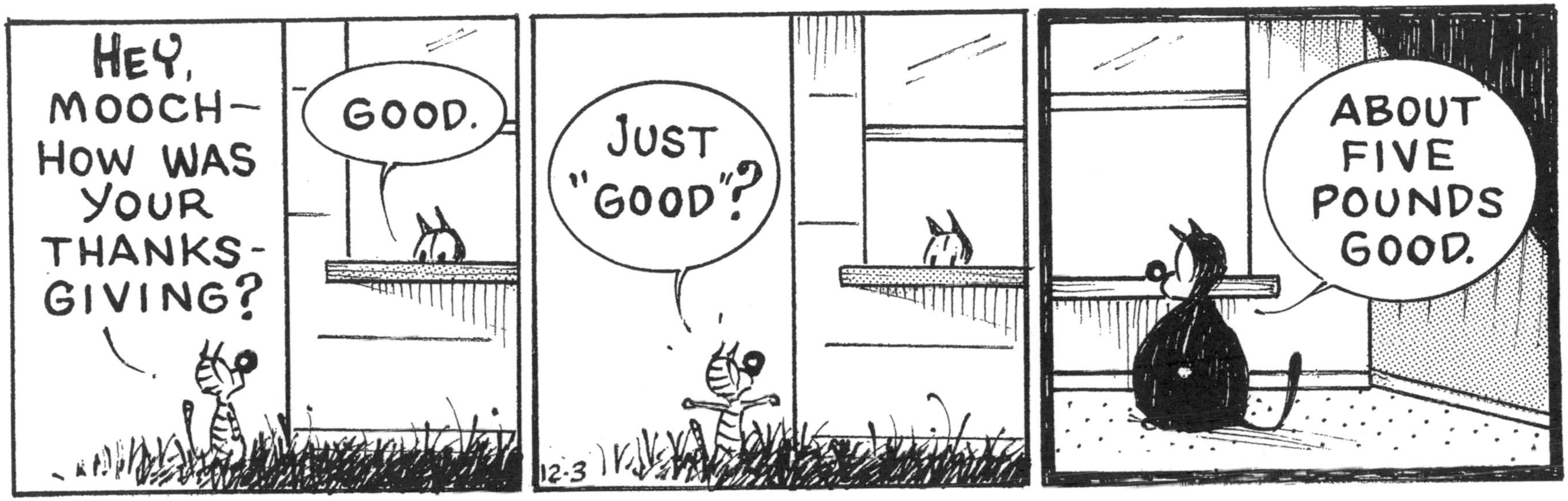
HEY, MOOCH— HOW WAS YOUR THANKS-GIVING?
GOOD.
JUST "GOOD"?
ABOUT FIVE POUNDS GOOD.
12·3

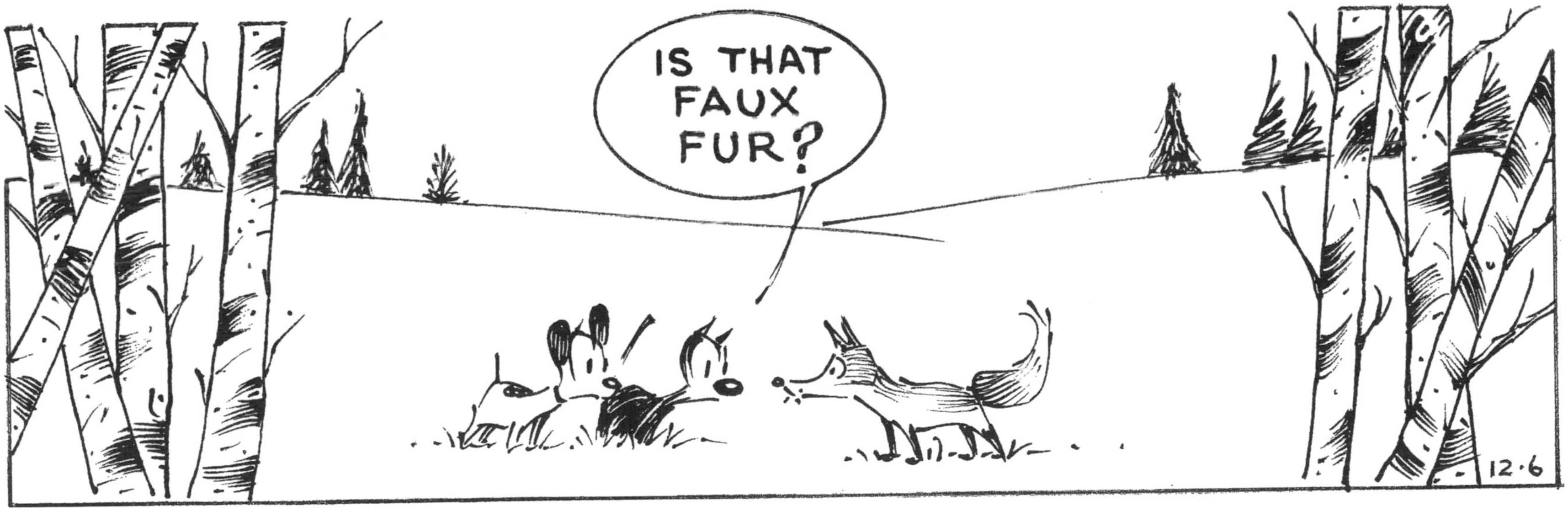
IS THAT FAUX FUR?
12·6

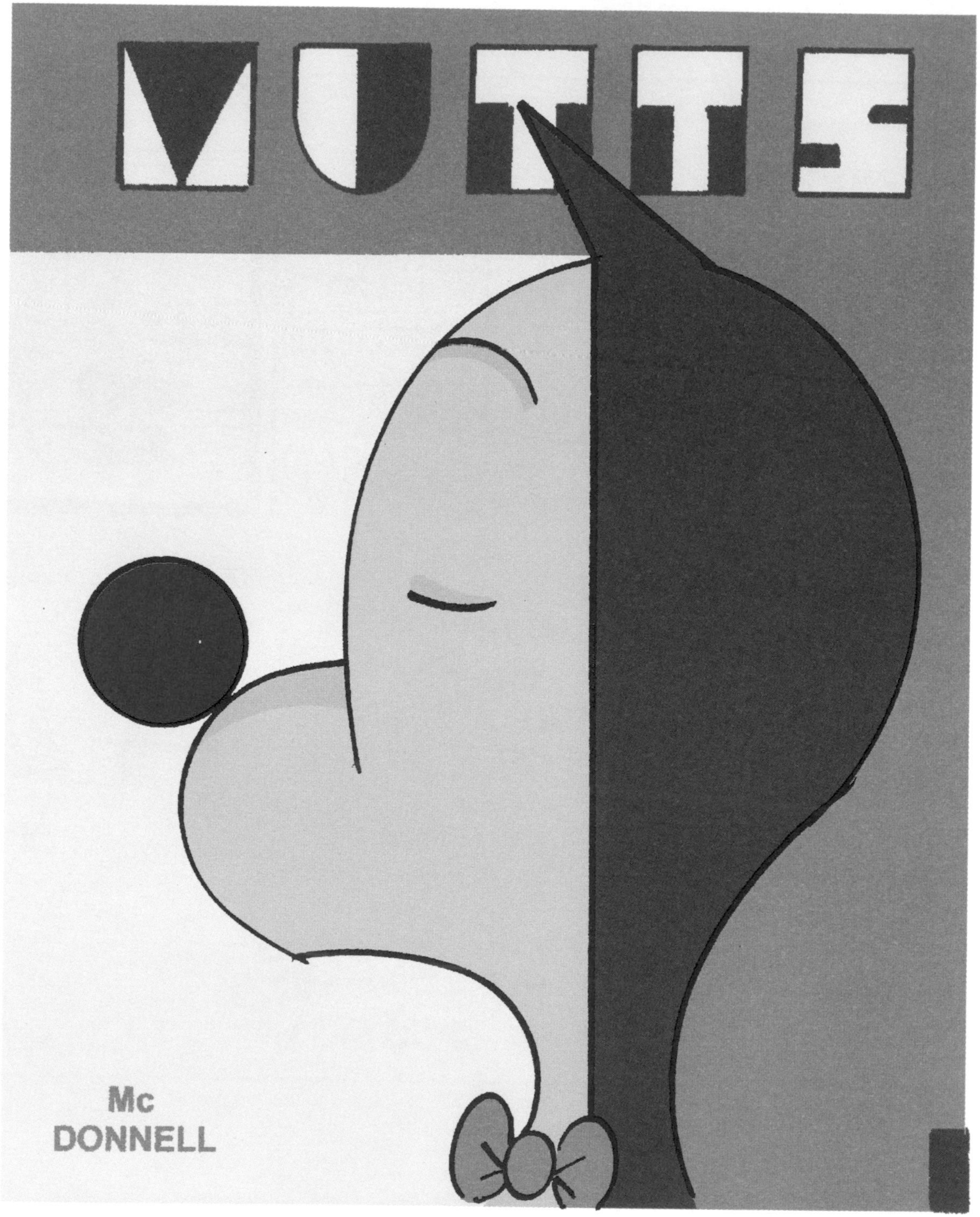
MUTTS
Mc
DONNELL

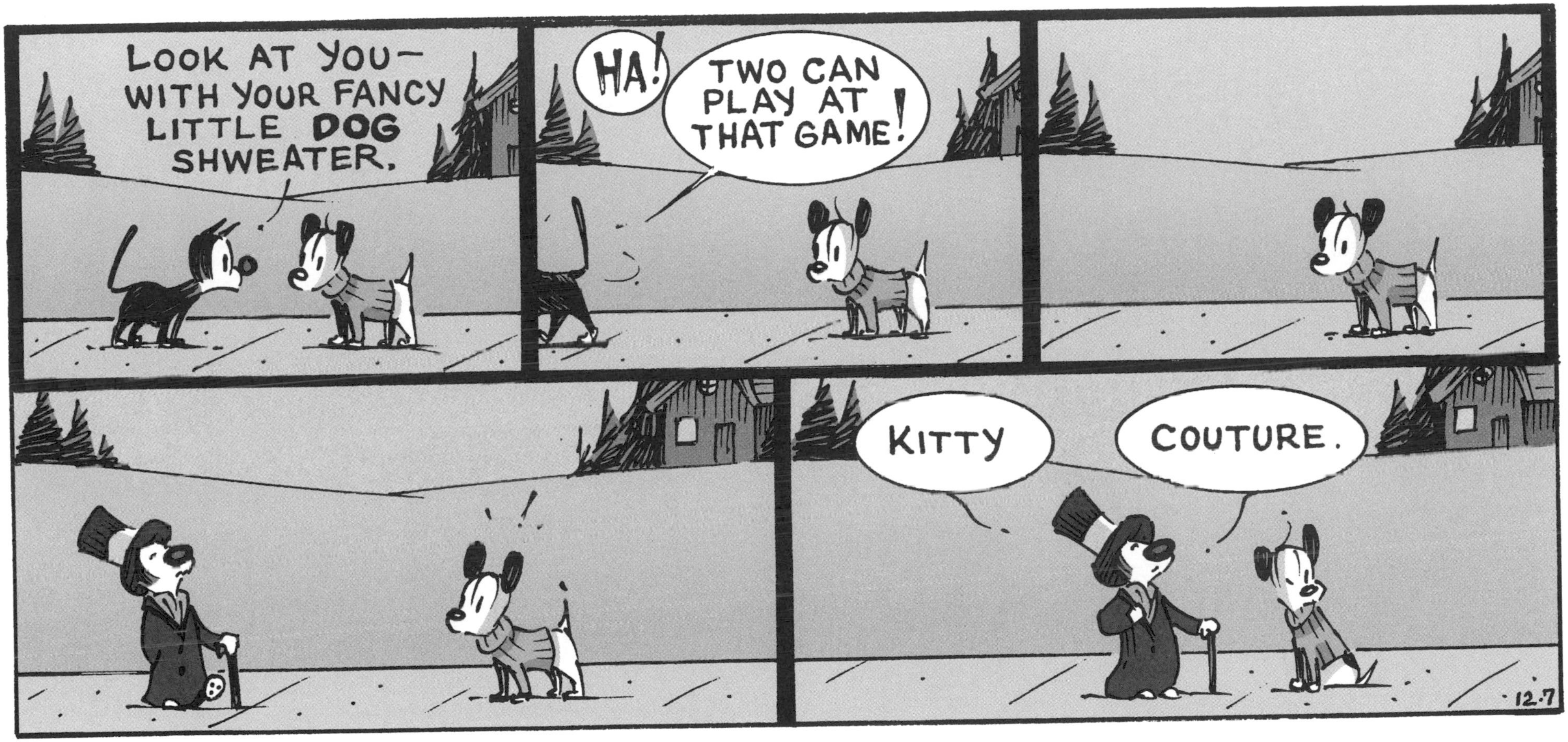
LOOK AT YOU—
WITH YOUR FANCY
LITTLE DOG
SHWEATER.
HA!
TWO CAN
PLAY AT
THAT GAME!
KITTY
COUTURE.
12·7

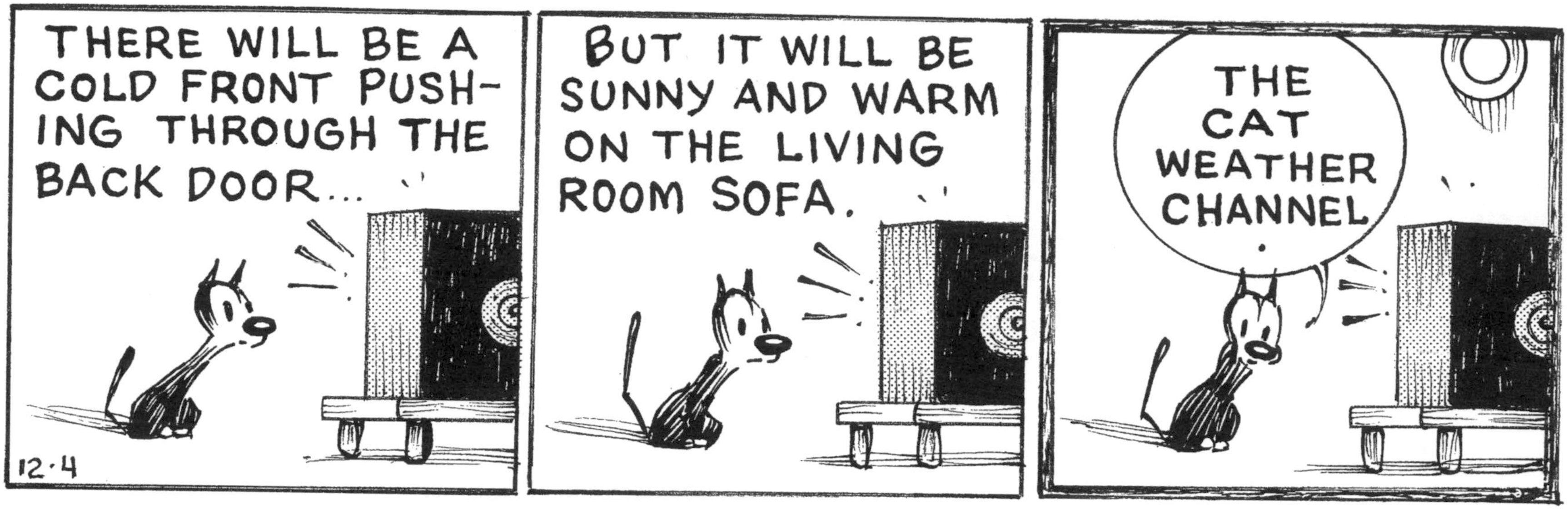
THERE WILL BE A COLD FRONT PUSHING THROUGH THE BACK DOOR...
12·4
BUT IT WILL BE SUNNY AND WARM ON THE LIVING ROOM SOFA.
THE CAT WEATHER CHANNEL.

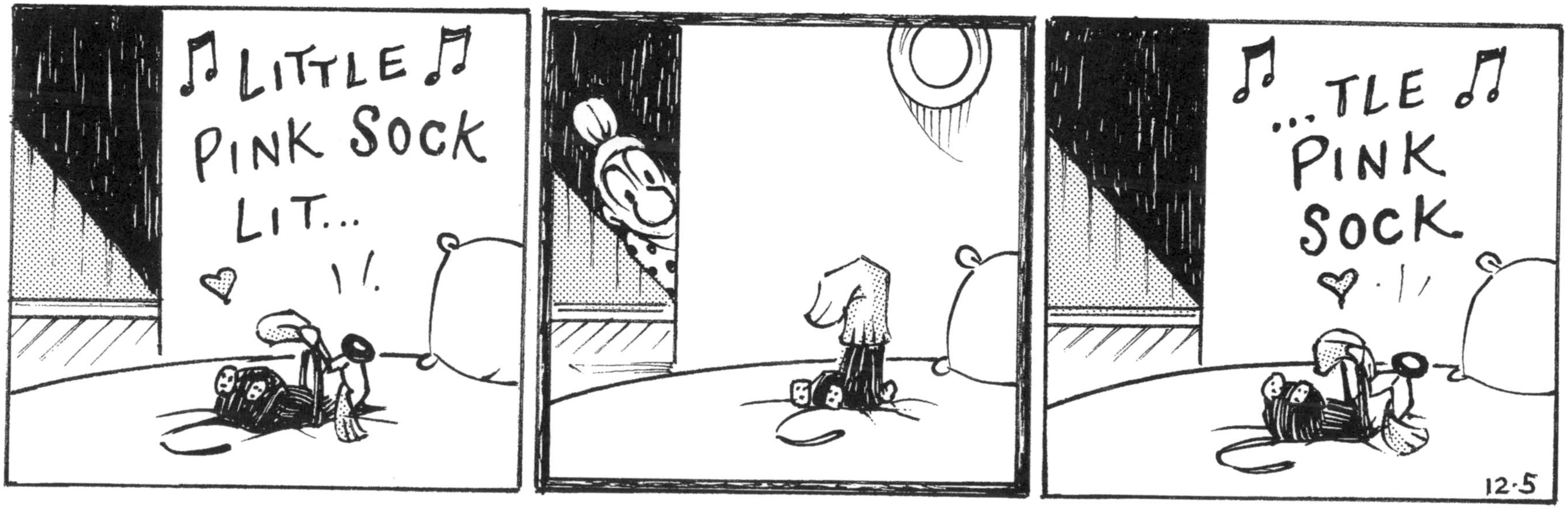
LITTLE
PINK SOCK
LIT...
...TLE
PINK SOCK
12·5

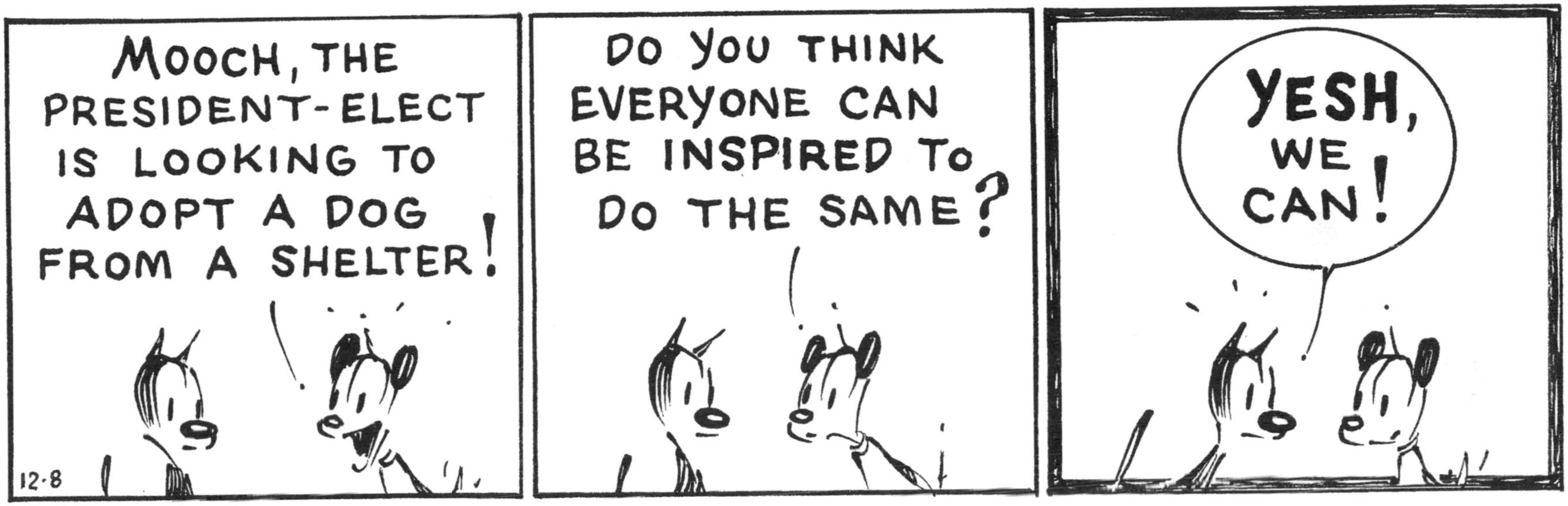
MOOCH, THE PRESIDENT-ELECT IS LOOKING TO ADOPT A DOG FROM A SHELTER!
12-8
DO YOU THINK EVERYONE CAN BE INSPIRED TO DO THE SAME?
YESH, WE CAN!

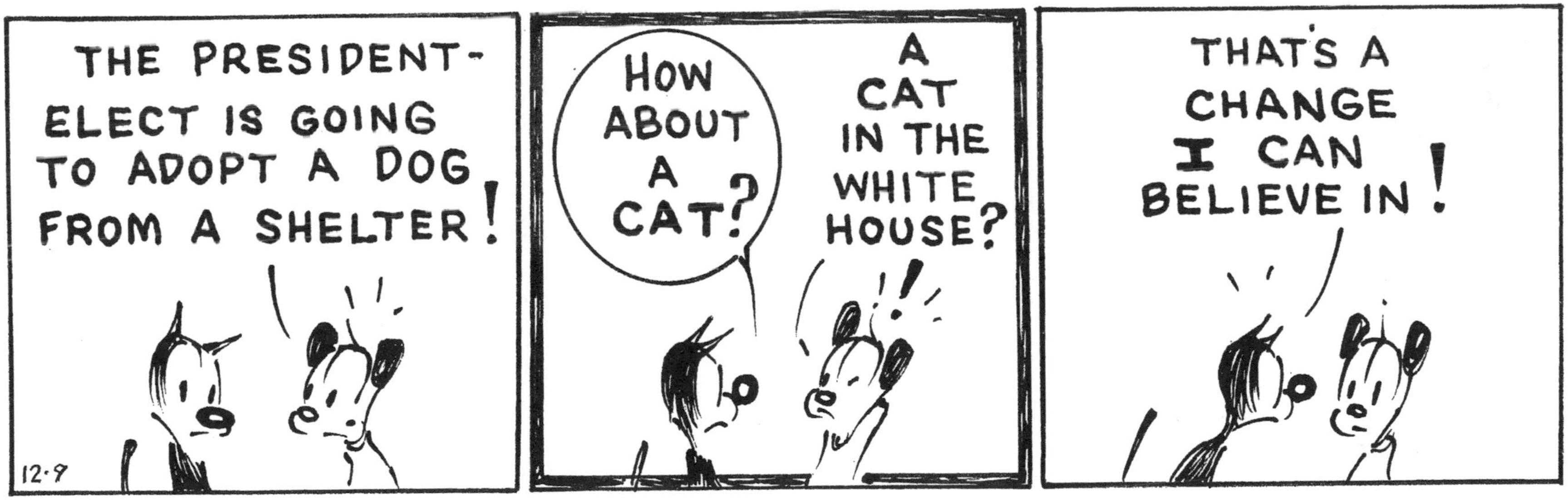
THE PRESIDENT-ELECT IS GOING TO ADOPT A DOG FROM A SHELTER!
12-9
HOW ABOUT A CAT?
A CAT IN THE WHITE HOUSE?
!
THAT'S A CHANGE I CAN BELIEVE IN!

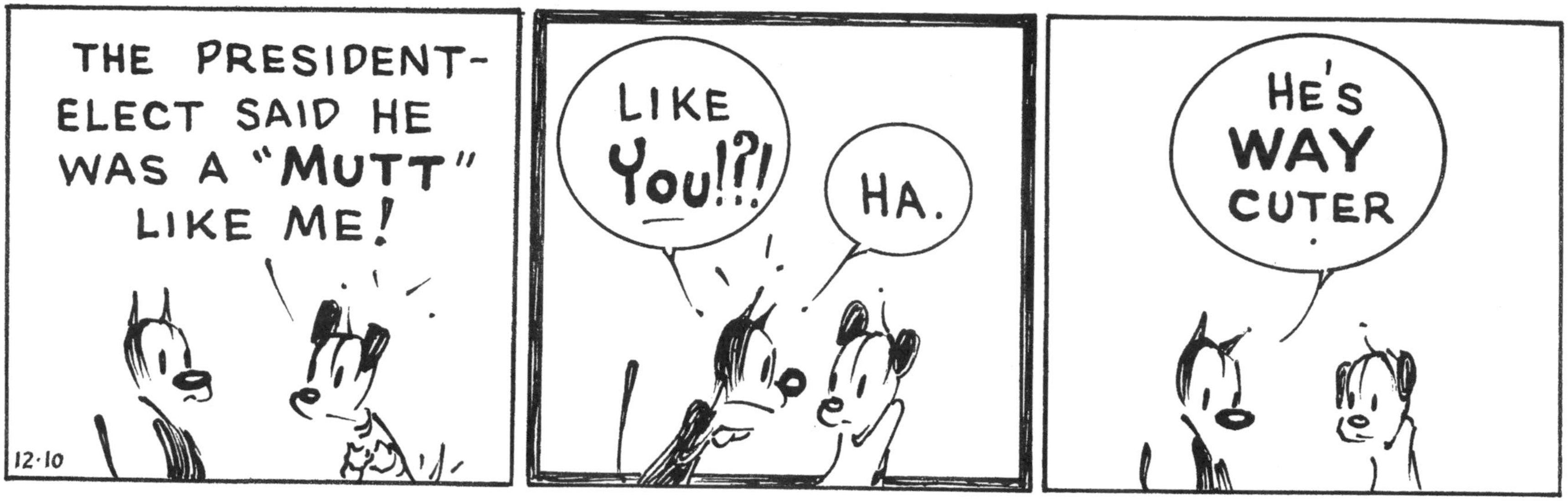
THE PRESIDENT-ELECT SAID HE WAS A "MUTT" LIKE ME!
12·10
LIKE YOU!?!
HA.
HE'S WAY CUTER

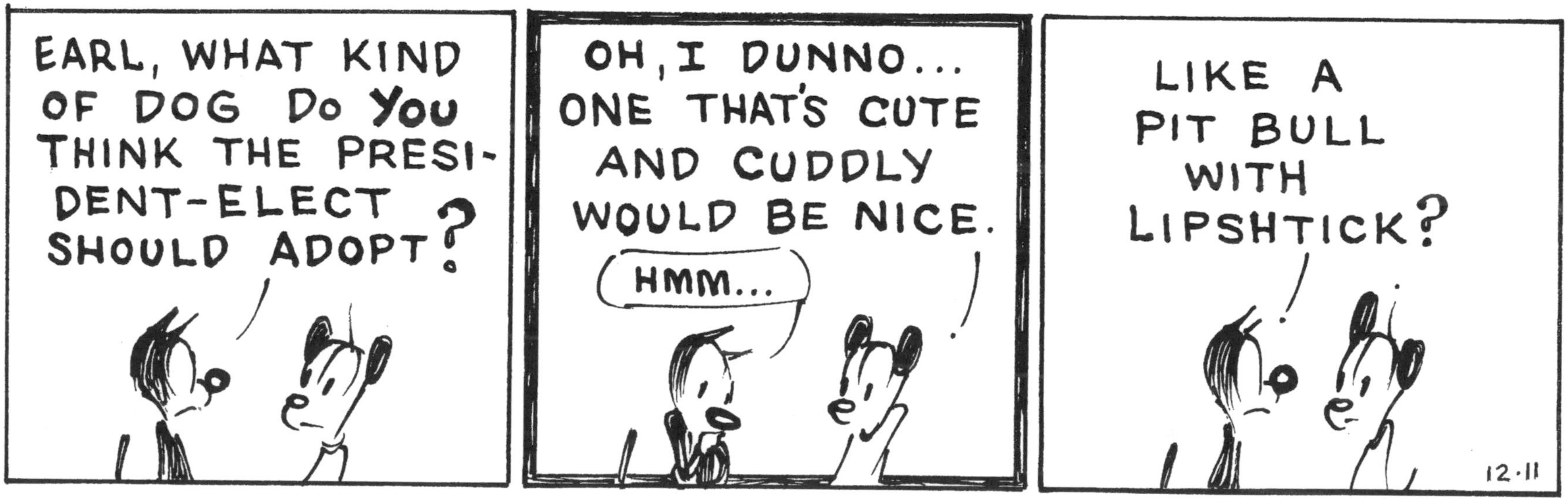
EARL, WHAT KIND OF DOG DO YOU THINK THE PRESIDENT-ELECT SHOULD ADOPT?
OH, I DUNNO... ONE THAT'S CUTE AND CUDDLY WOULD BE NICE.
HMM...
LIKE A PIT BULL WITH LIPSHTICK?
12·11

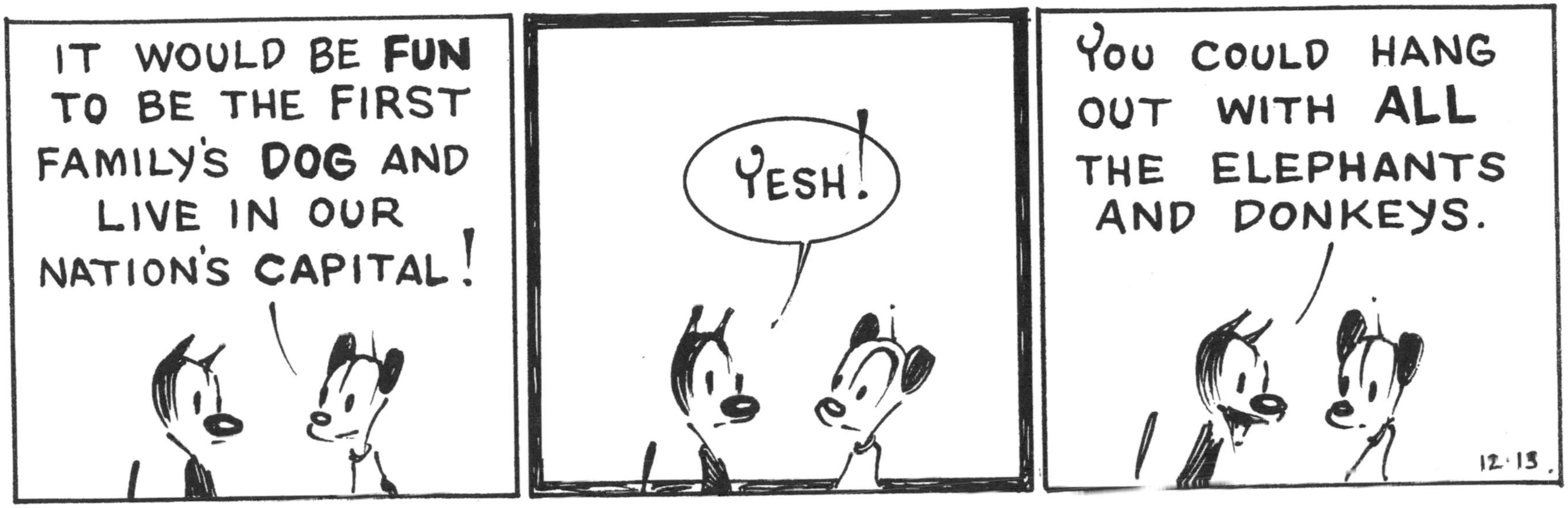
IT WOULD BE FUN TO BE THE FIRST FAMILY'S DOG AND LIVE IN OUR NATION'S CAPITAL!
YESH!
YOU COULD HANG OUT WITH ALL THE ELEPHANTS AND DONKEYS.
12·13

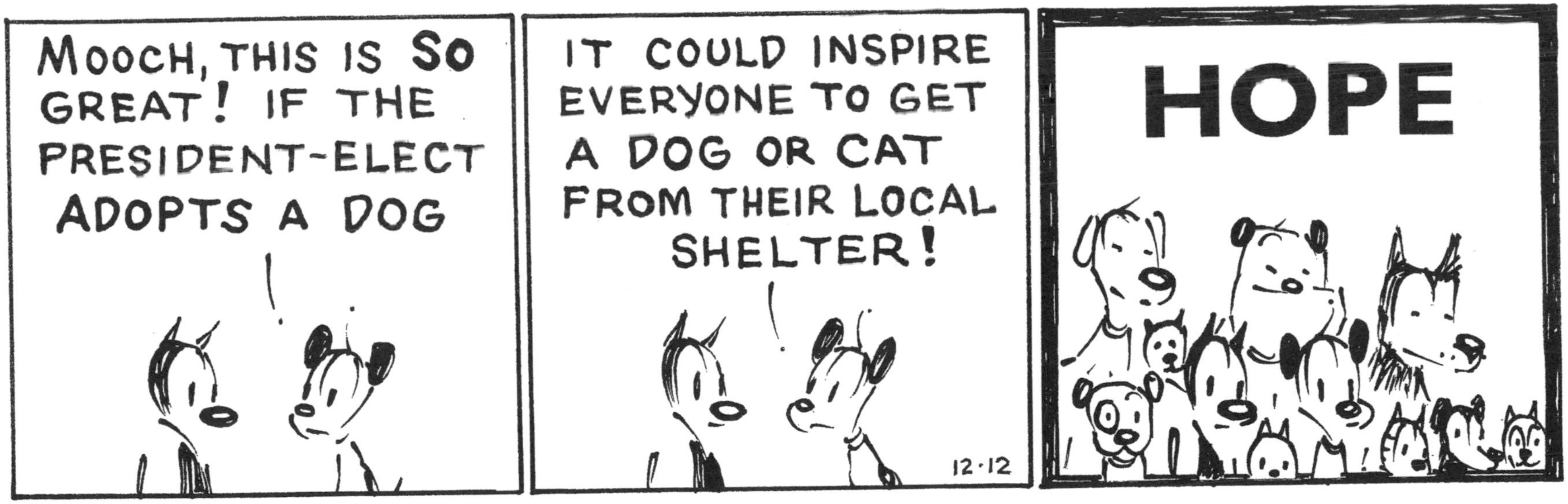
MOOCH, THIS IS SO GREAT! IF THE PRESIDENT-ELECT ADOPTS A DOG
IT COULD INSPIRE EVERYONE TO GET A DOG OR CAT FROM THEIR LOCAL SHELTER!
12·12
HOPE

Mutts
ARE WE THERE YET?
11·9

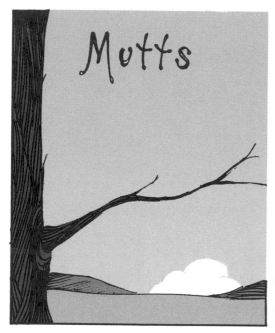

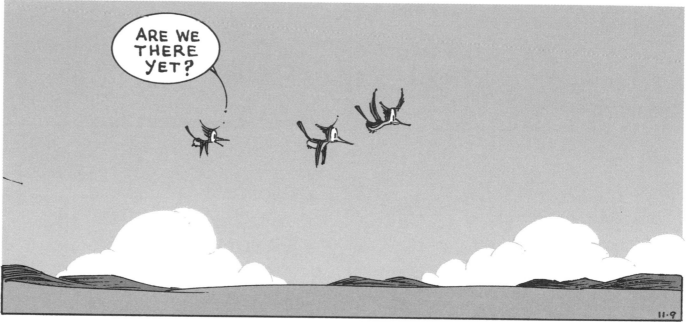

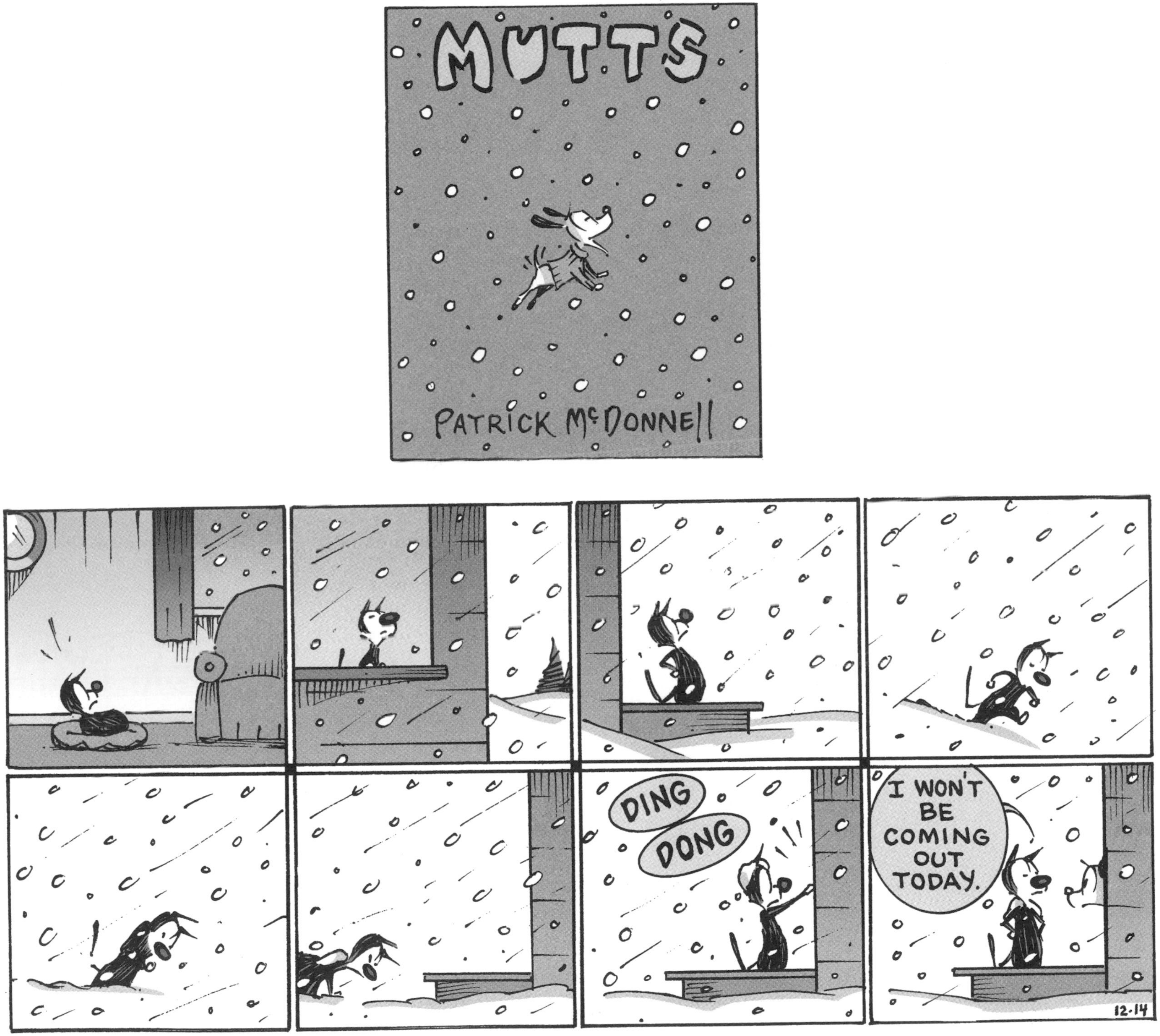
MUTTS
PATRICK McDONNELL
DING
DONG
I WON'T BE COMING OUT TODAY.
12·14

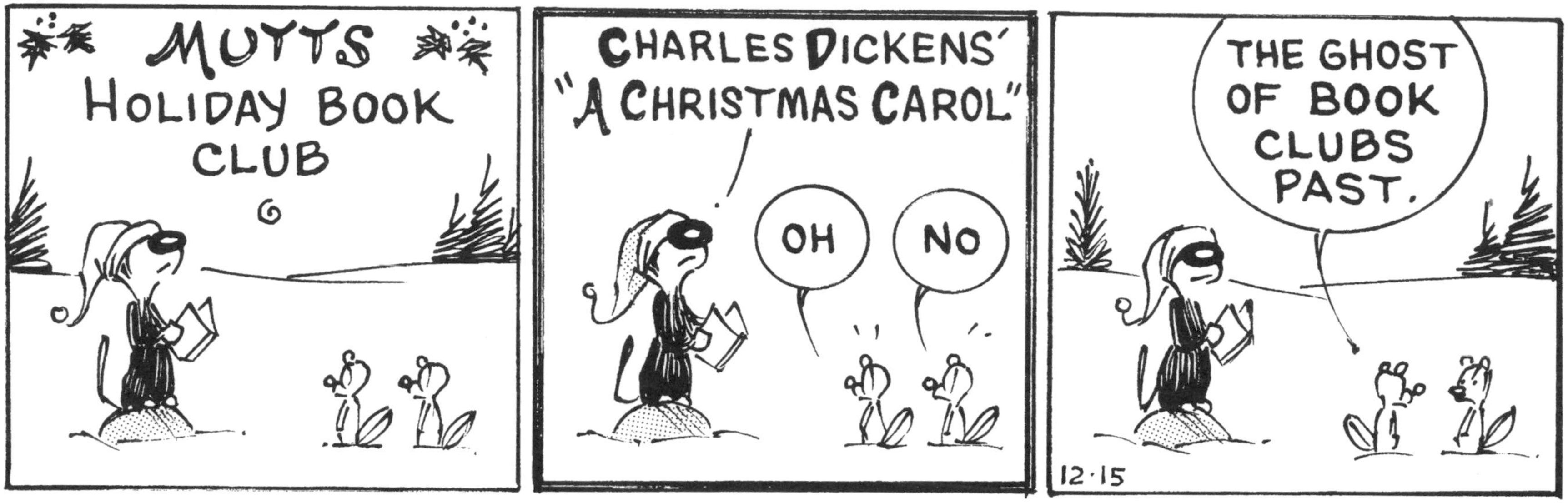
MUTTS
HOLIDAY BOOK CLUB
CHARLES DICKENS' "A CHRISTMAS CAROL"
OH
NO
THE GHOST OF BOOK CLUBS PAST.
12·15

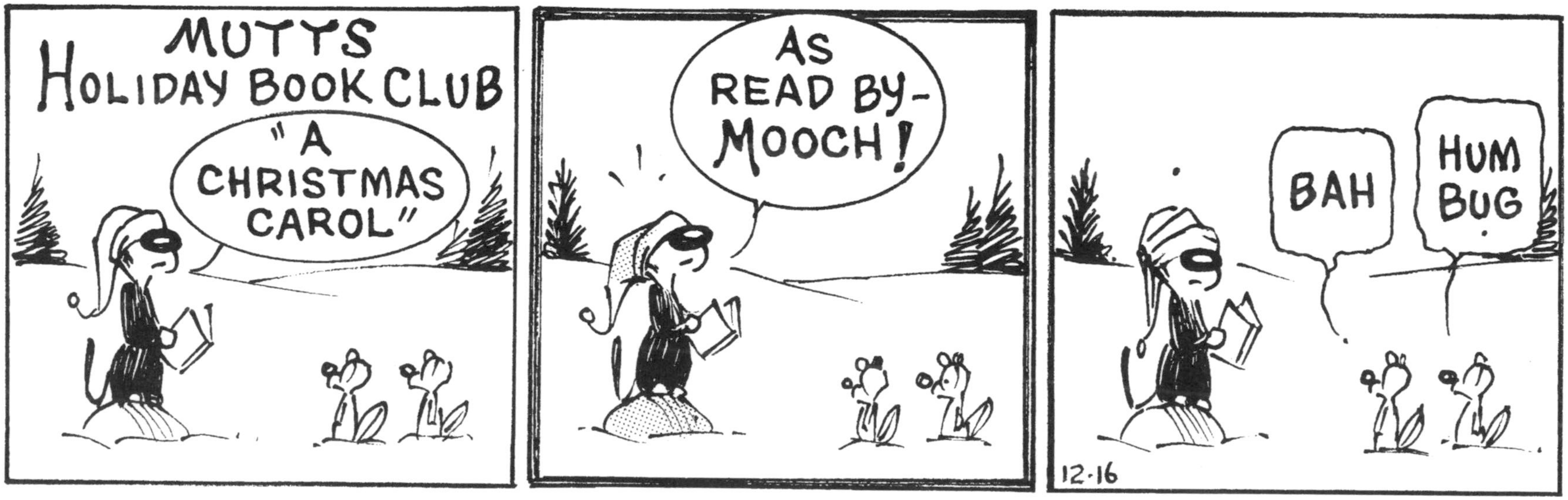
MUTTS
HOLIDAY BOOK CLUB
"A CHRISTMAS CAROL"
AS READ BY- MOOCH!
BAH
HUM BUG
12·16

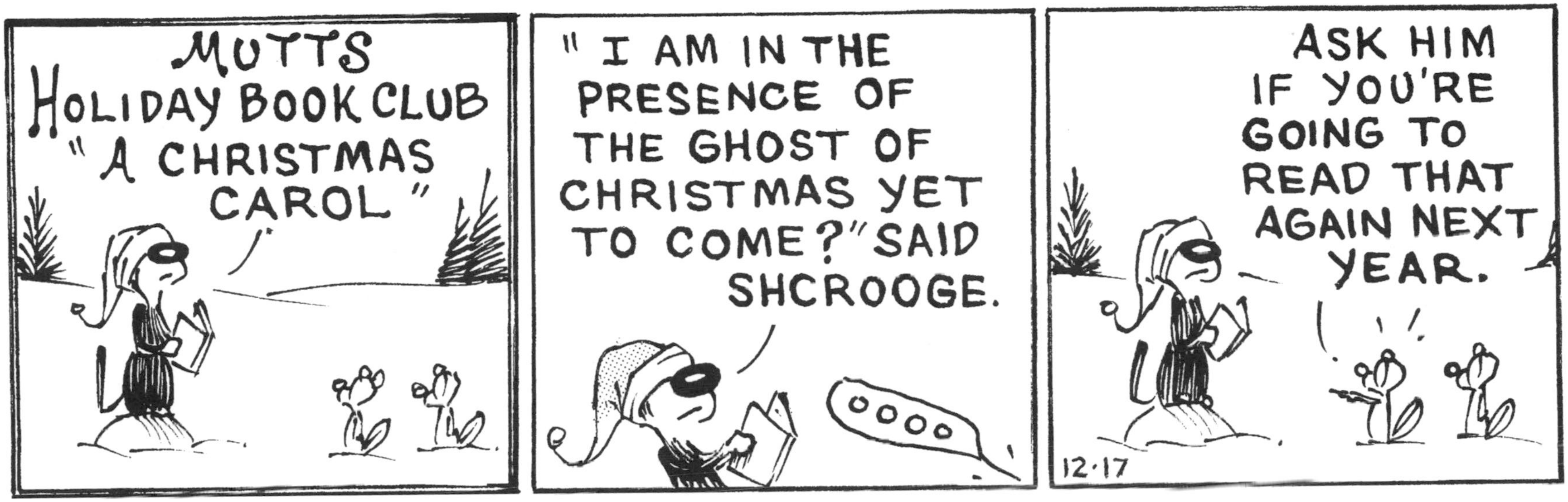
MUTTS
HOLIDAY BOOK CLUB
"A CHRISTMAS CAROL"
"I AM IN THE PRESENCE OF THE GHOST OF CHRISTMAS YET TO COME?" SAID SHCROOGE.
OOOO
ASK HIM IF YOU'RE GOING TO READ THAT AGAIN NEXT YEAR.
12·17

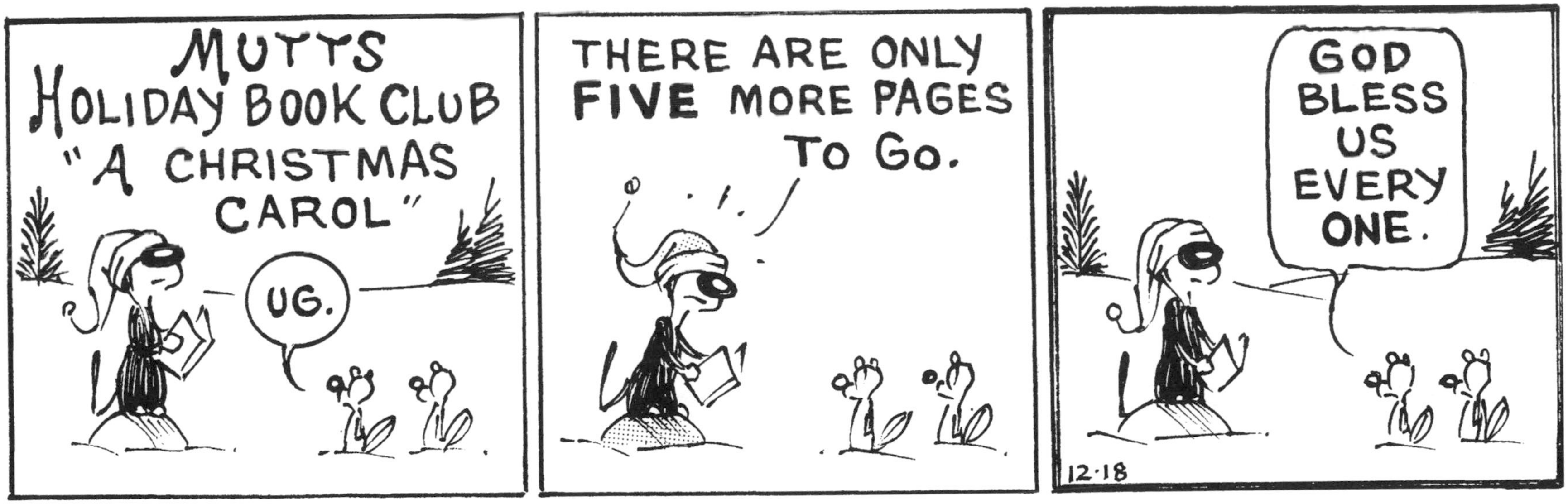
MUTTS
HOLIDAY BOOK CLUB
"A CHRISTMAS CAROL"
UG.
THERE ARE ONLY FIVE MORE PAGES TO GO.
GOD BLESS US EVERY ONE.
12·18

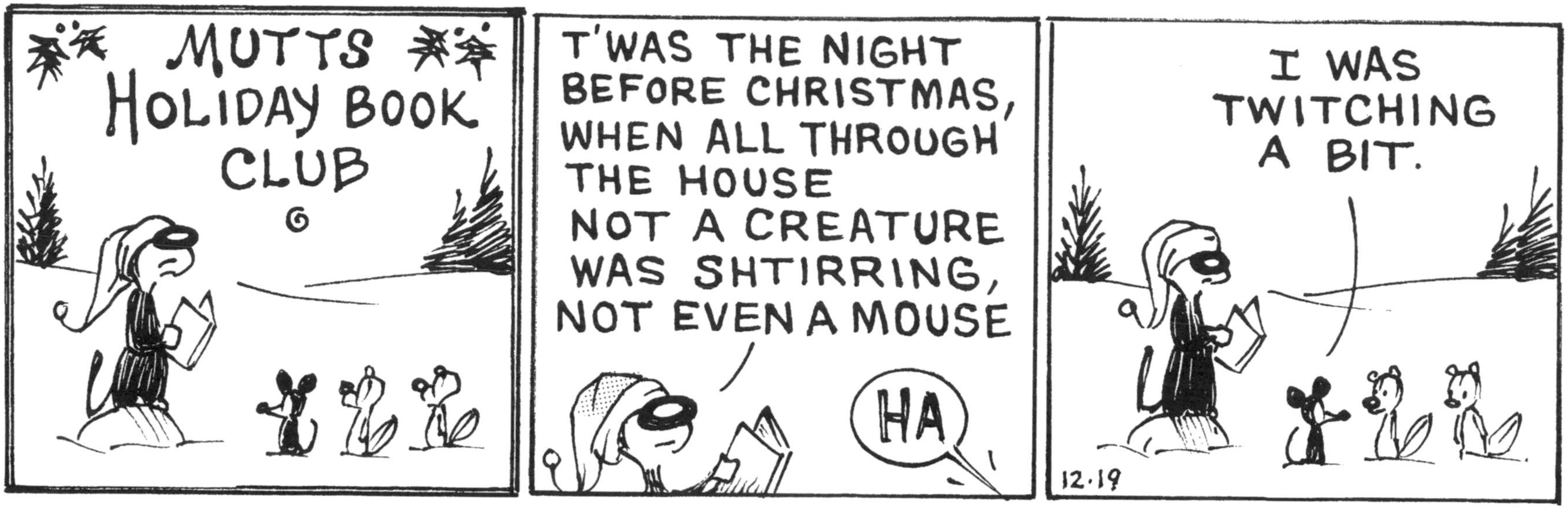
MUTTS HOLIDAY BOOK CLUB
T'WAS THE NIGHT BEFORE CHRISTMAS, WHEN ALL THROUGH THE HOUSE NOT A CREATURE WAS SHTIRRING, NOT EVEN A MOUSE
HA
I WAS TWITCHING A BIT.
12·19

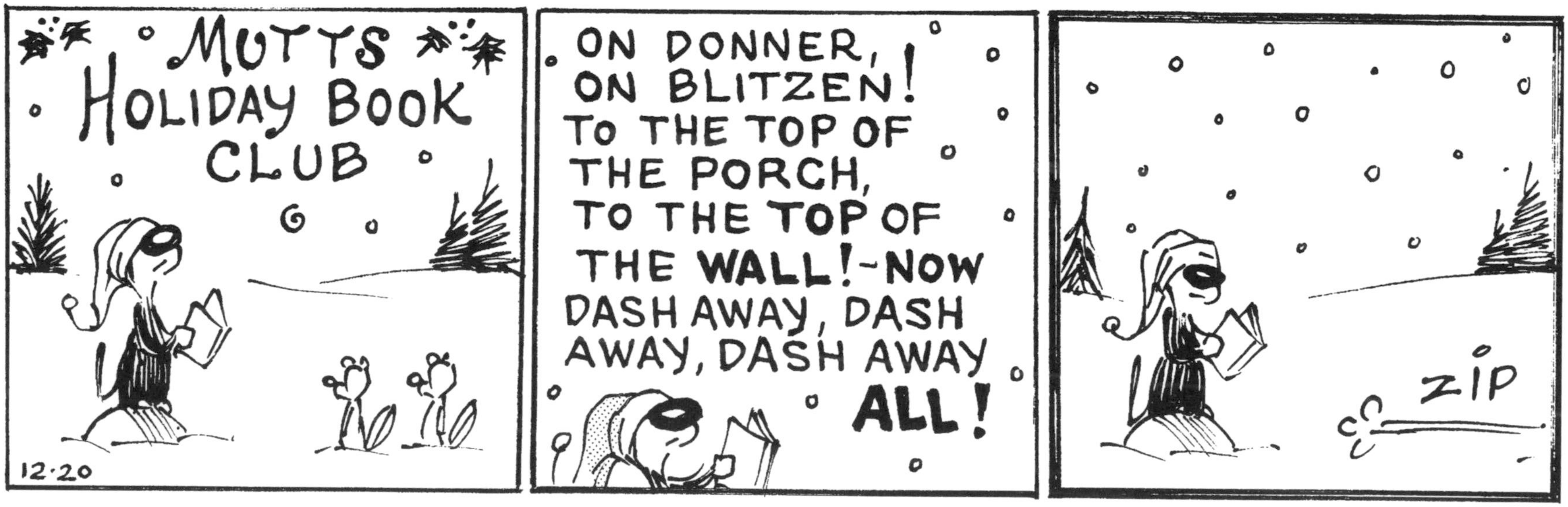
MUTTS HOLIDAY BOOK CLUB
12·20
ON DONNER, ON BLITZEN! TO THE TOP OF THE PORCH, TO THE TOP OF THE WALL!-NOW DASH AWAY, DASH AWAY, DASH AWAY ALL!
ZIP

MUTTS

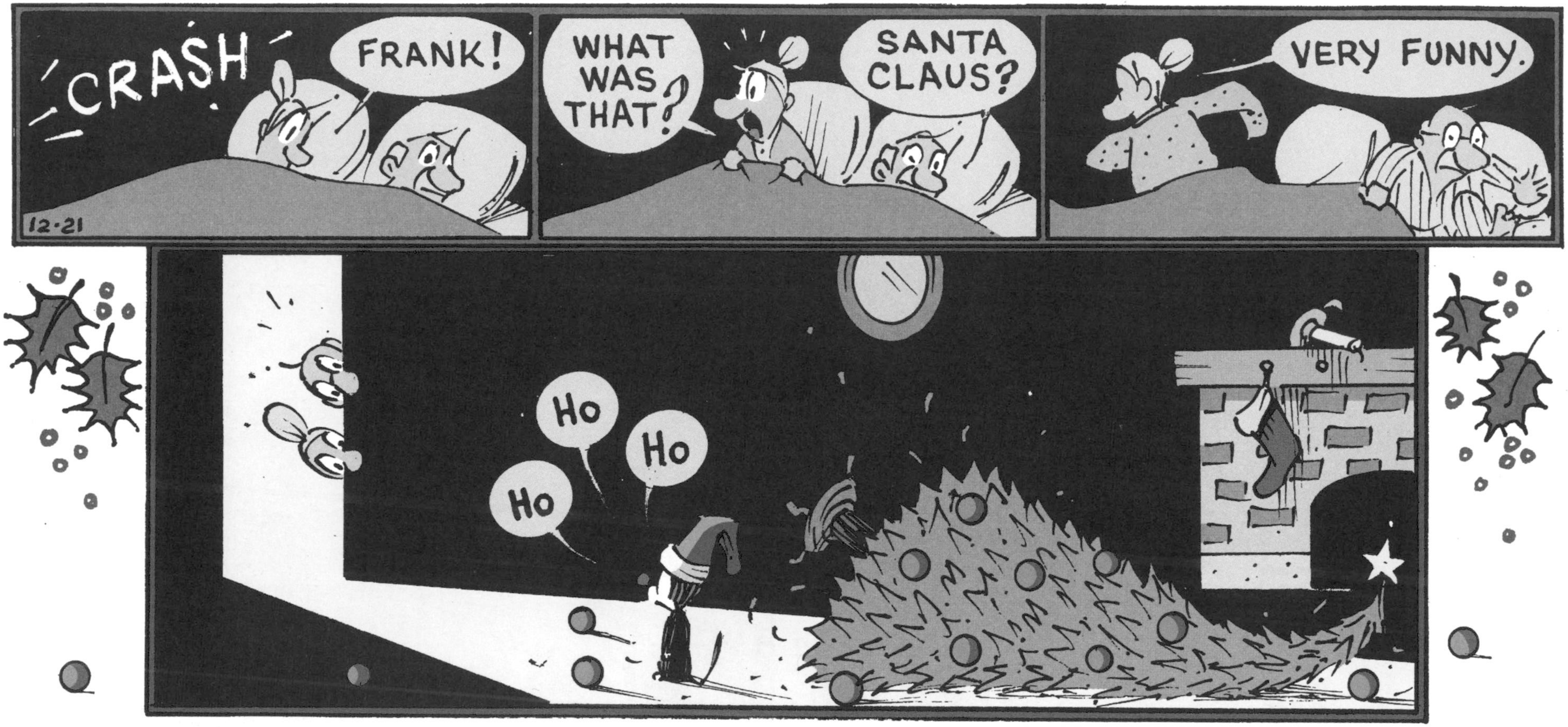
CRASH
FRANK!
12-21
WHAT WAS THAT?
SANTA CLAUS?
VERY FUNNY.
Ho
Ho
Ho

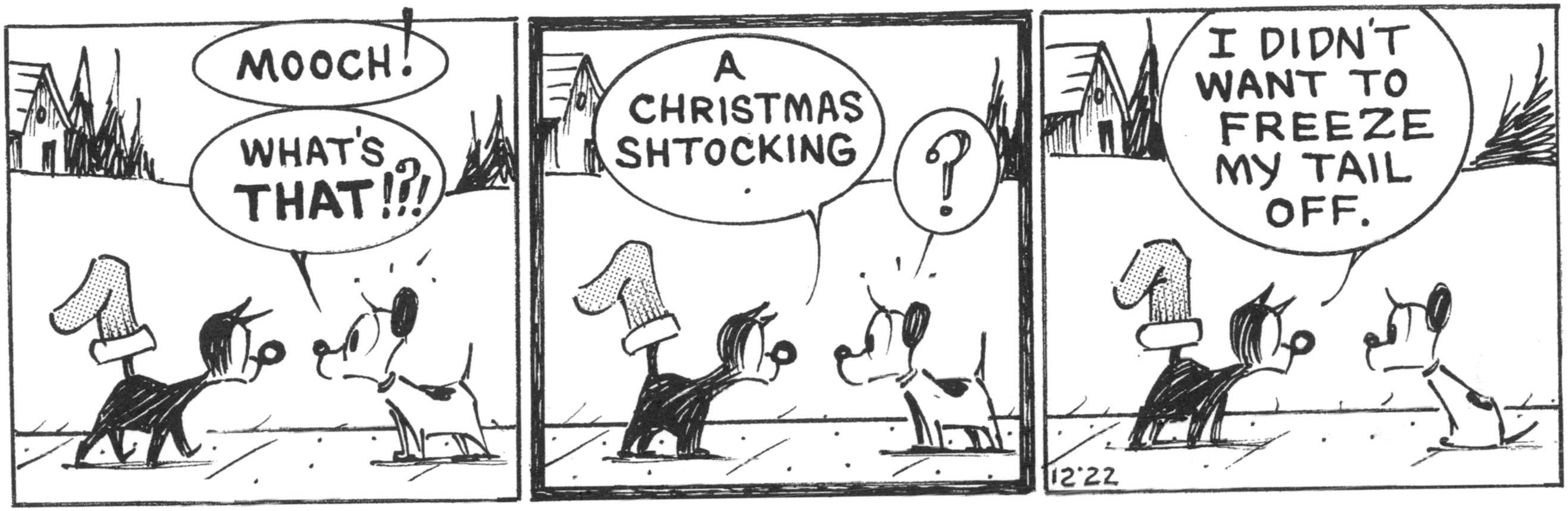
MOOCH!
WHAT'S THAT!?!
A CHRISTMAS SHTOCKING.
?
!
I DIDN'T WANT TO FREEZE MY TAIL OFF.
12·22

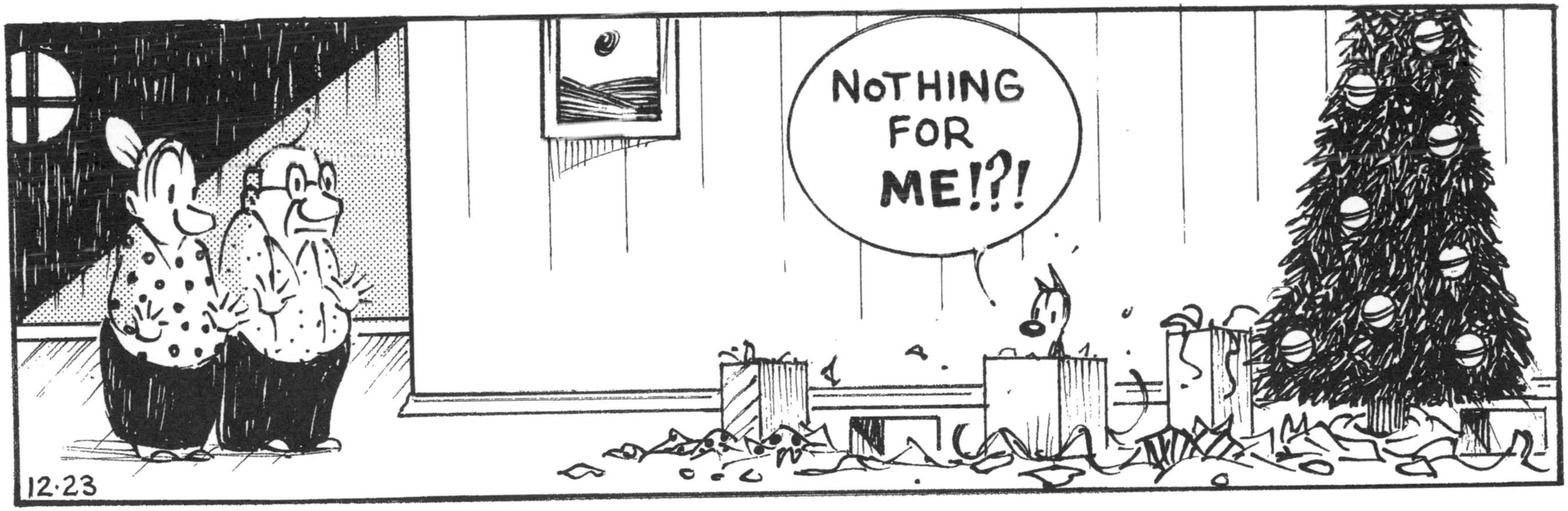
NOTHING FOR ME!?!
12·23

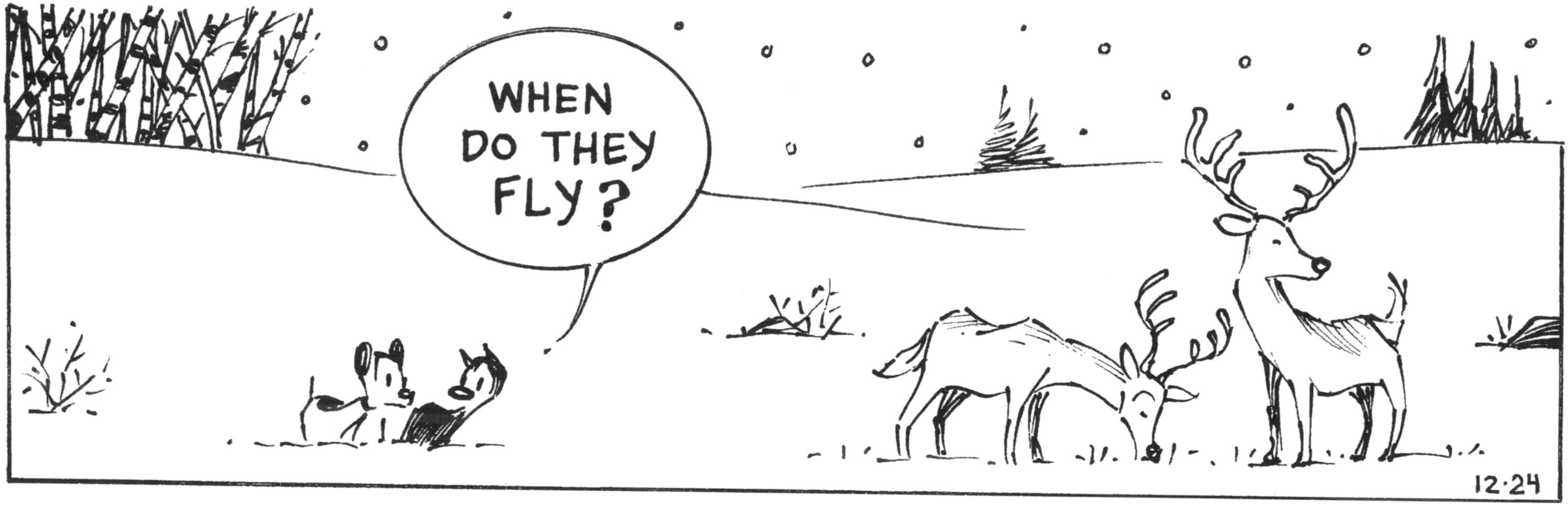
WHEN DO THEY FLY?
12·24

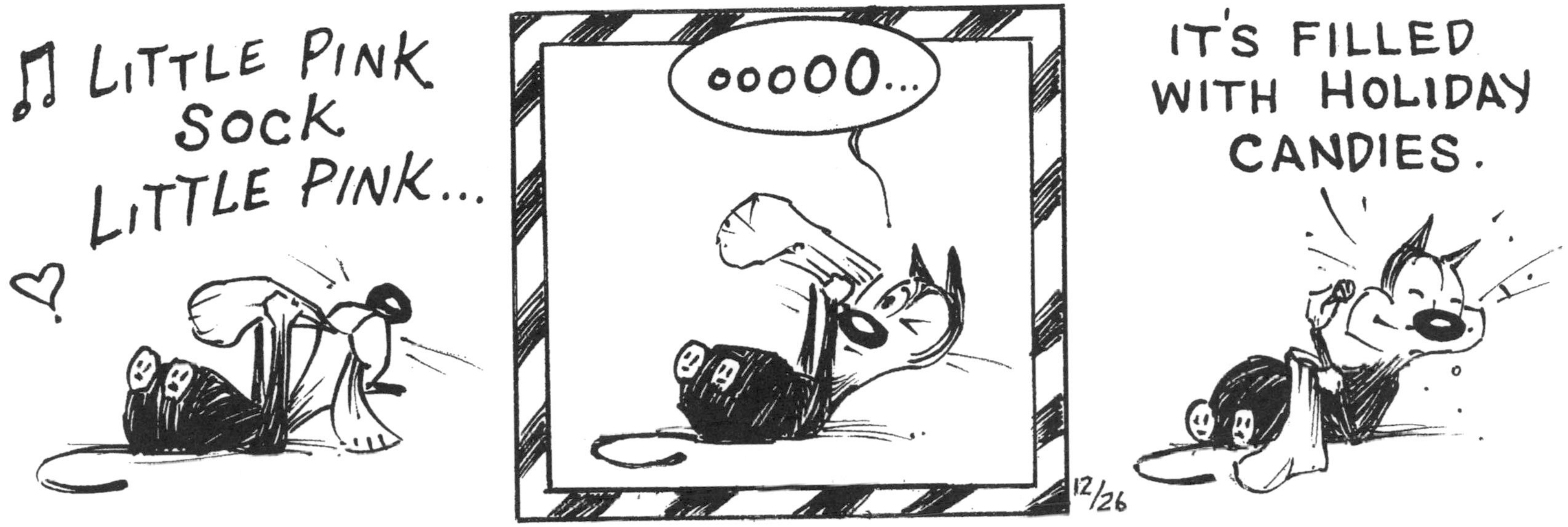
LITTLE PINK SOCK LITTLE PINK...
oooOO...
IT'S FILLED WITH HOLIDAY CANDIES.
12/26

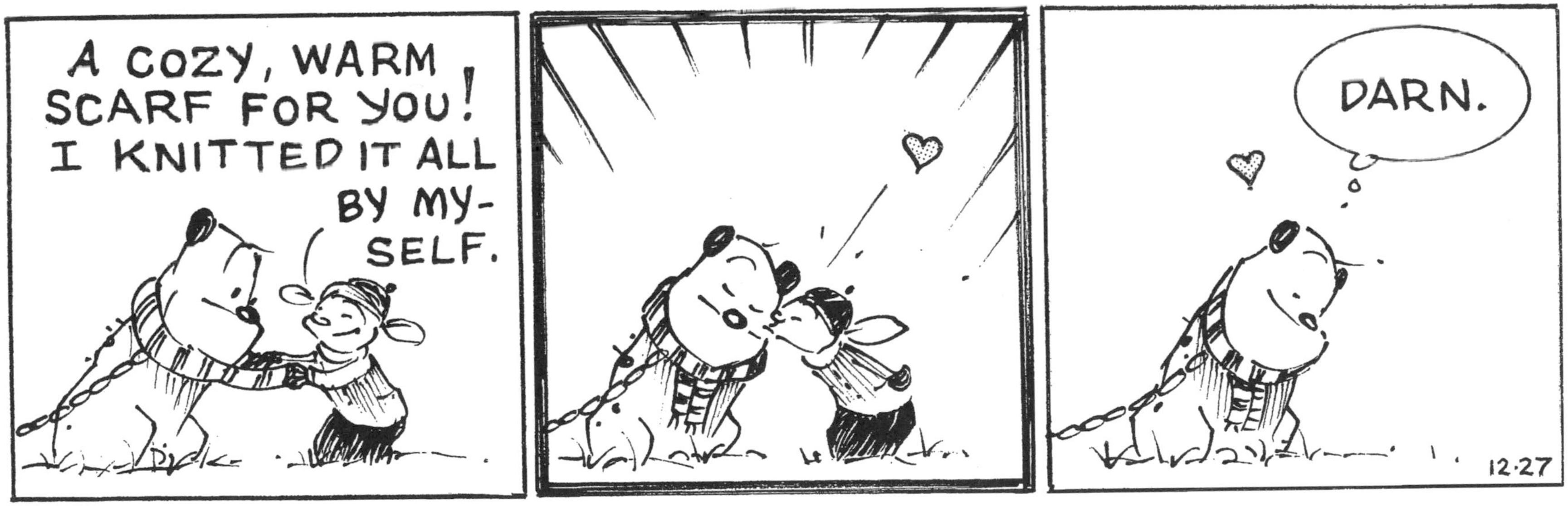
A COZY, WARM SCARF FOR YOU! I KNITTED IT ALL BY MY-SELF.
DARN.
12·27

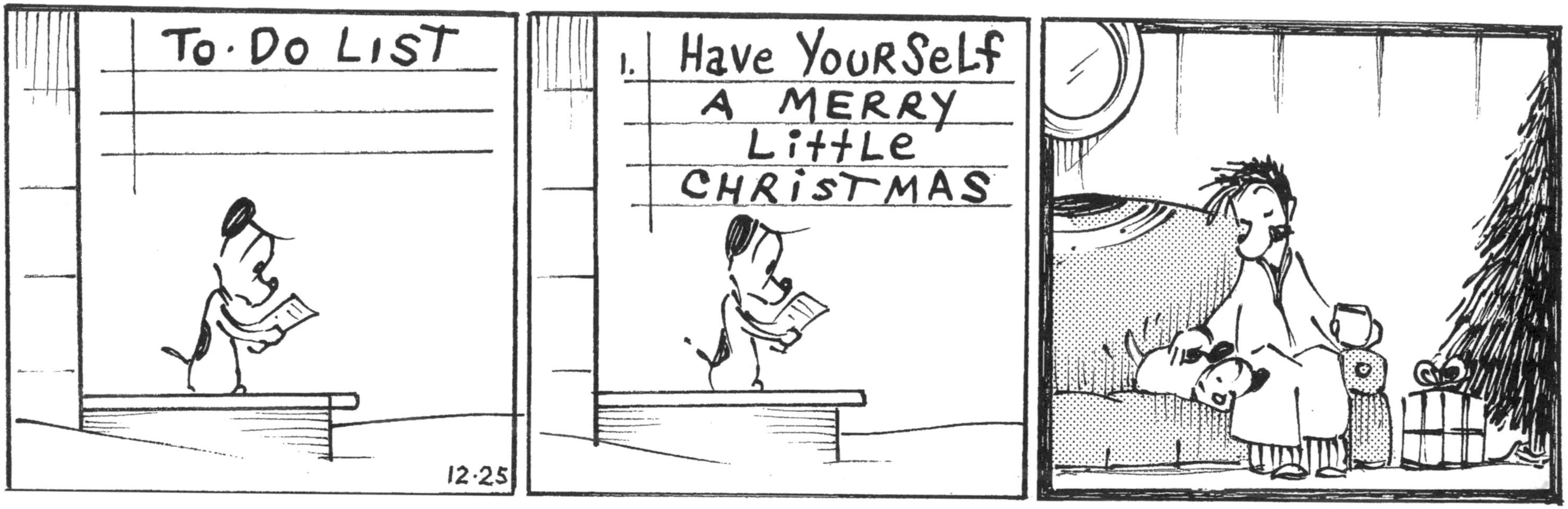
TO · DO LIST
12·25
1. Have YourSelf
A MERRY
Little
CHRISTMAS

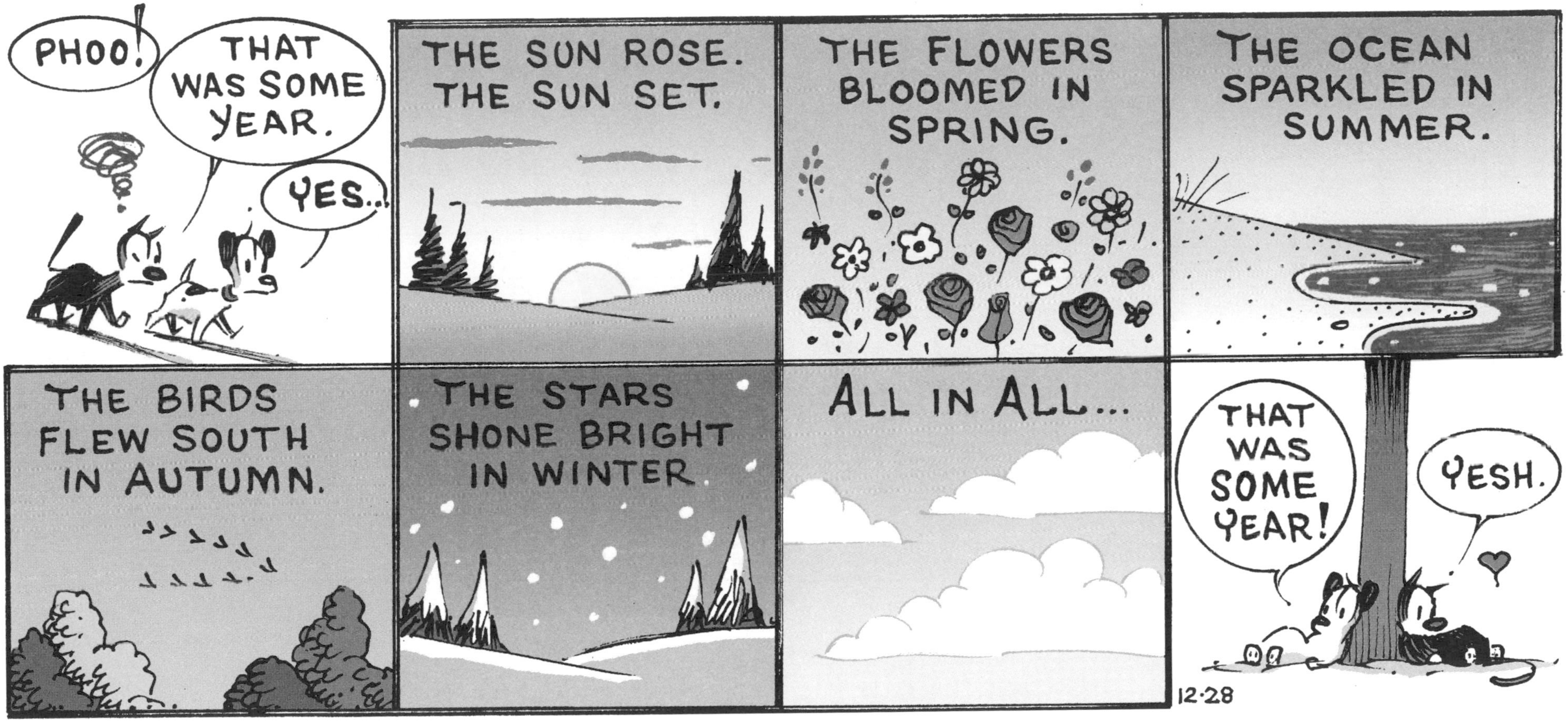
PHOO!
THAT WAS SOME YEAR.
YES...
THE SUN ROSE. THE SUN SET.
THE FLOWERS BLOOMED IN SPRING.
THE OCEAN SPARKLED IN SUMMER.
THE BIRDS FLEW SOUTH IN AUTUMN.
THE STARS SHONE BRIGHT IN WINTER
ALL IN ALL...
THAT WAS SOME YEAR!
YESH.
12-28

MUTTS

McDONNELL